The greatness of a nation and its moral progress can be judged by the way its animals are treated.—Mahatma Gandhi

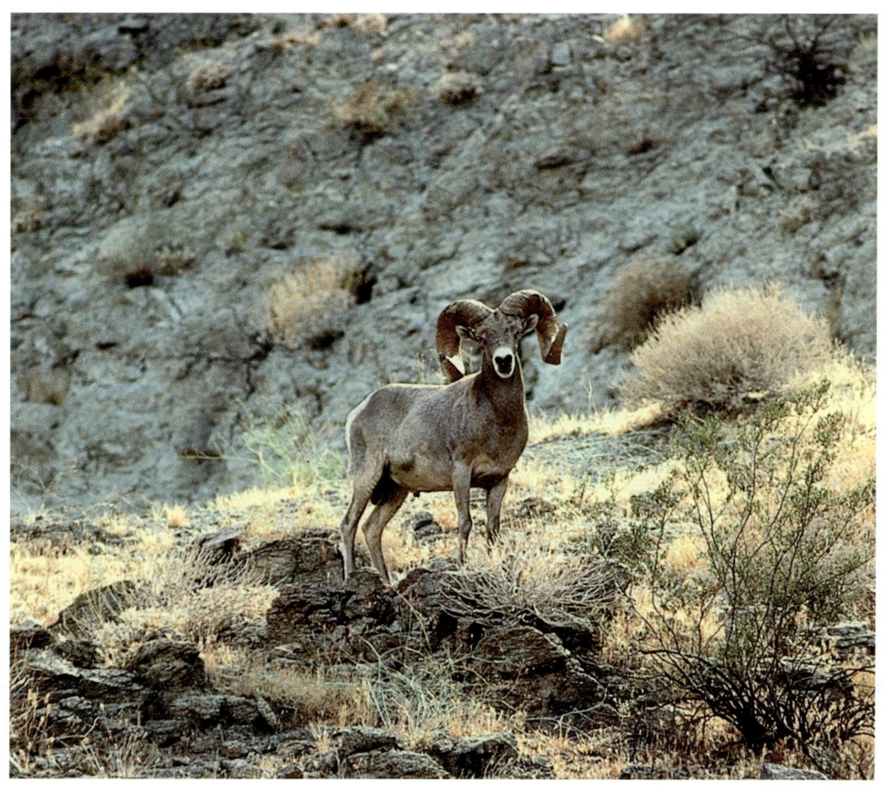

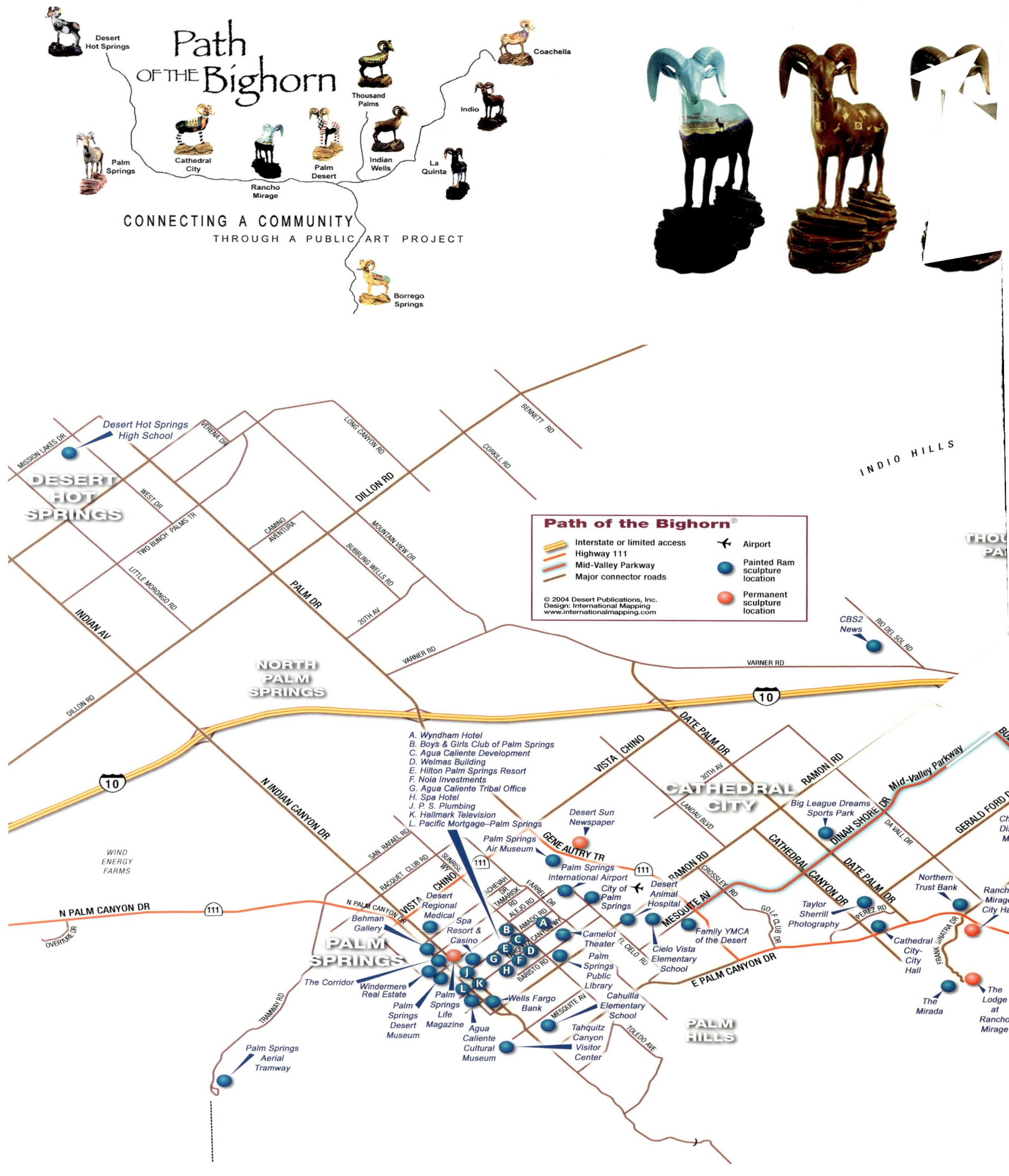

Path OF THE Bighorn
CONNECTING A COMMUNITY
THROUGH A PUBLIC ART PROJECT
Desert Hot Springs
Coachella
Thousand Palms
Indio
Cathedral City
Palm Springs
Indian Wells
La Quinta
Rancho Mirage
Palm Desert
Borrego Springs
Path of the Bighorn®
Interstate or limited access
Highway 111
Mid-Valley Parkway
Major connector roads
Airport
Painted Ram sculpture location
Permanent sculpture location
© 2004 Desert Publications, Inc.
Design: International Mapping
www.internationalmapping.com
DESERT HOT SPRINGS
NORTH PALM SPRINGS
CATHEDRAL CITY
PALM SPRINGS
PALM HILLS
INDIO HILLS
WIND ENERGY FARMS
MISSION LAKES DR
Desert Hot Springs High School
VERBENA DR
LONG CANYON RD
CORKILL RD
BENNETT RD
DILLON RD
WEST DR
TWO BUNCH PALMS TR
CAMINO AVENTURA
MOUNTAIN VIEW DR
BUBBLING WELLS RD
PALM DR
20TH AV
LITTLE MORONGO RD
INDIAN AV
DILLON RD
VARNER RD
VARNER RD
N INDIAN CANYON DR
RIO DEL SOL RD
CBS2 News
10
DATE PALM DR
VISTA CHINO
30TH AV
RAMON RD
LANDAU BLVD
Dinah Shore DR
Mid-Valley Parkway
DA VALL DR
GERALD FORD DR
CATHEDRAL CANYON DR
DATE PALM DR
FRANK SINATRA DR
A. Wyndham Hotel
B. Boys & Girls Club of Palm Springs
C. Agua Caliente Development
D. Welmas Building
E. Hilton Palm Springs Resort
F. Noia Investments
G. Agua Caliente Tribal Office
H. Spa Hotel
J. P. S. Plumbing
K. Hallmark Television
L. Pacific Mortgage–Palm Springs
Desert Sun Newspaper
GENE AUTRY TR
Palm Springs Air Museum
Palm Springs International Airport
City of Palm Springs
Desert Animal Hospital
Big League Dreams Sports Park
Northern Trust Bank
Rancho Mirage City Hall
RAMON RD
CROSSLEY RD
MESQUITE AV
GO LF CLUB DR
Taylor Sherrill Photography
PEREZ RD
SAN RAFAEL RD
RACQUET CLUB RD
SUNRISE WY
CHINO
VISTA
111
CHEVAH DR
TAMARISK RD
FARREL DR
ALEJO RD
Desert Regional Medical
Spa Resort & Casino
Behman Gallery
N PALM CANYON DR
N PALM CANYON DR
111
AMADO RD
INDIAN CANYON WY
Camelot Theater
Family YMCA of the Desert
Cielo Vista Elementary School
EL CIELO RD
Palm Springs Public Library
Cathedral City–City Hall
Northern
PALM SPRINGS
The Corridor
Windermere Real Estate
Palm Springs Desert Museum
Palm Springs Life Magazine
Wells Fargo Bank
BARISTO RD
Palm Springs
Cahuilla Elementary School
MESQUITE AV
Tahquitz Canyon Visitor Center
E PALM CANYON DR
The Mirada
The Lodge at Rancho Mirage
Agua Caliente Cultural Museum
TOLEDO AVE
OVERTURE DR
TRAMWAY RD
Palm Springs Aerial Tramway

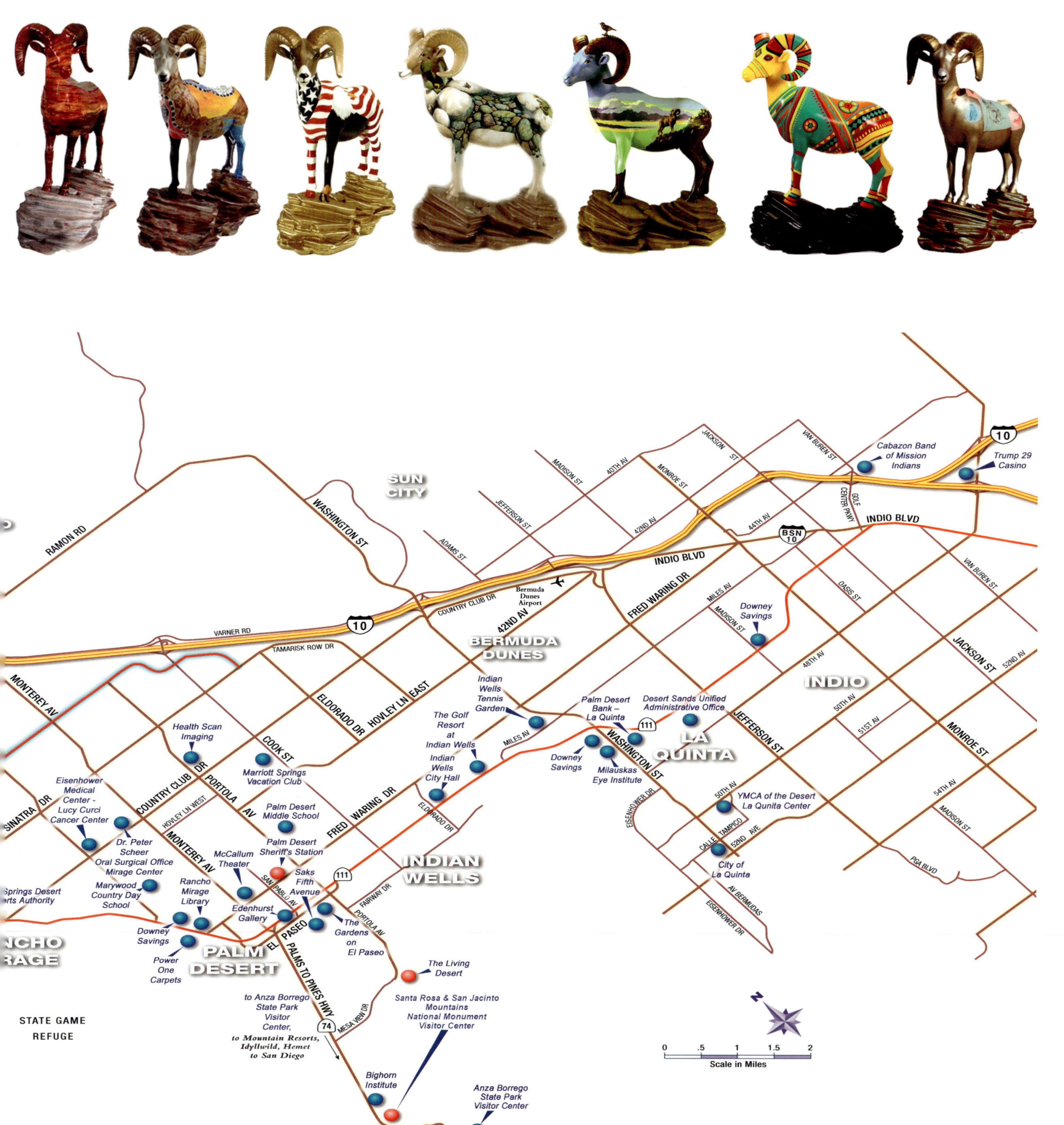

10
Cabazon Band of Mission Indians
Trump 29 Casino
JACKSON ST
VAN BUREN ST
MADISON ST
40TH AV
MONROE ST
44TH AV
GOLF CENTER PKWY
INDIO BLVD
SUN CITY
WASHINGTON ST
JEFFERSON ST
ADAMS ST
42ND AV
BSN 10
INDIO BLVD
42ND AV
Bermuda Dunes Airport
VARNER RD
TAMARISK ROW DR
10
COUNTRY CLUB DR
FRED WARING DR
MILES AV
Downey Savings
OASIS ST
VAN BUREN ST
BERMUDA DUNES
42ND AV
INDIO
JACKSON ST
52ND AV
MONTEREY AV
ELDORADO DR
HOVLEY LN EAST
Indian Wells Tennis Garden
MADISON ST
48TH AV
Palm Desert Bank – La Quinta
Desert Sands Unified Administrative Office
50TH AV
JEFFERSON ST
51ST AV
MONROE ST
Health Scan Imaging
COOK ST
The Golf Resort at Indian Wells
MILES AV
111
LA QUINTA
COUNTRY CLUB DR
PORTOLA AV
Marriott Springs Vacation Club
Indian Wells City Hall
WASHINGTON ST
Downey Savings
Milauskas Eye Institute
EISENHOWER DR
50TH AV
YMCA of the Desert La Quinta Center
54TH AV
MADISON ST
SINATRA DR
Eisenhower Medical Center - Lucy Curci Cancer Center
HOVLEY LN WEST
Palm Desert Middle School
FRED WARING DR
ELDORADO DR
CALLE TAMPICO
52ND AVE
Dr. Peter Scheer Oral Surgical Office Mirage Center
McCallum Theater
Palm Desert Sheriff's Station
INDIAN WELLS
City of La Quinta
PGA BLVD
MONTEREY AV
Saks Fifth Avenue
111
Springs Desert Arts Authority
Marywood Country Day School
Rancho Mirage Library
SAN PABLO AV
Edenhurst Gallery
FAIRWAY DR
PORTOLA AV
AV BERMUDAS
EISENHOWER DR
RANCHO MIRAGE
Downey Savings
PALM DESERT
EL PASEO
The Gardens on El Paseo
PALMS TO PINES HWY
Power One Carpets
to Anza Borrego State Park Visitor Center,
The Living Desert
STATE GAME REFUGE
MESA VIEW DR
Santa Rosa & San Jacinto Mountains National Monument Visitor Center
to Mountain Resorts, Idyllwild, Hemet to San Diego
74
Bighorn Institute
Anza Borrego State Park Visitor Center
N
0   .5   1   1.5   2
Scale in Miles

This book is dedicated to the
Peninsular Bighorn Sheep ...
May they forever freely roam

Published on the occasion of
the public art project PATH OF THE BIGHORN
documenting sculptures completed as of
October 1, 2004.

Bighorn Institute
P.O. Box 262, Palm Desert CA 92261-0262
www.pathofthebighorn.com

ISBN 0-9763451-0-2

Photographs of sculptures by Taylor Sherrill
Photographs of bighorn sheep by Bighorn Institute
Design by Lilli Colton & Alexandra Sheldon
Printed by Typecraft, Inc., Pasadena, CA

Printed in the United States of America

First Edition

Table of Contents

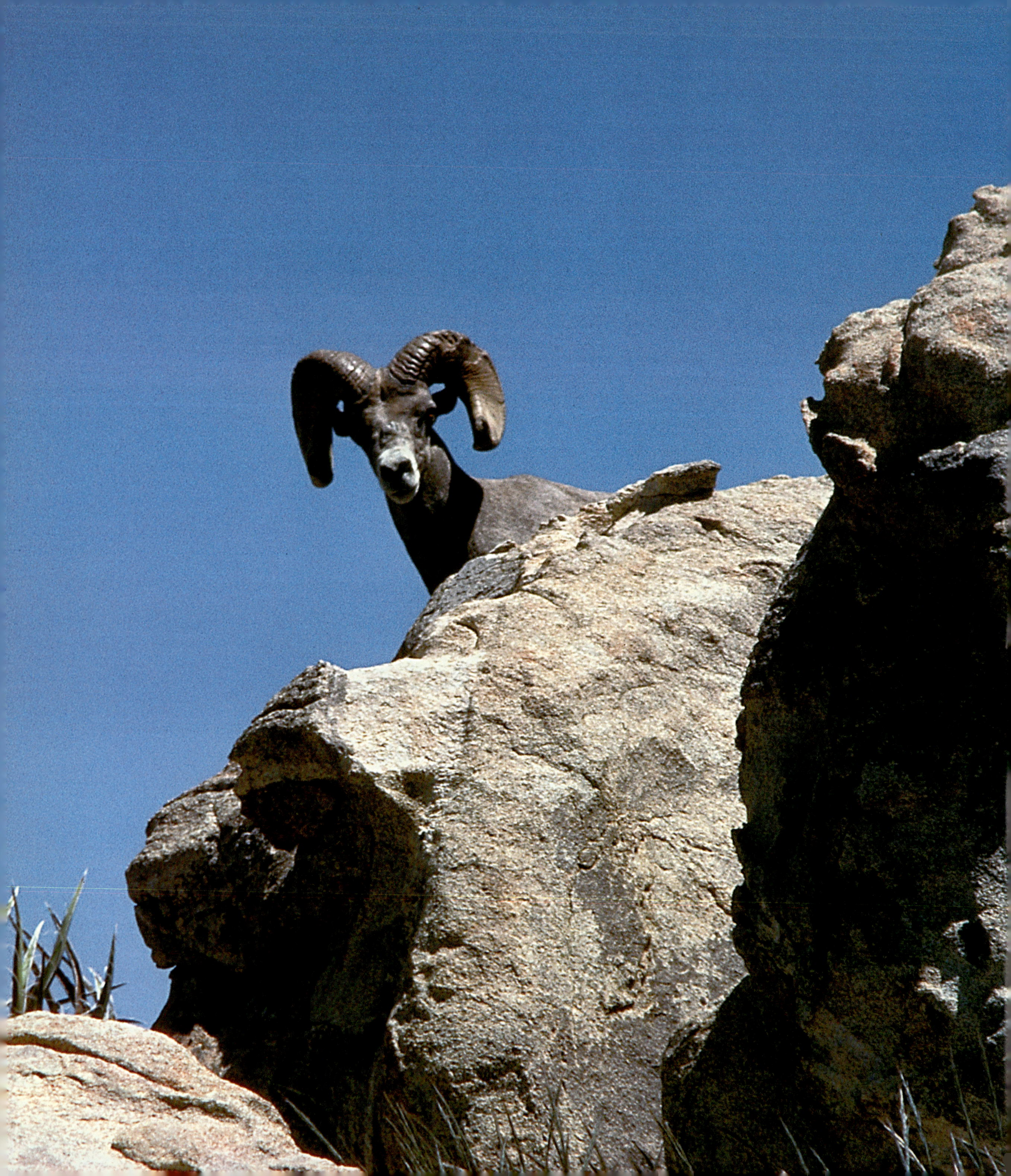

Path of the Bighorn

Jim DeForge
Executive Director
Bighorn Institute

As an undergraduate in biology, I became interested in wild sheep and later spent five years completing a Masters project on desert bighorn in the San Gabriel Mountains. I next focused on Peninsular bighorn at a time when most of the lambs were dying. The population was declining precipitously in the Palm Springs area, and the cause of decline was of the utmost concern to California wildlife officials. In February 1981, I came to the Coachella Valley to begin my research. Later that year, a small group of us formed Bighorn Institute, a non-profit conservation organization dedicated to wild sheep research and education.

The intervening years have been gratifying in what the Institute has been able to accomplish. The population of Peninsular bighorn has increased to approximately 600—still a precarious number but vastly improved from the 280 that it was estimated to be nearly a decade ago. There have also been moments of humor, challenge, and inspiration.

Bighorn Institute has been extremely successful with rehabilitation and release of Peninsular bighorn. Of the thirty-nine lambs that have been rescued, thirty-six have been successfully rehabilitated and reintroduced into the wild. In the early days of bighorn research, scientists did not think sick lambs could be saved. It was often said, "a sick bighorn is a dead bighorn." Disproving this mindset has been one of many proud accomplishments of the Institute, and it began with a two-month old lamb named Andrea. Andrea was overcome with viral-induced bacterial pneumonia and her blood and lab results suggested she was not going to survive. However, we've found that lambs will often respond if human caregivers take on the role of surrogate mother. We kept Andrea isolated and stayed with her, providing comfort and coaxing her to eat and drink. After several days of around-the-clock shifts, we were exhausted but Andrea showed little sign of improvement. She was still weak and often unwilling to stand. We ordered a pizza and had just sat down to eat, leaving Andrea bedded behind a four-foot high partition opposite us. To our astonishment, Andrea

came flying over the partition and landed in the middle of the
pizza. We looked at each other with tears of laughter, then called
to order another pizza explaining there was too much lamb on
the first one. Andrea went on to live a long and productive life.

Helicopters are essential tools for assessing any population of
wild sheep, and Bighorn Institute conducts an aerial survey each
October. As valuable as these censuses are for counting and evalu-
ating the condition of herds, they can be dangerous, occurring as
they do under harsh environmental conditions in remote regions.
I have lost several close friends to helicopter accidents; one recent
crew we had been working with didn't return from a survey in
Baja, and their crash site and bodies may never be found. My most
memorable ride happened several years ago over rough terrain in
the central Santa Rosa Mountains. Usually we fly light but, for
some reason that morning I decided to pack a few extra emergency
supplies. Throughout the day, I could hear an intermittent friction
noise, which I brought to the attention of the pilot, but otherwise
the helicopter operated well and the gauges suggested the same. At
four o'clock, we were alarmed by what felt like a bump to the rear
of the ship. Five hundred feet above the ground, we lost all power
in the engine and we began to fall. Our skillful pilot managed to
cushion the crash, and everyone got out just before the helicopter
caught fire. The aircraft was completely destroyed, but more
importantly no one was seriously injured. It took us six hours to
hike down to civilization, much to the relief of our colleagues.

Our work is relentless and difficult, but it is essential. For tens of
thousands of years. the Peninsular bighorn sheep have roamed
their lands from the San Jacinto and Santa Rosa Mountains,
through Anza Borrego Desert State Park, down into Baja
California. Southern California is the only place where Peninsular
bighorn can be found in the entire United States. Their population
must be increased from 600 to 750 for twelve consecutive years,
with at least twenty-five females in each of eight subgroups, before
they can be removed from the endangered species list.

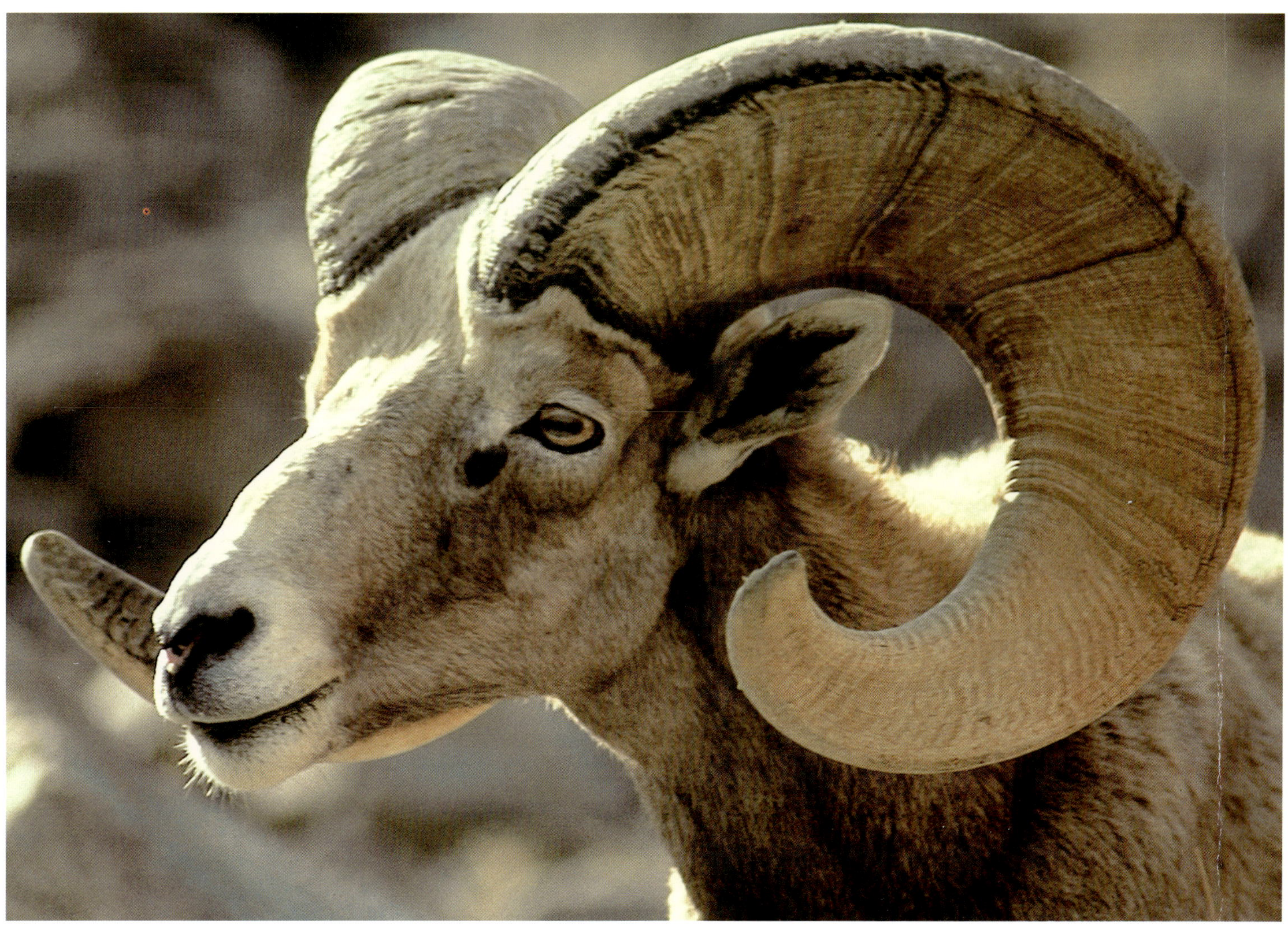

In conserving Peninsular bighorn, we are also conserving the animals and plants that dwell among them, not only for our own visual enjoyment, but also for future generations to come.

In our efforts, Bighorn Institute has been blessed with remarkable support from the general public as well as prominent citizens such as President Gerald Ford. We are especially grateful to our extraordinary Board of Directors; to special friends including Dick and Eloise Agee, Bob Howard, and Alexandra and Sidney Sheldon; and to the many biologists who care for the captive herd and who work in the field. With their continued help, the Institute can remain focused on and dedicated to the conservation of the endangered Peninsular bighorn. Through research and education, we look forward to the recovery of this magnificent creature—an emblem of all that is wild and free in nature.

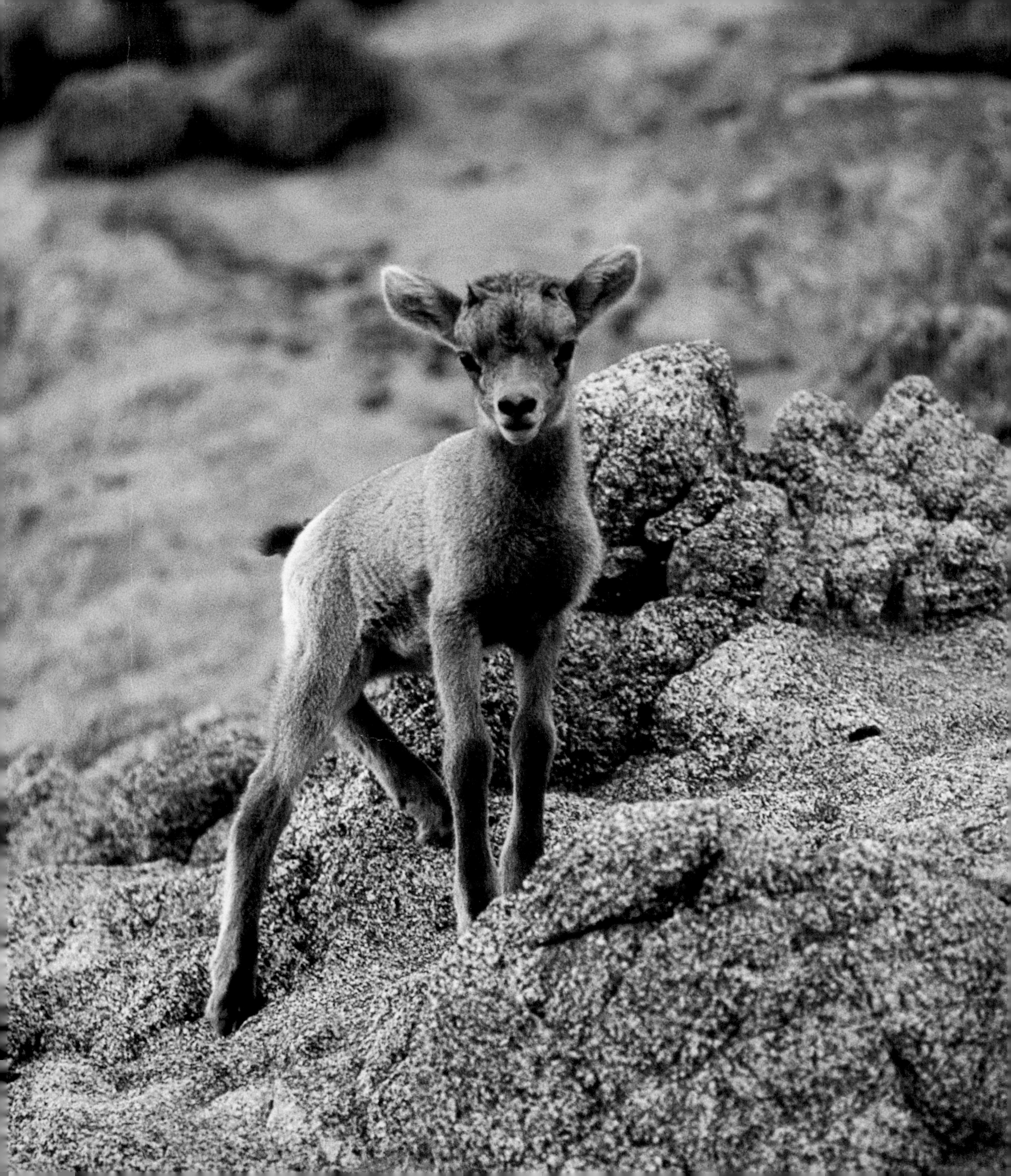

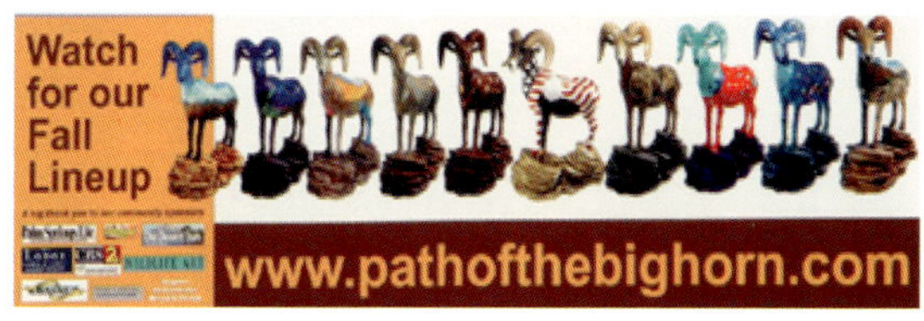

Today, nearly two years after the project was initiated, 107 painted sculptures have been completed. I am awed by the diversity and originality of the artists' visions and by the poignant, inspirational, and humorous experiences I've encountered during the process.

One of the most touching stories is that of the artist Paul Magloff, a cancer survivor. He believes that painting the rams have helped him to recover. His "Bighorn Sky Figure" is now at Desert Hospital Hospice.

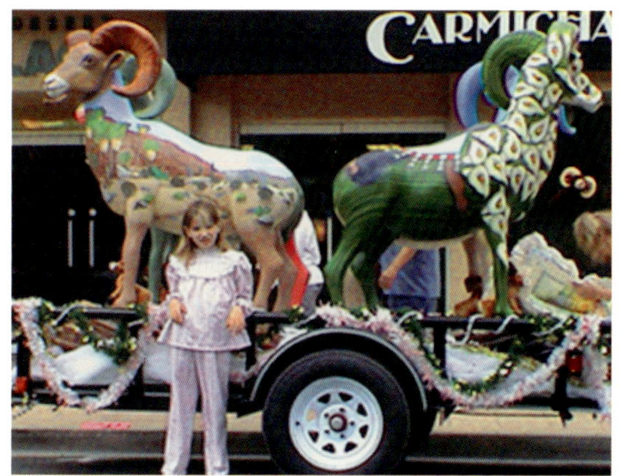

At the Cahuilla Elementary School unveiling of "Reaching out to the Bighorn," painted with over 300 hand prints by children from the school, Ron Oden, mayor of Palm Springs, spoke movingly to the second and third graders about the beauty of wild animals and why children are the future stewards of nature. He ended with the Native American saying: "We do not own the land that we walk upon; we only borrow it from our children, our grandchildren, and their grandchildren to come."

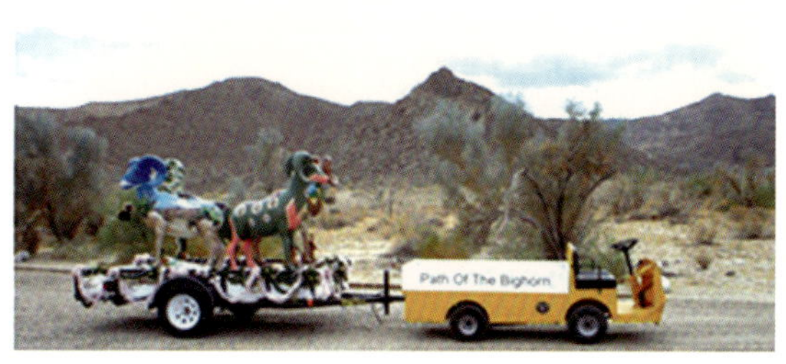

Another incredible experience occurred when my husband's granddaughter Rebecca and I dressed in pajamas and rode in the Palm Desert Golf Cart Parade. Titled "Bighorn Dreams," our float was decorated with angel hair to simulate a dream sequence, and the two of us squeezed in among five painted rams. As we rolled slowly along El Paseo which was lined with approximatly 33,000 spectators, we heard shouts of "Yea, bighorn sheep! We love the bighorn!" The magnitude of their response, along with the surprise presence of my husband, moved me to tears.

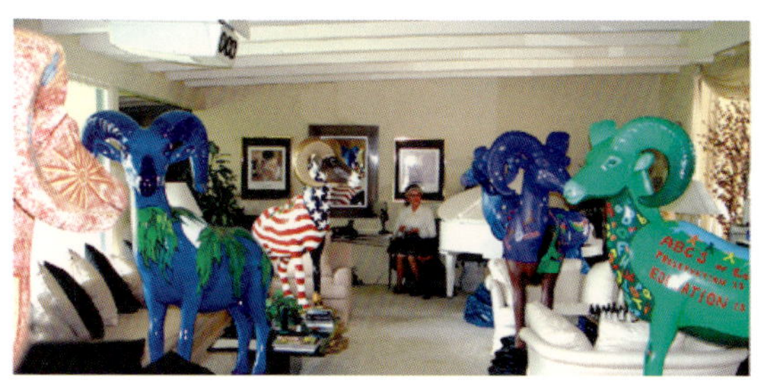

I believe the enormous interest in this project comes from the deep love of our community for the Peninsular bighorn. We are proud that the sheep dwell in our local mountain ranges, and we consider them to be one of our most magnificent natural treasures. This support has helped us accomplish our multi-faceted goals: to create awareness about the bighorn among residents and visitors, to bring attention to Valley businesses and points of interest along

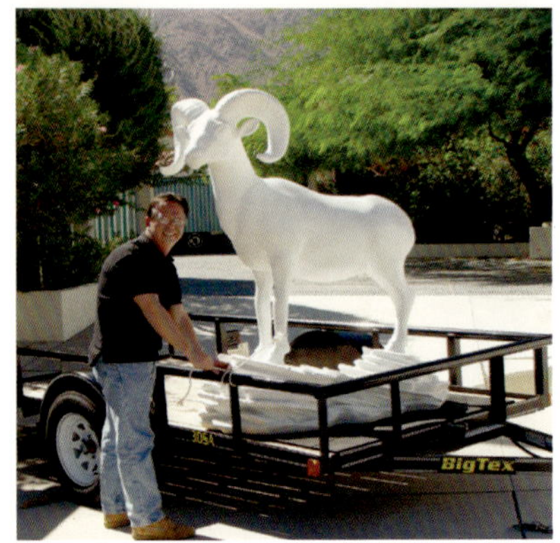

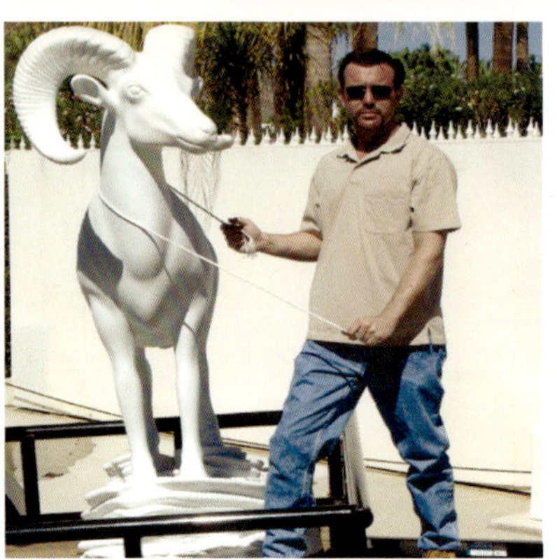

Gary Zornes moving a ram sculpture

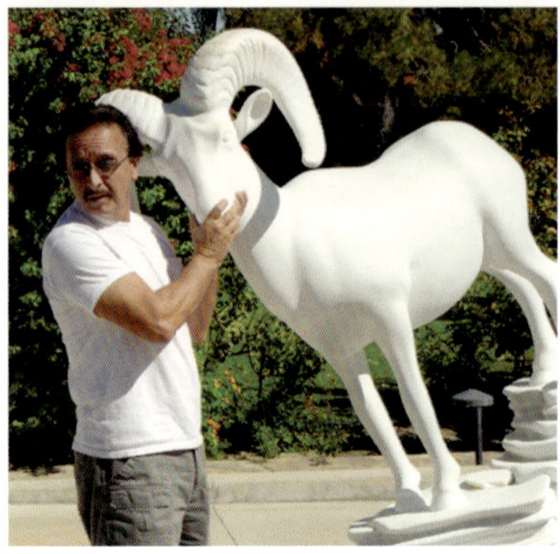

Bobby Zornes readying ram for delivery to artist

Kenny Zornes part of "Team Zornes" placing ram on the trailer

the path of the sculptures, and to fund the facilities that the Institute needs to pursue its mission.

On a personal level, I am gratified and touched by the "oohs" and "aahhs" at unveilings, the talent and thought behind every painted sculpture, the heart and soul that artists poured into their work, the excitement of our sponsors when they see their ram for the first time, and the anecdotes and responses that flow back to us by residents and tourists.

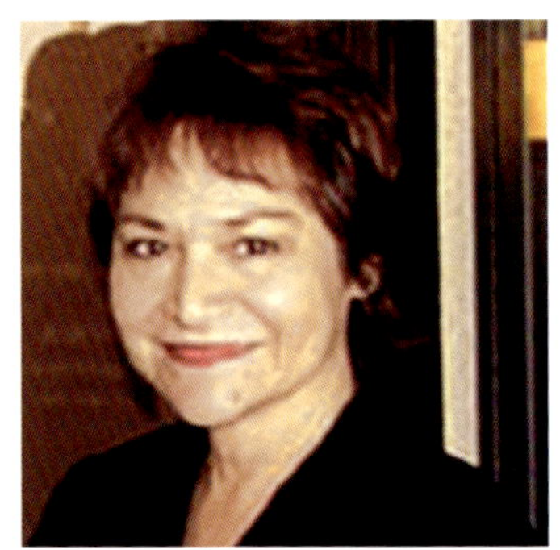

Path of the Bighorn media maven and Publicist Lydia Kremer

Path of the Bighorn was made possible by the work of an extraordinary team. Joe Wertheimer sculpted the model. Rod Barker, who heads Trail of the Painted Ponies in New Mexico, met with us at the beginning of our project and provided invaluable advice. I relied on the guidance of Jim DeForge, Executive Director, and Aimee Byard, Senior Biologist, and we had the support of the Board of Directors. Gary Zornes was a wonderful ambassador in contacting artists, sponsors, and locations and, with his tenacity and organizational skills, put together the pieces of a giant puzzle. Gary, his son Bobby, and Gary's brother Kenny sometimes referred to as "Team Zornes" moved rams between the foundry, the artists, the photographer, and the sites. The beautiful photography in this book is the work of Taylor Sherrill, who generously donated his talents. Our media maven, Lydia Kremer, is responsible for news stories and articles in the local and international press, for television coverage, and for a documentary by Women in Film. We took Path of the Bighorn to a bigger audience with the website created by Paul Helms. My dream of producing a beautiful book was realized through the work of writer-designer Lilli Colton and printer David Allen of Typecraft.

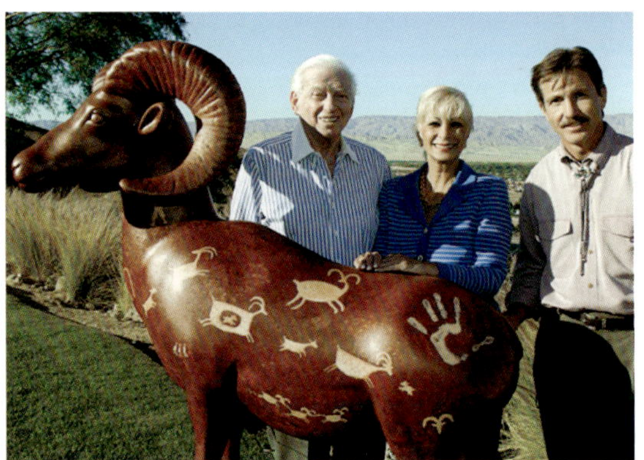

Sidney & Alexandra Sheldon by their painted ram, "The Storyteller" with Ron Barker, Director of Trail of the Painted Ponies

I continue to be thankful to the artists, sponsors, and civic leaders whose whole hearted support made this effort a reality. While the Coachella Valley is comprised of many independent cities, Path

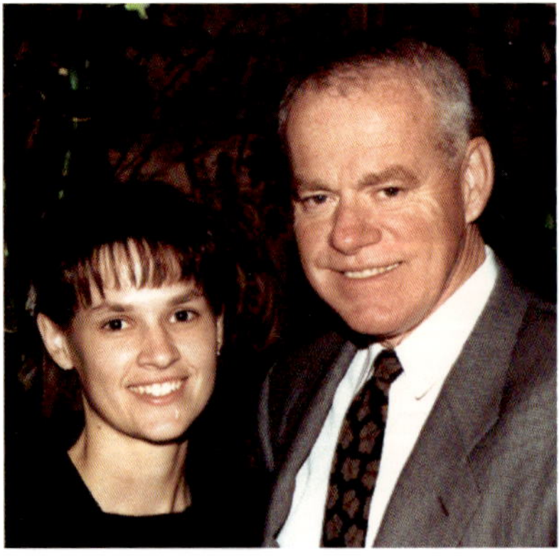

Bighorn Institute Staff Biologists Aimee Byard & Jim DeForge

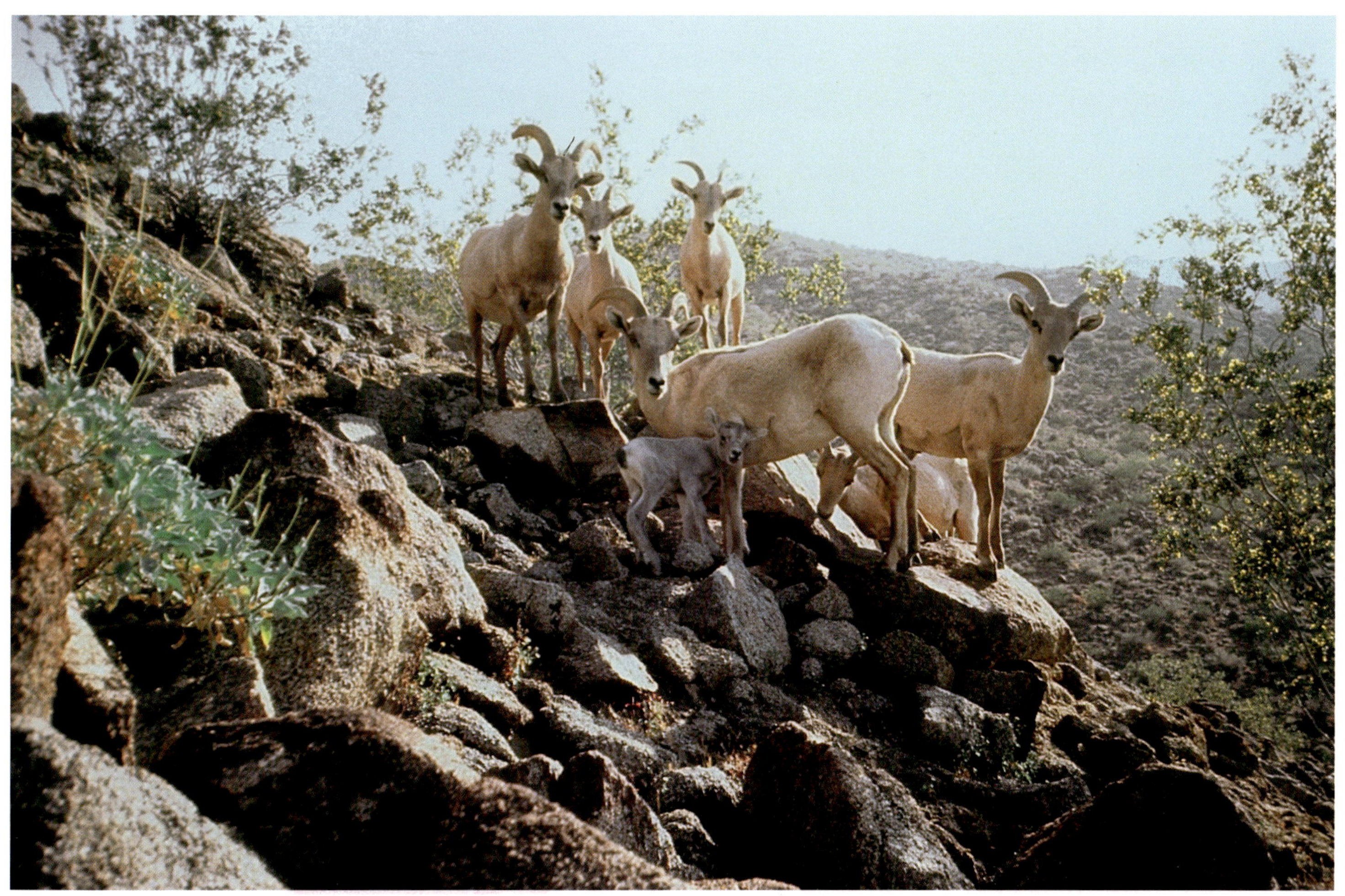

of the Bighorn connected them all, both physically and spiritually, as a public art project and as a community working toward a common goal.

Most of all, I am grateful to the staff of Bighorn Institute and to the recovery efforts that have rescued these animals from the brink of extinction. Thanks to their efforts, future generations will be graced by the presence of this noble creature. Because animals have no voice, we as humans are obligated to speak for them…to ensure that, for an eternity, they will be free to roam and to thrive.

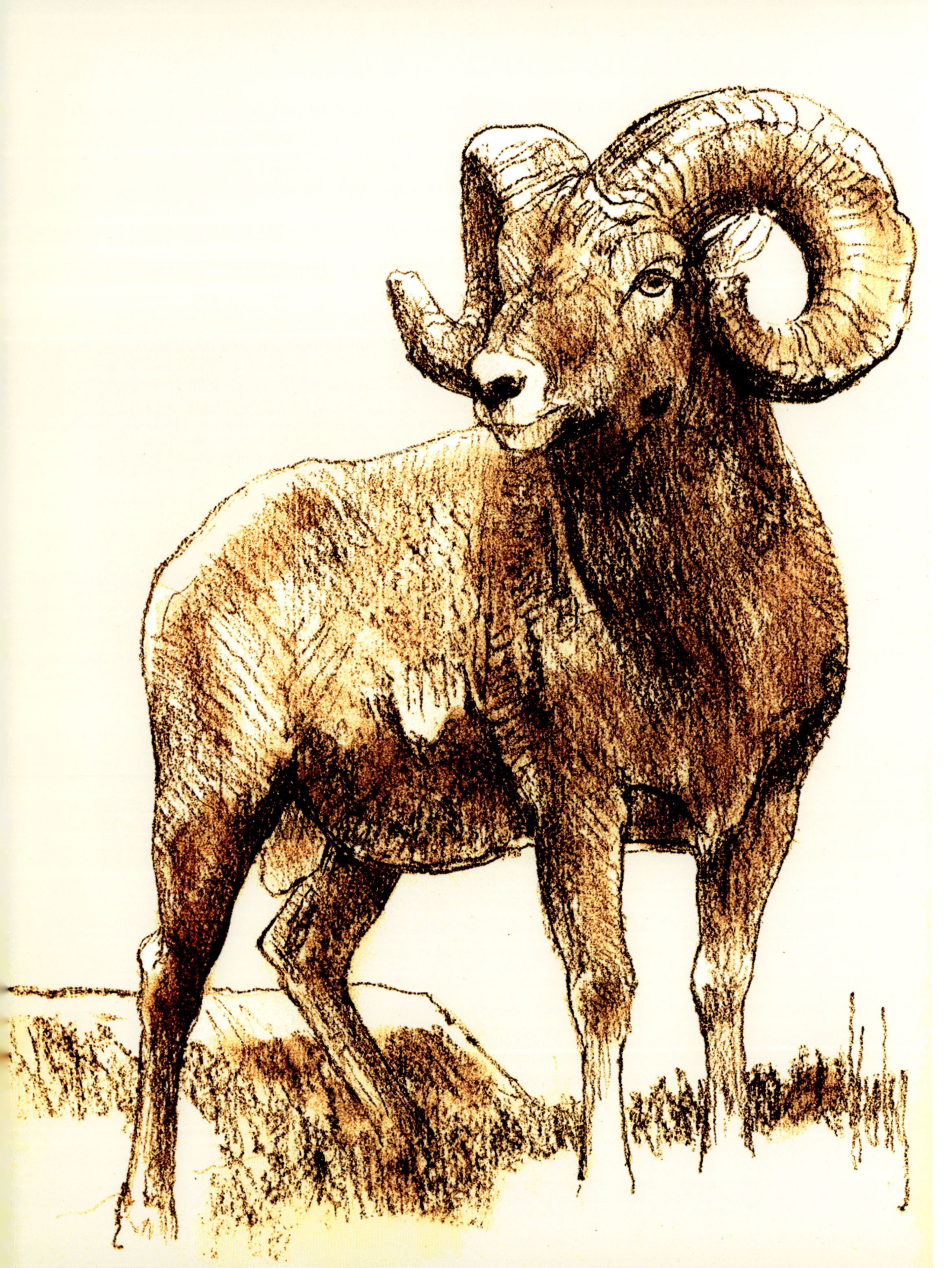

*Conté by
Wildlife Artist
Bob Kuhn*

The World of the Desert Bighorn

High on a barren mountaintop, silhouetted against the desert sky, the bighorn sheep stands as an icon of the American West. Climbing effortlessly over boulders and outcroppings, its noble head crowned by majestic spiral horns, it symbolizes the rugged independence of nature untamed. The extinction of this magnificent creature would herald a loss for all of us, and its preservation is a priority for everyone who values the quality of our world.

The bighorn's ancestors crossed from Eurasia over the Bering land bridge to the New World. Gradually moving southward while adapting to changes in climate, food, and the environment, the sheep evolved into new and distinct species. Today, bighorn sheep (*Ovis canadensis*) are found on high peaks as well as on low desert slopes; in steep, rocky terrain from Canada to Mexico. Over time, they have adapted to local habitats, and seven different subspecies are recognized, of which four are found in the dry southwest.

Desert bighorn are considered to be "relict" populations, descendants of animals stranded in isolated pockets by the retreat of glaciers and the formation of deserts. Unlike their northern counterparts, whose massive, blocky bodies conserve heat during cold temperatures, desert bighorn are uniquely adapted to hot, arid conditions. Lighter in color, their shorter, thinner coats maximize their surface area relative to body mass, thereby increasing their ability to disperse excess heat. Their digestive systems are extremely efficient at extracting liquid from their forage, and desert bighorn can exist for long periods without drinking water. When water is available, they can drink over two gallons in a matter of minutes and they have exceptionally large water retention organs. While they can tolerate losing up to one-third of their body weight from dehydration, desert bighorn perspire little. Instead, they rely on respiration and energy conservation to regulate body heat, and they can withstand internal temperatures up to 107°F.

Survival of the desert bighorn is also aided by a comparatively long breeding period that extends from July to December. Following a six-month gestation, a single lamb (twins are rare) is born. Weighing seven to ten pounds, the lambs can run among the cliffs within hours after birth. Although the steep terrain offers some degree of protection from predators, mortality is high among lambs, half of whom die before reaching six months of age. The mothers will often form a nursery, leaving one or more ewes in charge while the others forage. While ewes usually remain with the same group for life, young males are expelled during their second year and join bands of mature rams, learning the best places to feed and secure routes of travel. Ewes typically live ten to fourteen years and weigh 100–125 pounds, while rams may live nine to twelve years and reach 150–225 pounds. Adult bighorn stand thirty to thirty-six inches at the shoulders and are about sixty inches long.

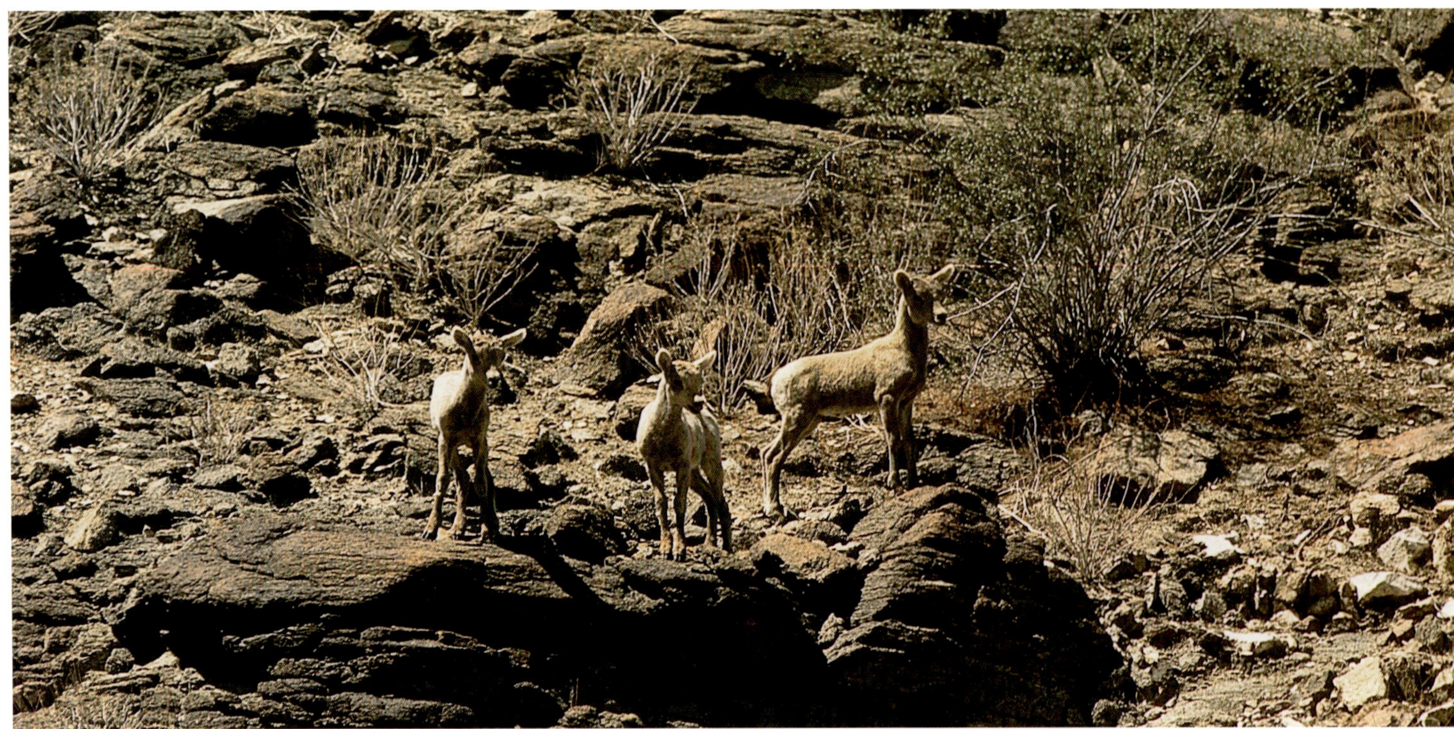

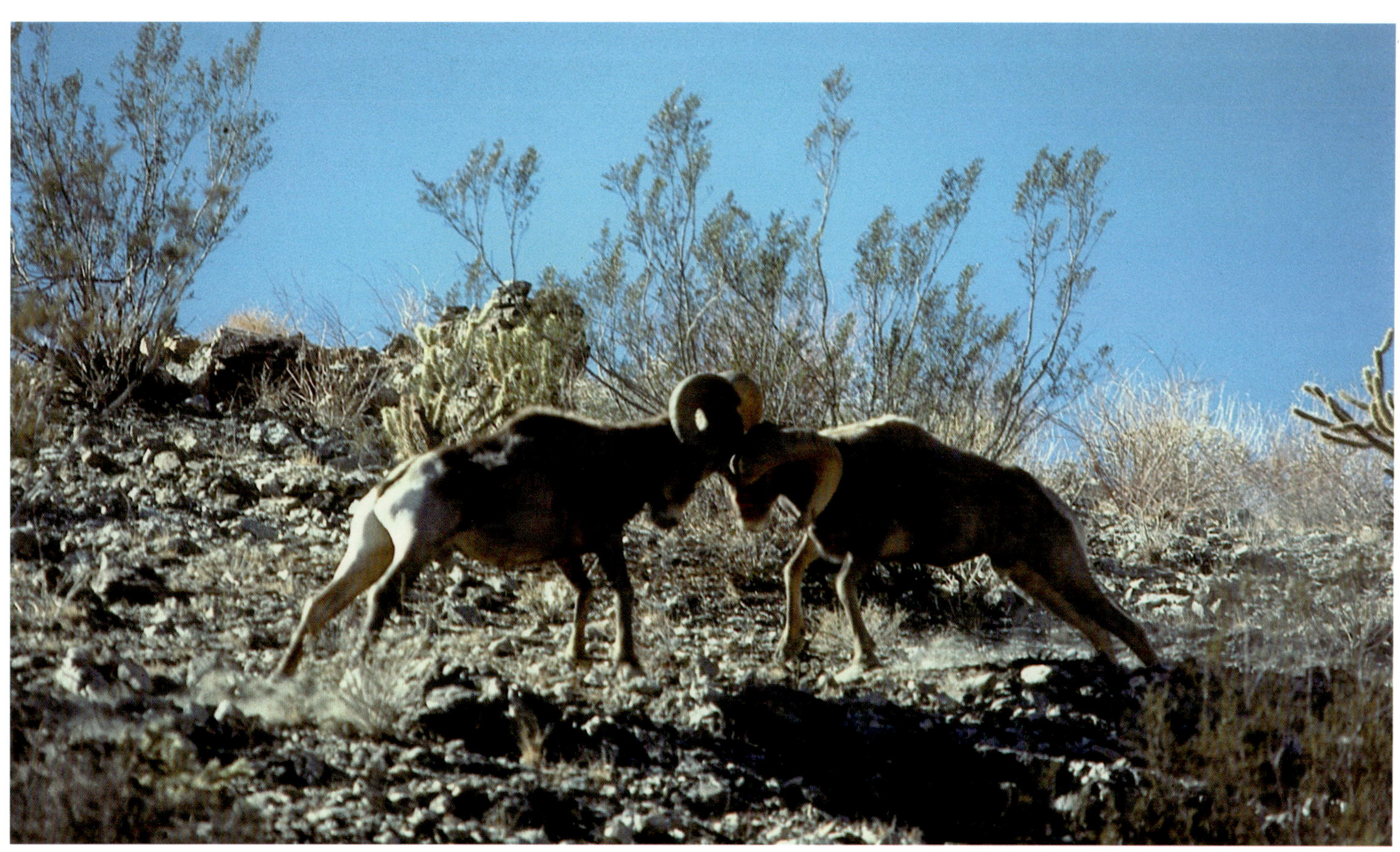

The desert bighorn's most distinctive feature remains its large, backward-curling horns that on males can reach over forty inches in length and can measure over sixteen inches in circumference at the base. Ewes sport straighter, more slender horns that are twelve to seventeen inches long. The horns are permanent and continue to grow throughout the sheep's life except during the annual breeding season, at which time a horn ring is formed, leaving a marker of the animal's age. During the breeding season, the horns are used in dramatic contests for dominance as rams clash heads and the sound of colliding horns echo off canyon walls. The higher-ranking rams do the majority of breeding, thus ensuring the continuation of the strongest genes.

Ironically, its magnificent horns contributed to the bighorn's decimation in early times as illegal hunters vied for impressive specimens. In addition to illegal hunting, competition with wild and domesticated animals, disease (often transmitted from livestock), opportunistic predation by coyotes, mountain lions and bobcats and low birthrates are also factors in the reduction of the bighorn population. However, the greatest impact by far has come from the encroachment of man and the ensuing loss of habitat. The endangered Peninsular bighorn—low-elevation sheep most often found between 400–4000 feet—are particularly vulnerable. It is estimated that approximately 600 Peninsular bighorn (*Ovis canadensis cremnobates*, the subspecies that live in the San Jacinto and Santa Rosa Mountains near Palm Springs) remain in the entire United States.

The Coachella Valley has seen unprecedented growth in recent years, a trend that has altered the environment irrevocably and that continues unabated. In an area that already has over 100 golf courses, more than fifteen additional golf courses and residential developments are currently proposed or have been approved for construction within the bighorn's habitat. Vast areas of open range—essential for adequate forage and water—have been lost. Peninsular bighorn have also been exposed to dangers at the urban-mountain interface. In the northern Santa Rosa Mountains between 1991 and 1996, Bighorn Institute documented bighorn struck and killed by cars, poisoned by ornamental landscape plants such as oleander, and strangled in illegal wire fences. The six-year

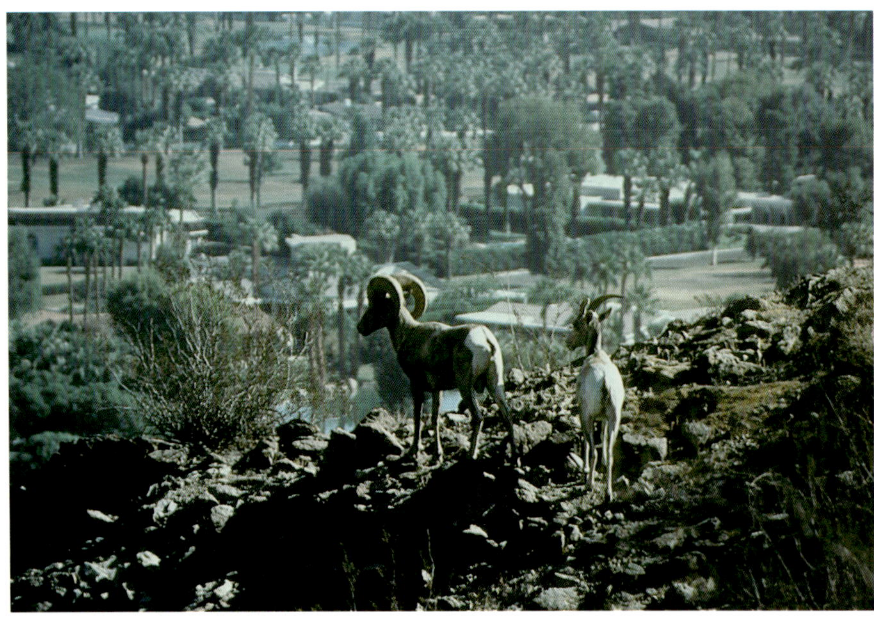

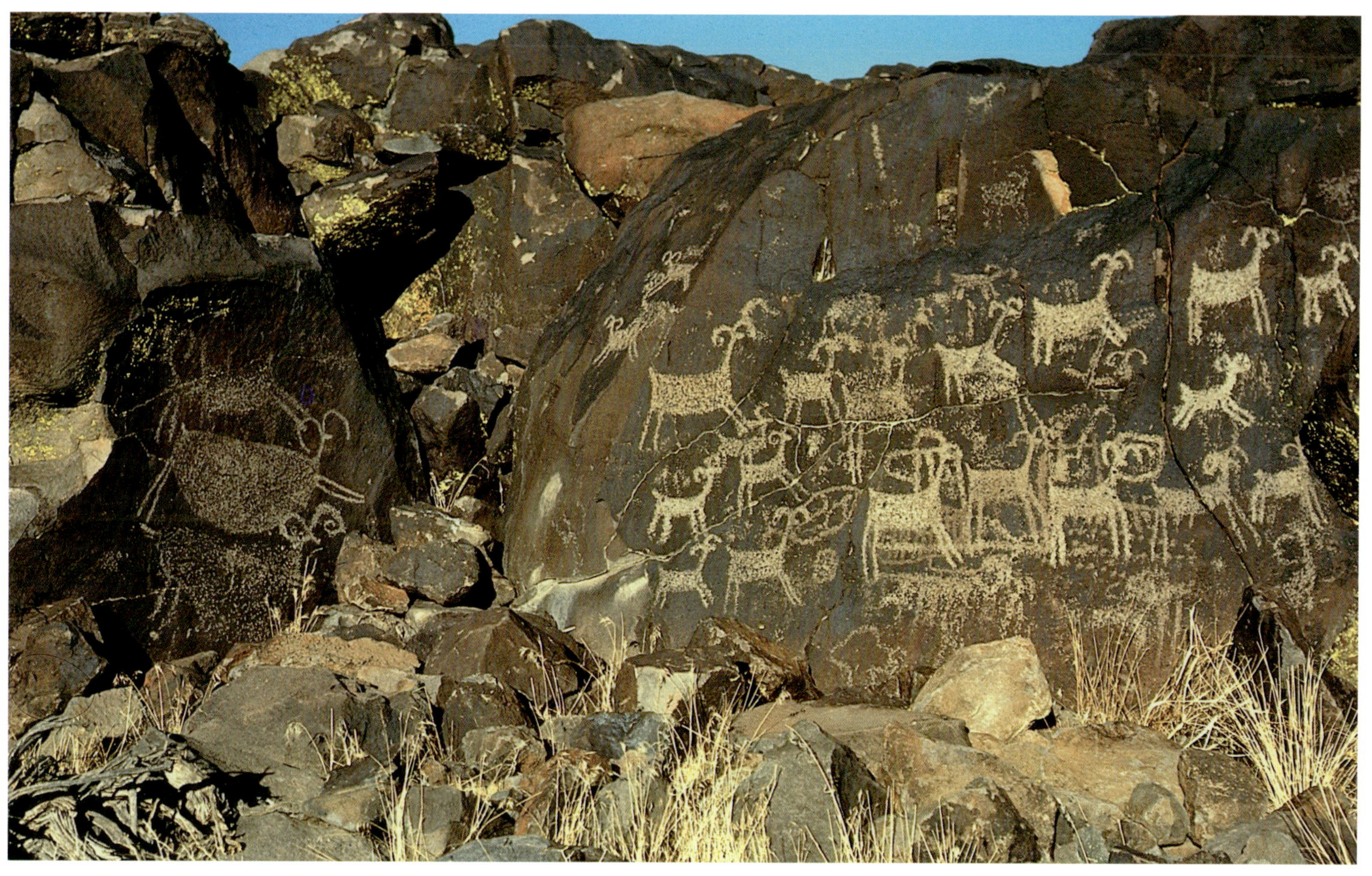

study found urbanization to be the leading cause of death for local Peninsular bighorn, accounting for 34% of adult mortalities.

As a result of this, the city of Rancho Mirage worked with the wildlife agencies and the Institute to construct a 4.5 mile 8-foot high bighorn-proof fence in 2002, which has elimated any further urban bighorn deaths.

The ecological importance of bighorn sheep was not always so misunderstood. Images of bighorn can be found painted and etched by Native Americans on rock surfaces in every Western state. *Kac-ko* is the sheep deity of the Acoma, and *Panwa* is the

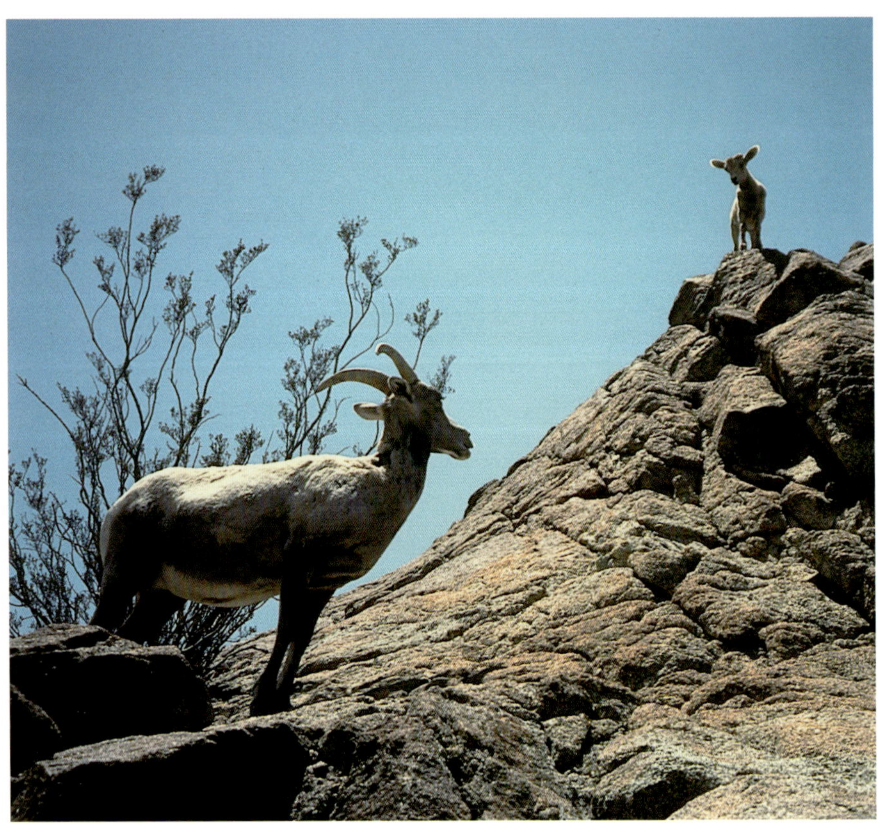

Hopi bighorn kachina. In the Navajo culture, *Ganaskidi*, who carried the seeds of the world's plants, is depicted with curving horns. The Papago believed that the horns of sheep killed by hunters must be piled together near water holes and venerated in order to control the wind and to prevent the air from leaving the earth. For the Cahuilla people, *Pem-tem-wha-ha* is the powerful protector of all hooved animals.

In the frantic pace of our modern world, it behooves us to pause and consider the significance of the bighorn sheep and its relationship to man. Wild sheep cannot alter their habitat; in order to survive in a changing world, bighorn must be able to find areas that provide at least the basic elements of food, water, and security from predators. Extinction is rarely a sudden or dramatic event. Rather, it is the inevitable outcome of changes in the environment that cause it to become too limited to support sustainable populations. Those of us who value wild sheep must find a way to ensure that our own population requirements and expansions incorporate consideration for all living things—to make certain that the grandeur of a bighorn outlined against a mountain peak never becomes the memory of a lost age and place.

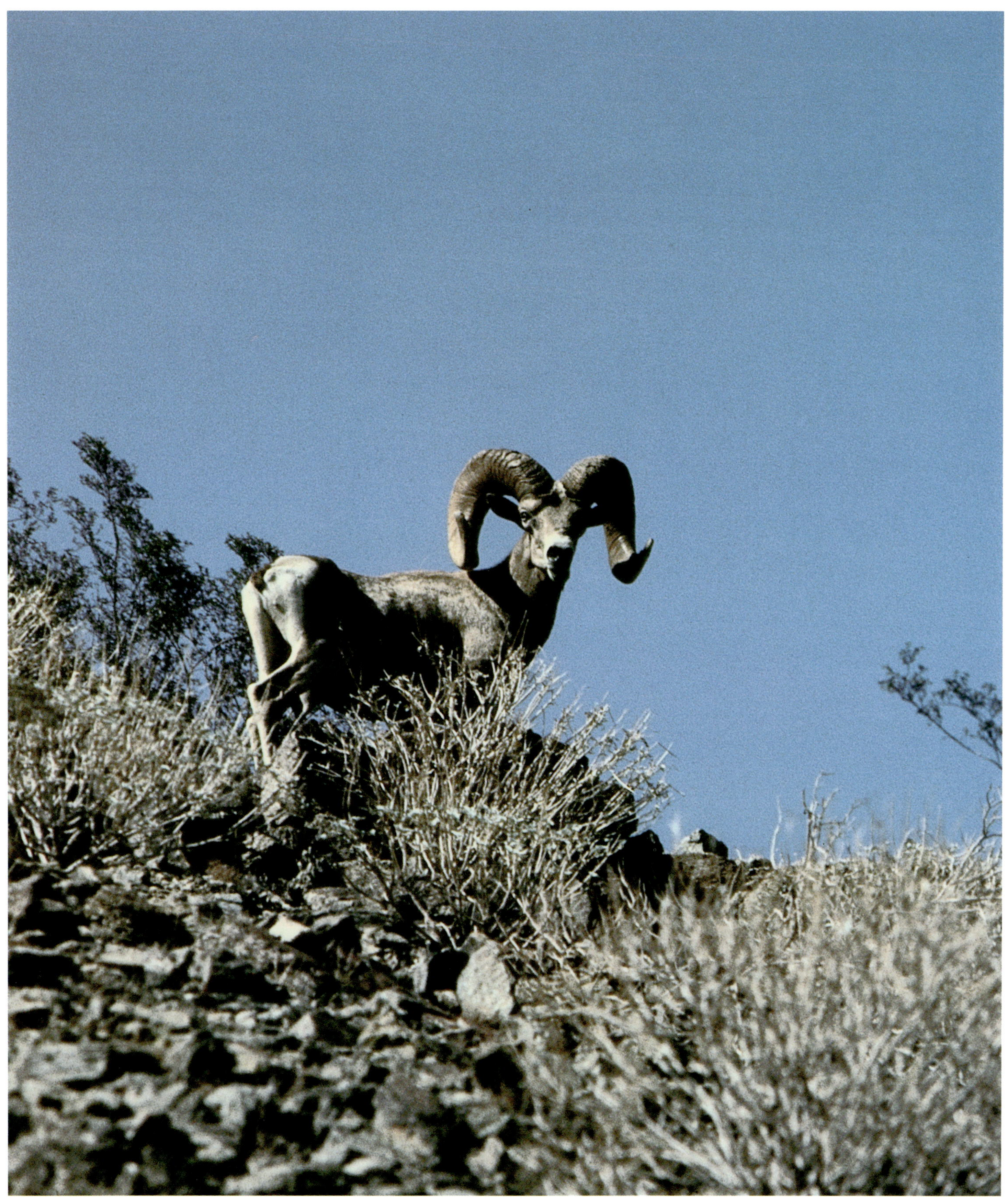

Connecting with Nature

Rising abruptly from the desert floor to an elevation of 10,800 feet on San Jacinto, the Santa Rosa and San Jacinto Mountains are a study of contrasts between the highly urbanized Coachella Valley at the base and the unpopulated wilderness at the peak. Palm trees and cacti frame distant snow-covered peaks, and manicured lawns push up against barren outcroppings.

The mountains contain five distinct climate zones, ranging from desert to alpine, and are home to more than 500 species of plants and animals. The hardiest occupants can be found in the rocky escarpments of the lower region, where annual rainfall can be less than $1/10$ inch while temperatures can soar above 120°F. Within this harsh environment, the Peninsular bighorn has adapted well. They are able to subsist on the sparse vegetation, foraging for grasses, shrubs, and forbs. While they favor acacia, catclaw, encelia, and mesquite, they are opportunistic feeders who adapt their diet to what is available. Bighorn can go for many days without drinking, extracting most of their required moisture from the plants they eat.

In turn, they provide a food source for mountain lions and coyotes. Predation is not a problem for healthy bighorn populations; however, when a herd is suppressed by other ecological factors, predation can potentially, help drive it to extinction.

Extraordinarily surefooted, bighorn are not challenged by the rough terrain and negotiate the steep cliffs and ravines without effort. Their light-colored coats allow them to virtually disappear into their arid surroundings. Bighorn are an integral part of their spartan world, and many Path of the Bighorn artists chose this theme to celebrate the balance and harmony that is possible in nature.

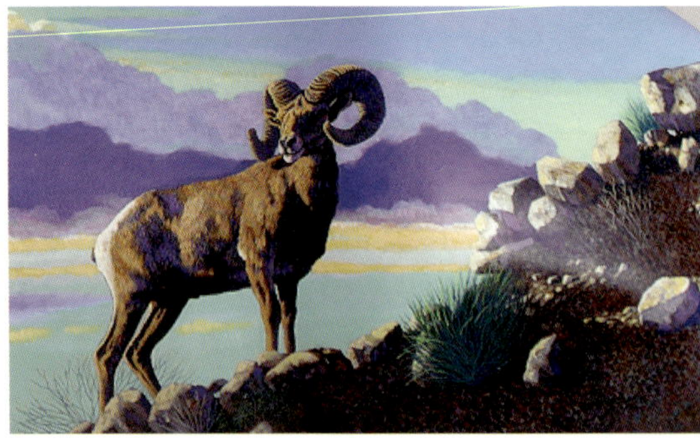

Detail from ram sculpture painted by Bill Ware

ABCs of Ecology

artist Carol Buck
sponsor Diane & Gary Zornes
inaugural site YMCA of the Desert—La Quinta Center

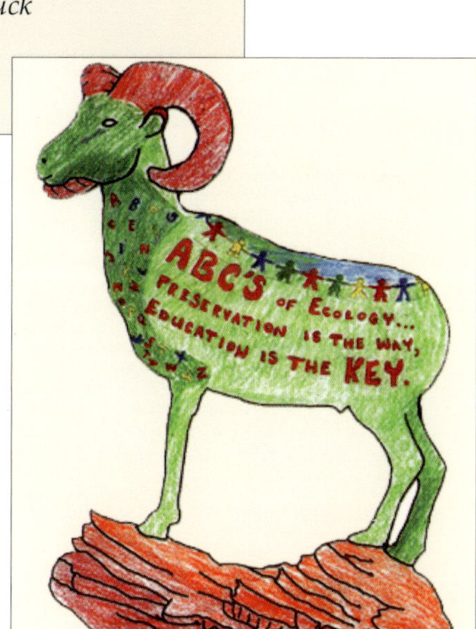

*Just as the
cycle of life
continues, so
does education. Our greatest
investment, and hope for our
earth, are the children of the
world and the generations to
come. — Carol Buck*

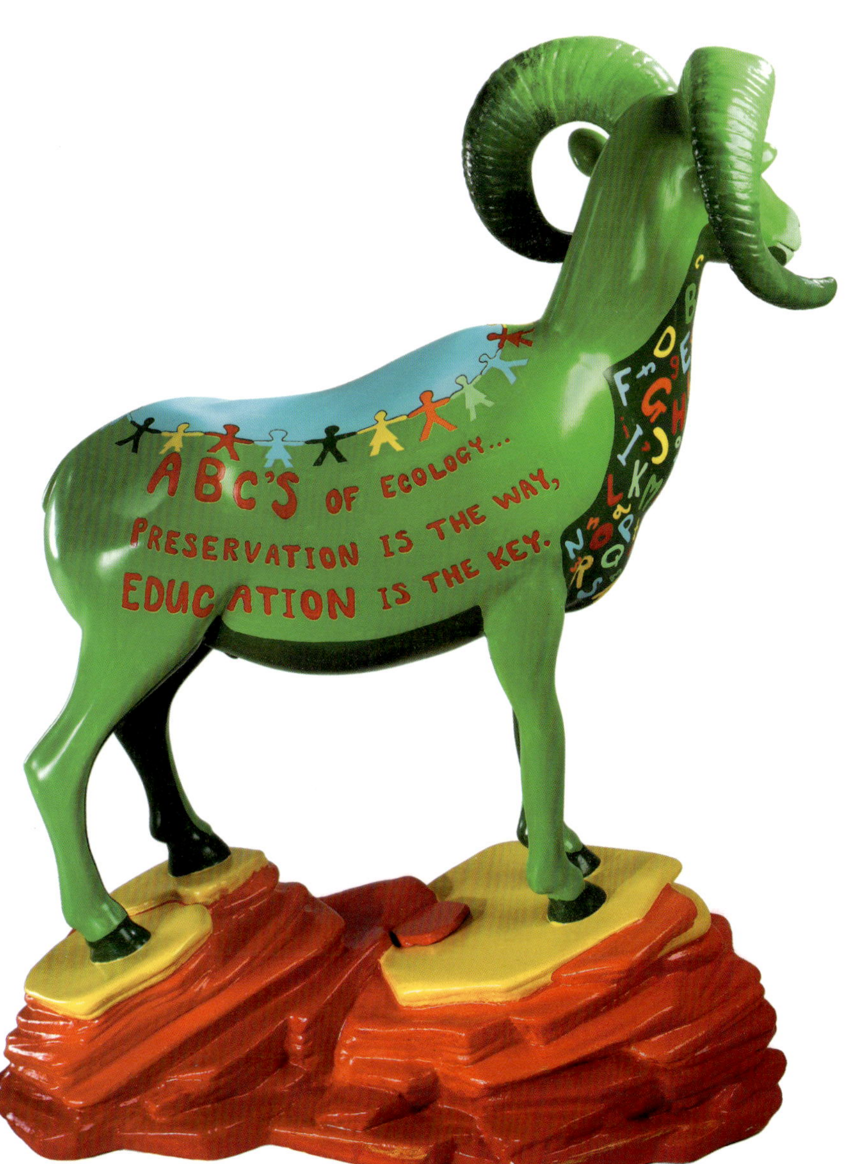

Above and Beyond

artist Bill Ware
sponsor The Mirada
inaugural site The Mirada

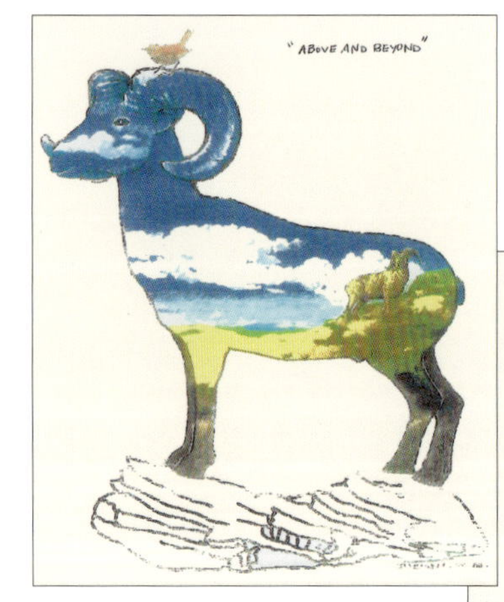

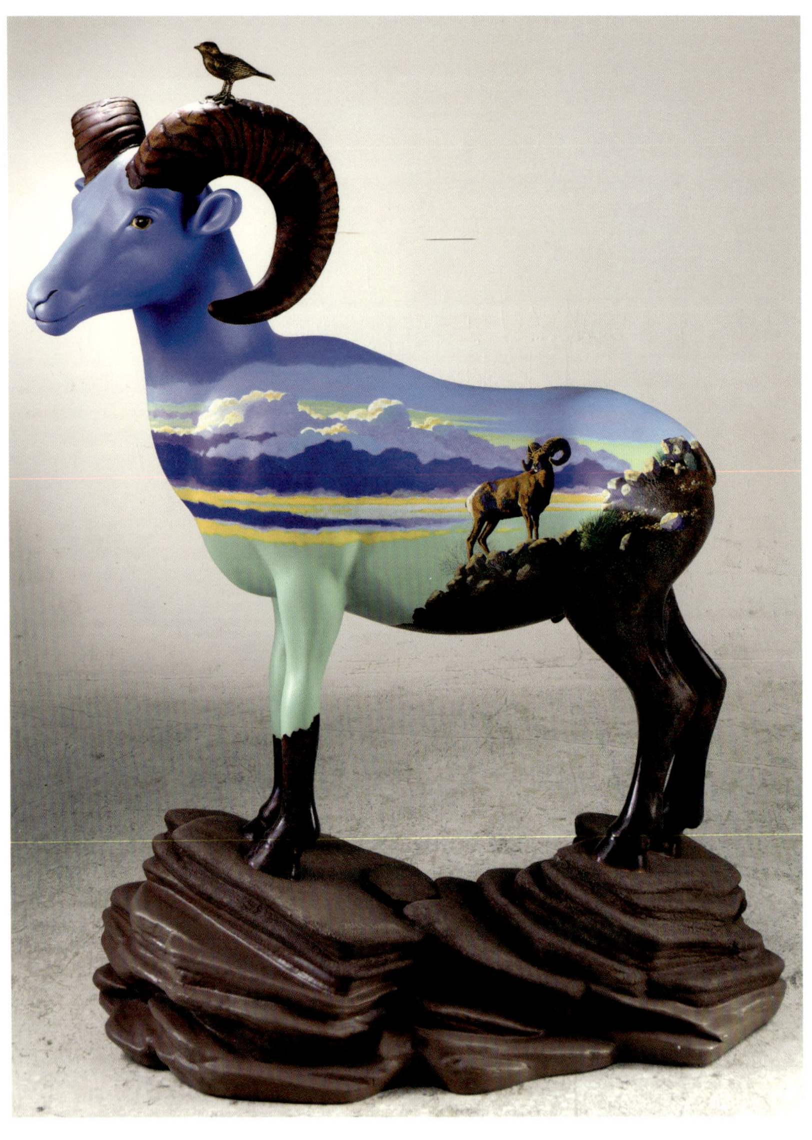

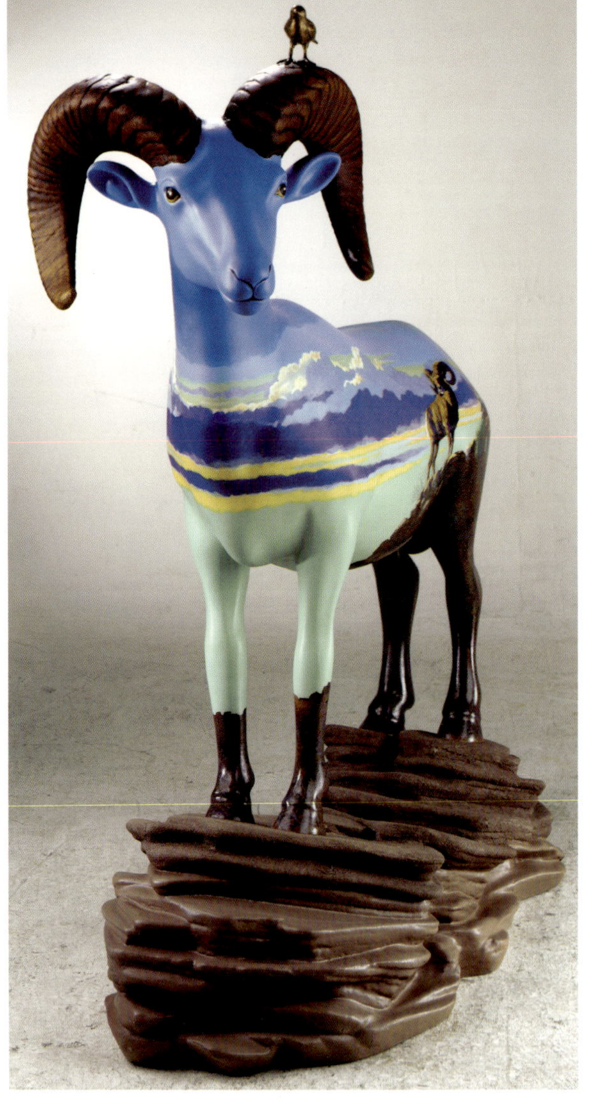

A New Beginning

artist William Cain
sponsor Indian Wells City Hall
inaugural site Indian Wells Tennis Garden

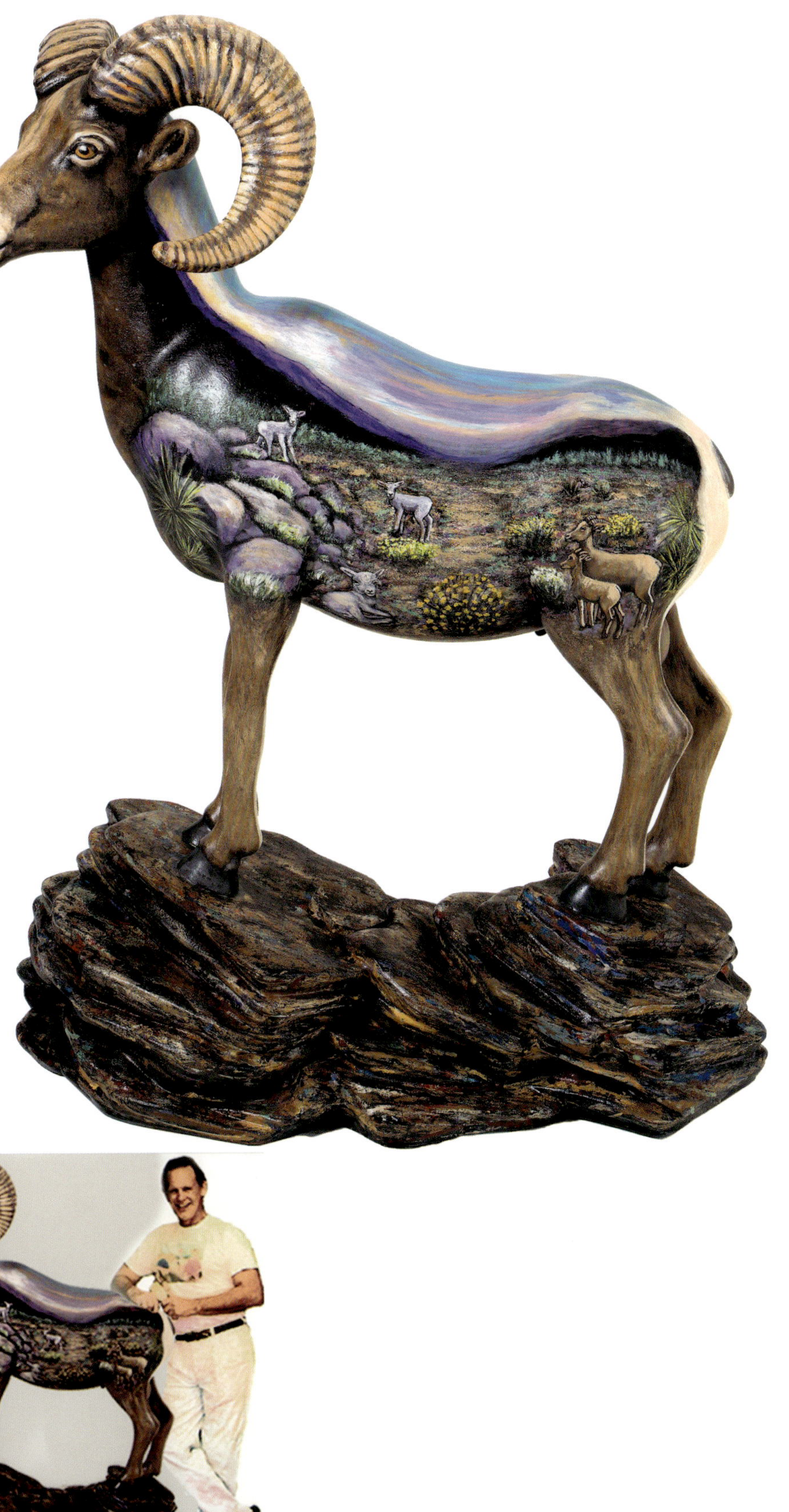

Alpha & Omega I

artist Kirstine Keel
sponsor Rebecca VanDusen
inaugural site Northern Trust Bank (stolen)

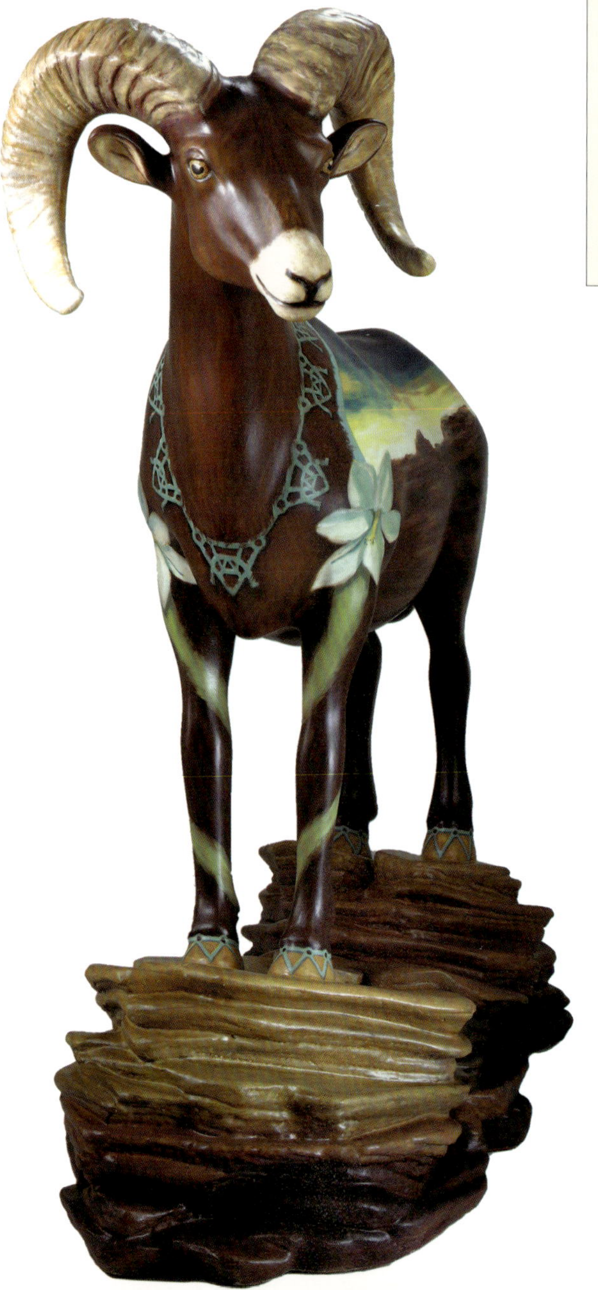

Every living thing in this mortal realm has a beginning and an end – Alpha and Omega. The path chosen creates our destiny. With our help, the Path of the Bighorn can be filled with life and hope.

The male bighorn has chosen a path of light. Around his neck is a pattern in turquoise that alternates between alpha and omega with the sign of the compass and eternal rings giving the ram a positive direction. His back carries the night sky with the Big Dipper pointing to the North Star signifying stability. A glowing sunrise gives the first light to the bighorn's natural habitat. The Desert Lilies guide his shoulders with purity and hope along nature's trail. His hooves are anchored, carrying the emblems of the direction toward eternity. – Kirstine Keel

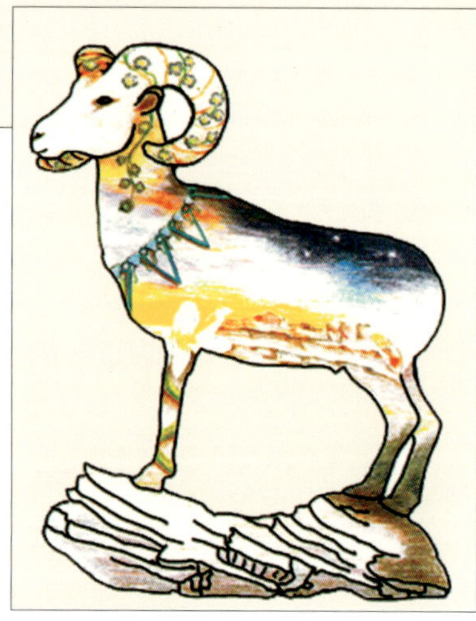

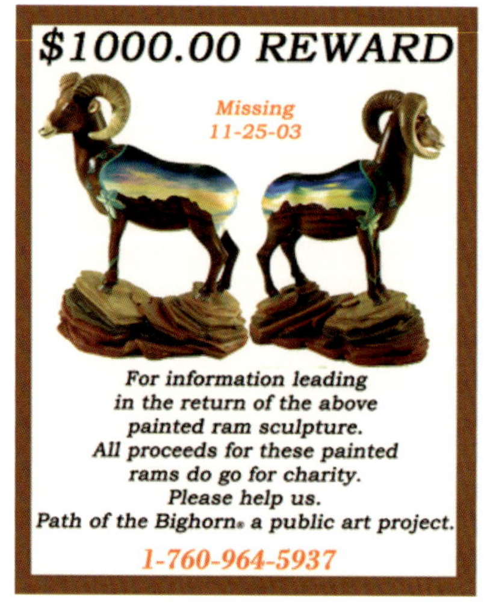

Alpha & Omega II

artist   Kirstine Keel
sponsor   Rebecca VanDusen
inaugural site   The Lodge at Rancho Mirage

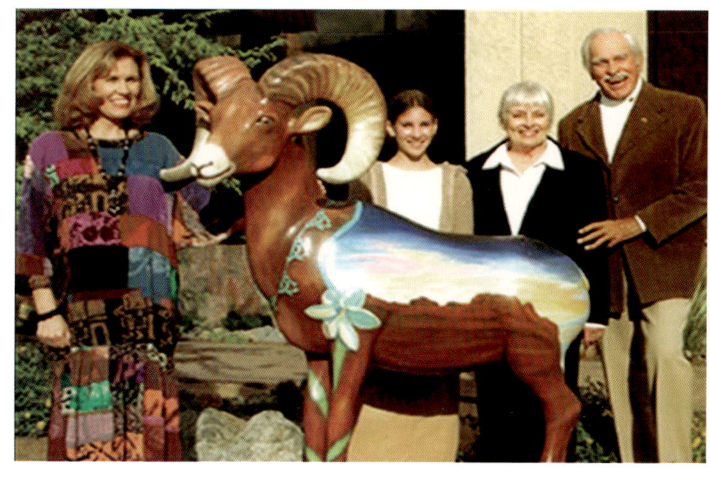

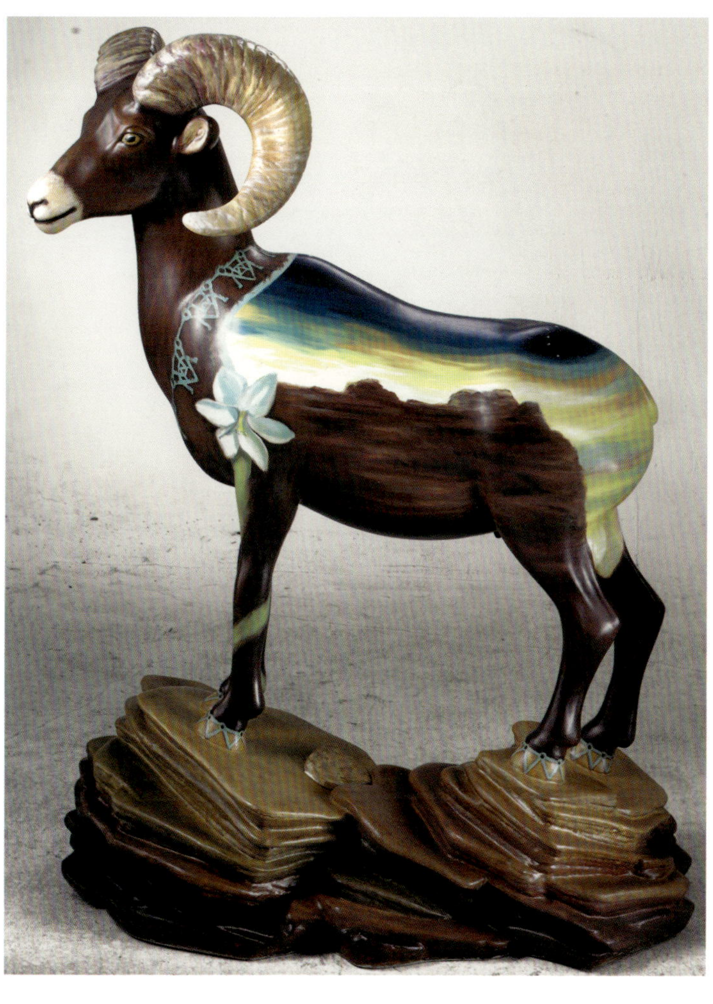

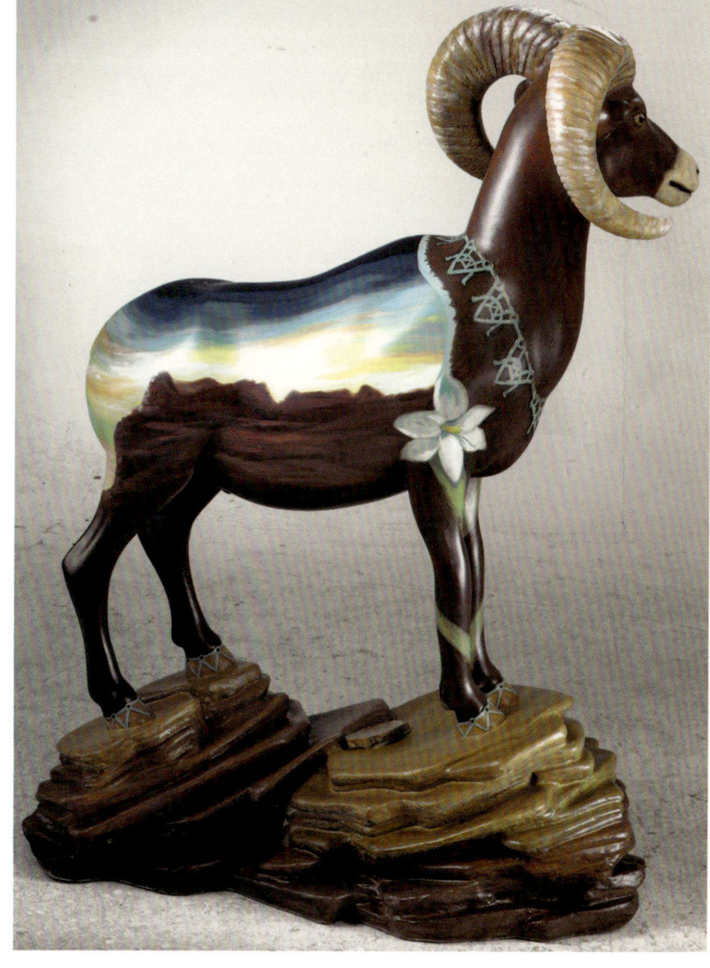

Animal Tracks

artist M. Goodwill
sponsor Dr. Mindy Byers & Dr. Roland Burbank
inaugural site Desert Animal Hospital

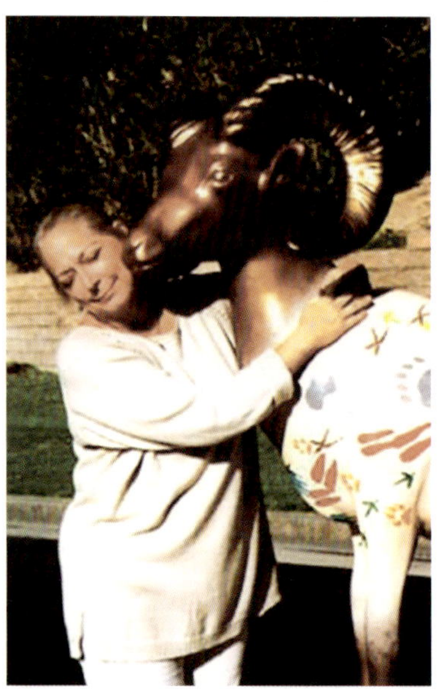

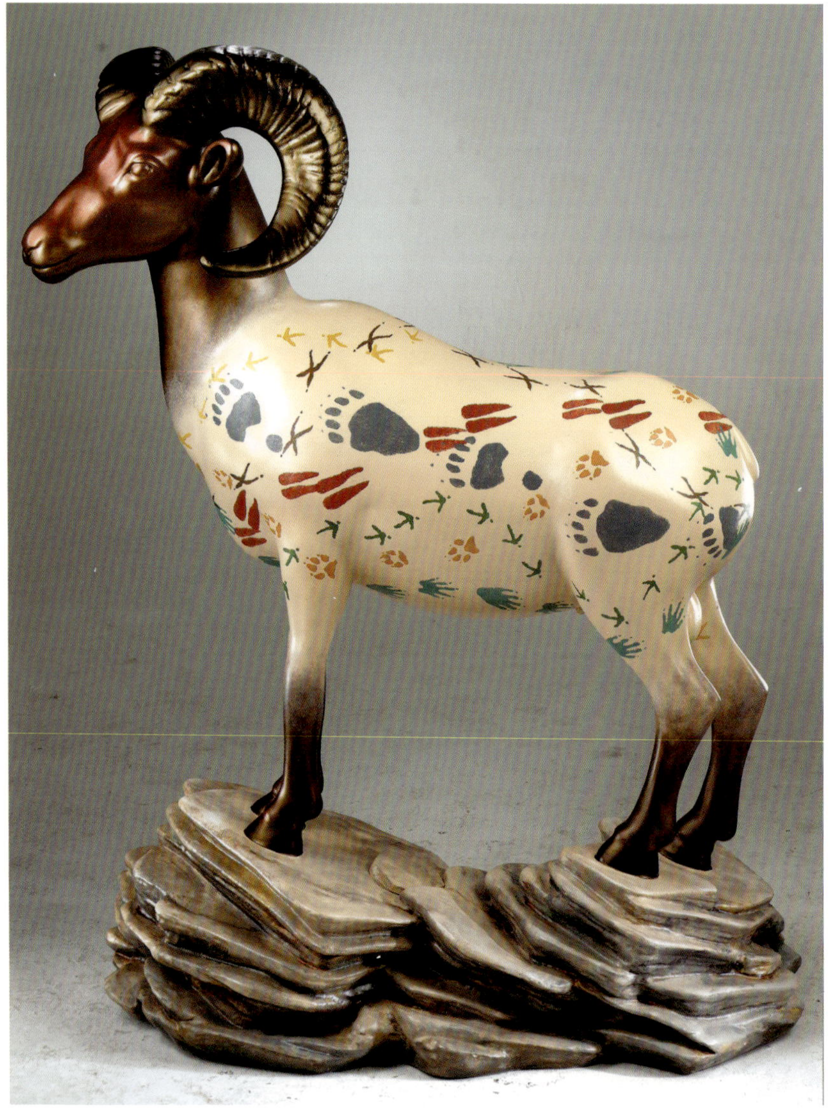

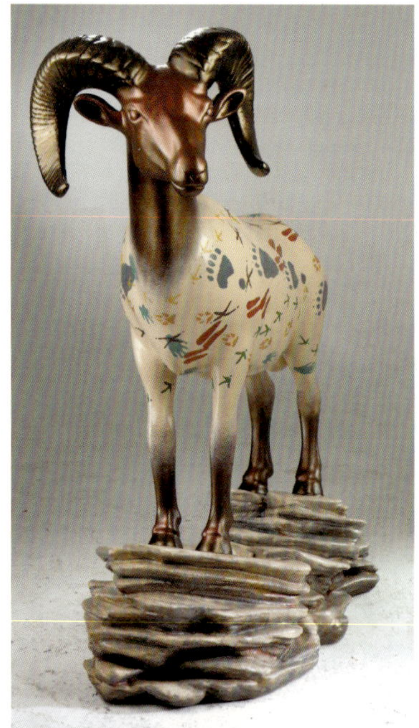

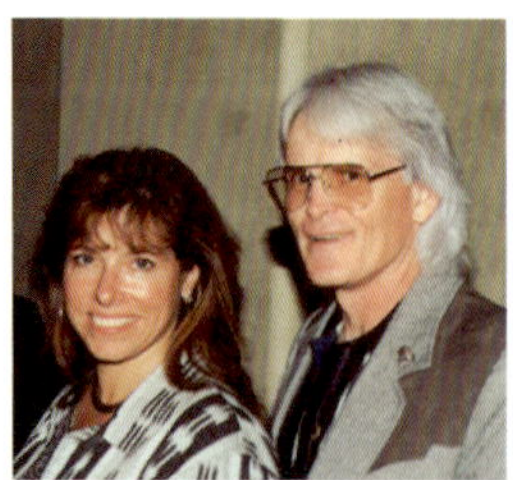

Sponsors
Drs. Mindy Byers
& Roland Burbank

A Piece of the Puzzle

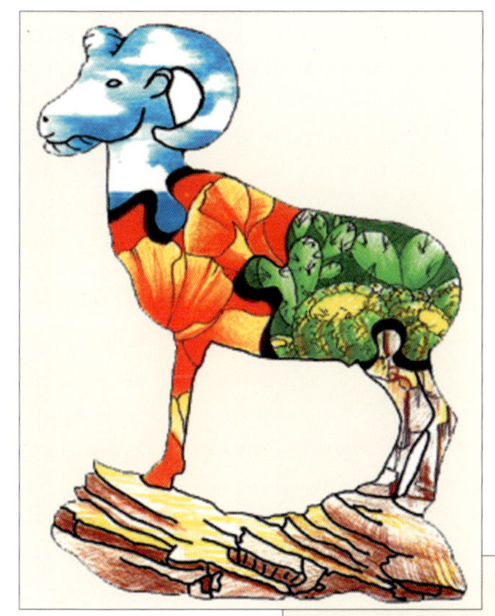

artist Craig D. Cynowa
sponsor Dr. William Kelly
inaugural site Health Scan Imaging

Each puzzle piece represents a local or regional environmental aspect of the bighorn's habitat. Together, the pieces suggest the inter-relationship of all things in nature.
— Craig Cynowa

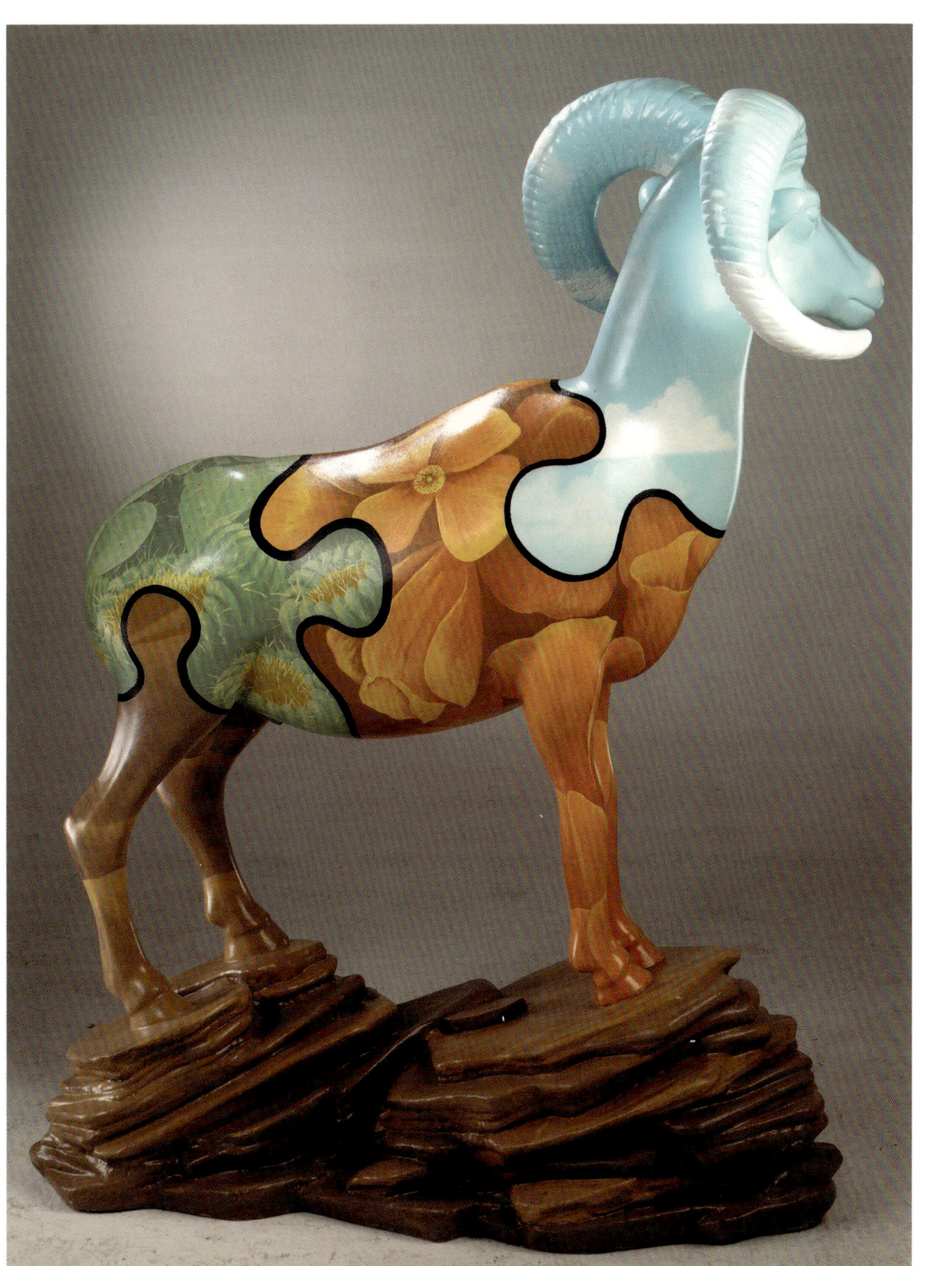

Aries

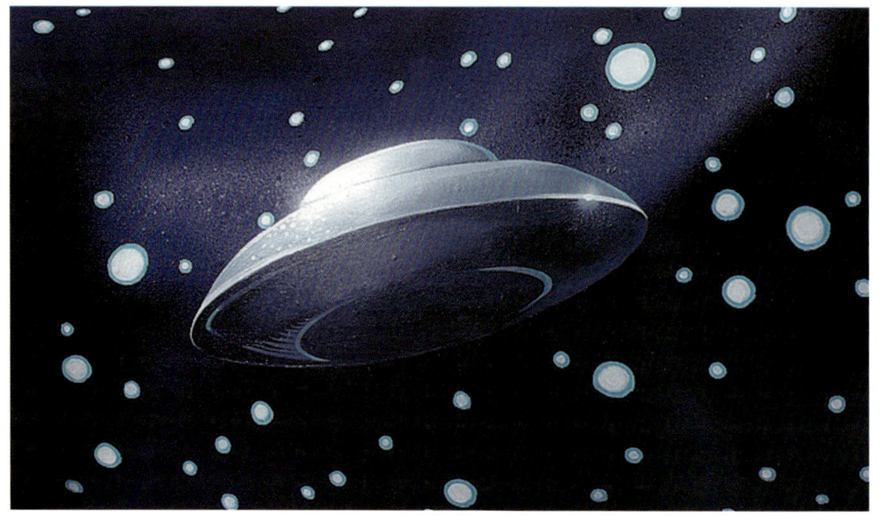

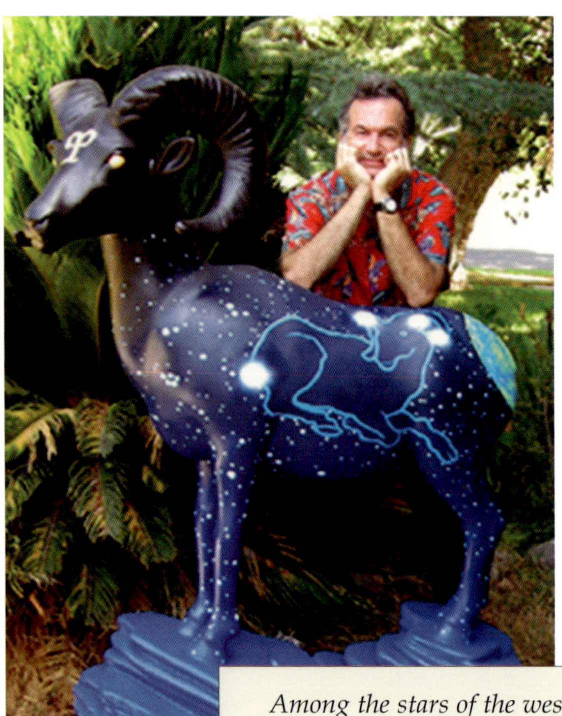

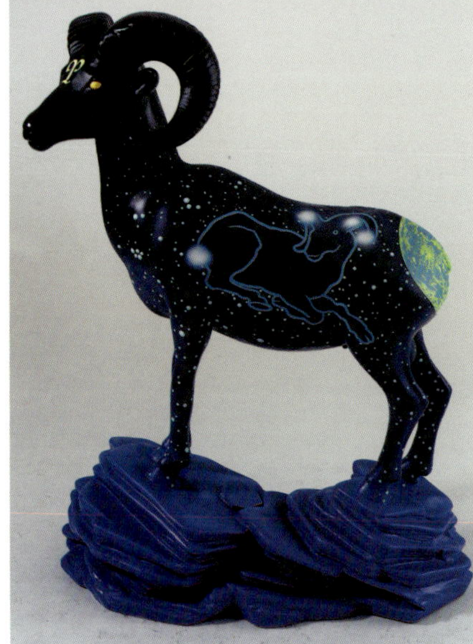

William Stout is an artist of extraordinary talent who has achieved success in a wide range of artistic media. At age 17, he won a full scholarship to the Chouinard Art Institute (now the California Institute of the Arts) where he obtained his B.A. degree. His early career began with work as an illustrator for books, newspapers and comic strips then segued into the music business. Following this he worked as an art director in the film industry creating advertisements for over 120 films. As a conceptual designer, he designed the production of Michael Crichton's "Jurassic Park" and Walt Disney's full-length computer animated feature "Dinosaurs." He won the 1984 Children's Choice Award for his design on Ray Bradbury's book "Dinosaur Tales" which was the basis for George Lucas' and Stephen Spielberg's joint film production "The Land Before Time." He was involved in the conceptual planning of several theme parks for Walt Disney Imagineering around the world, and later was chief designer for Lucasfilm/Industrial Light and Magic's first themed entertainment centers.

Stout has devoted a large part of his recent career to projects dealing with the natural world including a world-wide exhibition of his paintings depicting, "Dinosaurs, Penguins and Whales-The Wildlife of Antarctica" and a book project "Lost World-Modern and Prehistoric Life in Antarctica." He is currently continuing his work documenting the world's environments and our fragile natural world embodied by Path of the Bighorn.

Among the stars of the western American sky, the constellation Aries the Ram is the first sign of the Zodiac. Known as the pioneer and the adventurer, Aries is both energetic and courageous. Aries also represents the head of the human body. I hope that by using our heads, our human wisdom, we can solve the dilemma of the Peninsular bighorn sheep's survival. — William Stout

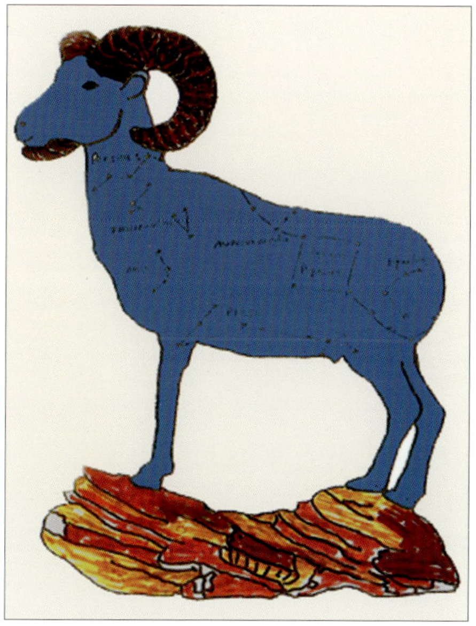

Aries the Ram

artist Pat Grimm
sponsor Cathy & Dave Stockton
inaugural site Downey Savings

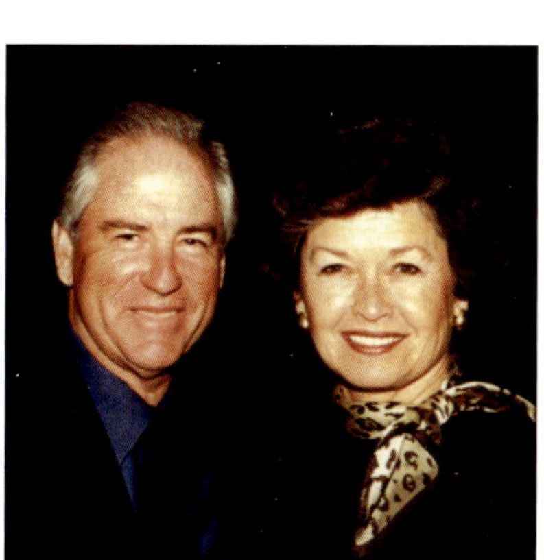

Sponsors Dave & Cathy Stockton

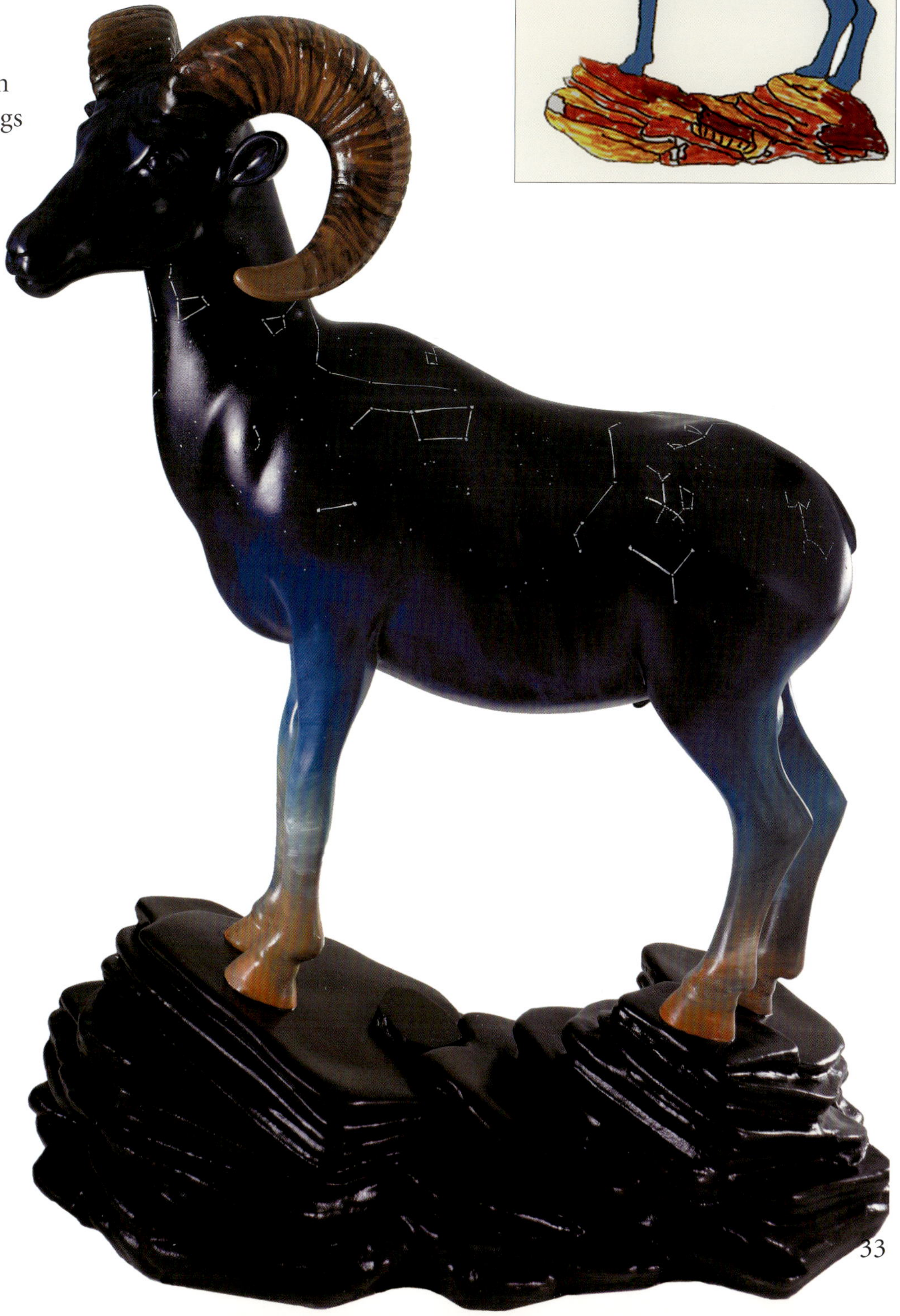

Bighorn Jack

artist Lori Musil
sponsor Palm Desert National Bank
inaugural site Palm Desert National Bank, La Quinta

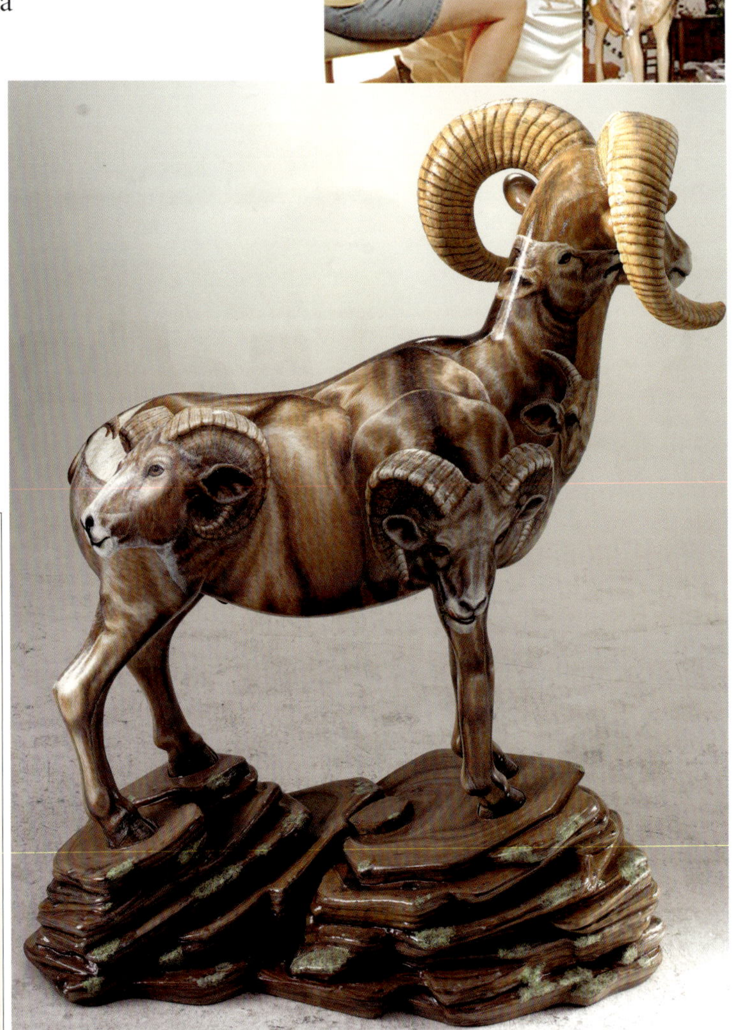

What fun! I've painted and drawn many a bighorn in my life…but never on a ram shape. I've hidden a jackrabbit amongst the many bighorns on this ram.

Charity projects that join businesses and sponsors, artists, and the public together are truly fantastic! It's a way to nurture the community. Happy Trails!
— Lori Musil

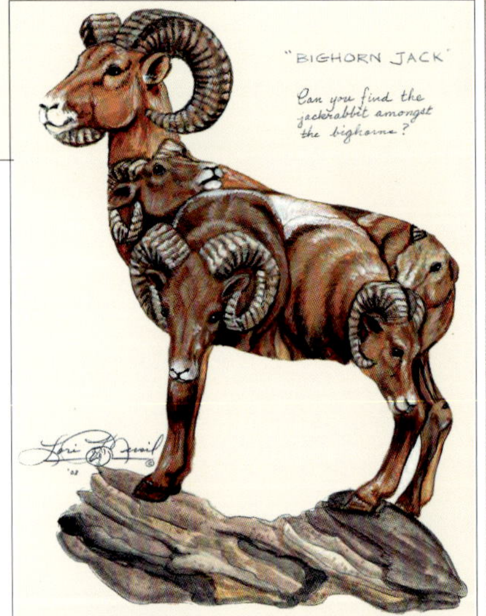

A native of Tucson, Az, Lori Musil now resides in the hills overlooking historic Cerrillo, New Mexico, just south of Santa Fe. A painter, potter, jeweler, and sculptor of the West and its wildlife, she is a self-taught artist with a keen sense of fine detail. While she spent 30 years in commercial art (textile color separations, logos, jewelry, sign painting), she began working with clay and ran a small pottery gallery.

Bighorn Moon

artist Wilberta Moulthrop
sponsor Mia & Bob Zornes
inaugural site Hallmark TV & Stereo

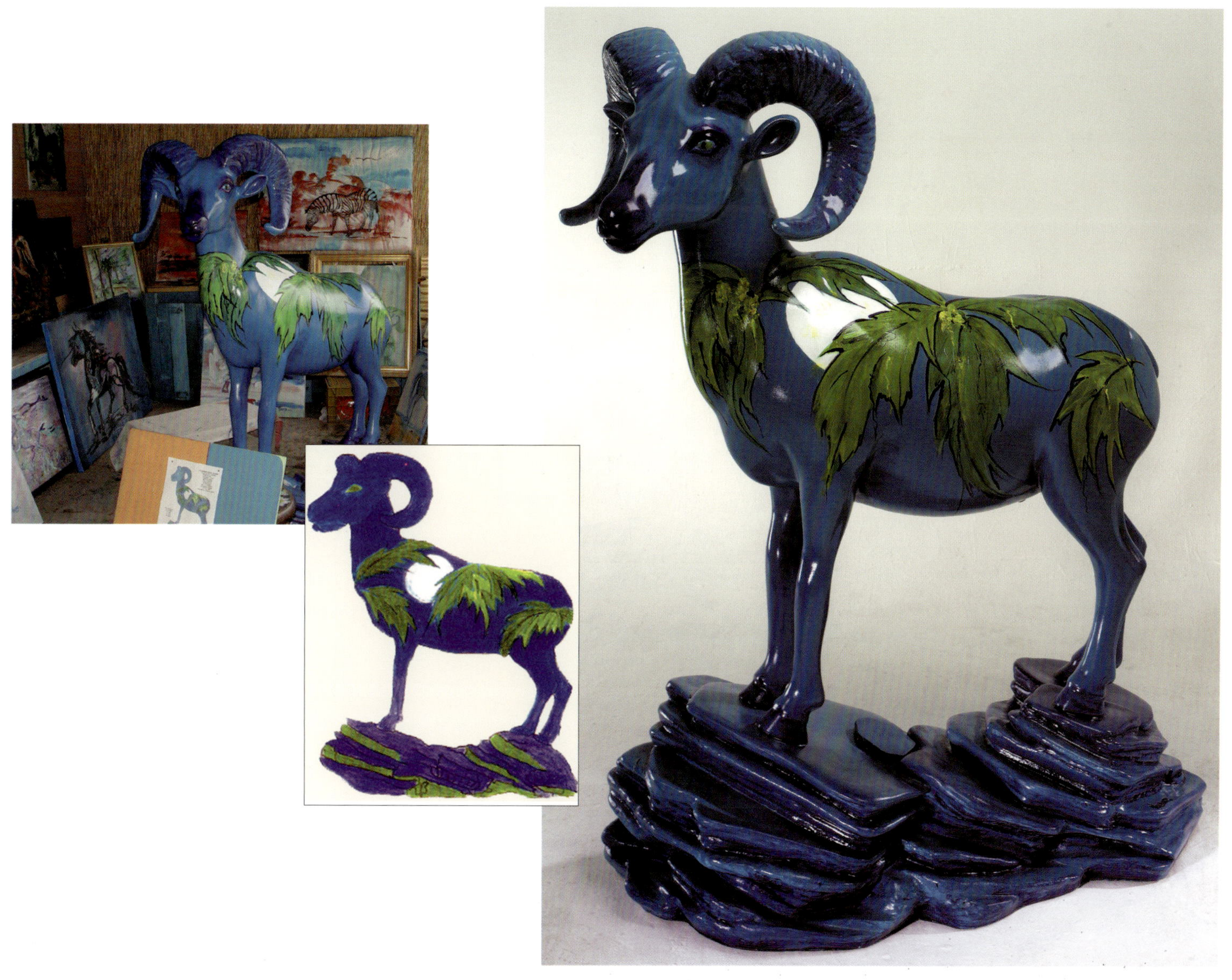

Bighorn Realm

artist Stuart Funk
sponsor Alexandra & Sidney Sheldon
inaugural site Bighorn Institute

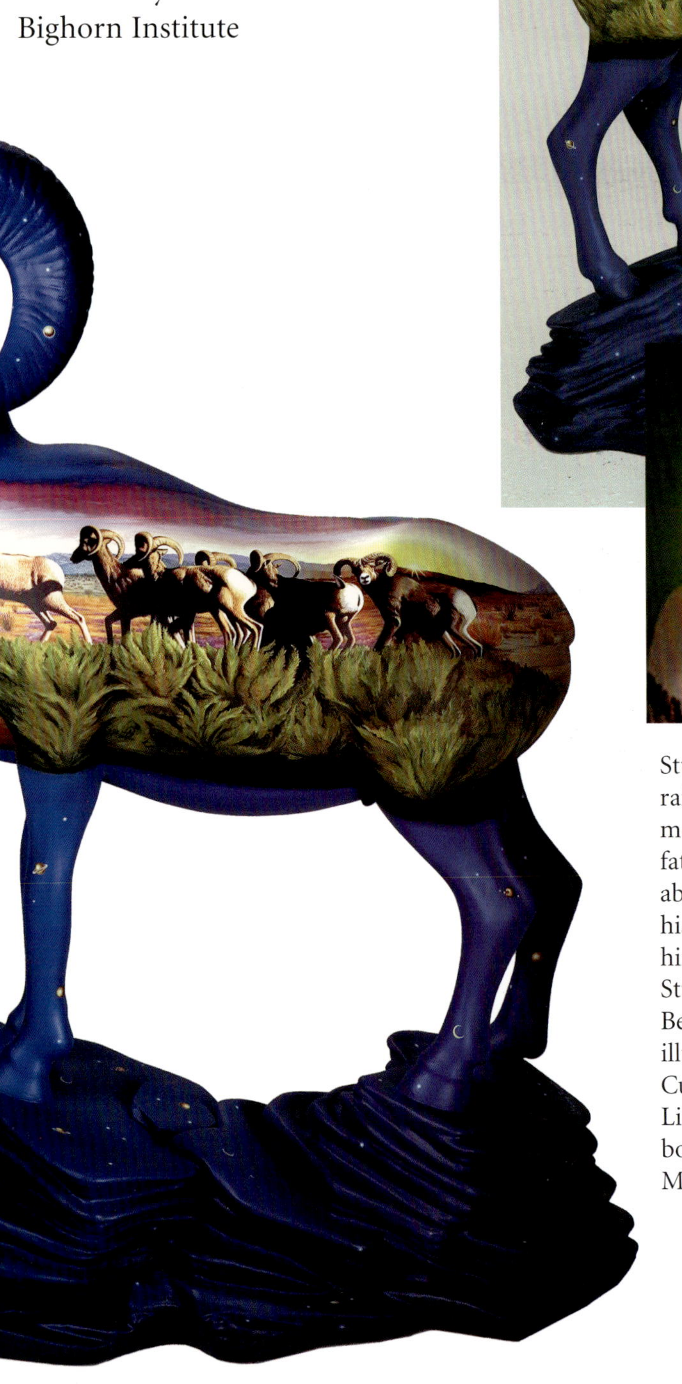

Stuart Funk was born in Harrisburg, PA, and raised in the South Bay area of Los Angeles. He moved to the Coachella Valley in 1997. Stuart's father was an artist and passed on his artistic ability to Stuart. One of his first memories is of his father taking his hand in his and teaching him to "shade".

Stuart studied drawing and painting at Long Beach State University and has worked as an illustrator for many national outdoor magazines. Currently he is the art Director of Palm Springs Life Magazine and is illustrating a children's book about the Santa Rosa and San Jacinto Mountains National Monument.

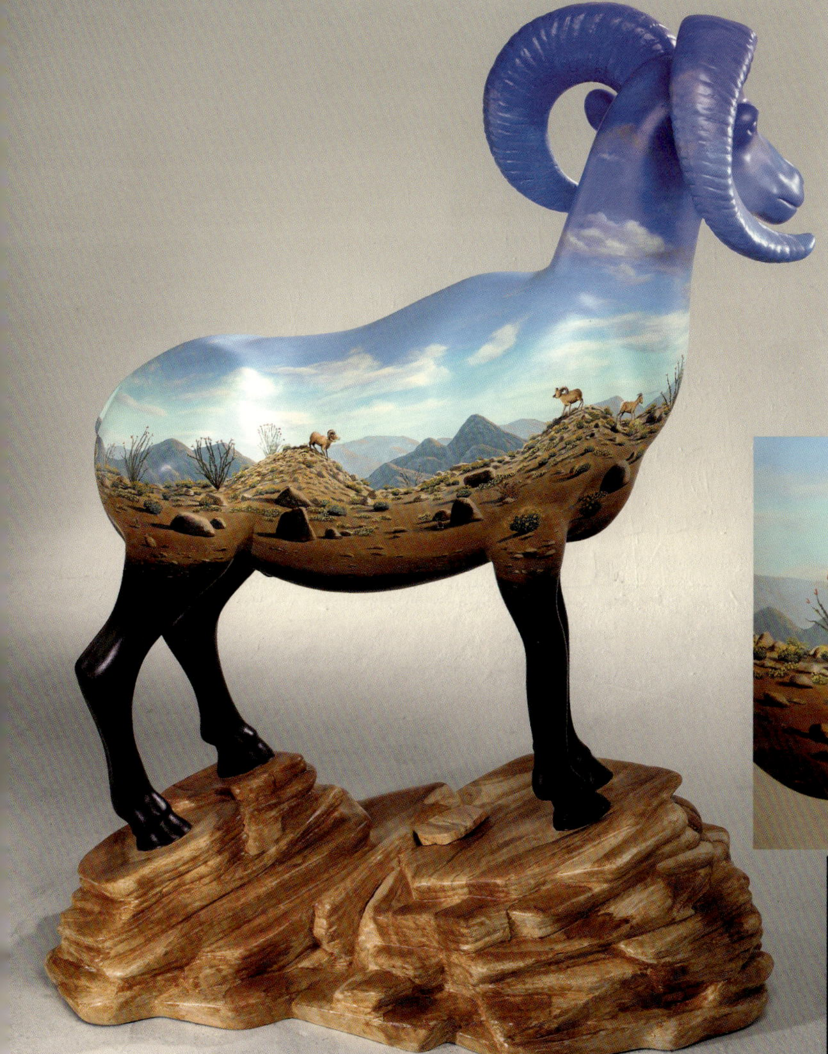

Bighorn Spring

artist Mark Junge
sponsor Dorothy & Kent Roberts
inaugural site Palm Springs International Airport

I have long been touched by the habitat of the Peninsular bighorn sheep — the rugged mountains, often sparse flora and brilliant spring color. The bighorn sheep themselves proclaim a grace and nobility that seem to contrast with their environment. My goal is to marry these opposing concepts by painting the habitat on the ram sculpture. The mountains are typical of the San Jacinto and Santa Rosa ranges with flowering ocotillo, brittlebush, cactus, and desert annuals. In the background is a family of bighorn sheep, the ewe and lamb partially obscured by encelia flowers. Other desert "critters" are waiting to be discovered by the viewer: native lizards, cottontails, and various birds. A few examples of earlier human habitation, such as the petroglyphs and Cahuilla pottery, can be found as well. From a distance, the painting seems uncluttered, but viewers who come close to the sculpture will see plenty of detail. The mountains, sky, and foreground wrap seamlessly around the entire sculpture.
— Mark Junge

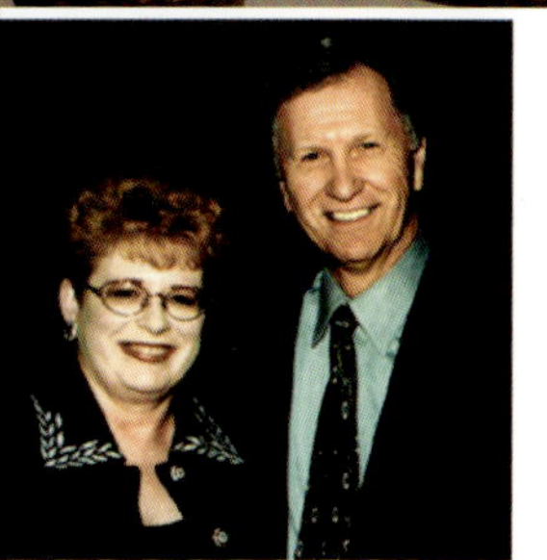

*Sponsors Dorothy
& Kent Roberts*

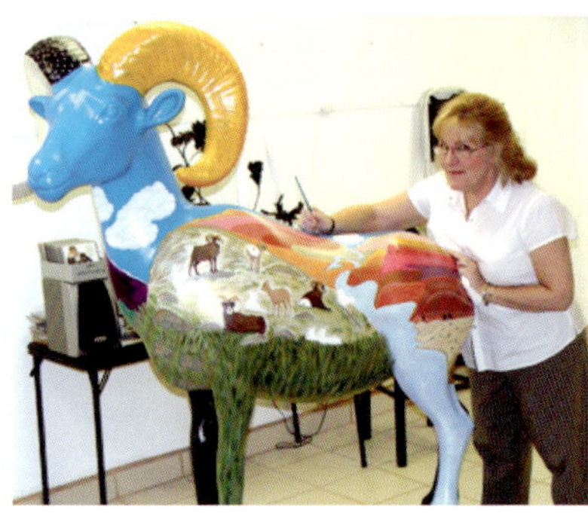

Born Wild, Live Free

artist   Brenda Johnson
sponsor   Sasha Sheldon
inaugural site   Windermere Real Estate

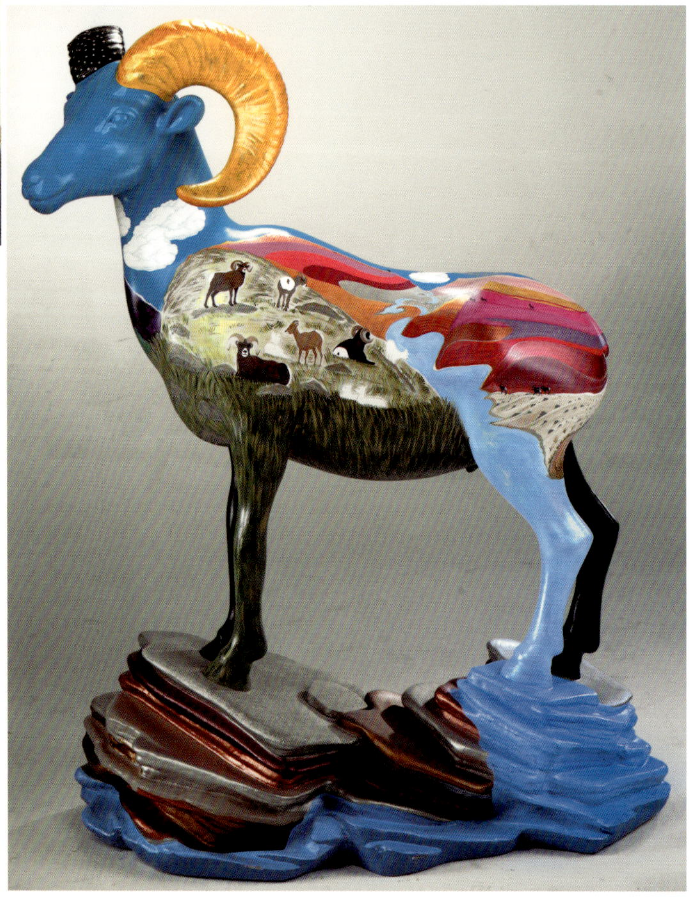

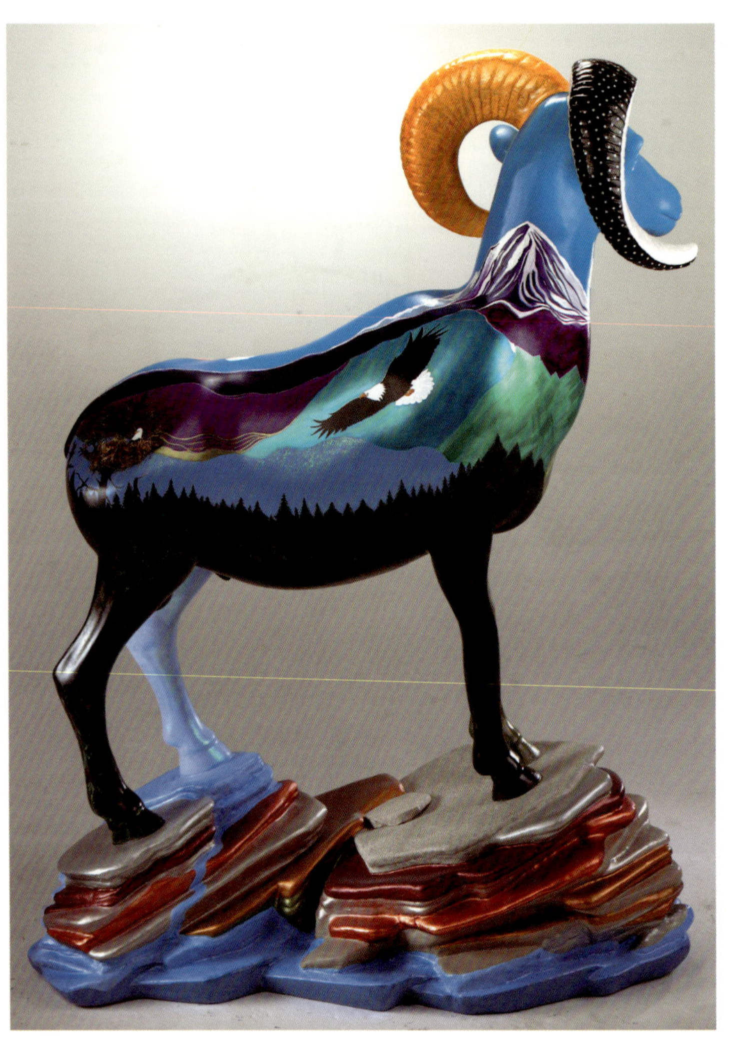

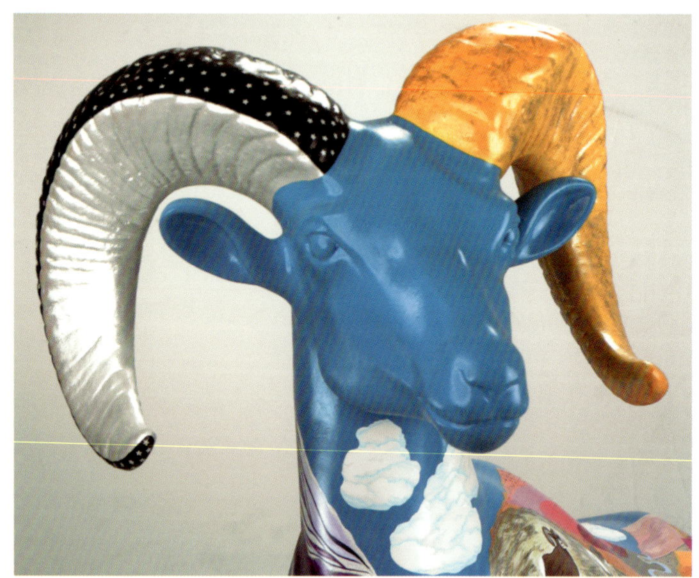

Borrego

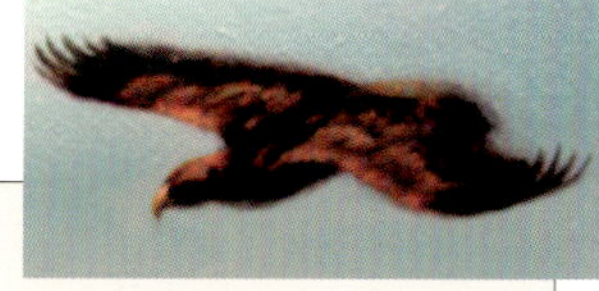

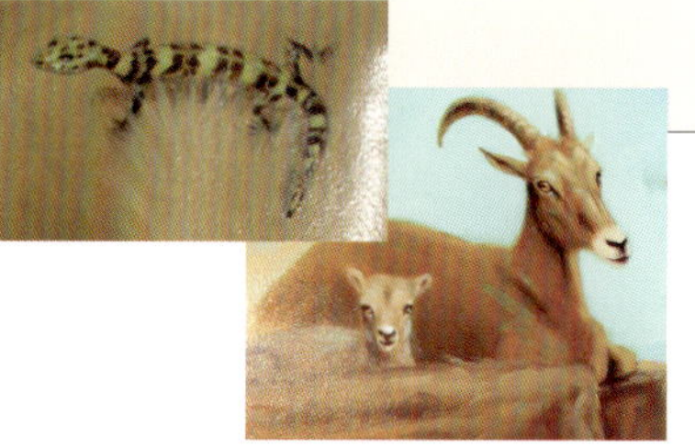

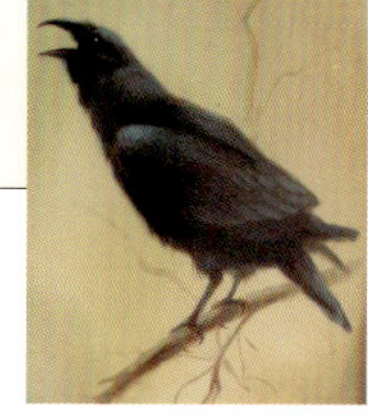

Painting the wildlife around us is very important to me. Since I live in Borrego Springs, my vision for the bighorn is to paint it with scenes and animals that are associated with the Anza Borrego Desert State Park. — Gail Anne

artist   Gail Anne
sponsor   Alexandra & Sidney Sheldon
inaugural site   Anza Borrego Desert State
                Park Visitors Center

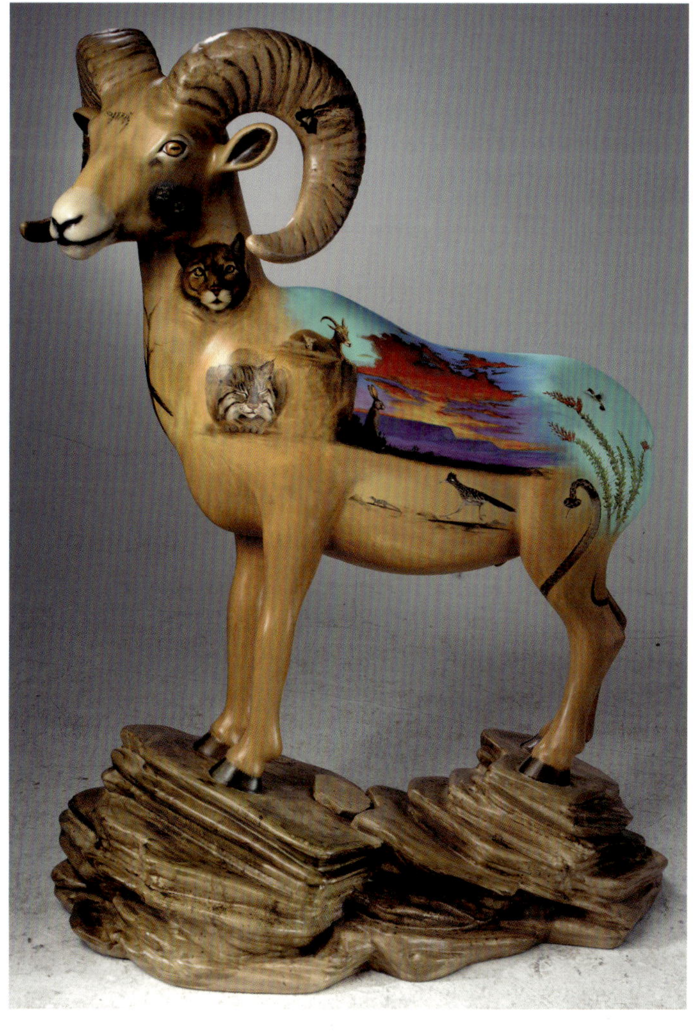

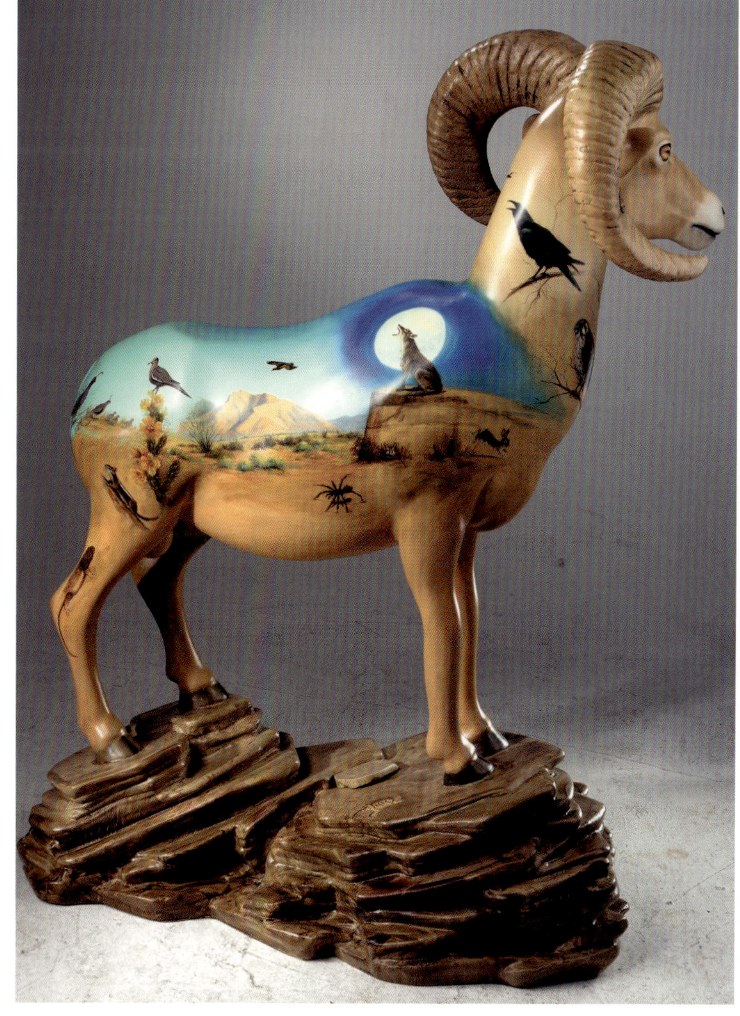

Bridging the Gap

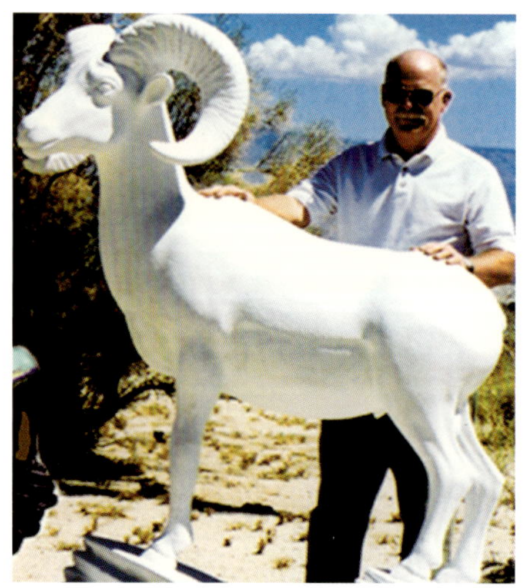

artist Joe Wertheimer
sponsor Alexandra & Sidney Sheldon
inaugural site Rancho Mirage City Hall

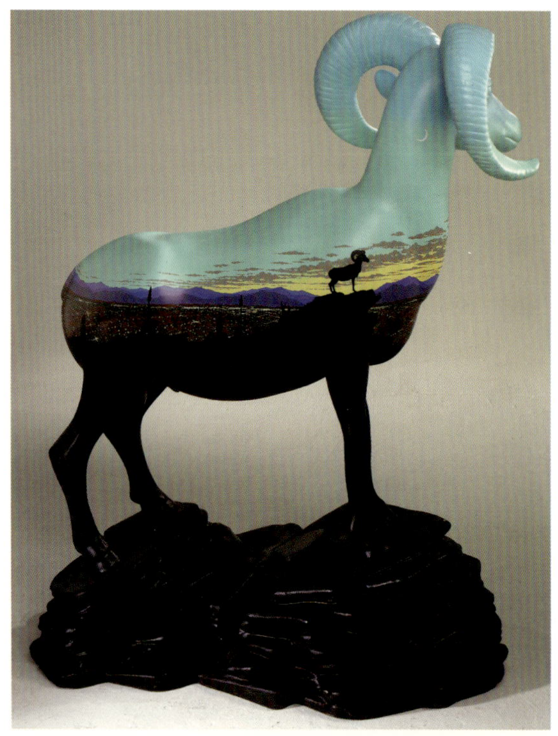

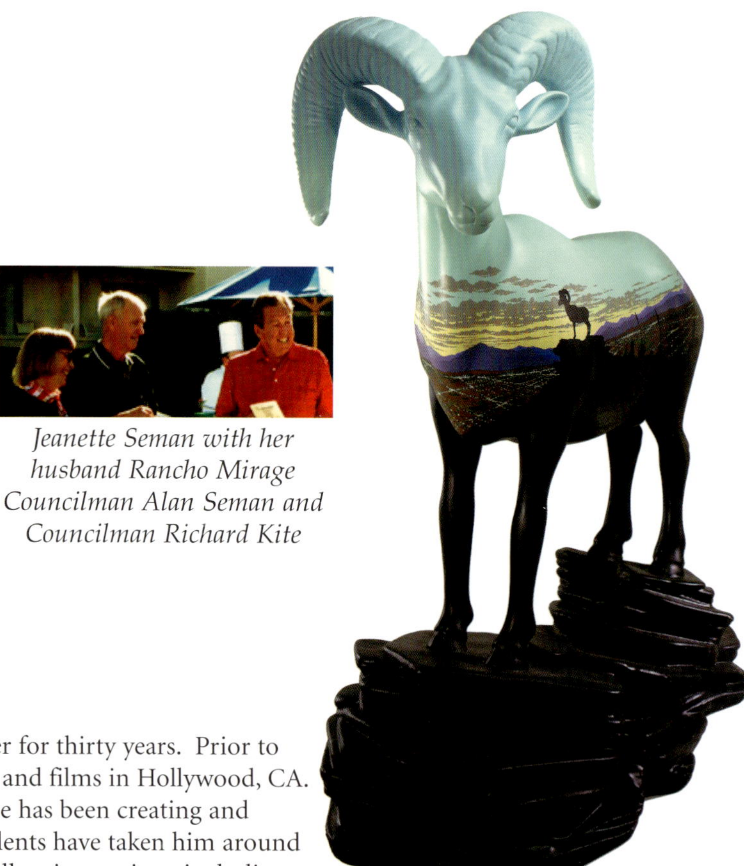

Jeanette Seman with her husband Rancho Mirage Councilman Alan Seman and Councilman Richard Kite

Joe Wertheimer has been a Sculptor and Conceptual Designer for thirty years. Prior to that, Joe was a Production Designer on various commercials and films in Hollywood, CA. Joe and his family moved to Palm Springs, CA in 1990 and he has been creating and developing projects out of his studio there ever since. His talents have taken him around the world, where he has worked on many interesting and challenging projects including The Palace of the Lost City Hotel in Sun City, South Africa. There he sculpted 18 African animals, life-size and larger, as well as hundreds of architectural details on the walls, ceilings and columns for interior and exterior portions of the project. At Atlantis, Paradise Island, Bahamas, he sculpted numerous pieces for the largest marine habitat in the world, as well as exterior pieces for the Mayan Temple water slide. Most recently, Joe sculpted two life-size figures of the Madonna and St. Francis, as well as the original of the bighorn sheep for Bighorn Institute's Path of the Bighorn. Bridging the Gap is the first painted ram sculpture in the series and is in a permanent location in Rancho Mirage City Hall.

Bright Future

artist   Rick Farrell
sponsor   Mary & Wm Wilcox
inaugural site   Noia Investments

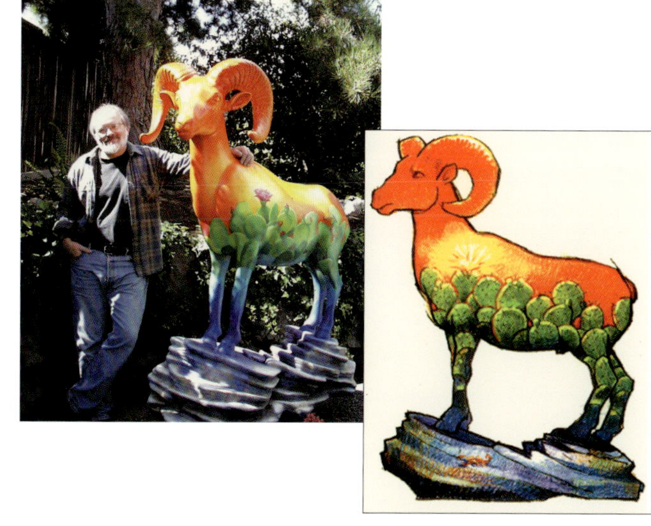

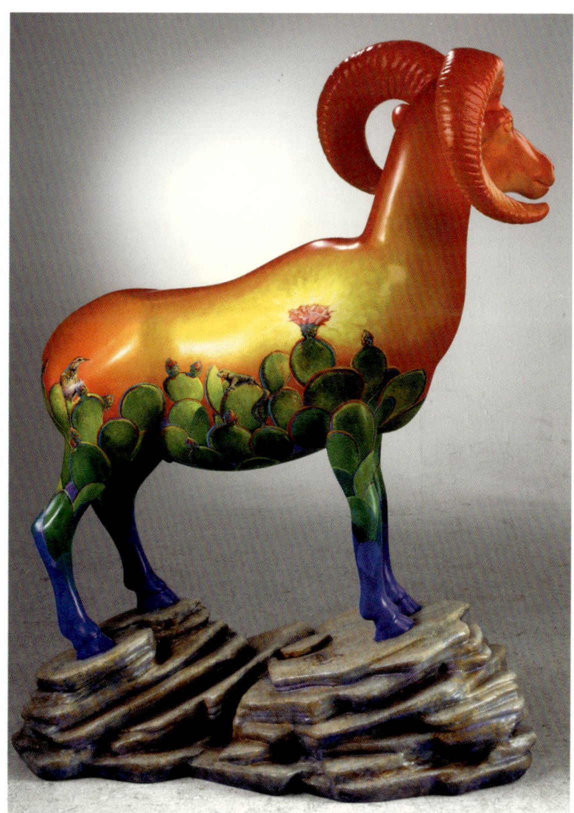

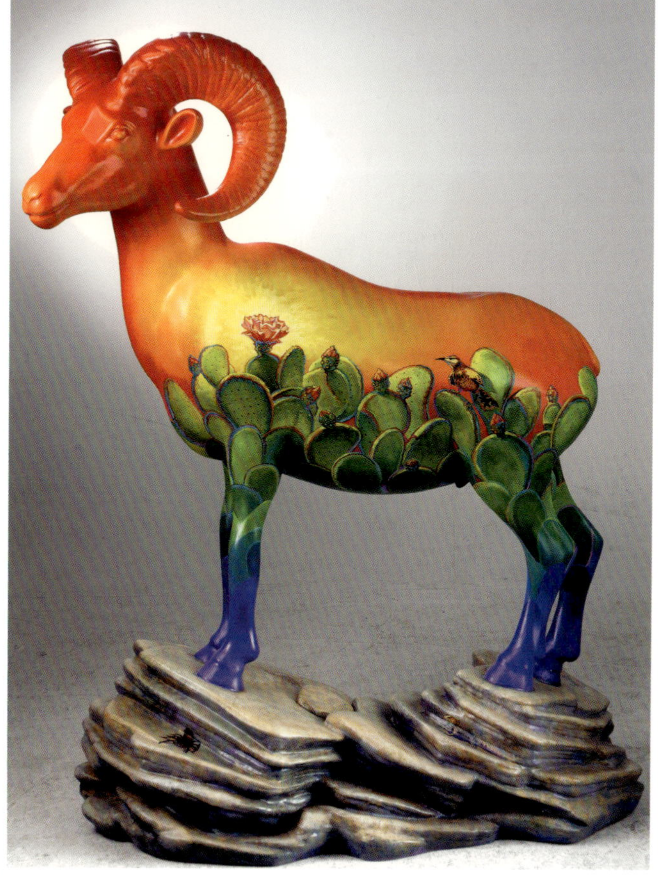

From actors to tractors, Rick Farrell has supplied artwork to clients in a wide range of style and subject matter. A professional illustrator since 1976, with a very wide range of corporate, editorial, entertainment, sports, and private commissions, art has been virtually a lifelong vocation. Clients include the History Channel, Columbia Pictures, Universal Pictures, MGM, Warner Brothers, Paramount Pictures, Disney, the NFL, the LA Dodgers, the Chicago White Sox, Deere & Company, McDonald's, Pillsbury, AT&T, Caterpillar, Road & Track, American History, Harcourt Brace, Random House, Bantam House, most major advertising agencies in the U.S., and many other corporate and private commissions. Using virtually all physical art media, including graphite and pastels, watercolors, acrylic, and oil paints, Farrell has made a conscious decision to avoid digital production of artwork, and enjoys the process of producing artwork as much as ever. "Bright Future", the title of Rick Farrell's painted ram is Rick's wish for the endangered Peninsular bighorn sheep.

Desert Majesty

artist Snake Jagger
sponsor Dr. Peter & Susan Scheer
inaugural site The Mirage Center

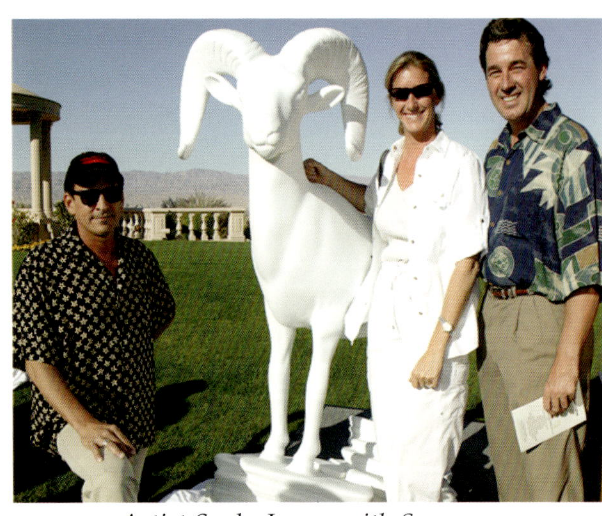

Artist Snake Jagger with Sponsors
Dr. Peter & Susan Scheer

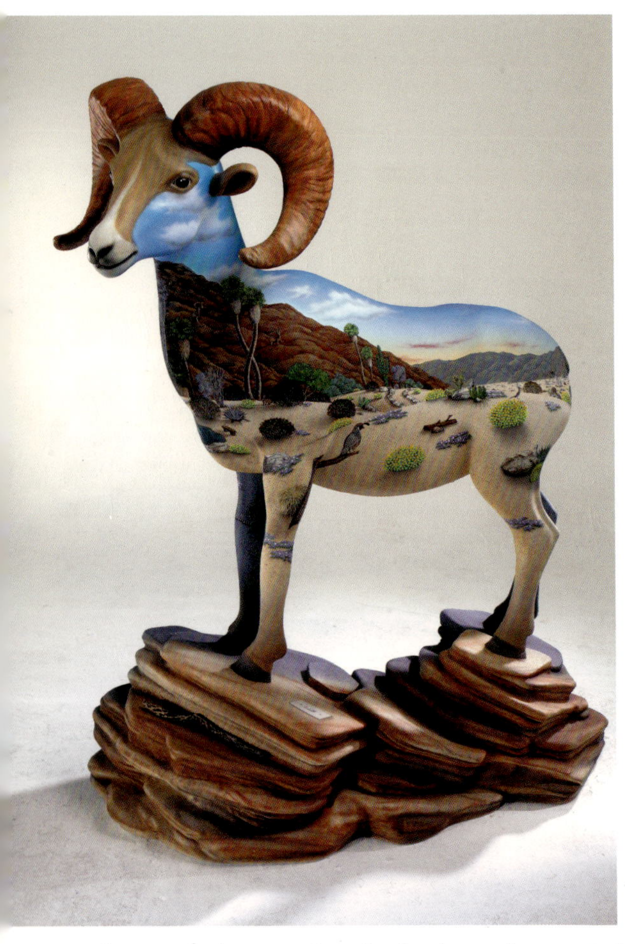

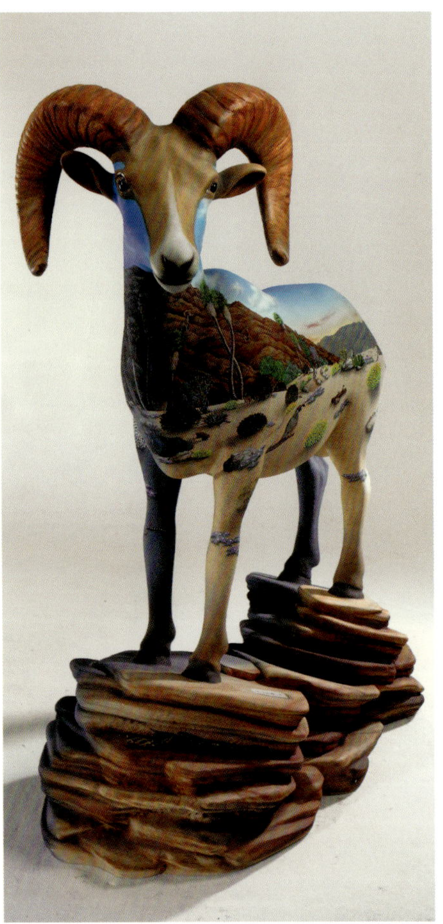

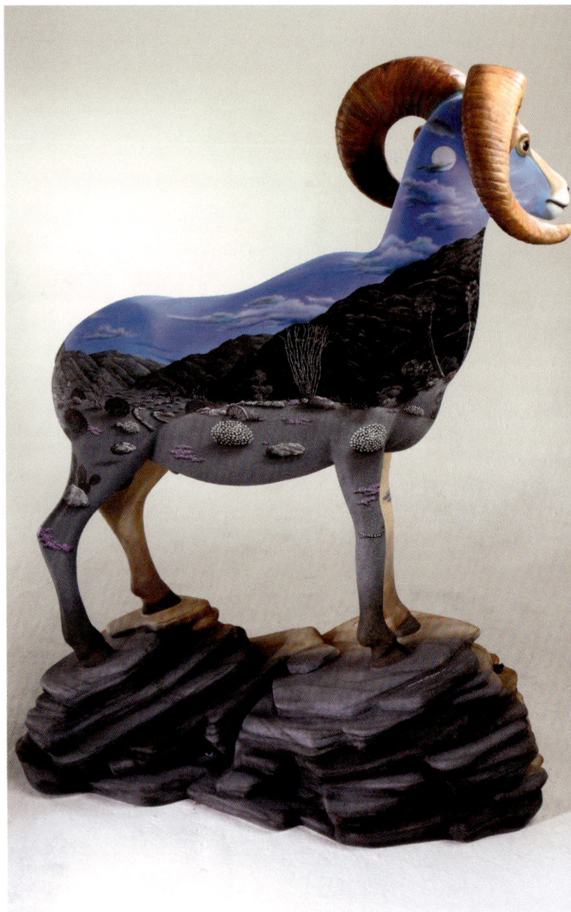

Snake Jagger chose to sleep in the desert for nearly five years. He took baths in hot springs, had the companionship of his two domestic cats and relied on his own basic instincts for comfort and safety. For years Snake observed everything around him - the wild flowers, the incredible changing beauty of the desert landscape and all the variety of animals that dwelled around him. He watched the ever changing patterns and light that played across the mountains, and watched the beautiful sunrises, sunsets and cloud formations and thought about the meaning of everything. When he left his solitude of dwelling in nature, he decided to paint the beauty that was his domain for so long. Now Snake Jagger's paintings are found in major collections and grace the walls of many establishments in the United States and as far as Hensley, England.

Desert Oasis

artist Snake Jagger
sponsor City of Indian Wells
inaugural site Indian Wells Golf Resort

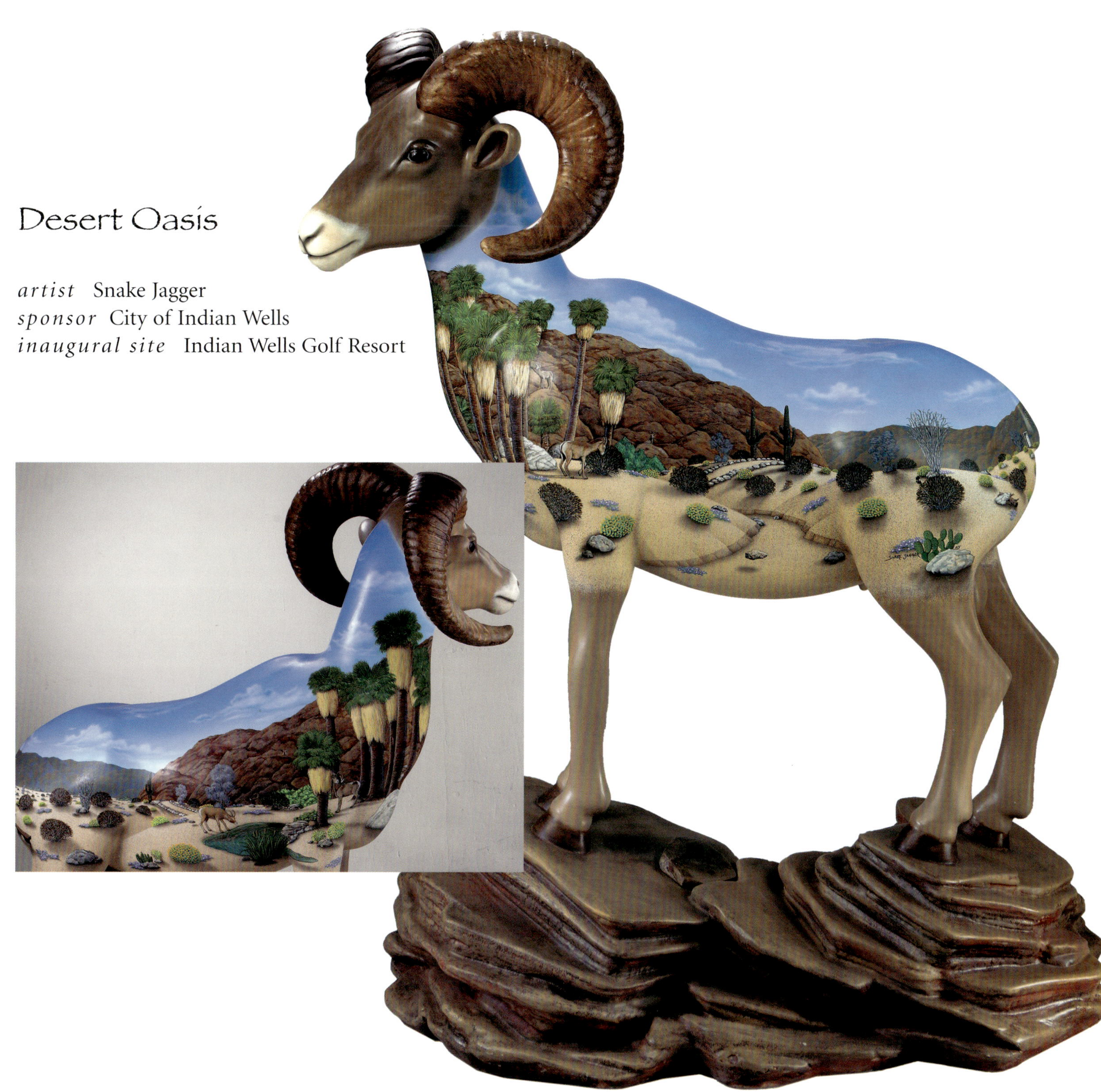

Desert Patches

artist   Regina Murphy
sponsor   Newman's Own & Family
inaugural site   The Lodge at Rancho Mirage

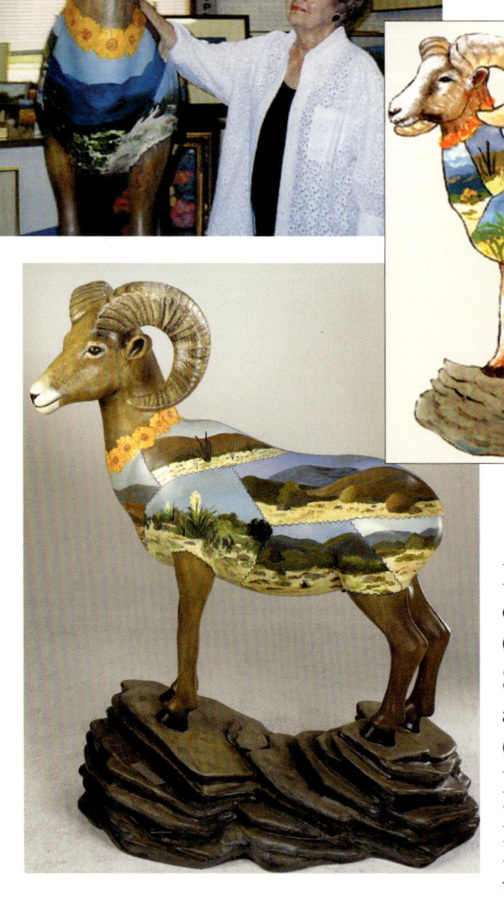

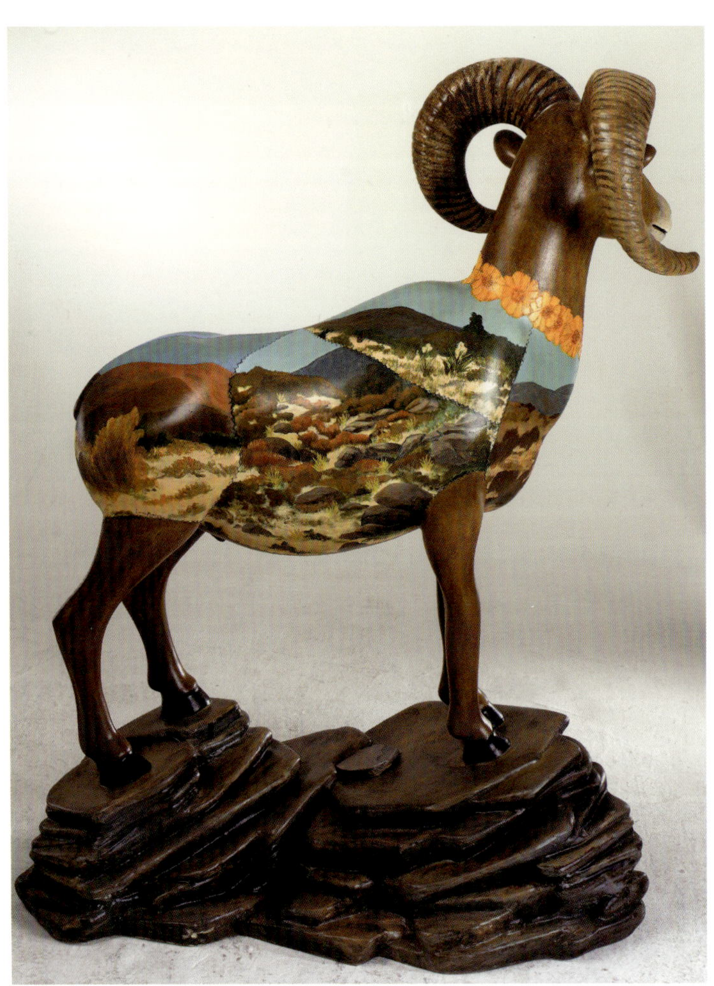

Regina is a resident of Oklahoma City. She has studied at Oklahoma City University, Louisiana Tech in Ruston and in Rome, Italy, as well as with many prominent art instructors. She has explored a wide range of subject matter in many different media. Her most recent work deals with landscapes depicting special places through both traditional and abstract compositions in bright or muted colors, using oil or acrylic on canvas or paper. Regina holds signature membership in both the National Watercolor Oklahoma and Kansas Watercolor Society. She is past president of Oklahoma Watercolor Association, a member of Oklahoma Art Guild, Individual Artist of Oklahoma and Oklahoma Visual Arts Coalition. She has had many solo exhibits and has participated in a number of juried and invitational shows. Regina is represented in numerous corporate collections. Her work is in many private collections including those of Paul Newman & Joanne Woodward, Arthur & Patty Newman, Dee & Joseph Wambaugh, Ann & David Yost and Don & Phyllis Paulsen.

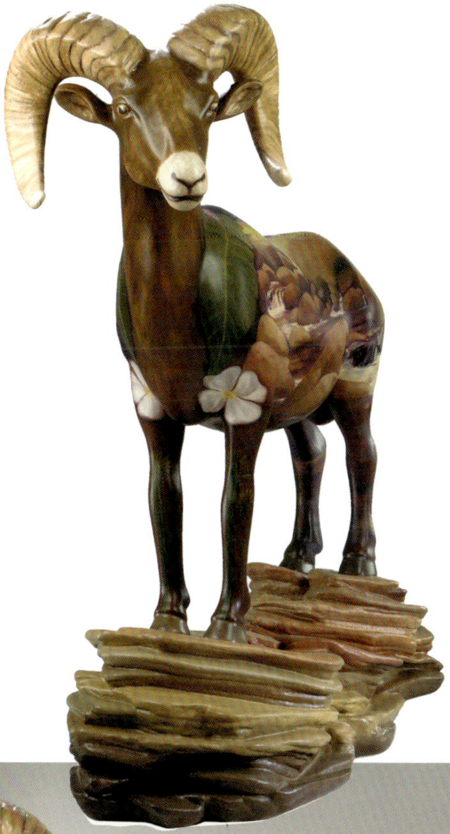

Evening Oasis

artist Kirstine Keel
sponsor Teri & Paul Helms
inaugural site Northern Trust Bank

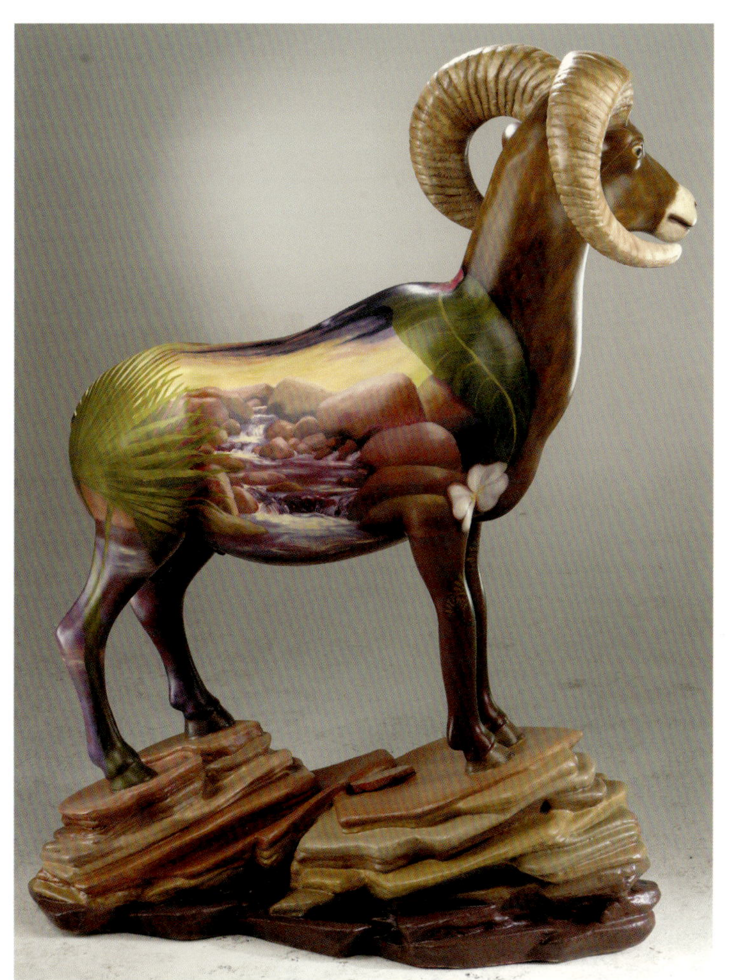

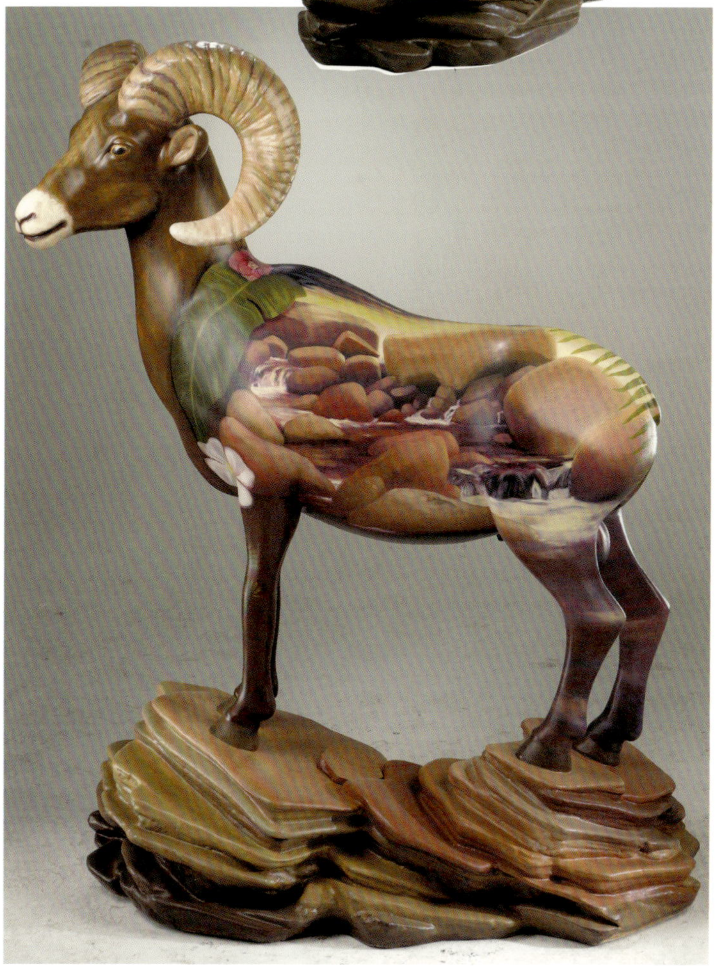

Follow the Leader

artist Joe Wertheimer
sponsor Rita & Tom Martin
inaugural site Agua Caliente
Development Authority

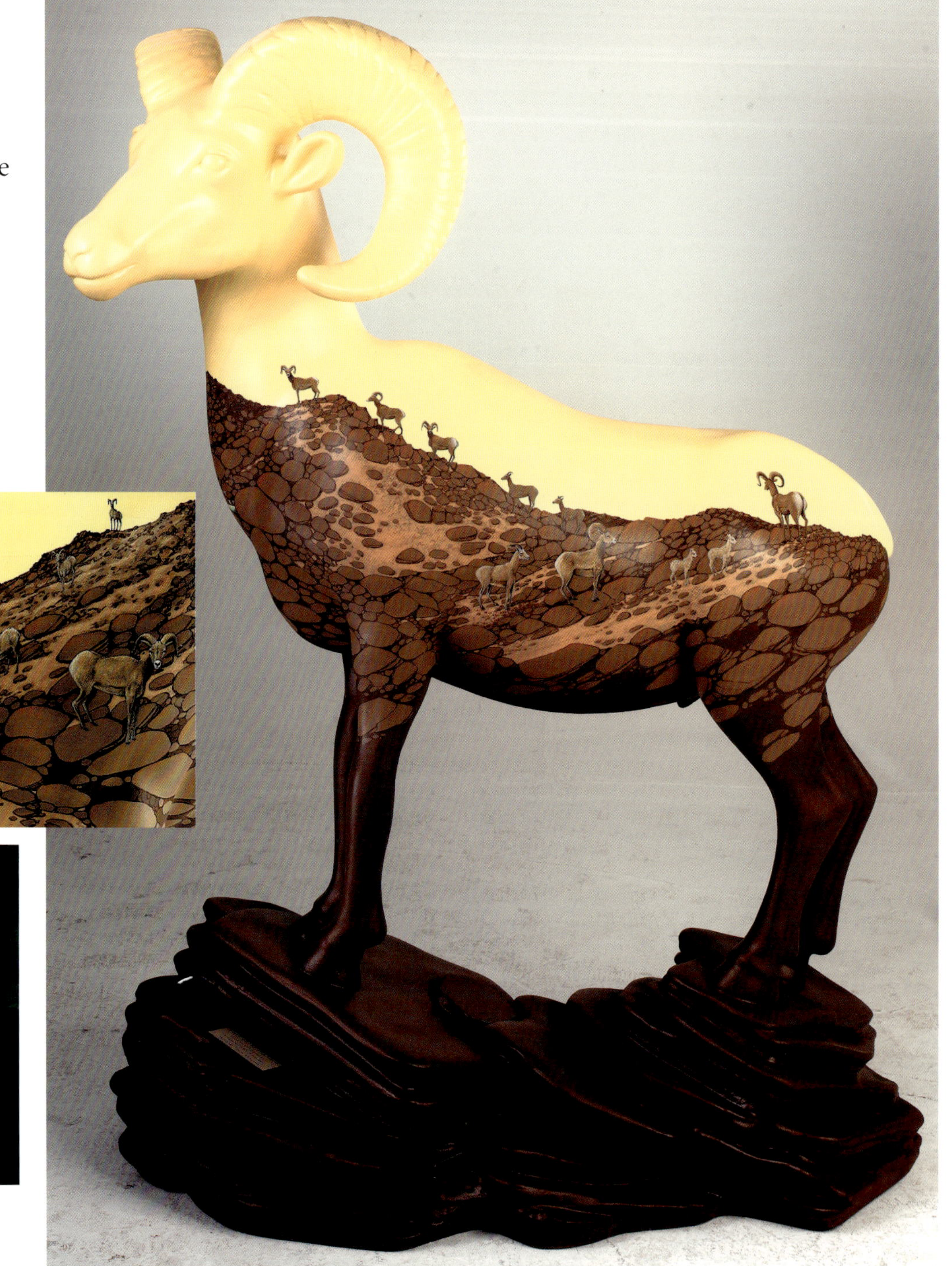

Sponsors Rita & Tom Martin

Guardian of the Oasis

artist Family YMCA of the Desert
sponsor Alexandra *&* Sidney Sheldon
inaugural site Family YMCA
        of the Desert

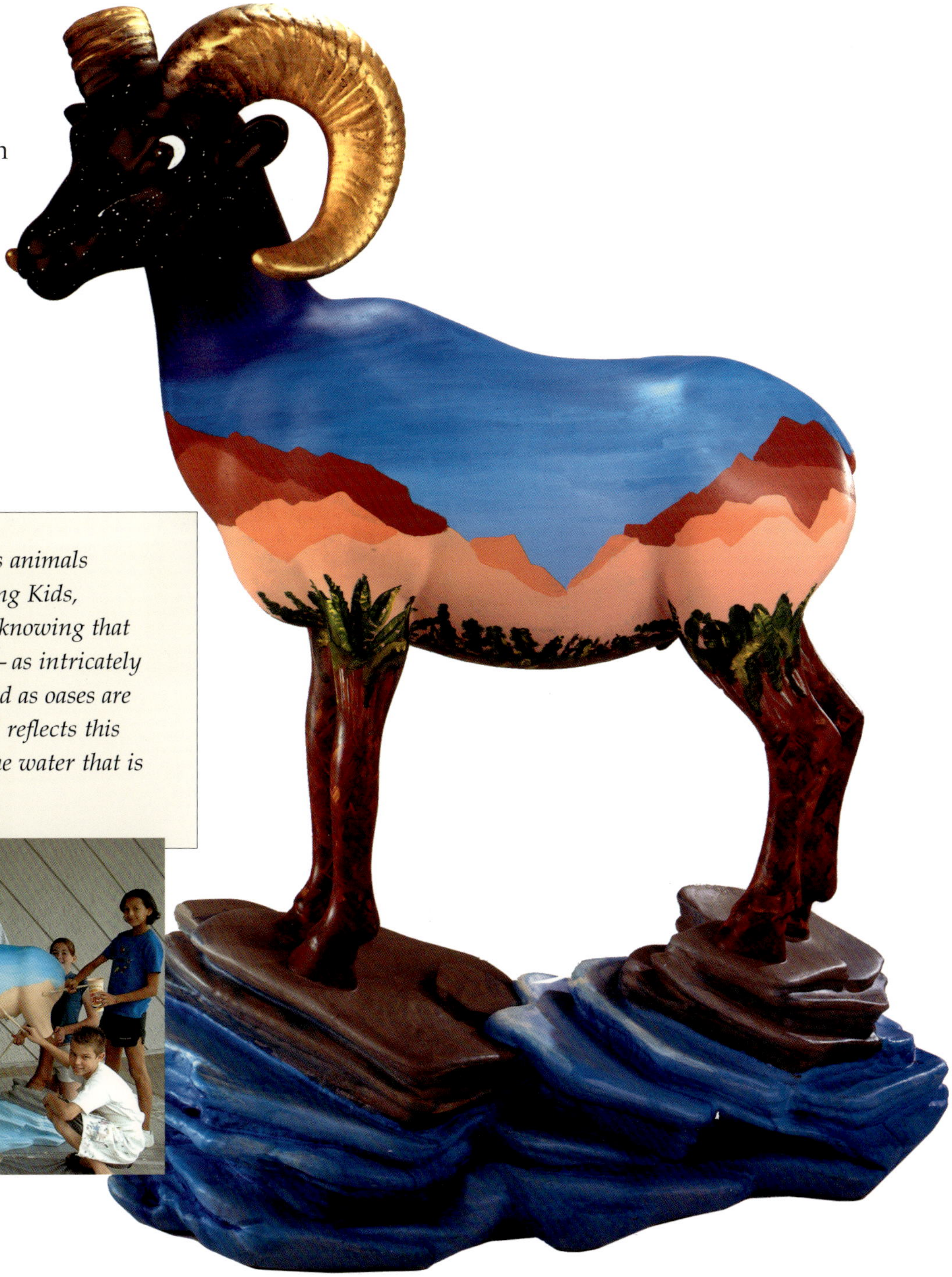

In the desert, the water of an oasis brings animals together. At the YMCA, "We build Strong Kids, Strong Families, Strong Communities," knowing that those elements are intricately connected — as intricately connected as bighorn are to the desert, and as oases are to the animals. "Guardians of the Oasis" reflects this need to be caretakers of the earth, from the water that is the basis of life, to the life that it waters.

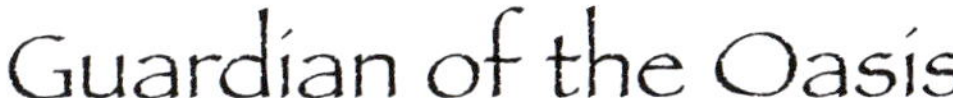

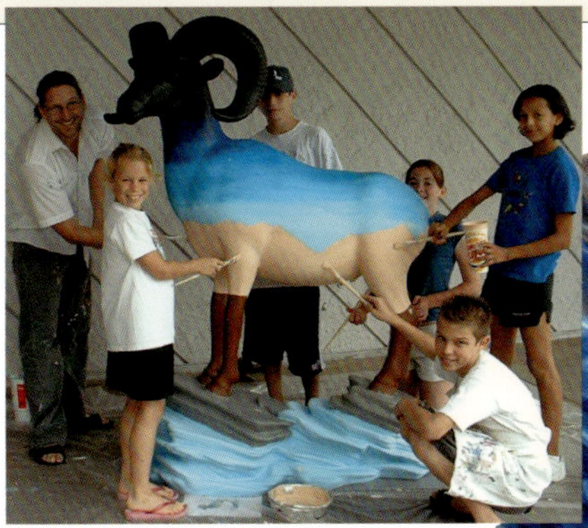

From the Earth

artist   Timothy Kroe
sponsor   Alexandra & Sidney Sheldon
inaugural site   Palm Springs Convention
& Visitors Authority

"From the Earth" is about the bighorn's connection to the earth and the need for modern civilization to realize that we are connected to it as well. Since the dawn of Cartesian Duality, western man has become increasingly separated from the earth, believing that he is somehow superior to his environment. Instead of being blind conquerors, we need to become caretakers. The green in "From the Earth" represents our potential to transcend old modes of thinking and to embrace our new role. The gold symbolizes the divinity that exists within all of Earth's creatures. — Timothy Kroe

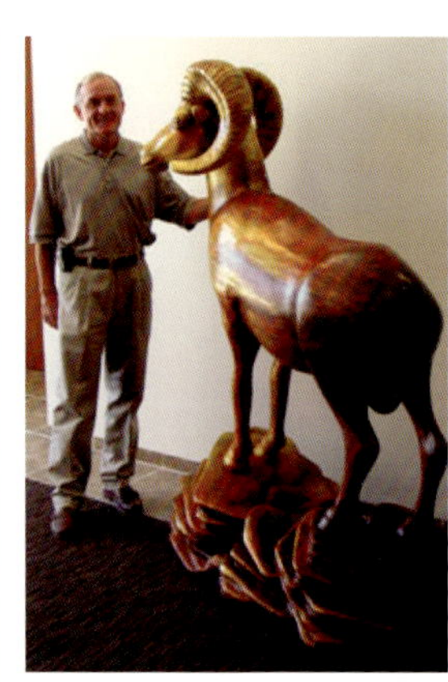

Mike Fife, President of the Palm Springs Convention & Visitors Authority, proudly displays "From the Earth"

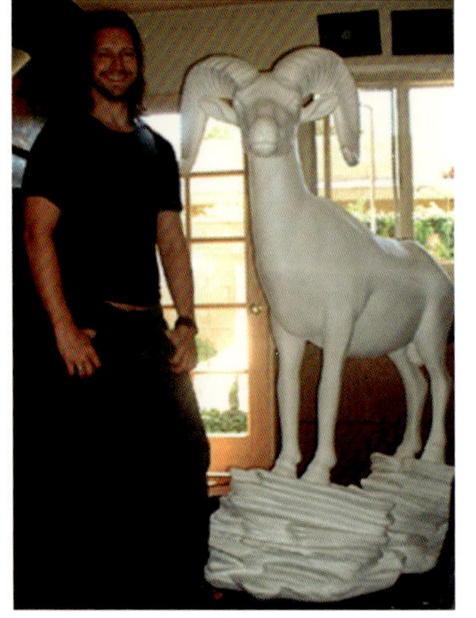

I continually sought ways to express my connection with the imaginable reality of childhood. It wasn't, however until a fateful brush with death in 1993 (an electrocution that sent 2600 volts of electricity through my foot and out my fingertips) that the desire to communicate the naturalistic world of the divine became increasingly important to me.

48

Genesis

artist   Jayne Behman
sponsor   Desert Fine Arts Academy
inaugural site   Behman Gallery

The design is an abstract representation of evolution. In the beginning there was light which I interpret to be "dawn." Sunrise is a beginning, as is this project — to enlighten public awareness of the threatened extinction of the bighorn sheep and to educate the public on how to protect them and their habitat. — Jayne Behman

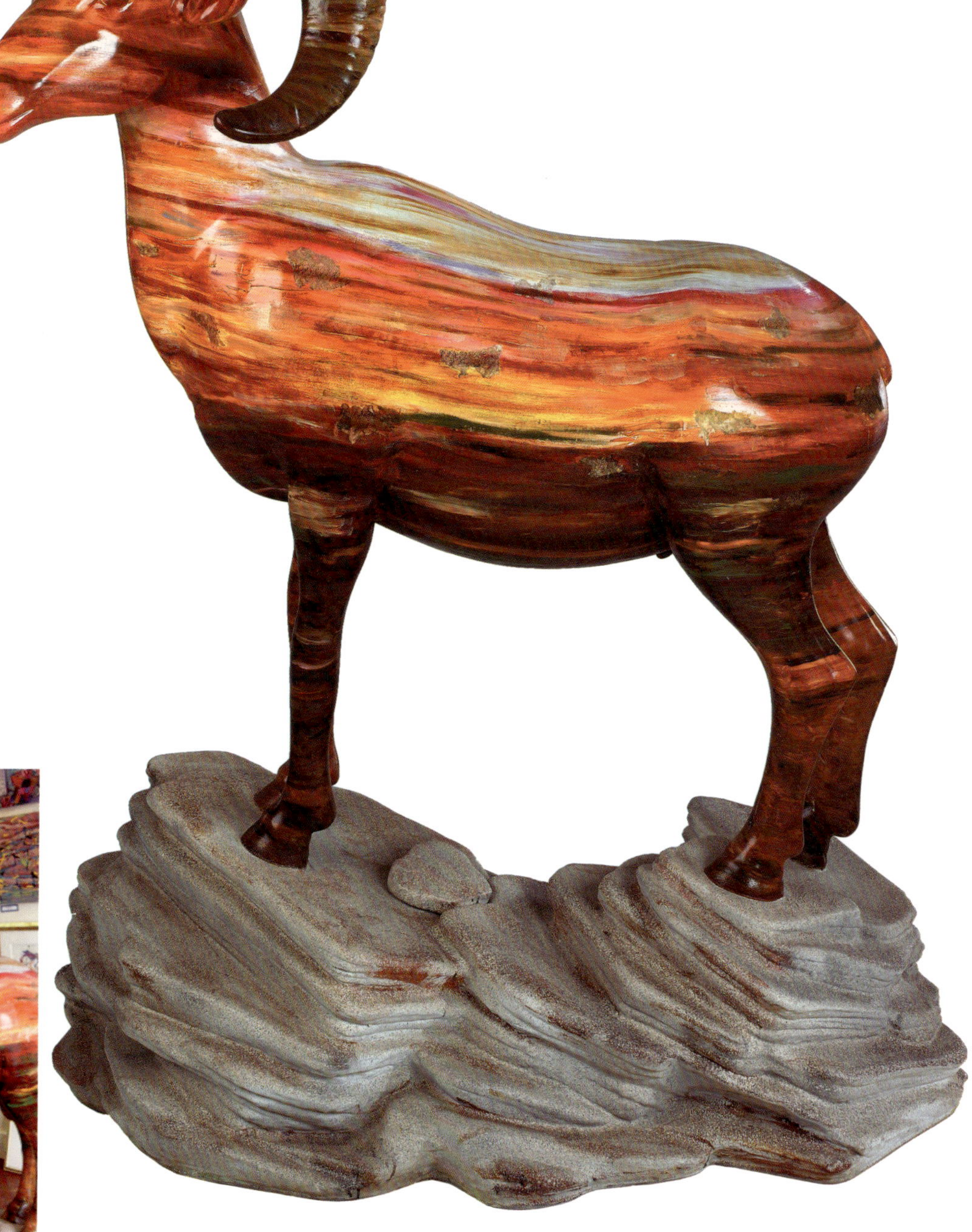

In the Still of the Night

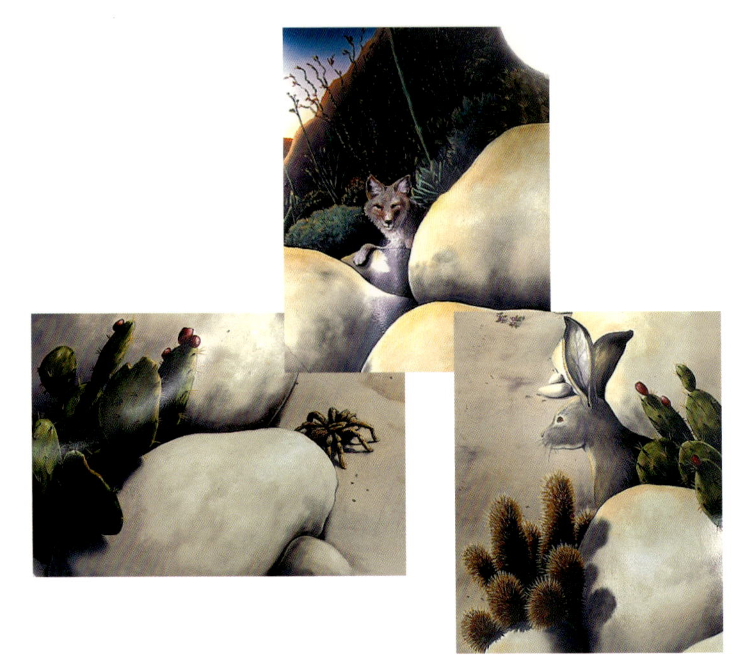

artist Sue Clark
sponsor Alexandra Sheldon
inaugural site La Quinta City Hall

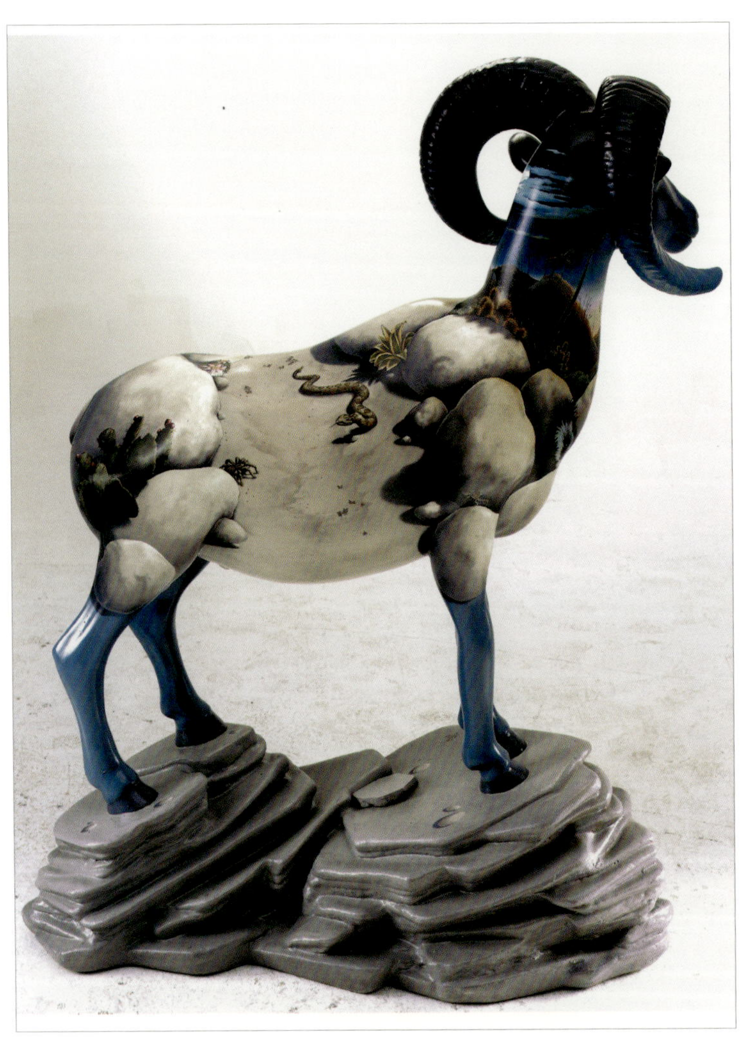

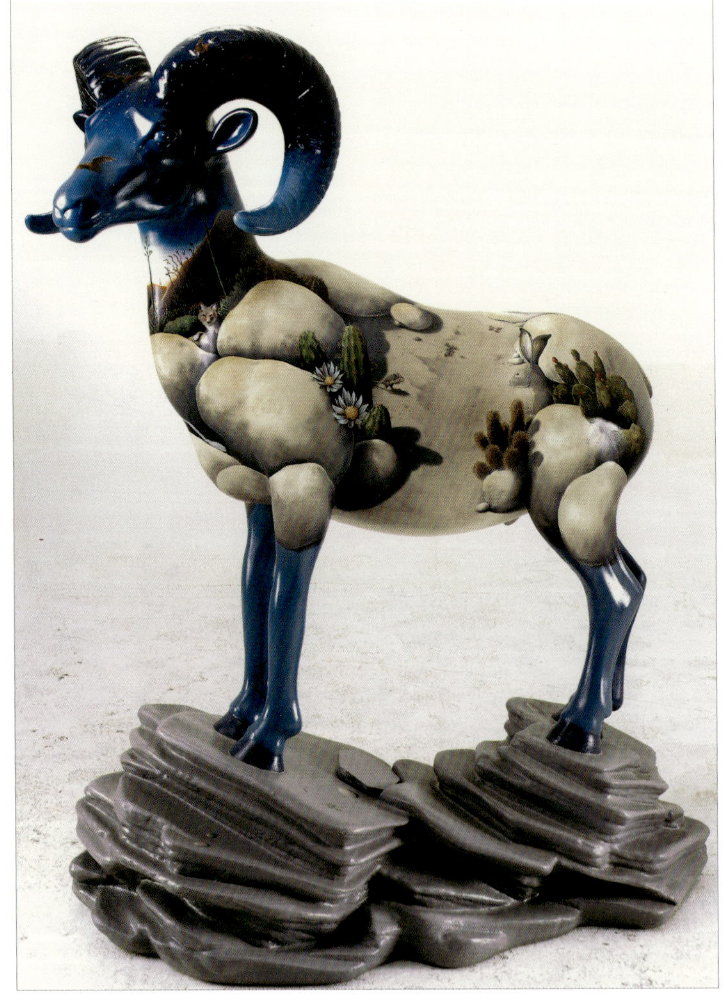

A Bighorn's Dream

artist   Sue Clark
sponsor   Alexandra Sheldon
inaugural site   Agua Caliente Band
of Cahuilla Indians Tribal Administrative Office

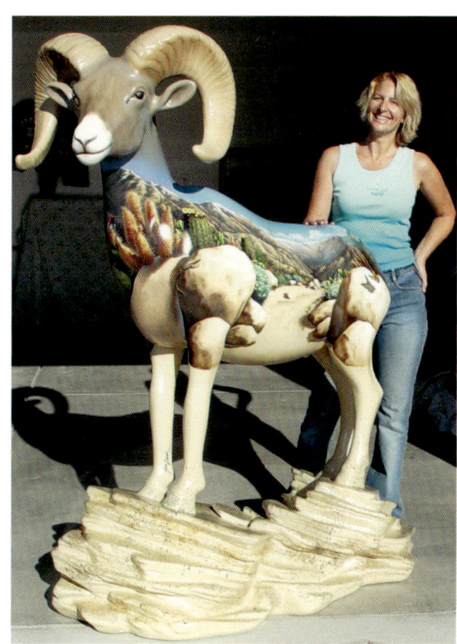

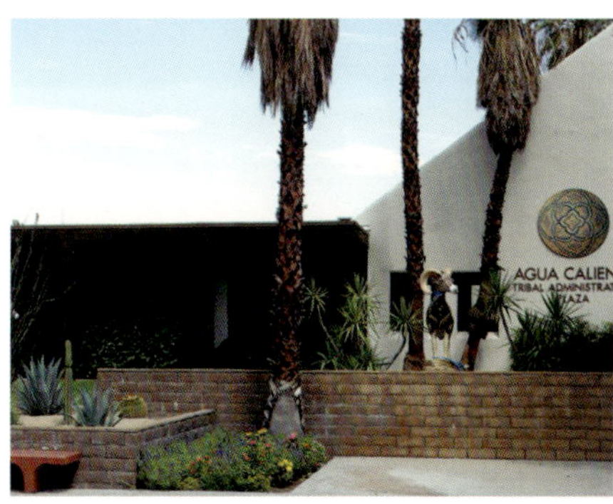

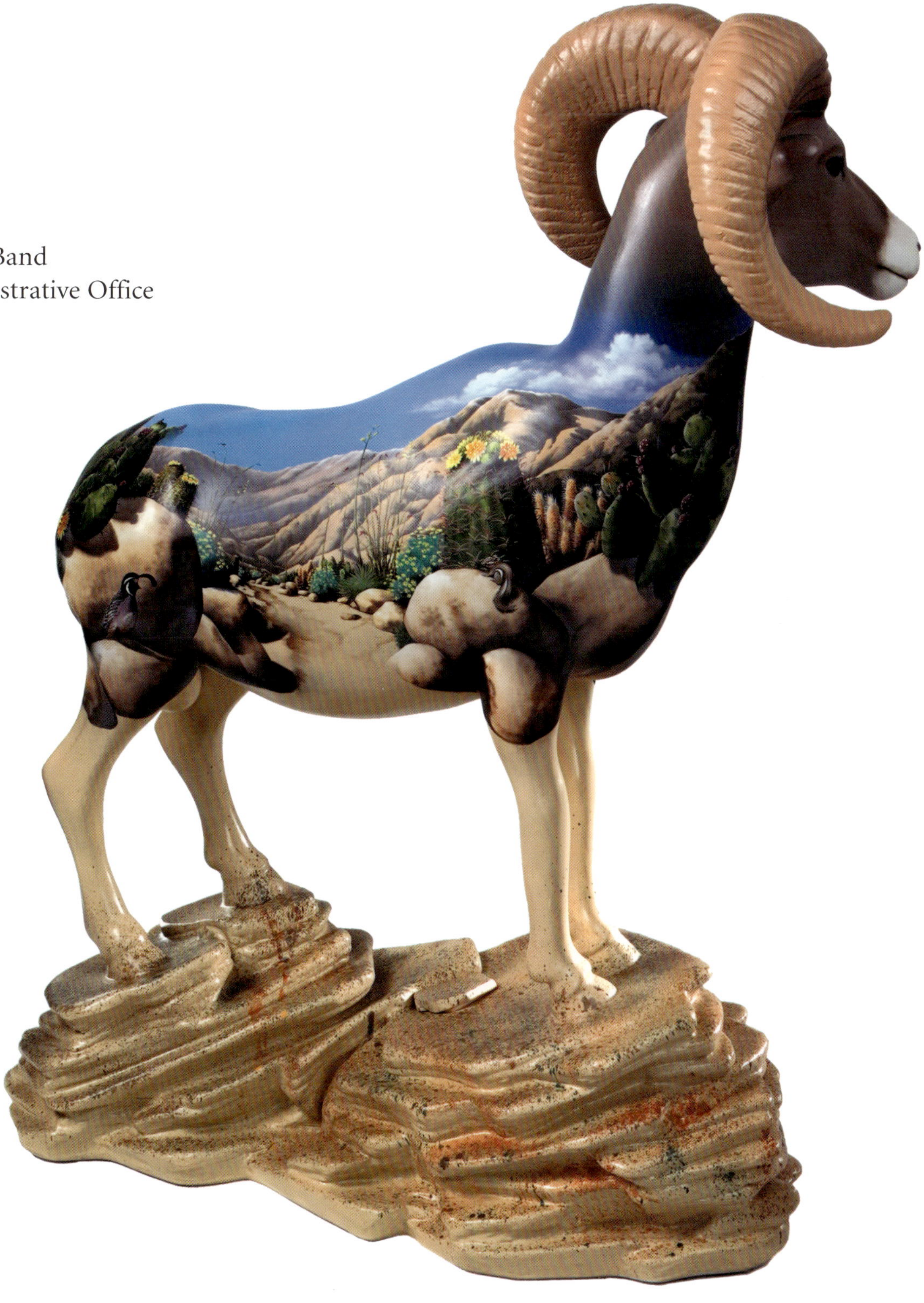

Horns of Plenty

artist Mona Shafer Edwards
sponsor Dr. Charlie & Shirley Jenner
inaugural site Downey Savings

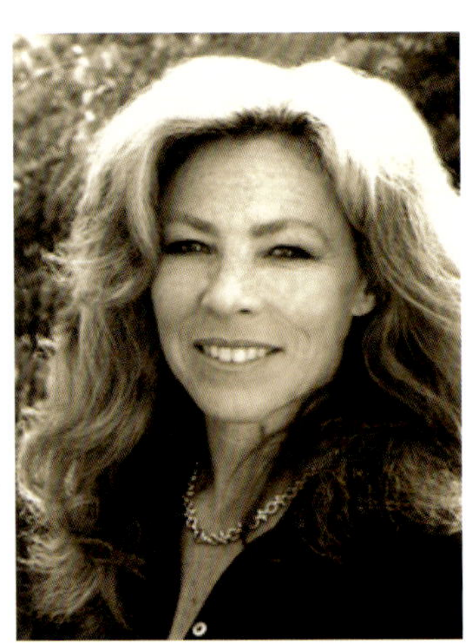

Mona Shafer Edwards is a freelance illustrator specializing in Fashion and Courtroom Illustration. She is a native of Los Angeles, California, and was one of the youngest graduates of the Art Center College of Design, where she completed her Bachelor of Fine Arts with Honors. Mona has illustrated children's books and has done artwork for major department stores and manufacturers, and regularly donates her artwork to various charities. Her courtroom illustrations for ABC News have been seen worldwide, and many of her drawings have been featured in foreign print publications. In the nearly twenty years of sketching in the courtroom, she has witnessed hundreds of high profile trials from Richard Ramirez and the McMartin Preschool cases to Rodney King and O.J. Simpson. Her colorful and emotional drawings are in many private collections in the U.S. and abroad.

Keeper of the Canyon

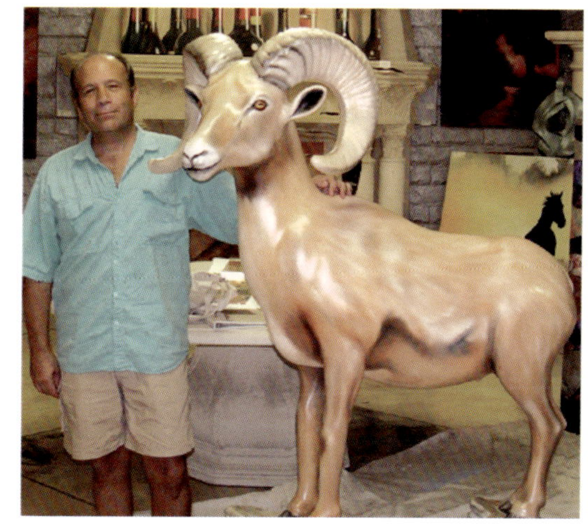

artist Randyn Harris
sponsor Dr. & Mrs. Roland Reinhart
inaugural site Palm Desert Middle School

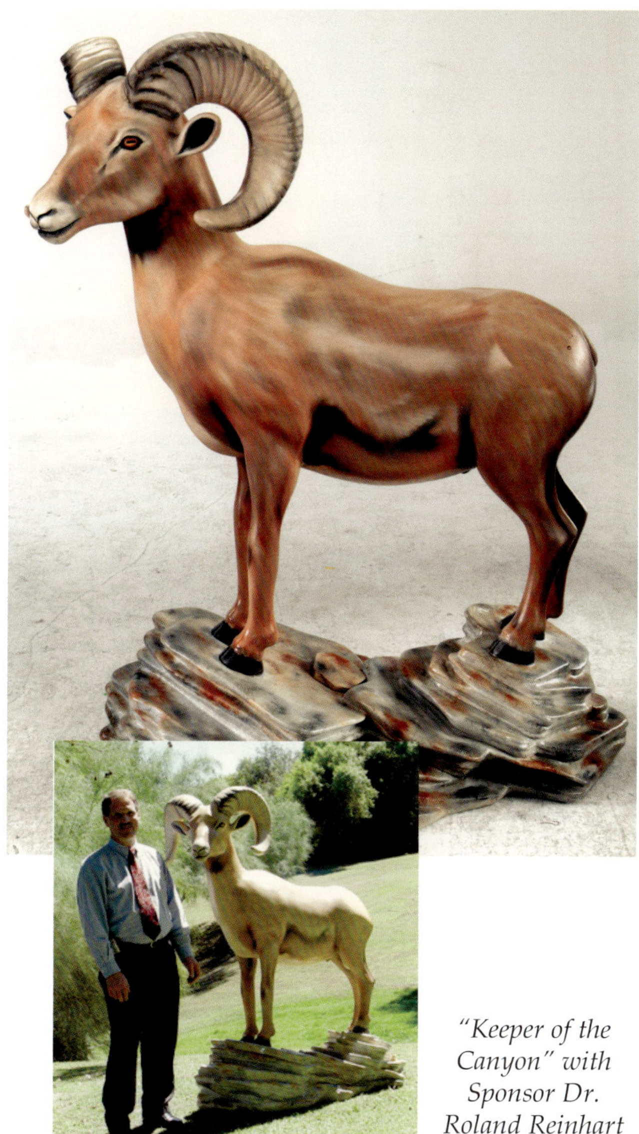

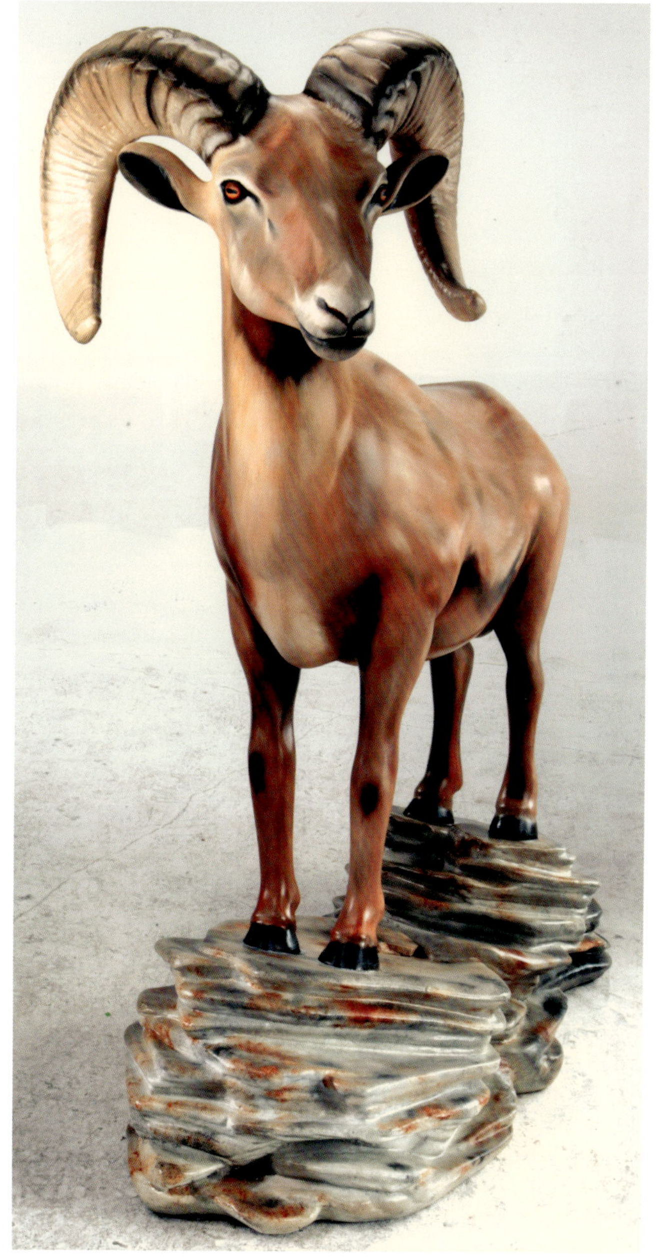

"Keeper of the Canyon" with Sponsor Dr. Roland Reinhart

Jewel of the Desert

artist Donald Dyar
sponsor Lydia & Alex Kremer
inaugural site The Gardens on El Paseo

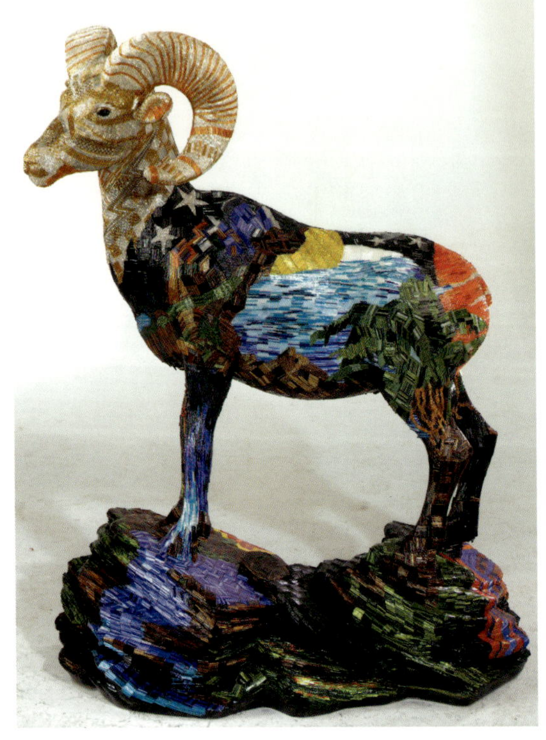

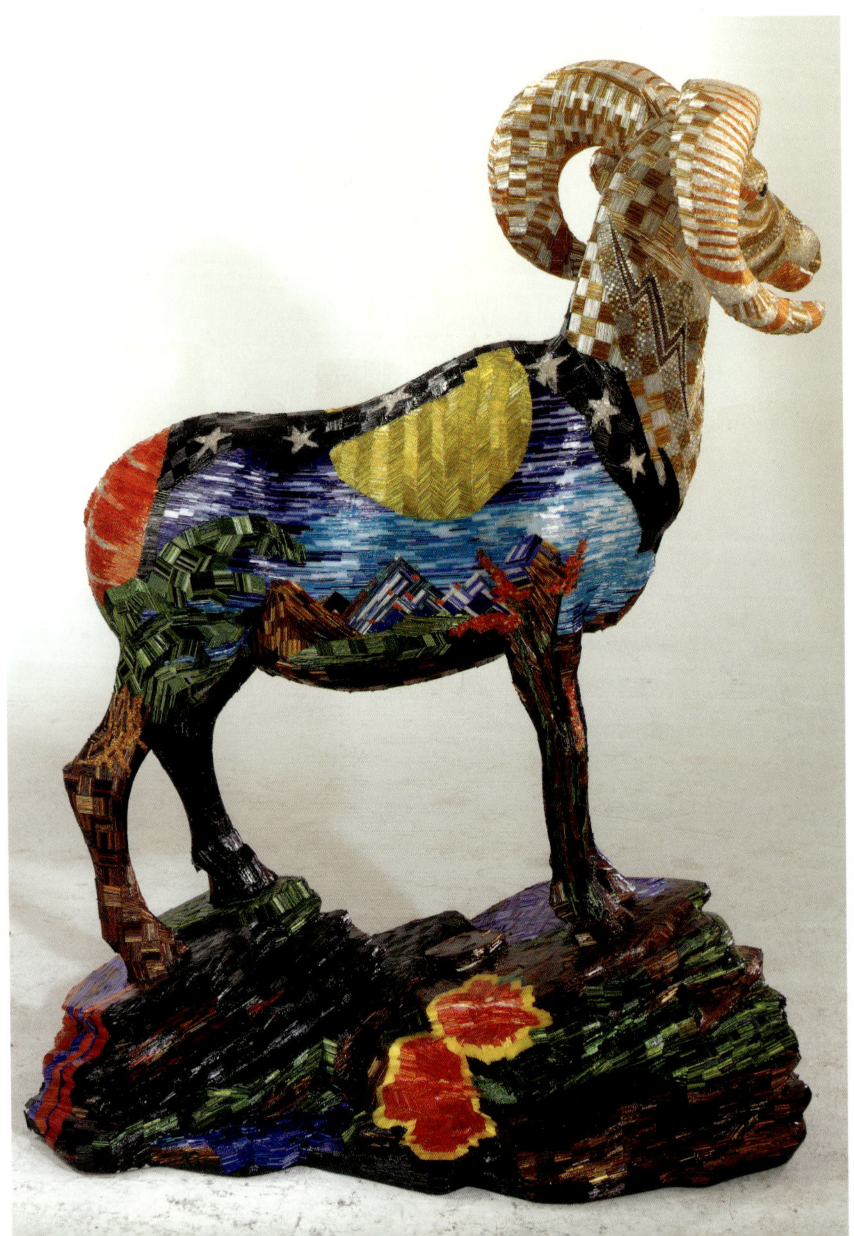

My statue is a jewel-incrusted landscape of the desert, a three-dimensional tribute to our bighorn sheep roaming the mountains throughout history. They were here first. — Donald Dyar

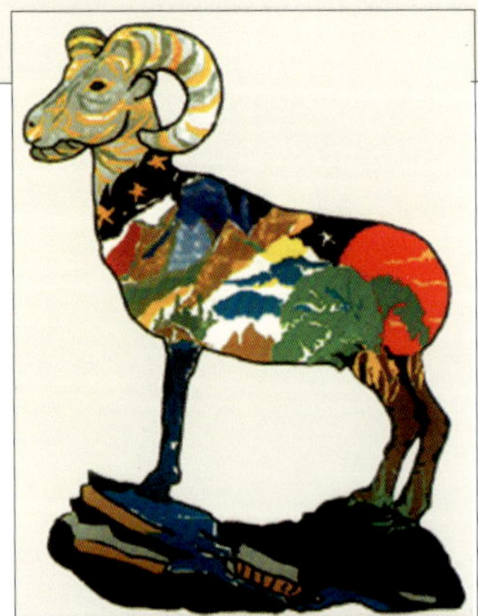

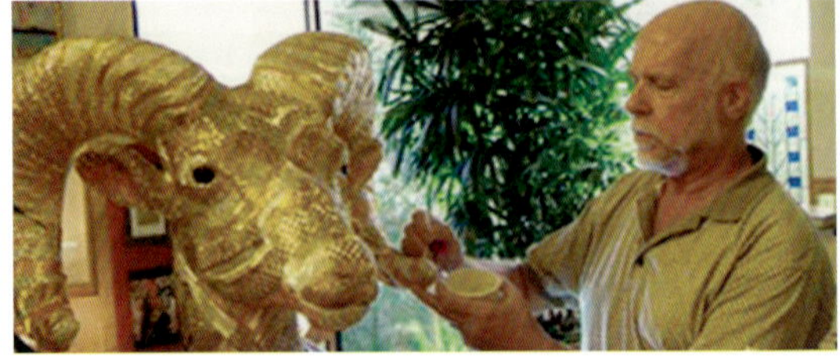

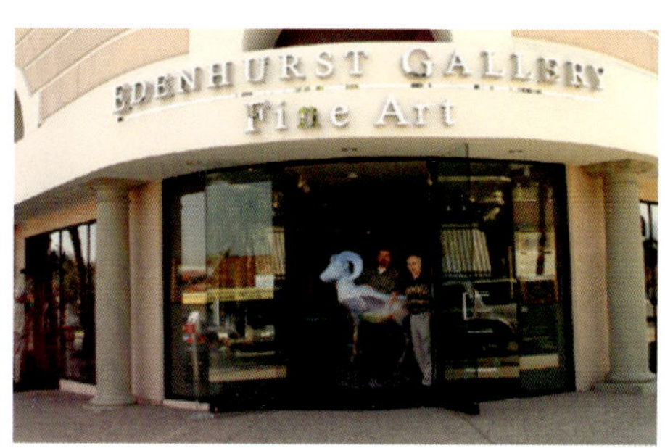

Lasting Impression

artist Carl Ramsey
sponsor Edenhurst Gallery
inaugural site Edenhurst Gallery

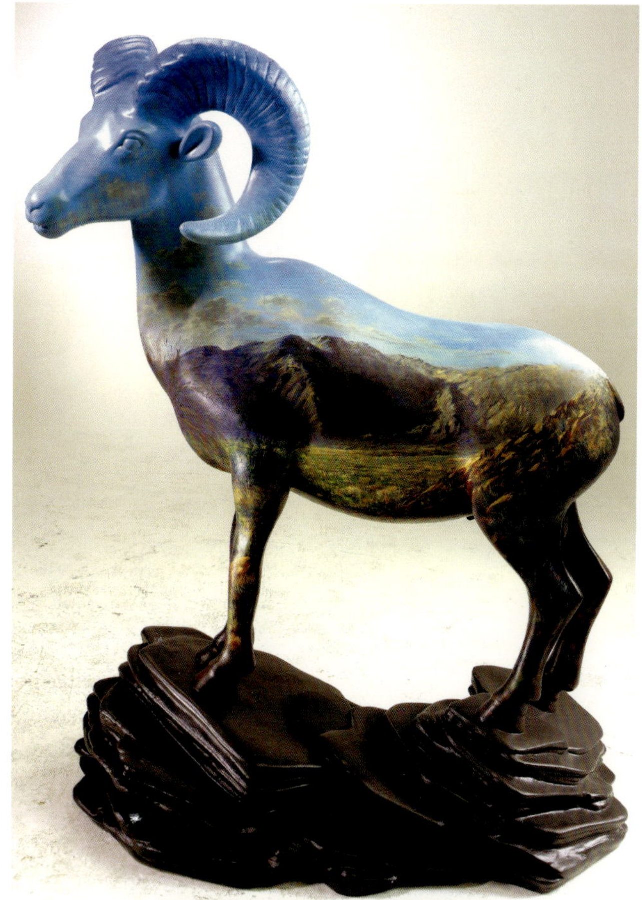

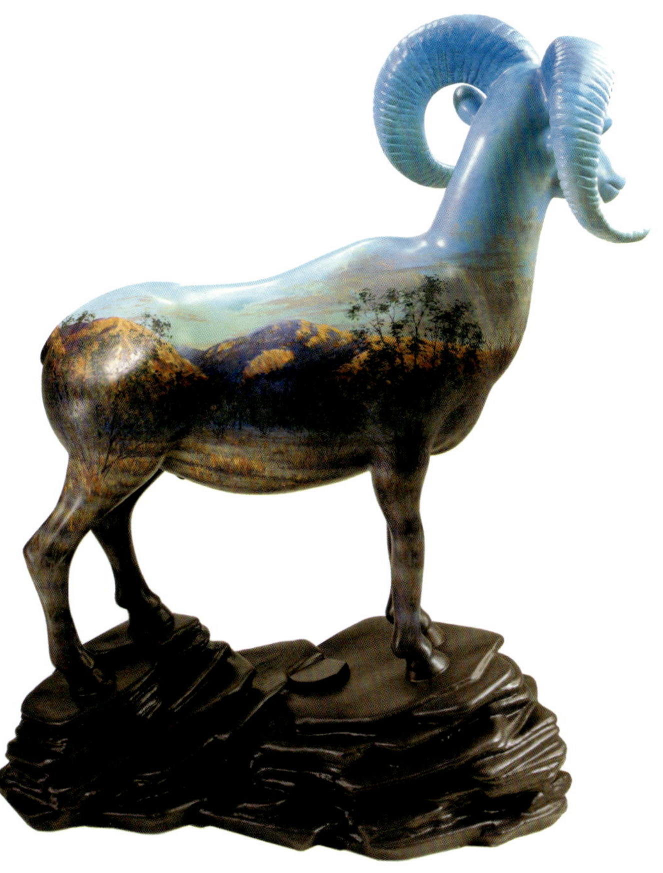

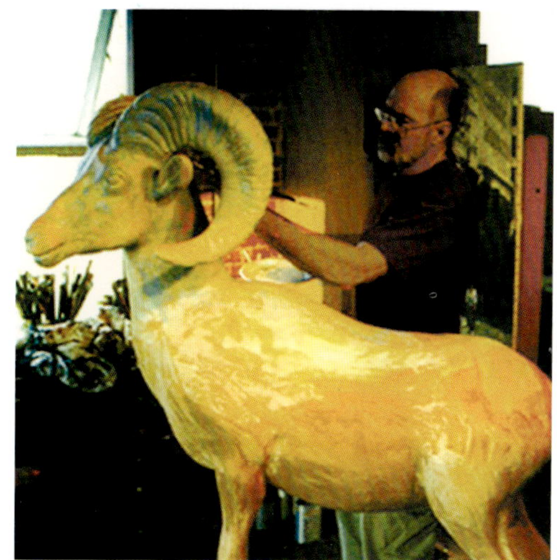

Carl Ramsey was an accomplished illustrator for many years before turning to painting. At Southwestern College he came under the guidance of an excellent art department faculty, including the conceptual artist John Baldessari, who suggested late nights at Barney's Beanery and classes at Chouinard Art Institute. Four years later Ramsey began a career in illustration. Advertising agencies, Motor Trend Magazine, album cover designers, and eventually motion picture studios supplied the assignments and tight deadlines for the next two and a half decades. Baseball and fly fishing supplied the sanity. One-sheet illustrations, including the final art for films such as Quest for Fire, One Crazy Summer, Risky Business, Police Academy 4, Return of the Living and Beetlejuice, along with innumerable drawings, sketches and other paintings were produced for film releases during the 1980's and early 1990's. Landscape painting and figurative work now provide the painter's daily activity.

Looking for Ewe

artist Sue Clark
sponsor Alexandra & Sidney Sheldon
inaugural site Sold in auction to
   Mr. and Mrs. Roger Snellenberger

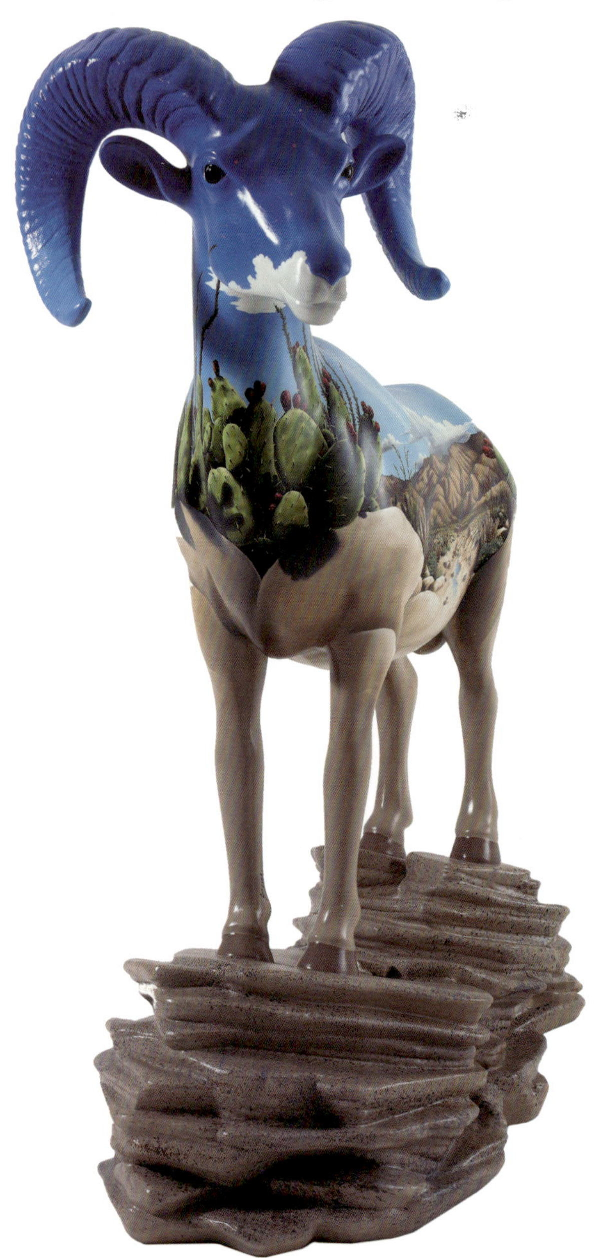

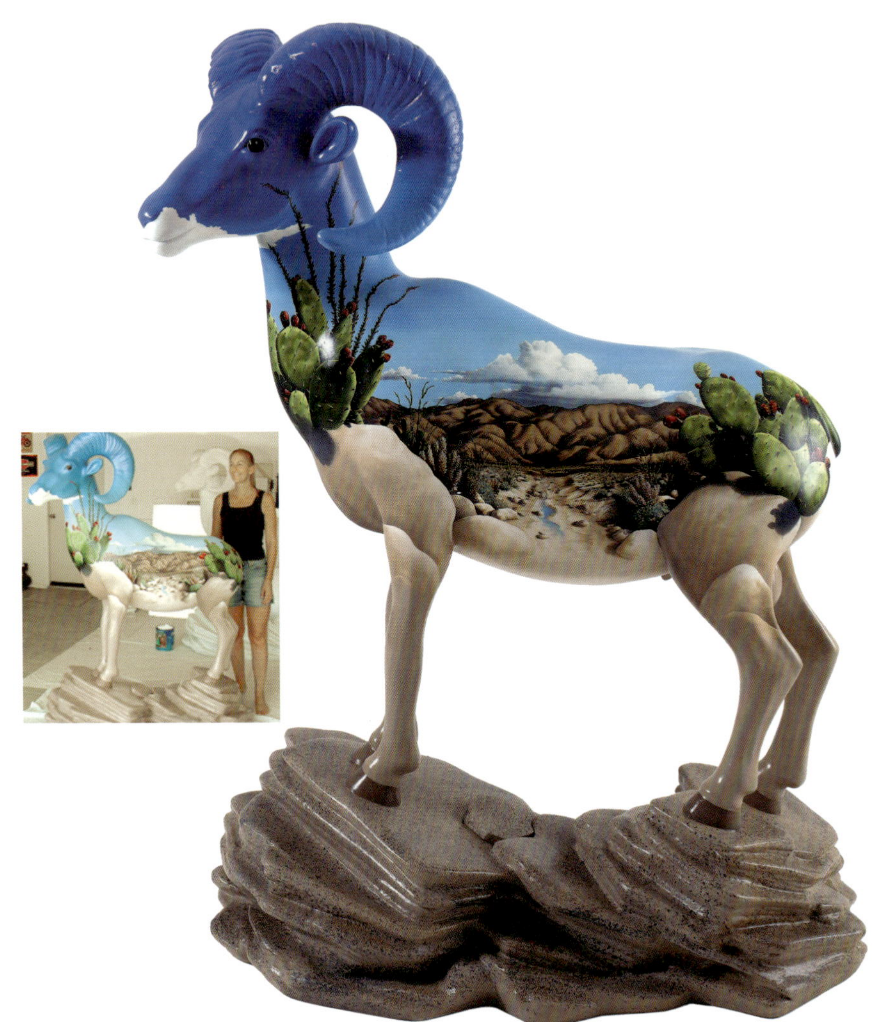

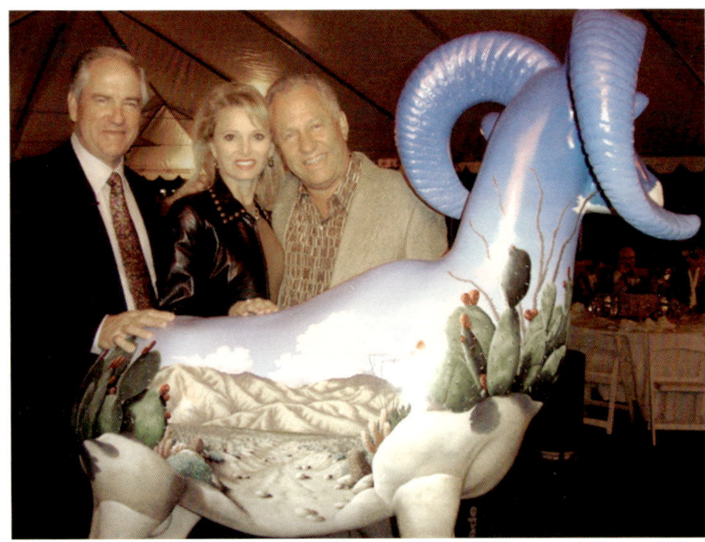

*Golf Pro Dave Stockton with proud
owners, Mr. & Mrs. Roger Snellenberger*

Moon Over the Mountain

artist Stan Stokes
sponsor Taylor Sherrill & Associates
inaugural site Taylor Sherrill & Associates

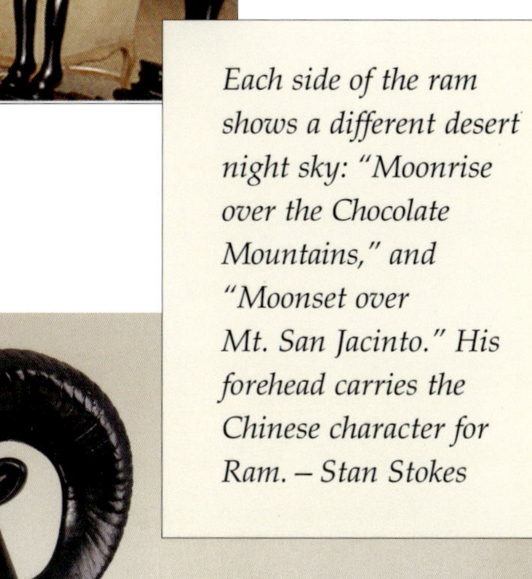

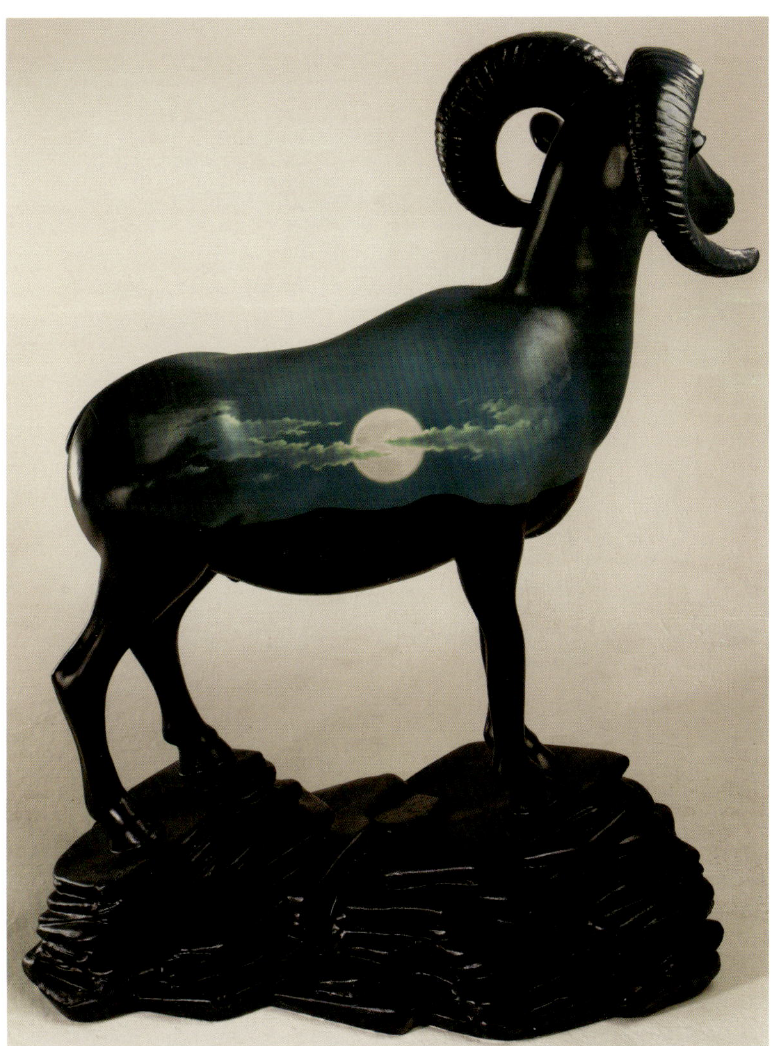

Each side of the ram shows a different desert night sky: "Moonrise over the Chocolate Mountains," and "Moonset over Mt. San Jacinto." His forehead carries the Chinese character for Ram. — Stan Stokes

"Incredibly accurate", that's what many say about the art of Stan Stokes. His work is known for infinite detail, the rare ability to create magnificent three-dimensional effects, and most importantly-the feeling that you are right there! Stan is a prize-winning California painter who, because of his artistic ability and precise attention to detail, is considered to be one of the world's foremost aircraft artists.

artist   Sue Clark
sponsor   Alexandra Sheldon
inaugural site   Agua Caliente Band of Cahuilla Indians
                Tribal Administrative Office

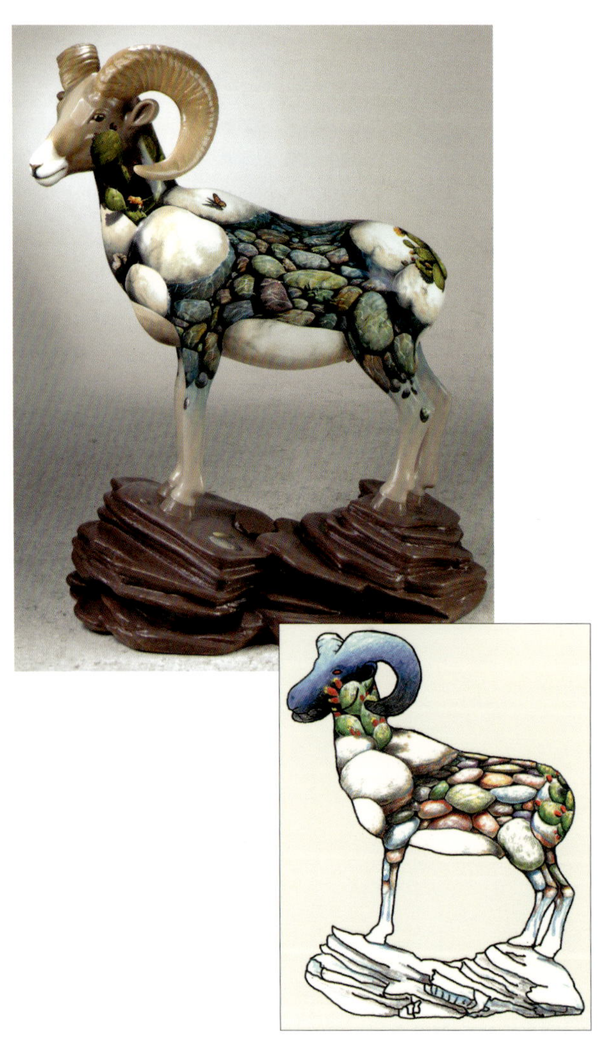

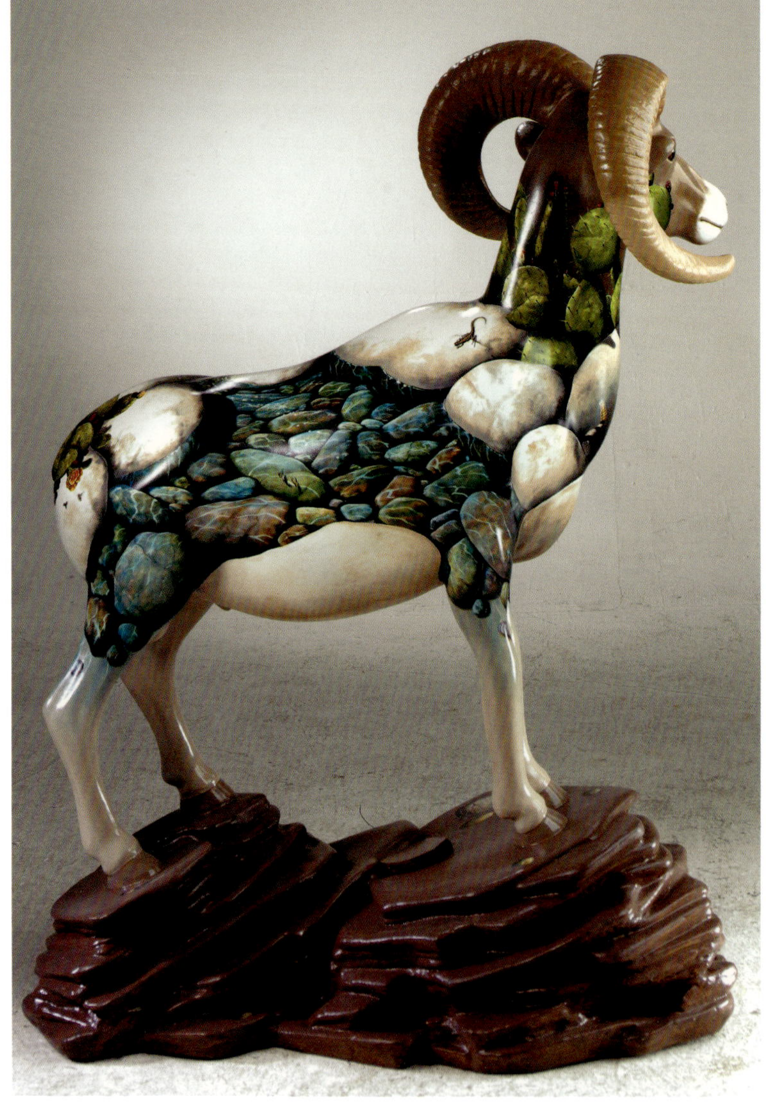

Spikehorns

artist Richard Meyers
sponsor Bureau of Land Management
inaugural site Santa Rosa & San Jacinto Mountains
         National Monument Visitors Center

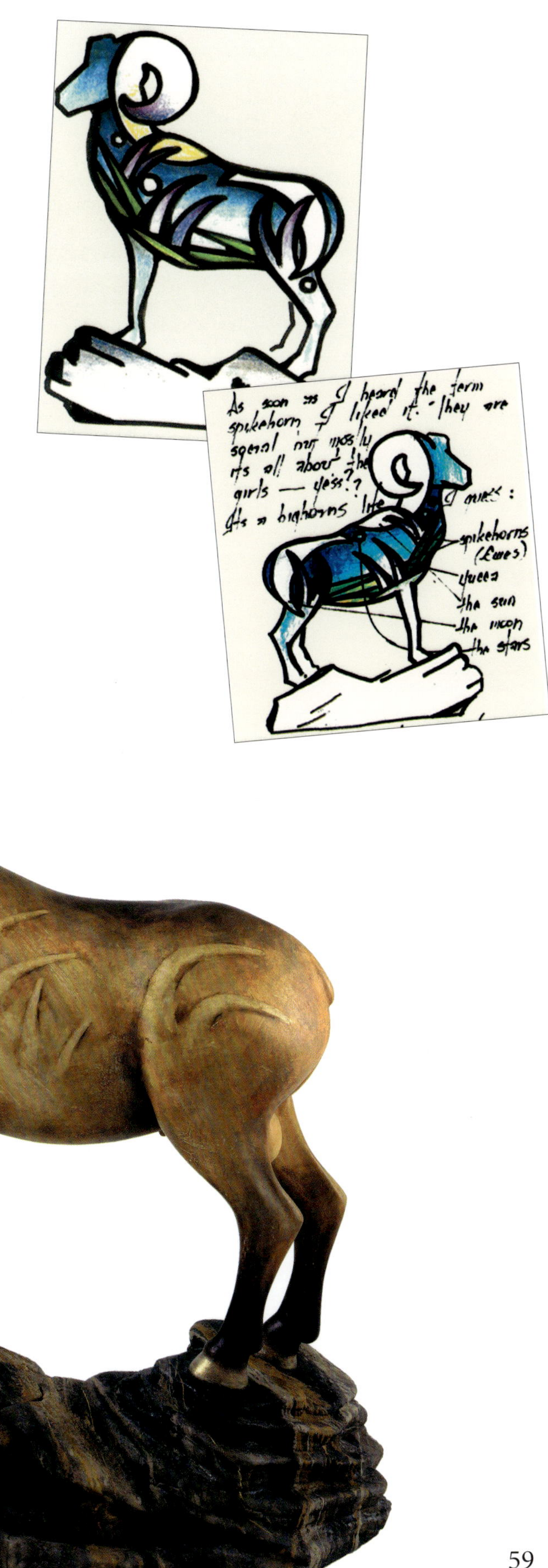

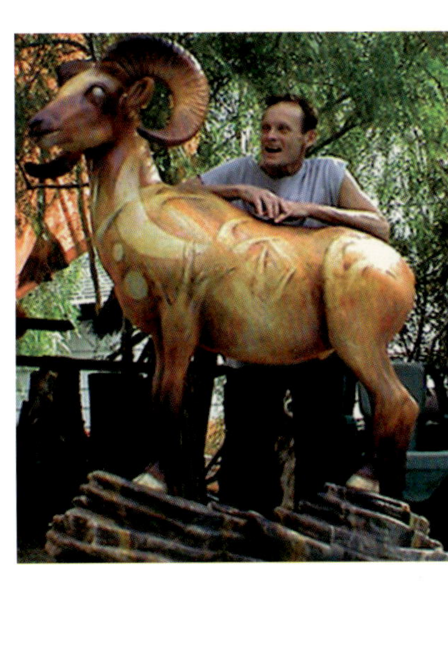

Pa'at 1

artist   Regina Murphy
sponsor   City of Indian Wells
inaugural site   Indian Wells City Hall

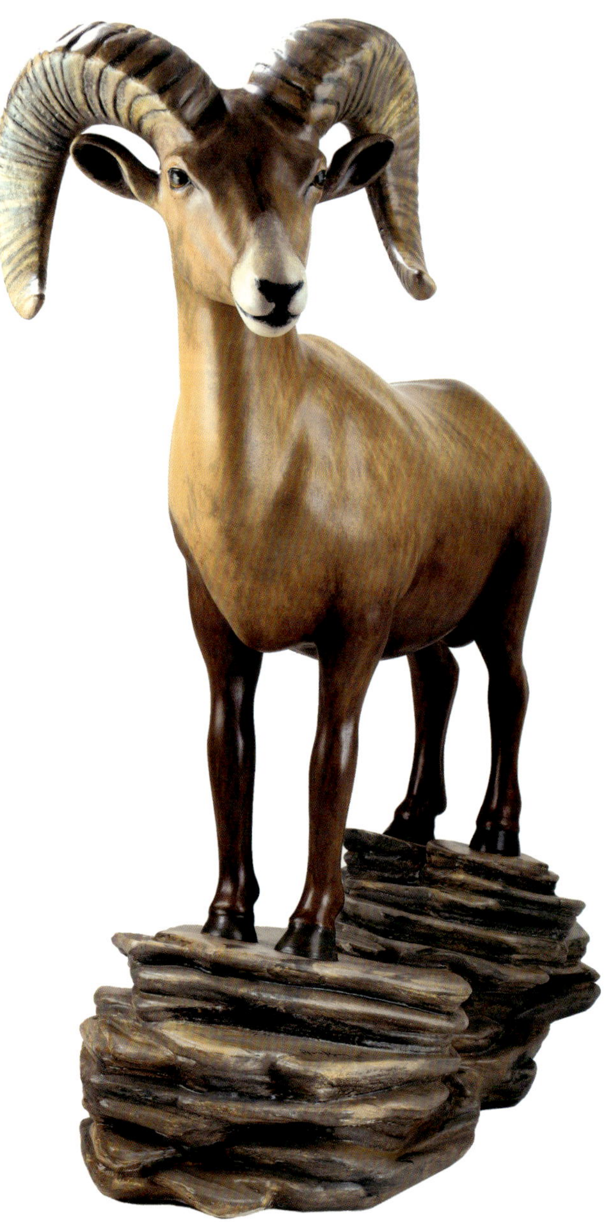

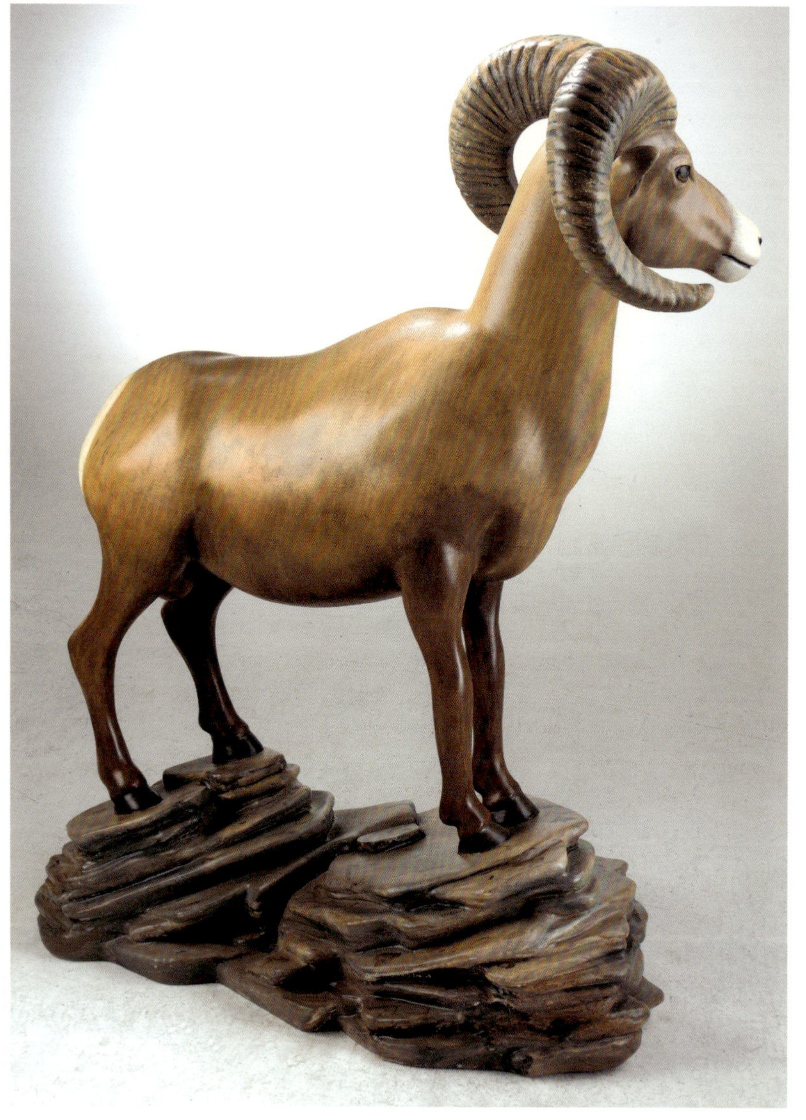

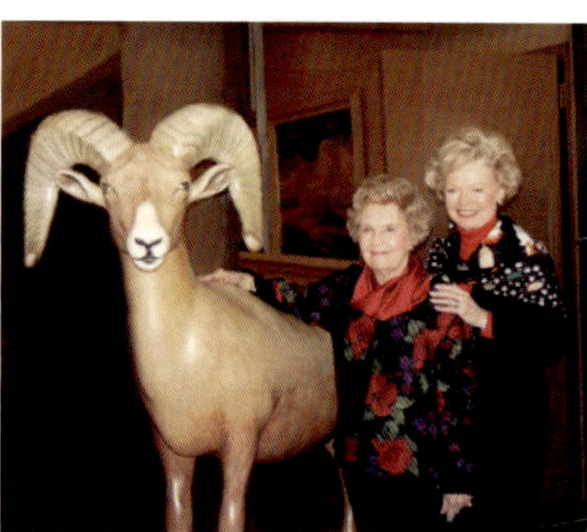

Artist Regina Murphy at the unveiling ceremony for Pa'at at Indian Wells City Hall shown with her daughter, Patty Newman

Pa'at II

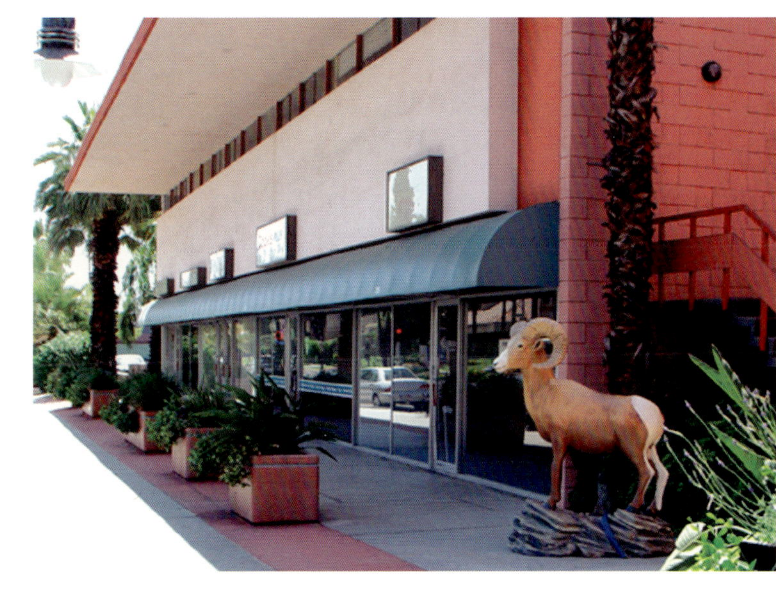

artist Regina Murphy
sponsor Alexandra & Sidney Sheldon
inaugural site Welmas Building

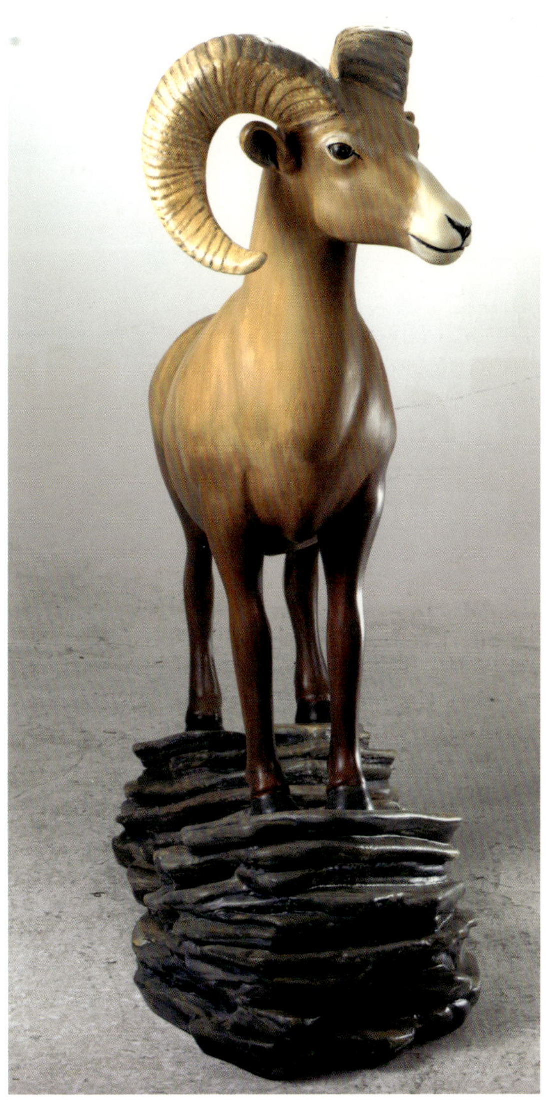

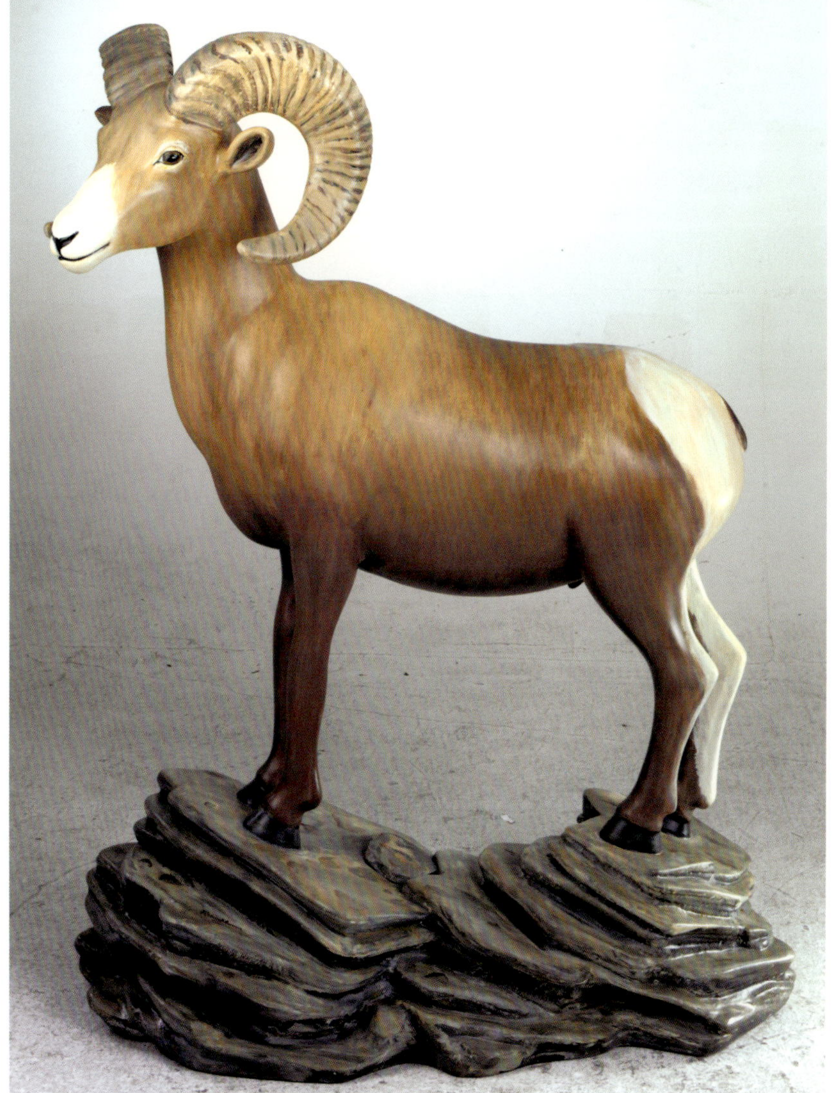

Preserve the Vision

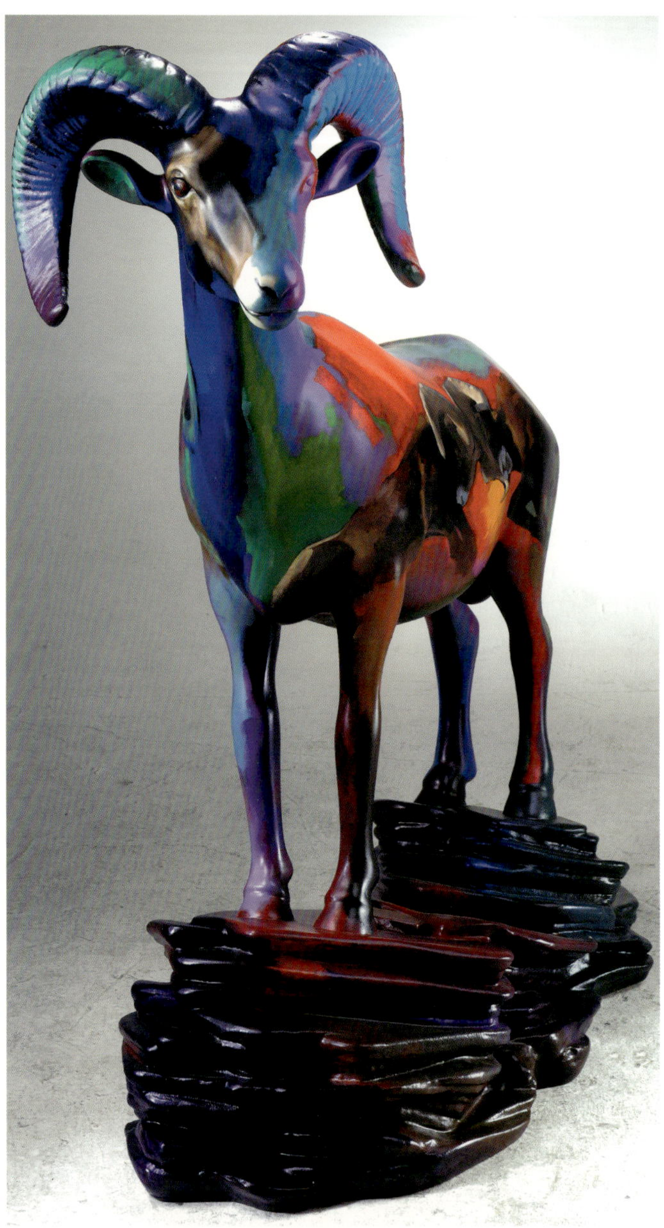

artist Gregory Manchess
sponsor Alexandra & Sidney Sheldon
inaugural site Bighorn Institute

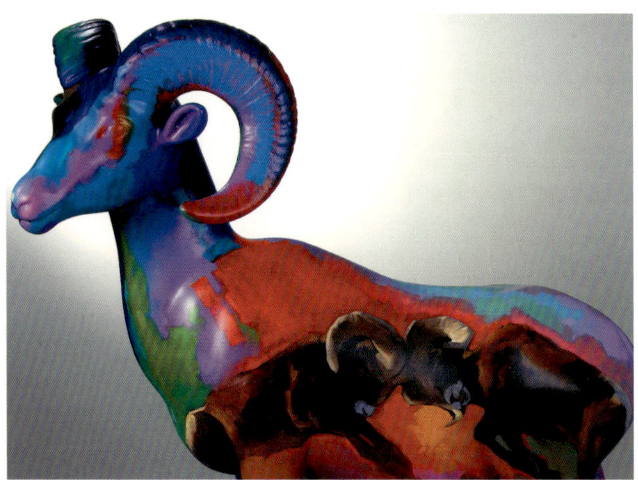

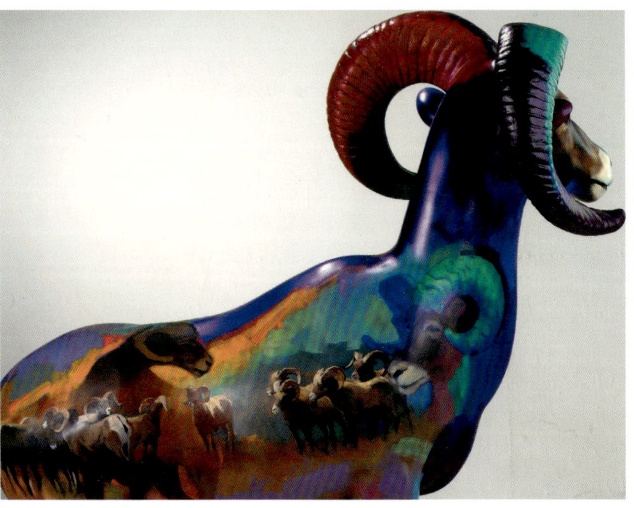

The recipient of numerous awards for his artwork including half a dozen gold and silver medals from the Society of Illustrators, Gregory Manchess has painted covers for Time and The Atlantic Monthly and interior art for Newsweek, Playboy, Omni, and Smithsonian. He has also painted movie posters for Paramount and Disney, as well as a portrait of the young Sean Connery for Warner Brothers' "Finding Forrester". Manchess has worked for the National Geographic Society on many occasions, has illustrated three children's books, and has exhibited his paintings in galleries around the world. Aside from his illustration work, Manchess pursues interests in environmental issues, hiking and ninjutsu, a 900-year-old rare form of Japanese martial arts.

Sharing the Desert

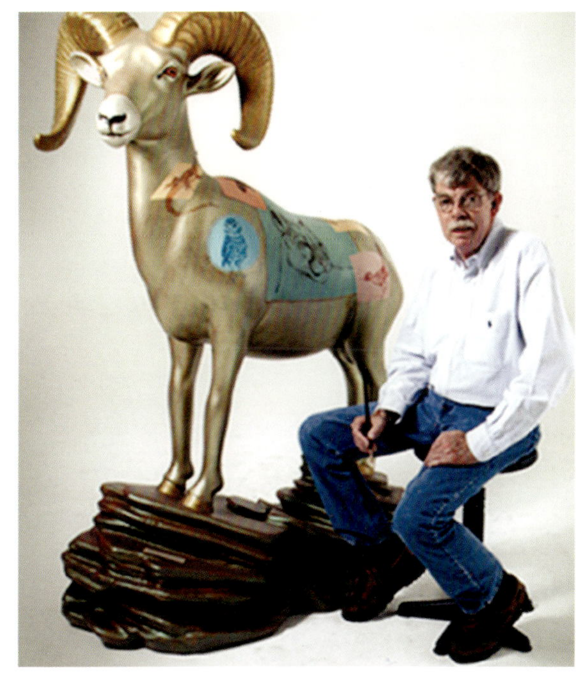

artist   Ken Carlson
sponsor   Alexandra *&* Sidney Sheldon
inaugural site   The Lodge at Rancho Mirage

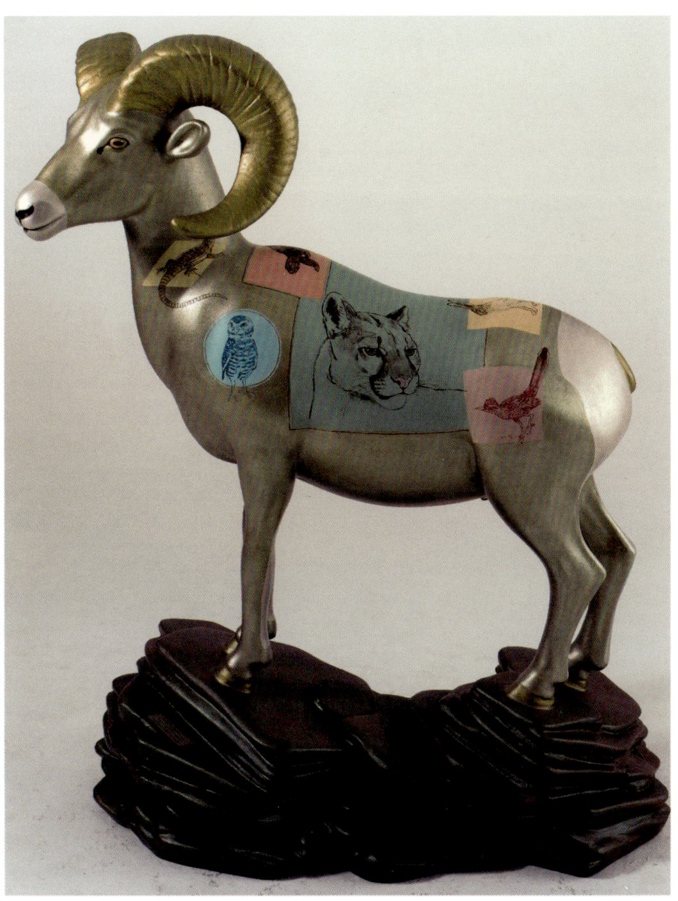

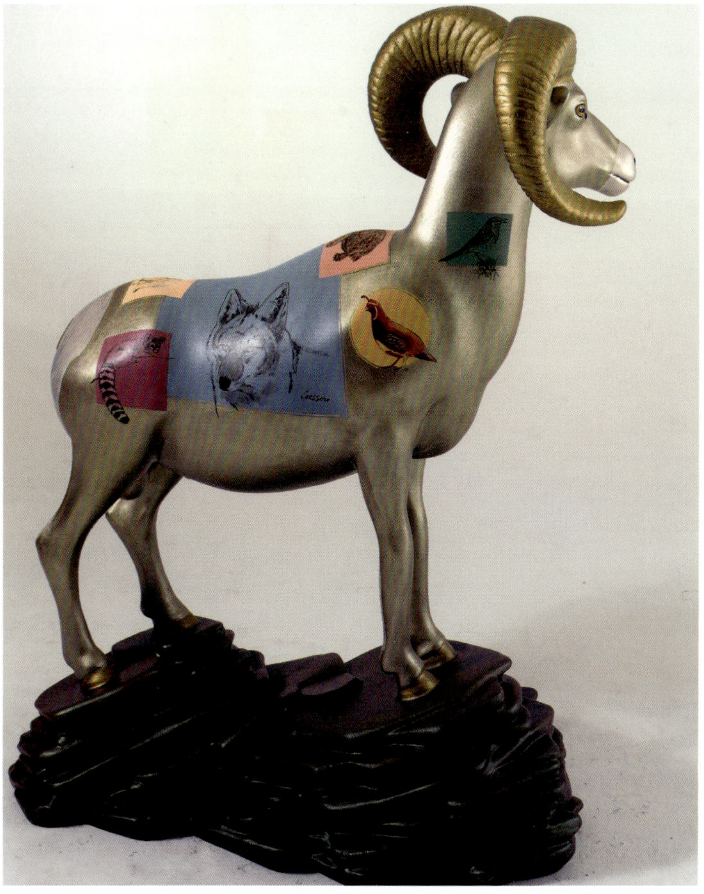

Ken Carlson's work is exhibited in the Glenbow Museum, Calgary, Alberta; National Museum of Wildlife Art, Jackson, Wyoming; Genesee Country Museum, Mumford, New York; and the Leigh Yawkey Woodson Art Museum, Wausau, Wisconsin. His paintings have helped raise funds for conservation organizations including Bighorn Institute. In 1996, Collectors Covey of Dallas, Texas published From The Tundra To Texas: The Art Of Ken Carlson. Included are more than 100 paintings and sketches, with text provided by author Tom Davis, who described Carlson's work as 'an eloquent testimony to the fact he has transcended the boundaries of genre painting.'

Spirit in the Sky

artist Stuart Funk
sponsor Palms Springs Life Magazine
inaugural site Palm Springs Life Magazine

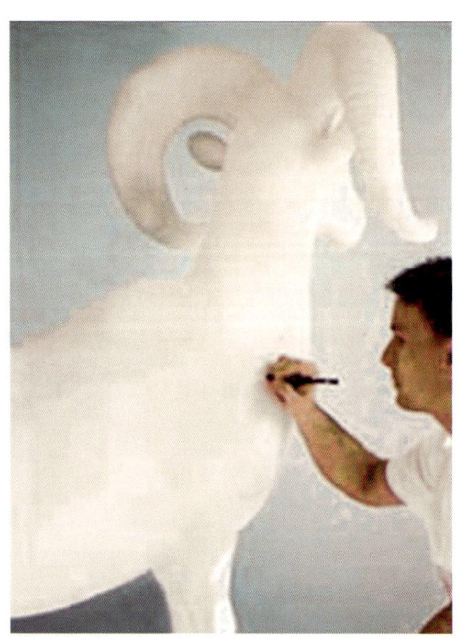

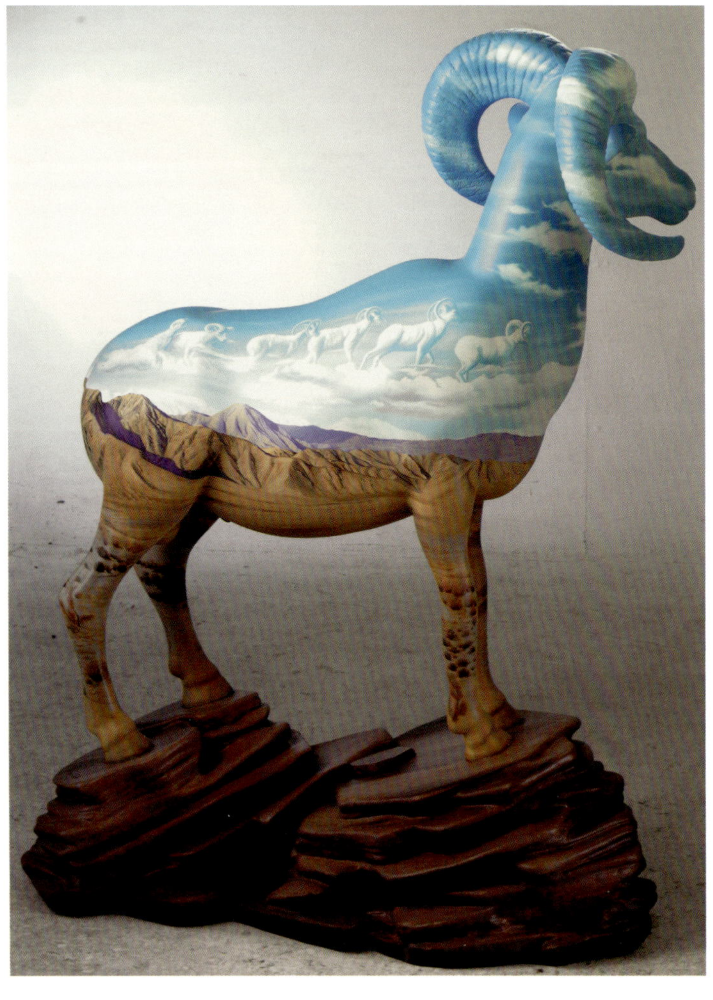

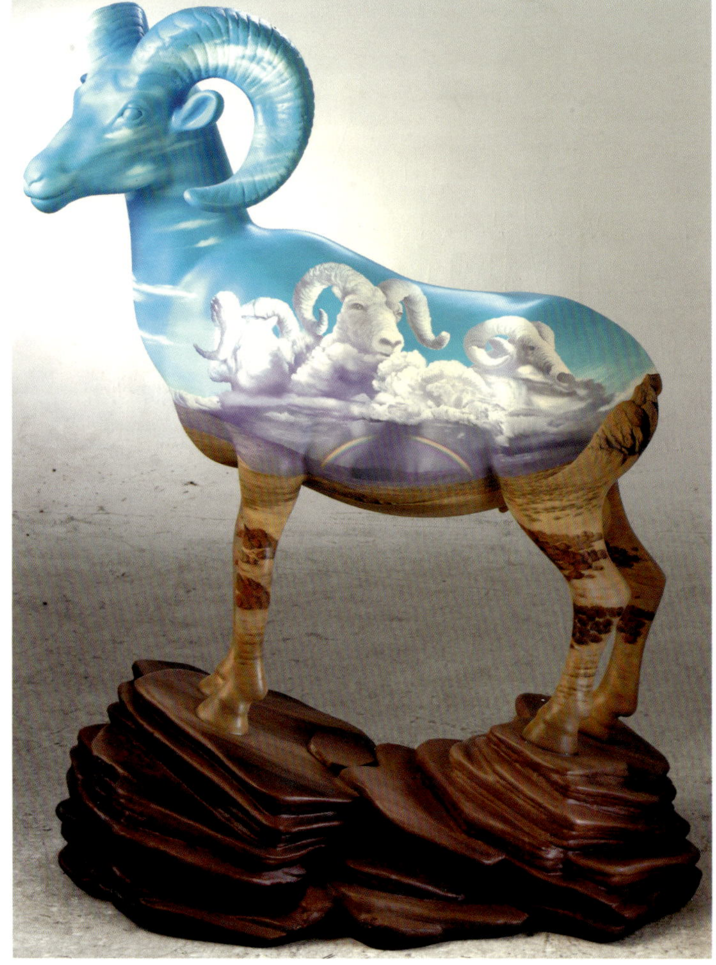

The Sands of Time

artist Jane Wooster Scott
sponsor The Lodge at Rancho Mirage
inaugural site The Lodge at Rancho Mirage

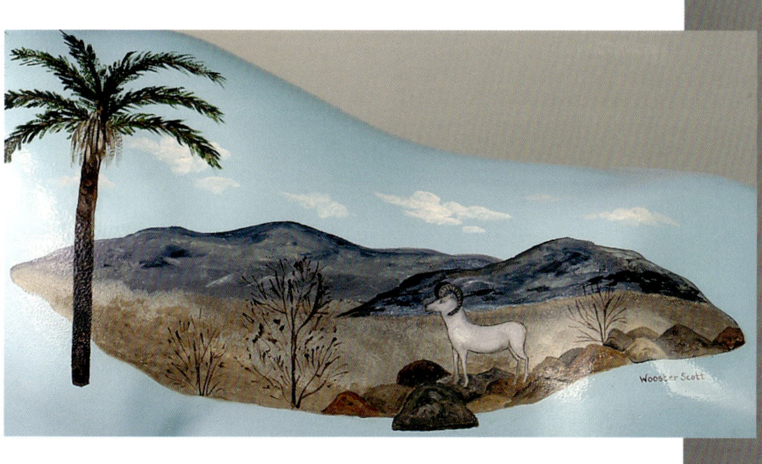

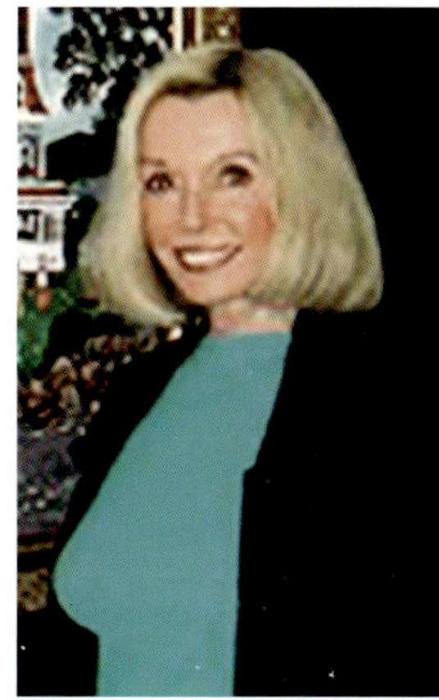

With gaiety, color and grandeur, Jane Wooster Scott's intricate paintings celebrate American life at the dawn of the 20th Century. Her award-winning paintings touch the heart, stir memories of simple pleasures, and burst with optimism. Art Business News, March 2002 Emory R. Geisz states: "Jane Wooster Scott has been recognized as the finest and most productive oil painter of Americana in the world." In fact, she has been named by the Guiness Book of World Records as the most reproduced artist in America. Her paintings have always celebrated American ideals when life seemed to be simpler in the early 1900's.

Trece'

artist Snake Jagger
sponsor Marcella & Peter Murphy
inaugural site Private residence

This ram was commissioned by Marcella and Peter Murphy and depicts the grounds around their home: the desert landscaping on one side and the golf course on the other. The title "Trece'" (thirteen) was chosen because their house is on the 13th hole on the golf course.

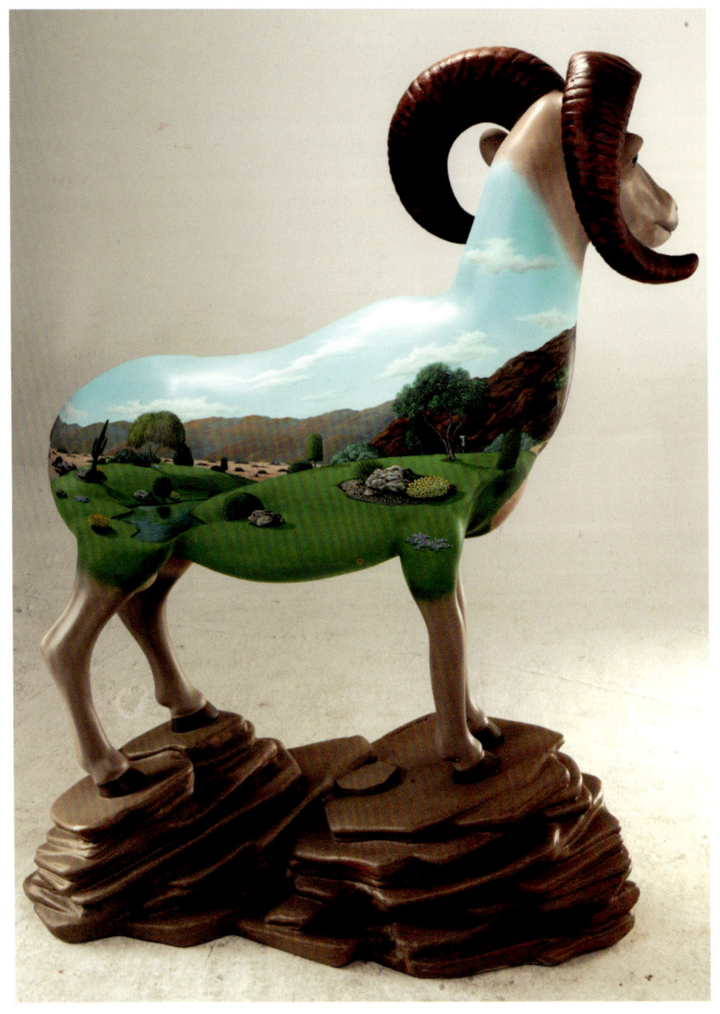

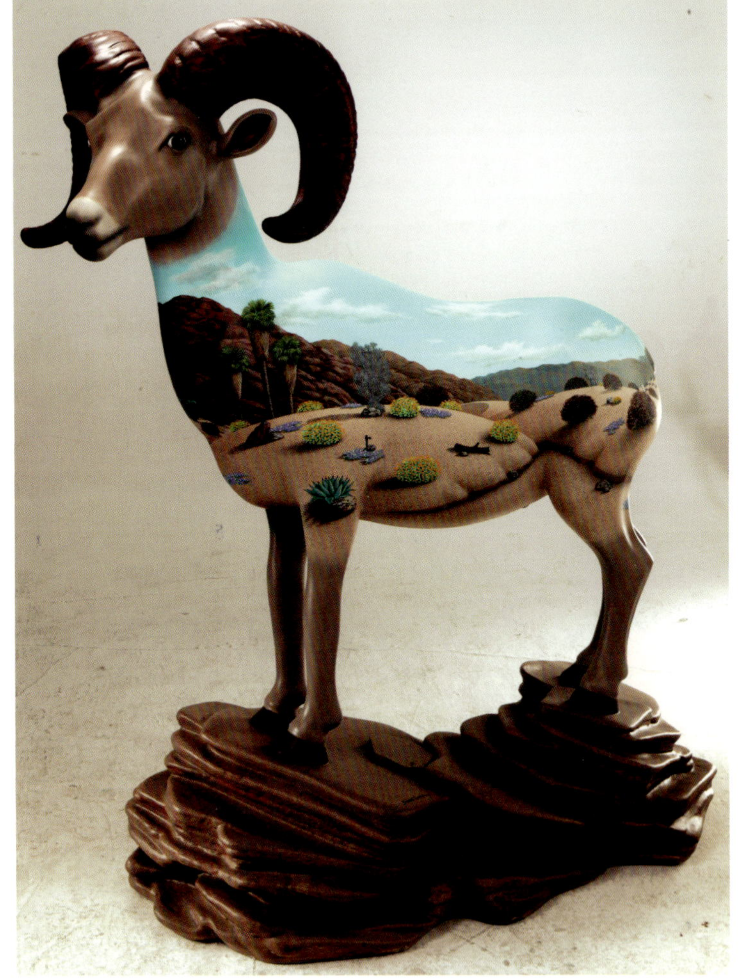

We Are Many, We Are One

artist Brenda Johnson
sponsor Sidney Sheldon
inaugural site Downey Savings

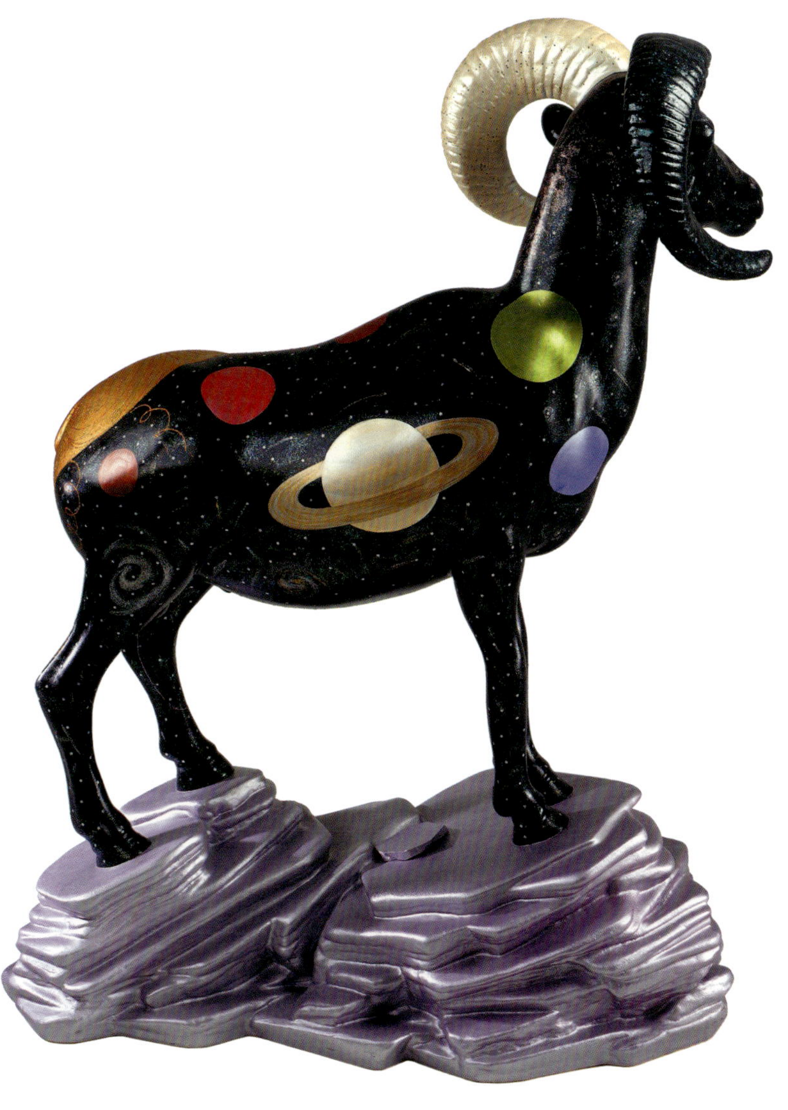

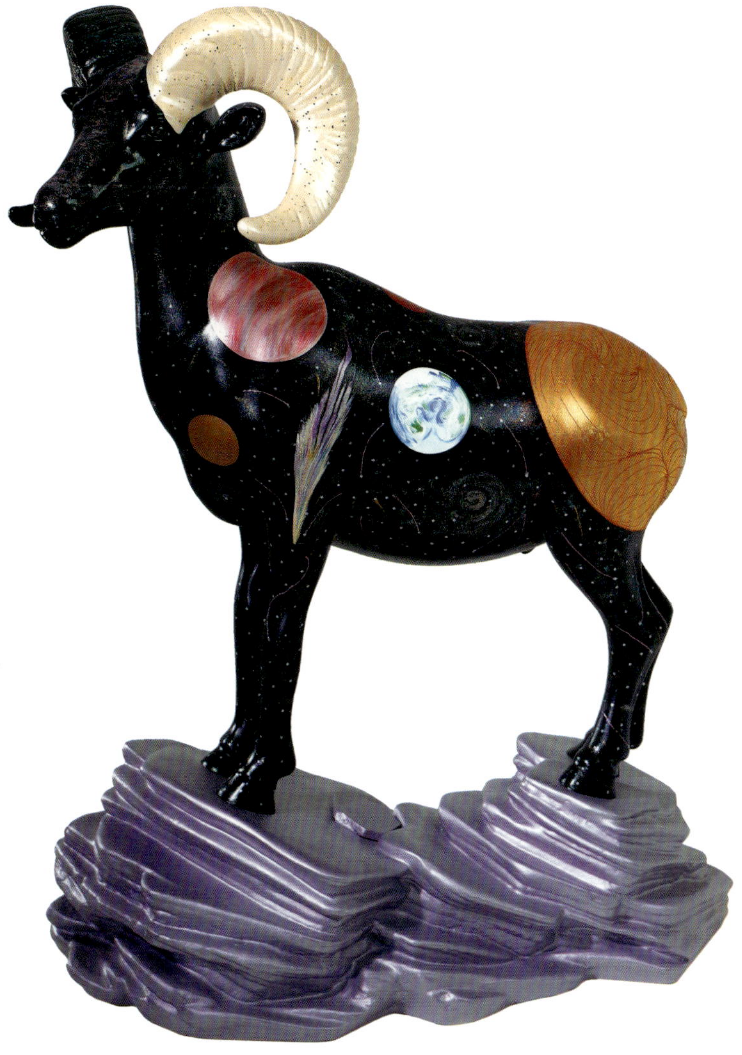

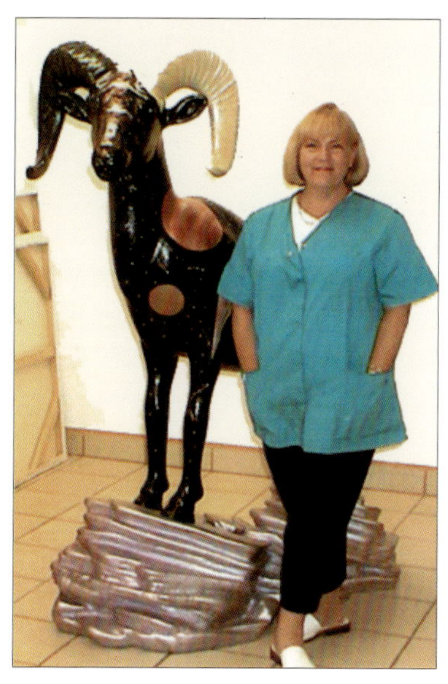

Connecting with Our Heritage

Most of the aboriginal rock art in the United States is found west of the Mississippi River. From the Rocky Mountains to the Pacific Coast, there are numerous painted and carved sites, particulary in the canyons created by major rivers, in wind-eroded caves, and on patinated volcanic rocks.

Of all the designs made by western Native Americans, the image of the bighorn is by far the most abundant animal figure. It is clear that, for thousands of years, sheep were an essential component in the life of early man. A valued game animal, the sheep were hunted for food; their hides were cured for clothing, blankets, bags, and thongs; and their horns and bones were used for a variety of tools, utensils, and ornaments.

The petroglyphs and artifacts testify to the respect and esteem with which Native Americans held the bighorn. A number of Path of the Bighorn artists have interpreted this motif, in homage to the past and to the rich heritage that all of us have been blessed with.

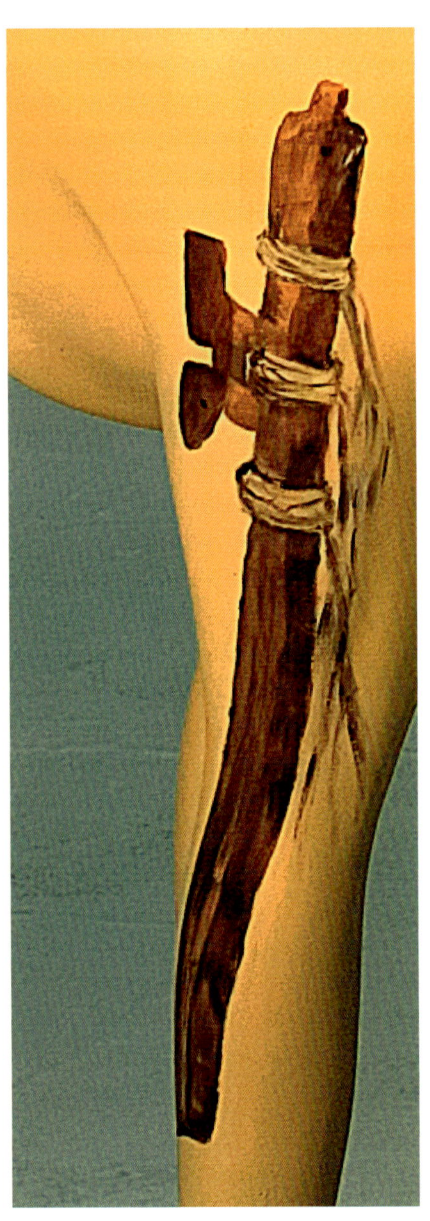

*A flute detail from "Kokopelli" by
Mary Wilcox*

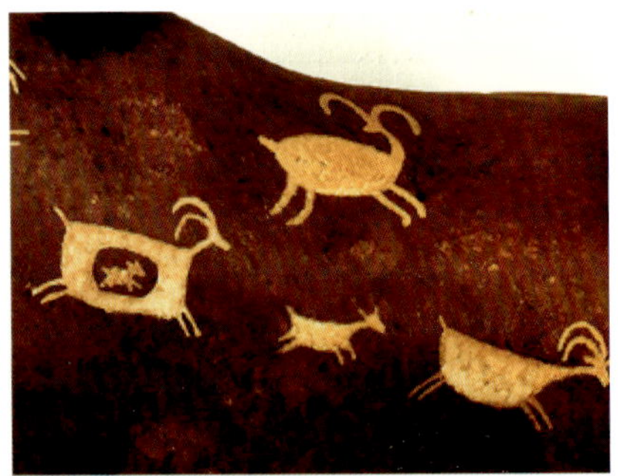

*A rock art detail from
"The Storyteller"
by Alexandra & Sidney Sheldon*

American Odyssey

artist Gregg Deam
sponsor Grant, Tani, Barash & Altman
inaugural site The Gardens on El Paseo

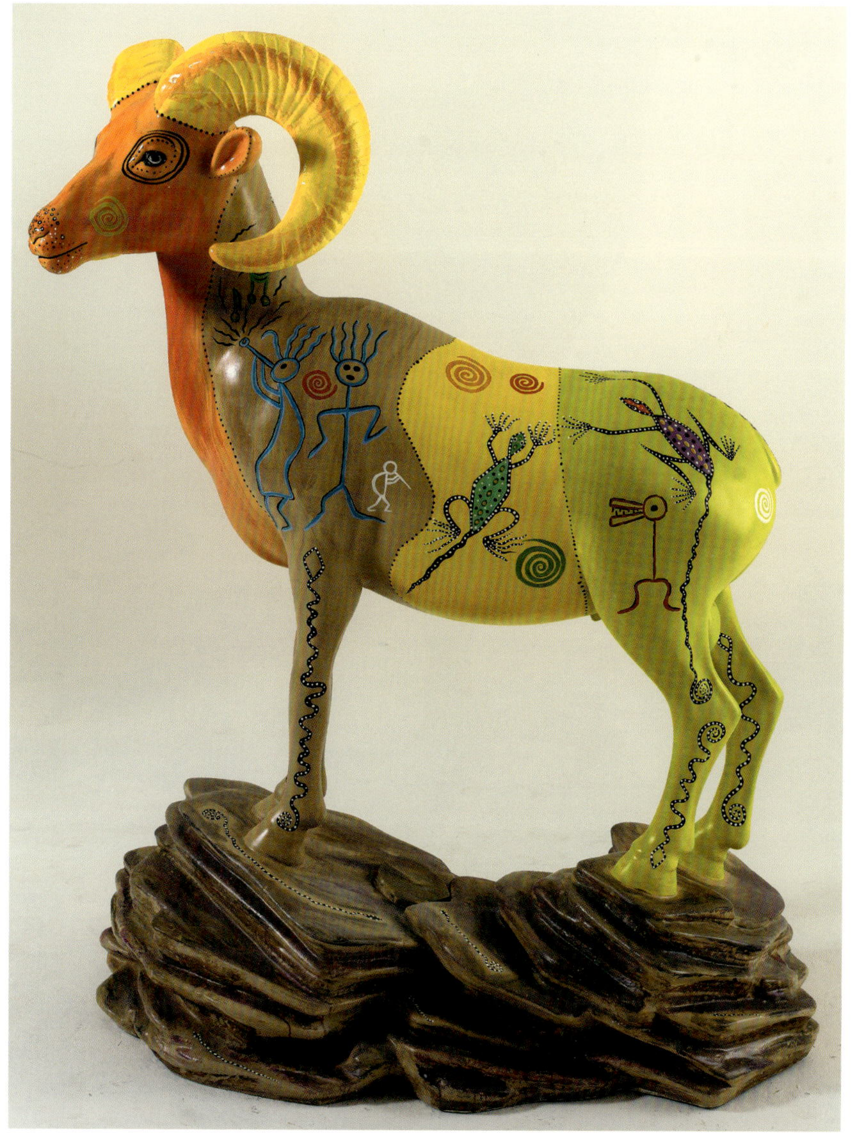

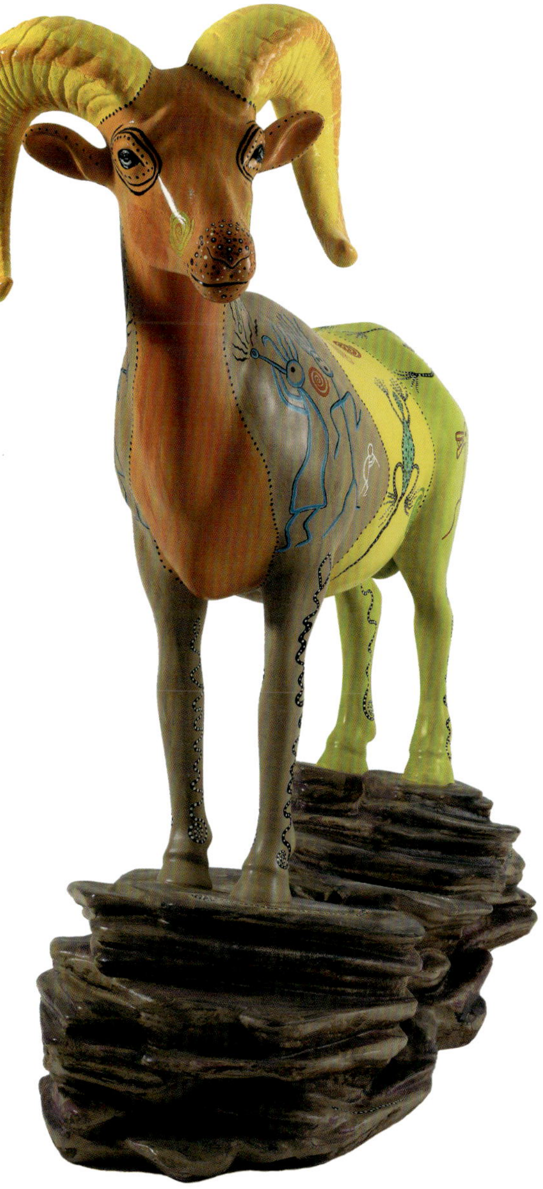

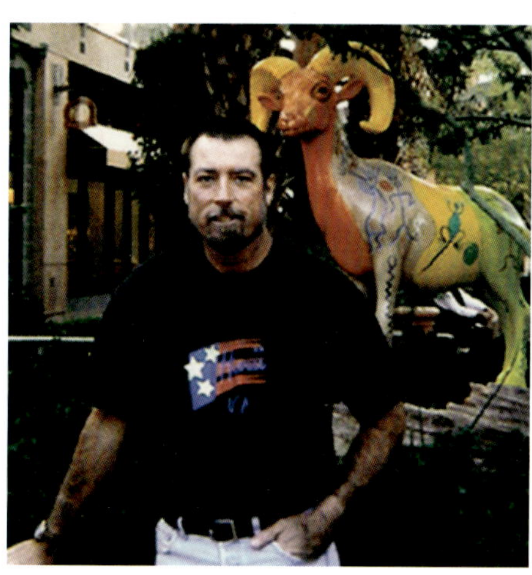

Ancient Art

artist Donnaldo Smolens
sponsor Fay & Dick McClung
inaugural site McCallum Theater

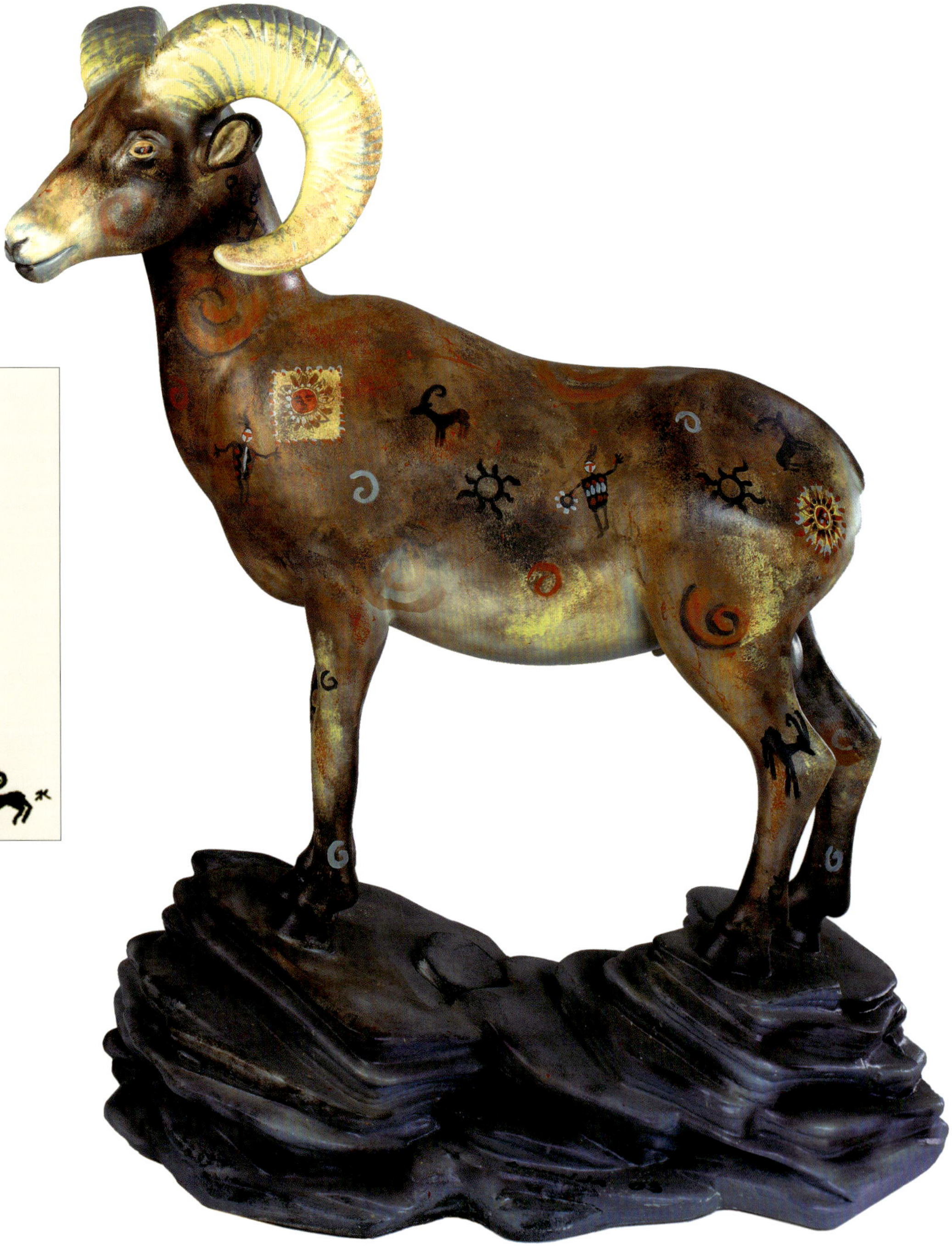

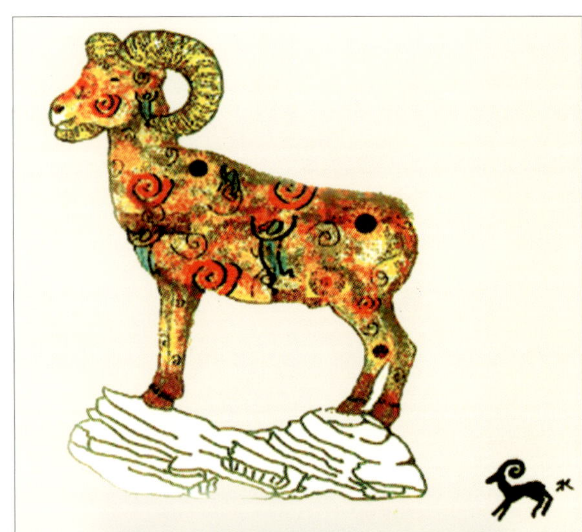

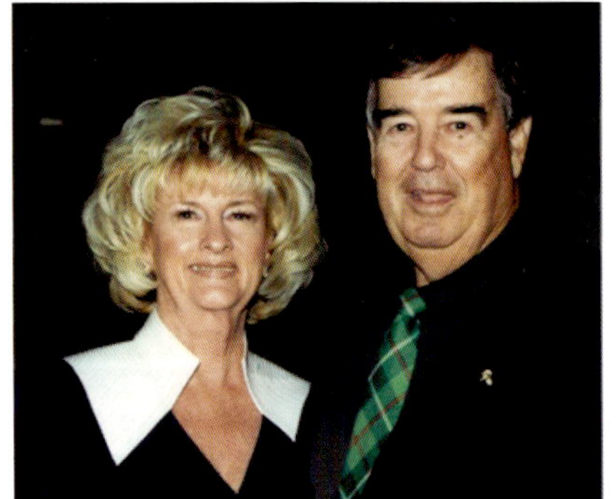

Sponsors Fay & Dick McClung

Big Blue—Miró Series

artist   Steven Maloney
sponsor   Jackie Lee & Jim Houston
inaugural site   Palm Springs Air Museum

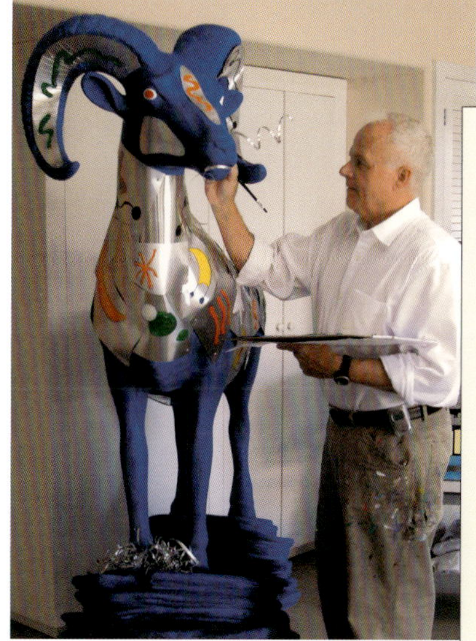

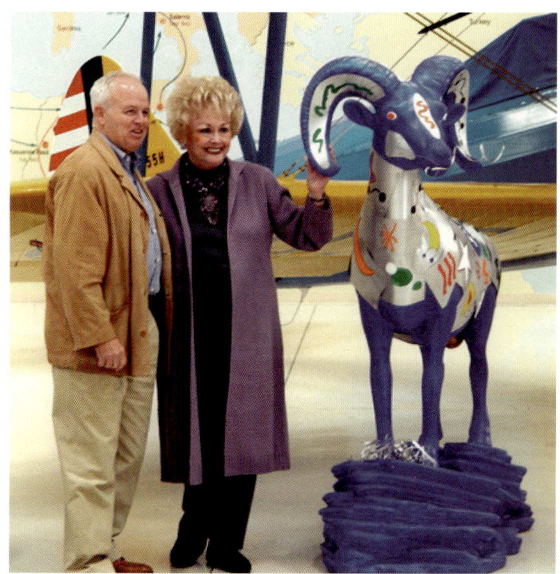

*Steve Maloney with sponsor
Jackie Lee Houston at the unveiling of Big Blue
at the Palm Springs Air Museum*

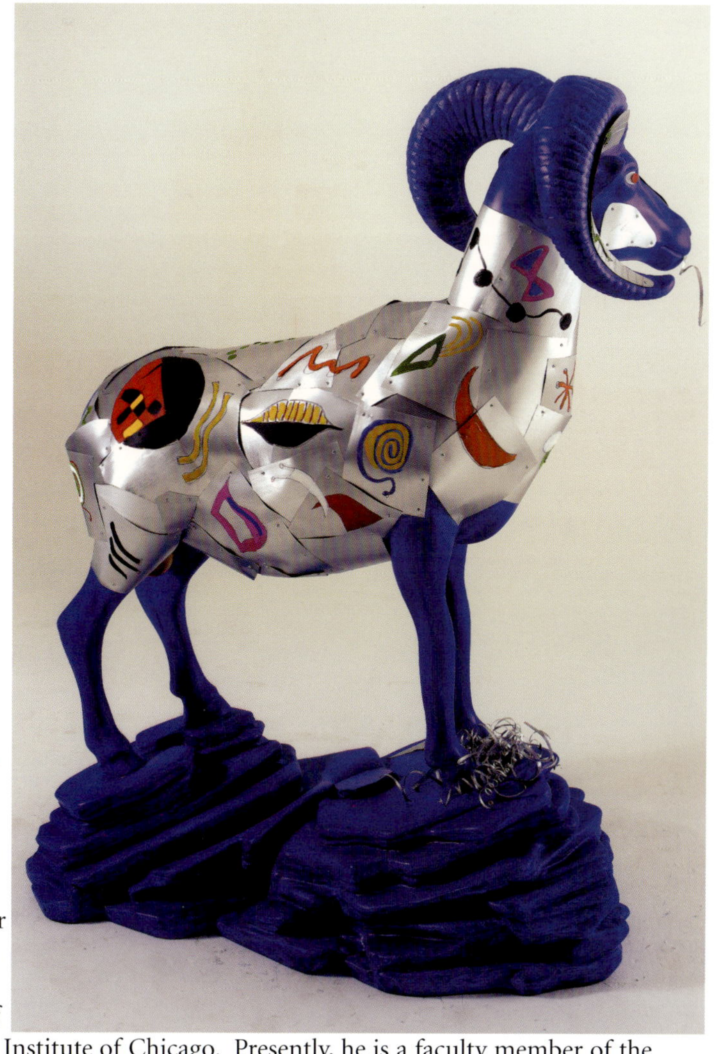

Maloney, a direct descendant of W.E. Upjohn, spent many years as a high fashion textile retailer working with color, pattern, texture and style. He later became an entrepreneurial owner of a machine tool manufacturing business. In both professions an American aesthetic sensibility was a must. He now dedicates his time to contemporary art. "Currently, I enjoy the art of Red Groom, whose sense of humor I find profoundly inspiring, and Gerhard Richards and Frank Stella. I am delighted by the creativeness and exuberance of their work." Maloney has studied under Kwok Wai Lau, a past faculty member of the International Art School of Hong Kong, and Lecturer at The Art Institute of Chicago. Presently, he is a faculty member of the Palm Spring Desert Museum in Palm Springs, California. Maloney has shown his work around the United States.

Bighorn Ghost Dance

artist Paul Magloff
sponsor Diane & Gary Zornes
inaugural site Palm Springs Plumbing

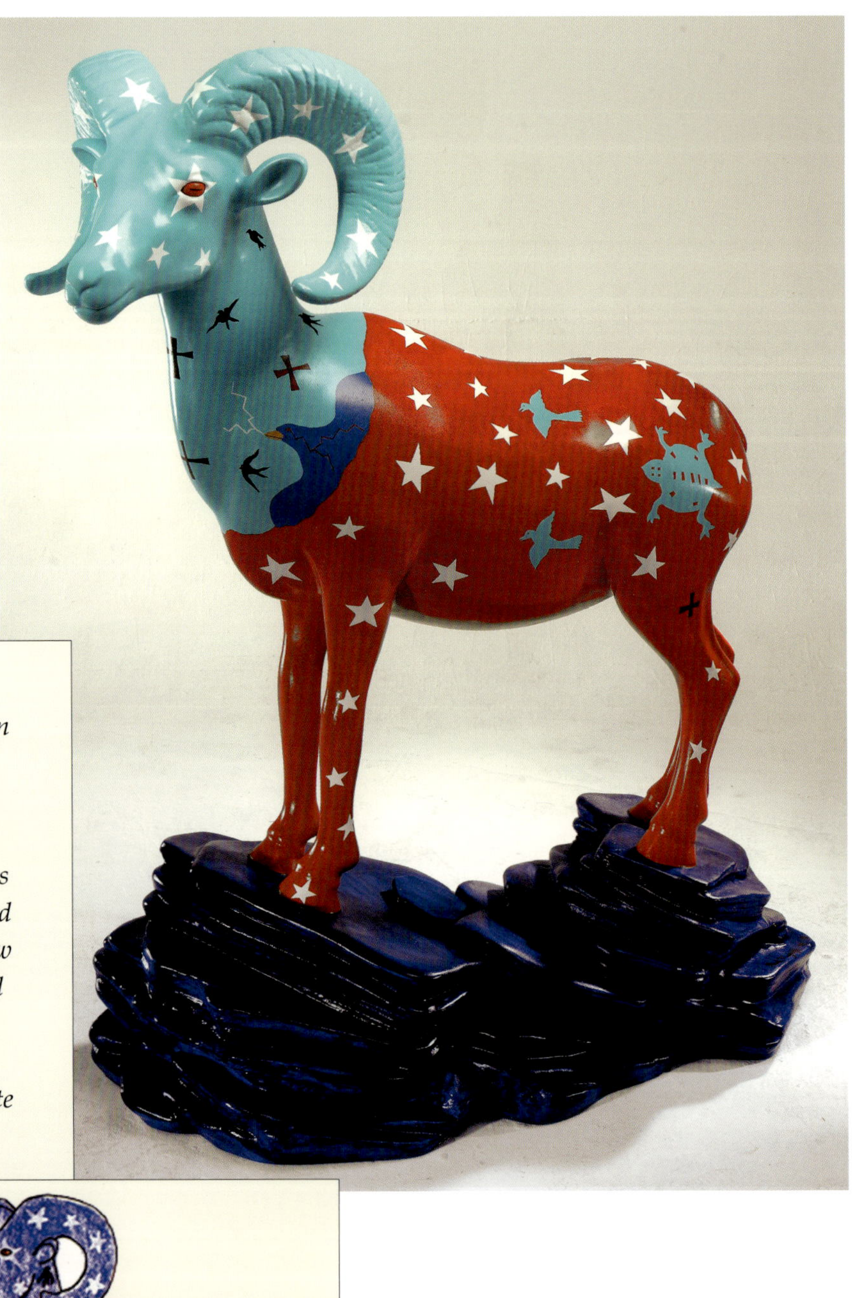

At the end of the 19th century, a religious cult known as the Ghost Dance flowered briefly. This was an indigenous response to the cultural holocaust taking place throughout the vast lands of the West. Its immediate inspiration was a series of religious visions by Wovoka, a Paiute holy man. In 1889 he proclaimed that if Indian people lived peacefully, performed a new dance that he introduced called the Ghost Dance, and sang the Ghost Dance songs, their world would be transformed into an ideal place populated by buffalo herds and the ancestral dead. Most importantly, white people, their goods, and the troubles they had caused would disappear. This hopeful message spread across many Western tribes, and was adapted according to the cultural practices of each group. Notably, the Ghost Dance movement also incorporated some features of Christianity, including recognition of a "Messiah." Hauntingly beautiful painted clothing was made for Ghost Dance participants which incorporated many celestial and avian symbols. — Paul Magloff

Bighorn Pow Wow

artist Charlie Schridde
sponsor Shellie Read *&* Harold Matzner
inaugural site Wyndham Hotel

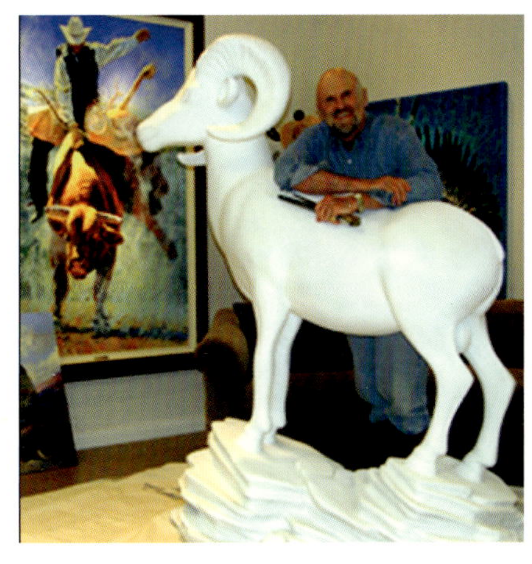

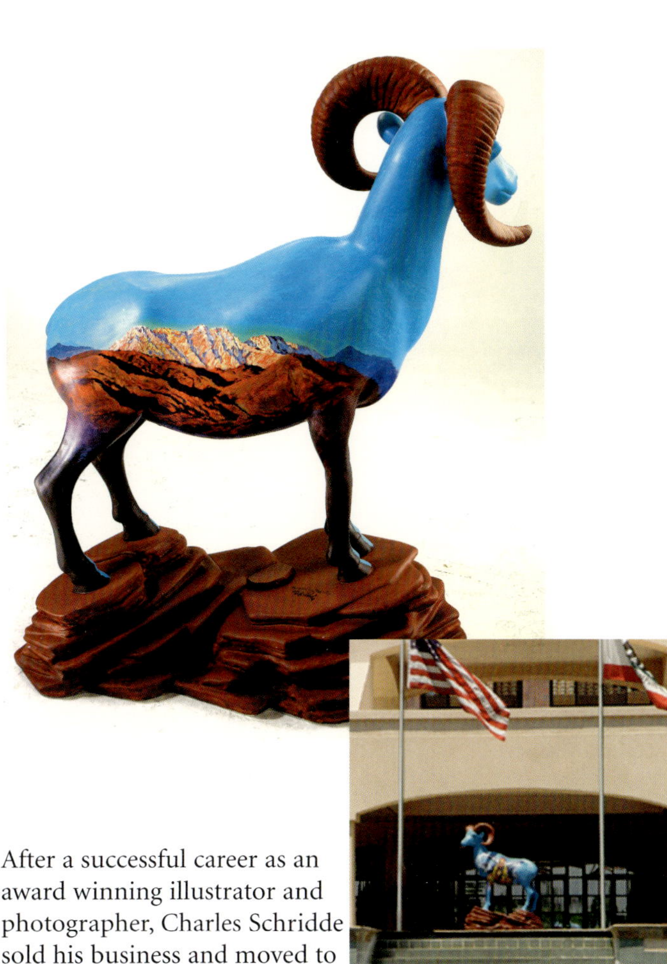

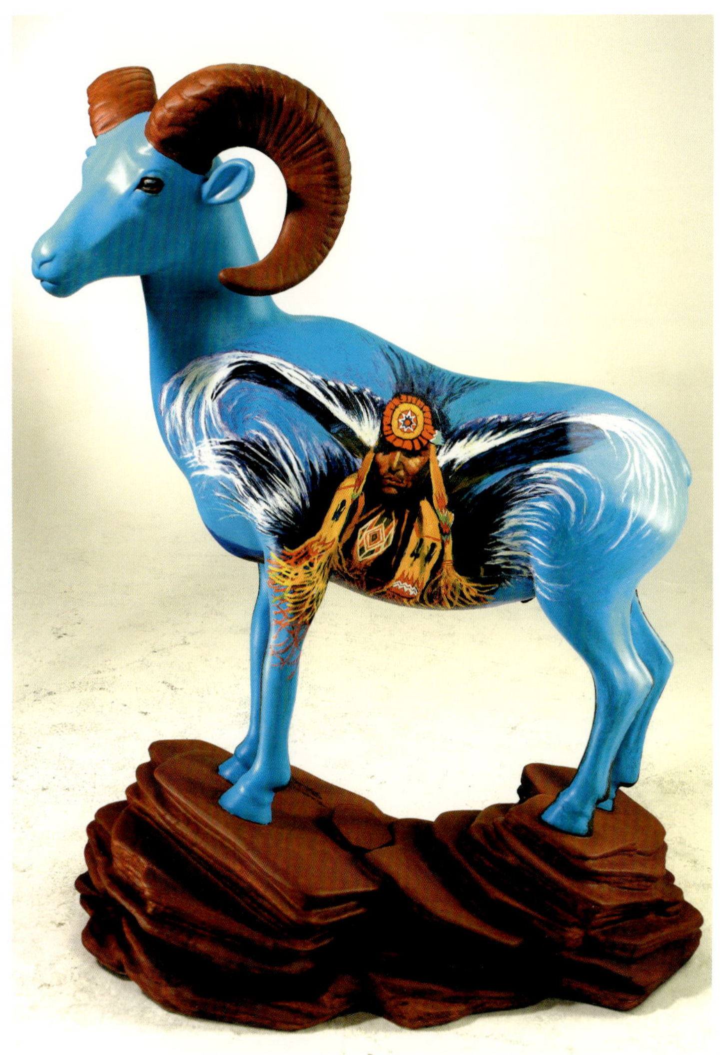

After a successful career as an award winning illustrator and photographer, Charles Schridde sold his business and moved to Laguna Beach, California, to concentrate on painting. Although he began drawing as a child and attended art school in Illinois, Michigan, and California, Schridde had to put his painting on hold, first to serve in the Navy for two years and later to earn a living. Southwest Art writes, "Schridde has become equally skilled at painting landscapes and figures, achieving dramatic effects of light, color and movement." He is a regular on the rodeo circuit, where he finds much of his subject matter. He starts the process by taking all of his own photos. After many hours of viewing, he chooses the images that capture his passion and spirit. Schridde and his wife have recently relocated to South Africa.

Bighorn Sky Figure

artist   Paul Magloff
sponsor   Mary, Anastasia & Alexandra
inaugural site   Desert Hospital Hospice

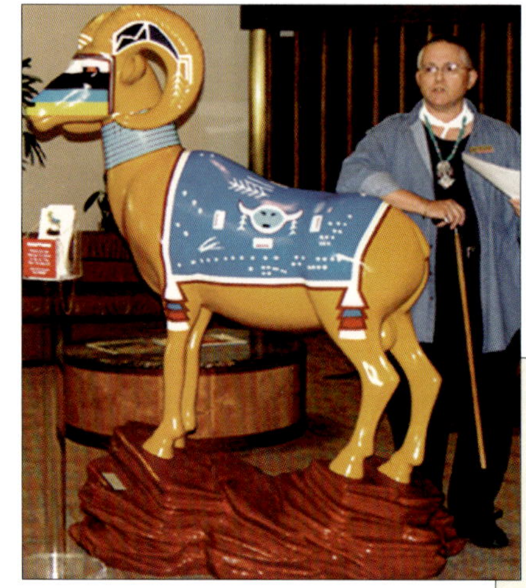

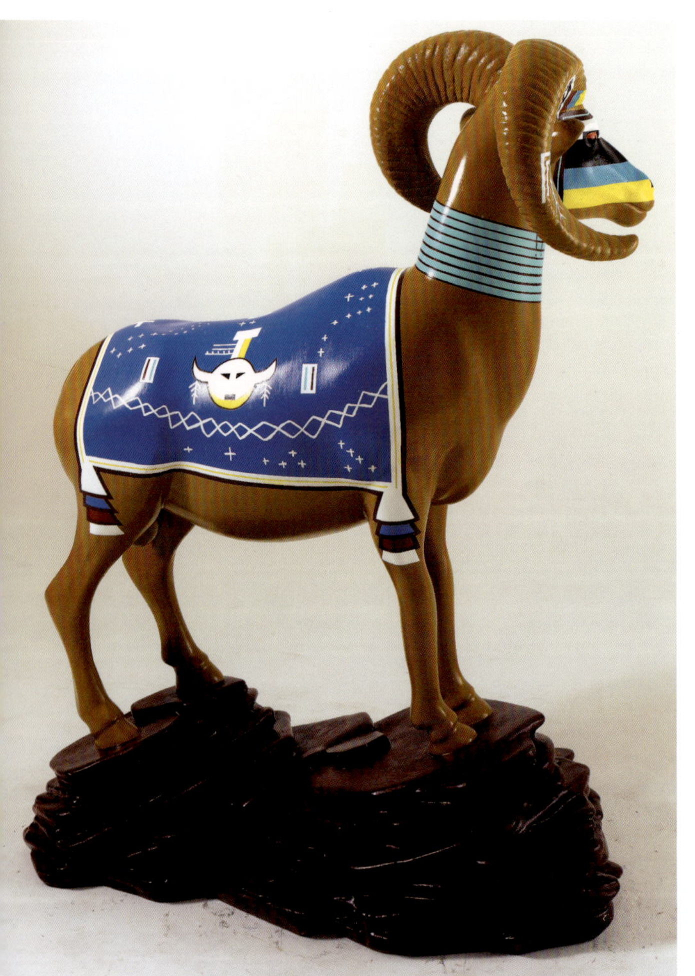

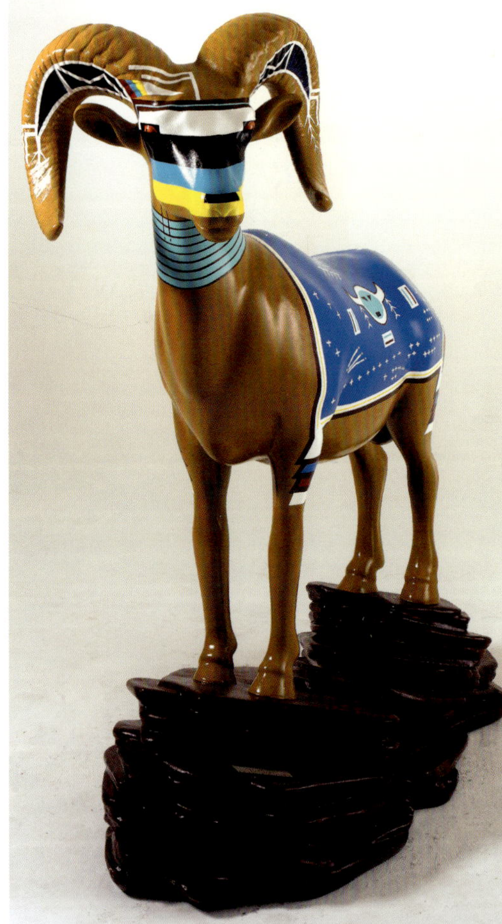

Navajo sandpaintings form part of the religious ceremonies performed by medicine men to heal a sick person. They are called chants and usually last several days. A sandpainting is made early in the morning and is destroyed by sundown.

This is the Sky figure from the Emergence or Upward-Reaching Chant. In the sky we see the sun and the moon both bearing the horns of omnipotence and guarded by red and blue rain spots. Above the moon's head is the Eastern Star; just below, going from left to right across the painting is the zig-zagging Milky Way. The remaining star patterns include the "Turkey Tracks" and other groupings that the Navajos use as hunting guides. Above the sky blanket is the head representing One Intelligence over all.

Cahuilla Dreams

artist Morgan Weistling
sponsor Alexandra & Sidney Sheldon
inaugural site The Lodge at Rancho Mirage, &
                          Agua Caliente Casino

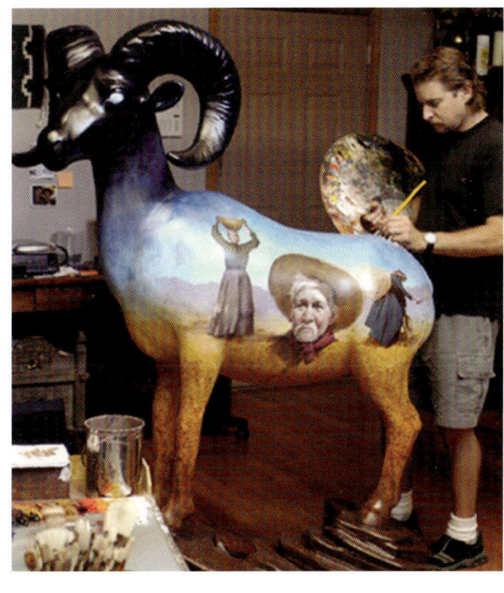

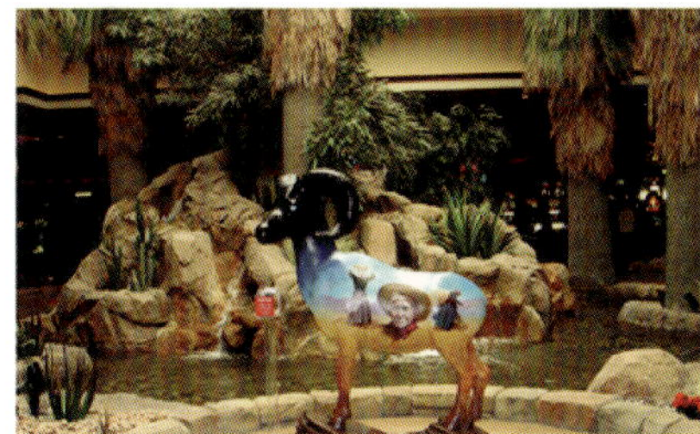

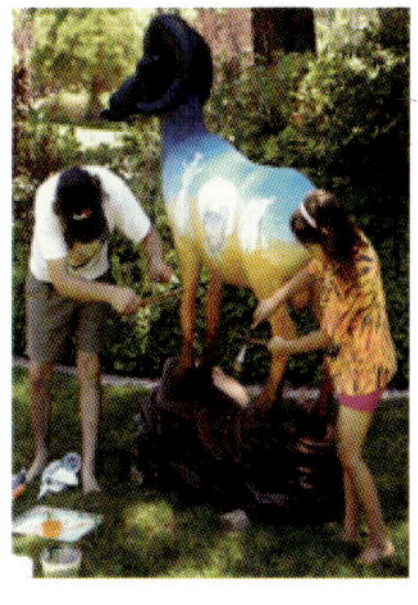

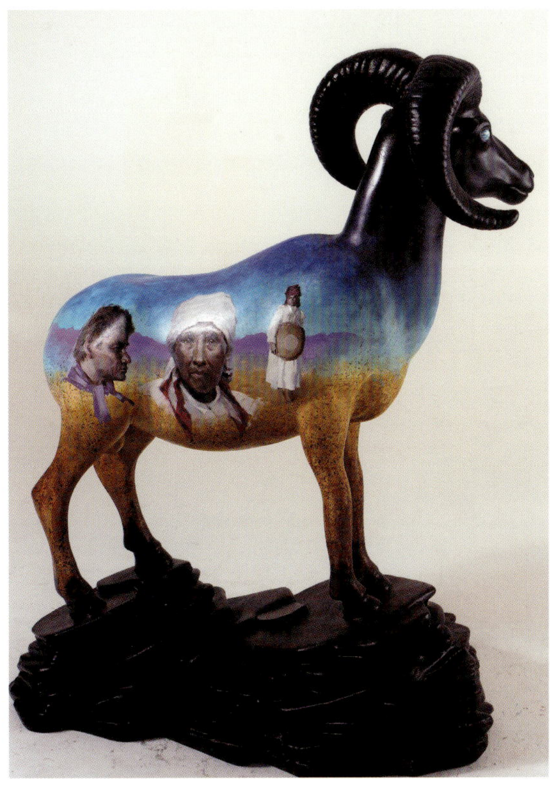

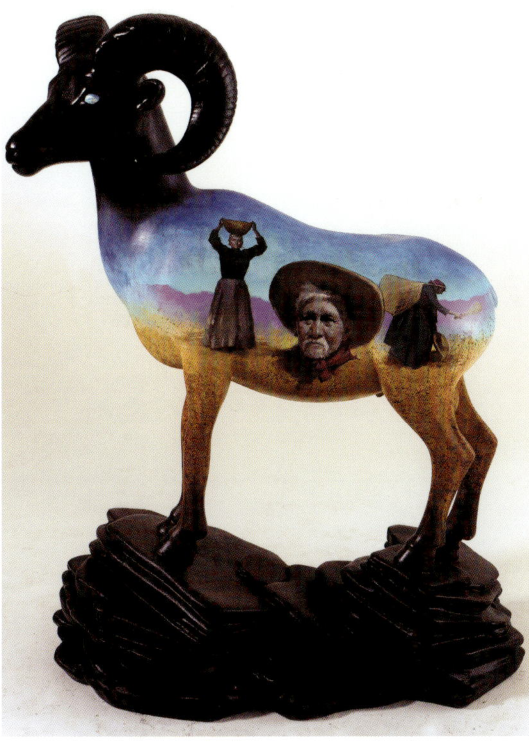

Working in a Los Angeles art supply store while attending art school, Morgan Weistling often showed some of his own work to noted artists whenever they came in. One such customer was a famous movie poster artist. As a result of their chance encounter, at the age of 19, Weistling began a notable career as an illustrator. Weistling became well-known in the film industry for his illustrations whose amazing celebrity likenesses promoted movies and their merchandise (such as Anastasia, The Santa Clause, Last Action Hero, The Lost World and countless action thrillers). The list of movie stars whose features Weistling has flawlessly captured reads like a stroll down the star-studded sidewalks of Hollywood Boulevard, and his clients have included many major studios.   After being art directed for years, Morgan needed to paint something for himself. He took time out to produce a painting of two children and brought it to Scottsdale, Arizona on the advice of a long time friend. The first gallery he walked into signed him on the spot, Trailside Galleries. "He would send his paintings to Trailside unframed and before they could get hung, they would be sold."   Soon a "draw" system for Weistling's paintings became necessary. His first one-man show had 26 paintings and all were sold opening night.

Boundary Lines

artist   Rebecca M. Hendrickson
sponsor   Howard Richmond
inaugural site   Rancho Mirage Library

My artwork signifies man's imposed order on the ram and his habitat. It has been said that straight lines do not exist in nature but are a result of man. I have painted and beaded this ram with rectilinear lines which encroach on the random and curvilinear planes of nature. — Rebecca M. Hendrickson

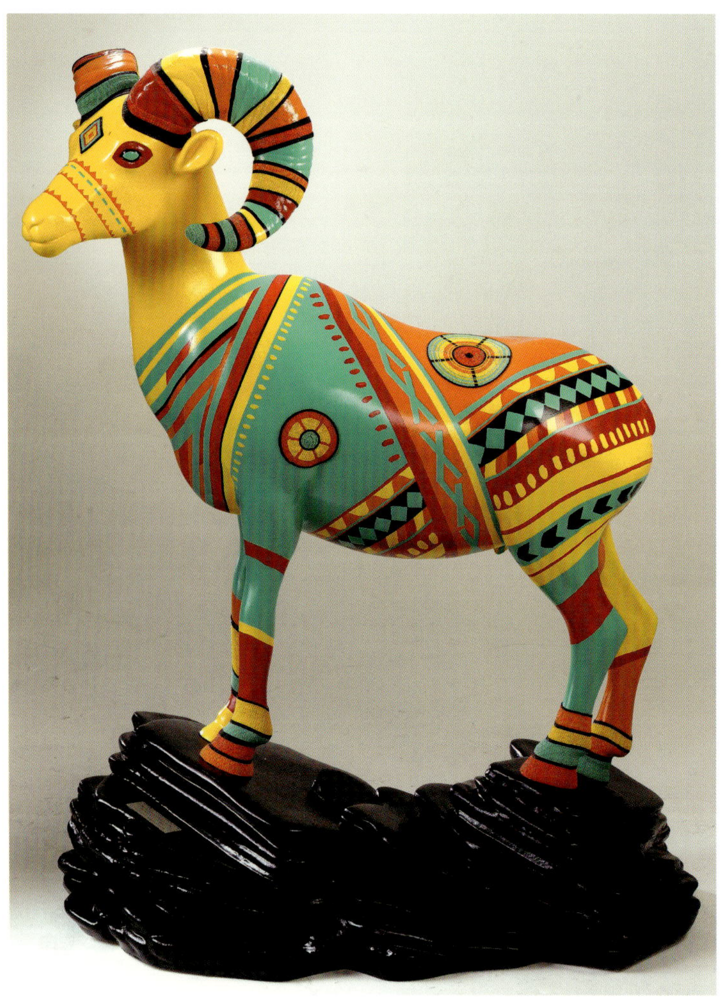

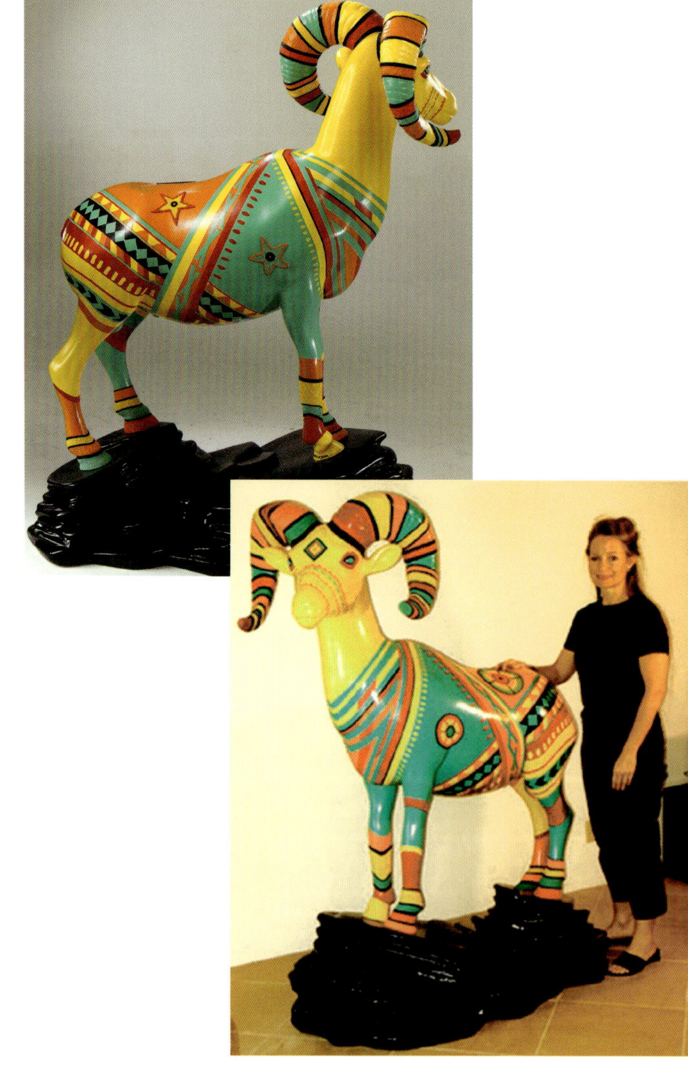

Cahuilla Life

artist Agua Caliente Young Adults
sponsor Agua Caliente Band of Cahuilla Indians
inaugural site Spa Hotel

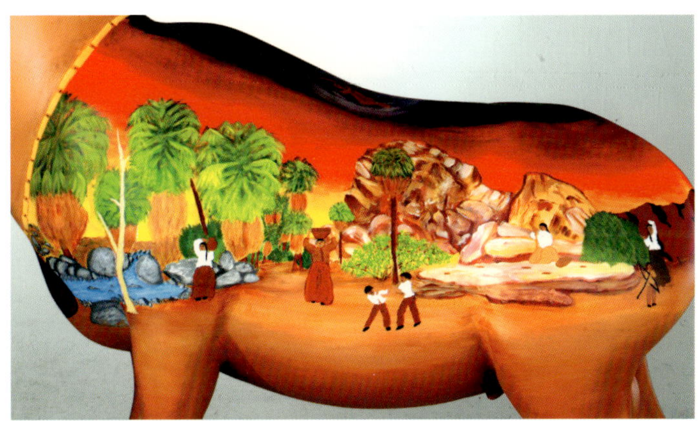

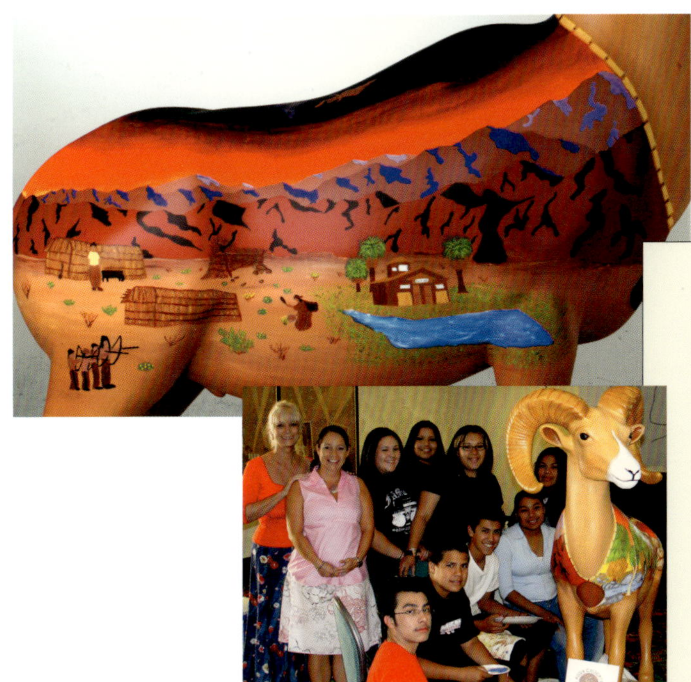

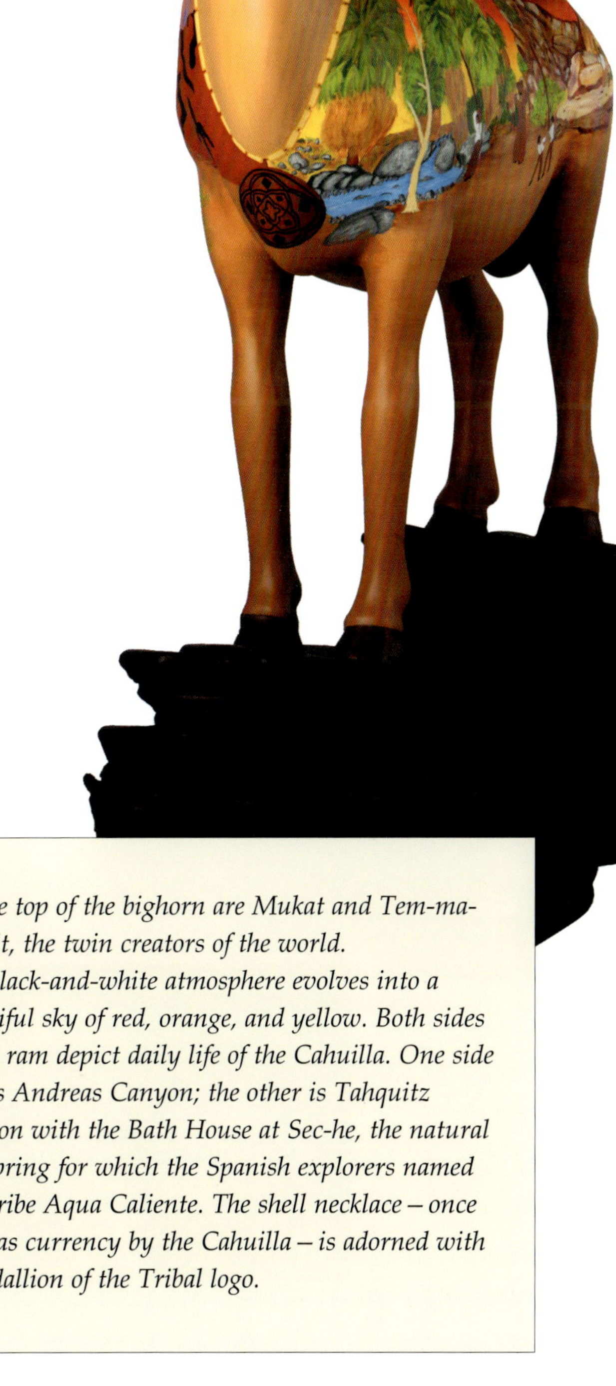

At the top of the bighorn are Mukat and Tem-ma-ya-wit, the twin creators of the world.
The black-and-white atmosphere evolves into a beautiful sky of red, orange, and yellow. Both sides of the ram depict daily life of the Cahuilla. One side shows Andreas Canyon; the other is Tahquitz Canyon with the Bath House at Sec-he, the natural hot spring for which the Spanish explorers named the Tribe Aqua Caliente. The shell necklace — once used as currency by the Cahuilla — is adorned with a medallion of the Tribal logo.

Chimayo

artist Carl Ramsey
sponsor Pauline & Neil Van Luven
inaugural site Spa Resort Casino

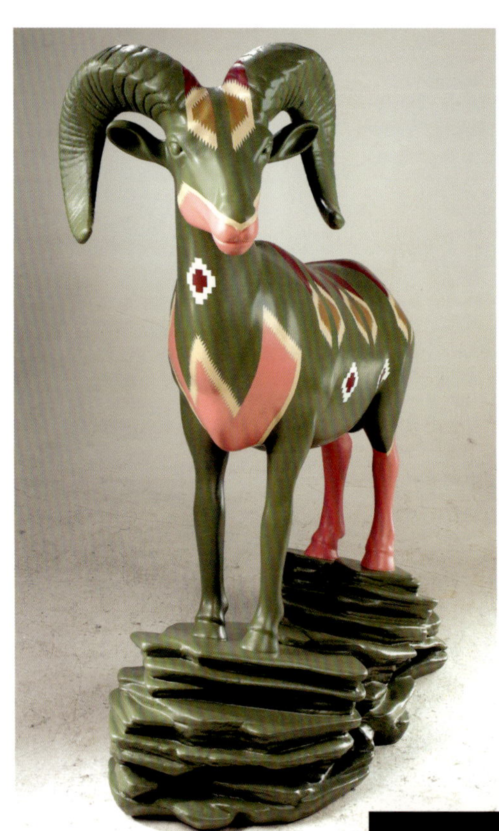

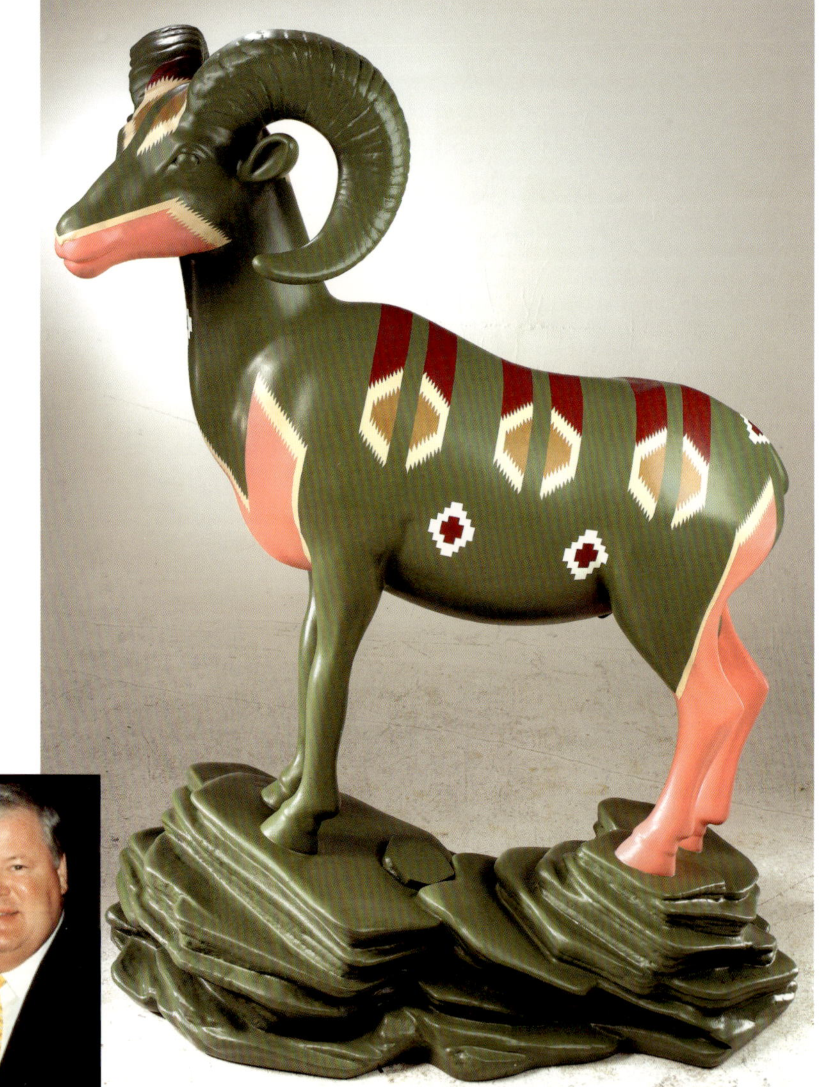

*Sponsors
Pauline & Neil
Van Luven*

Hail to the Chief

artist Carl Ramsey
sponsor Gary Powers
inaugural site Powers Carpet One

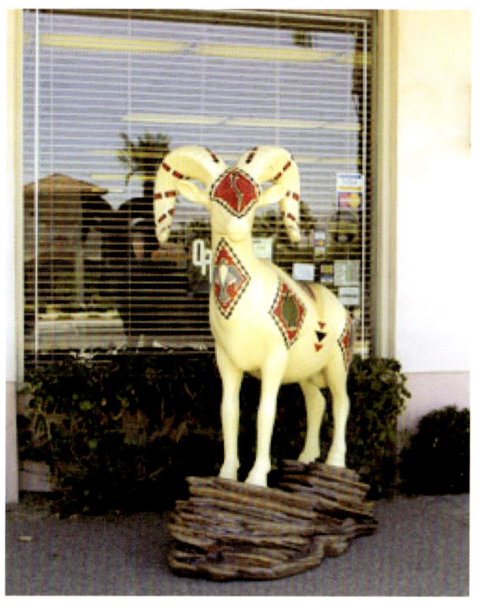

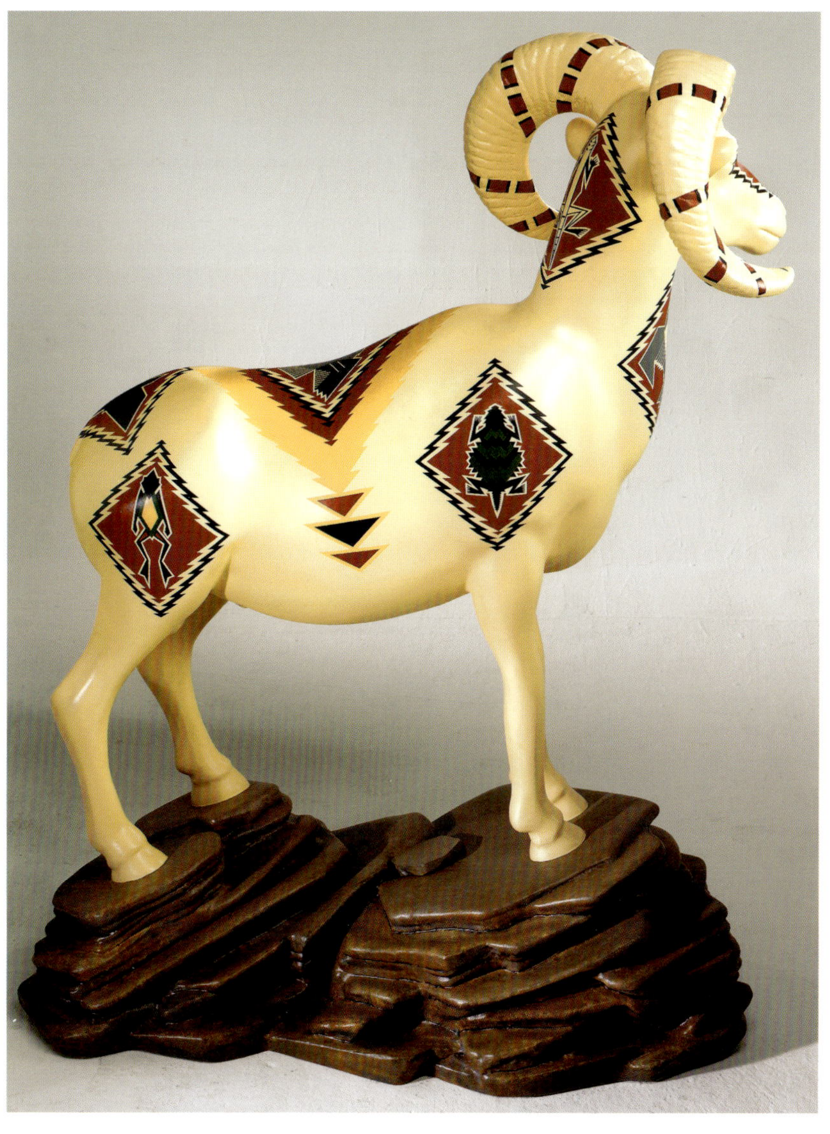

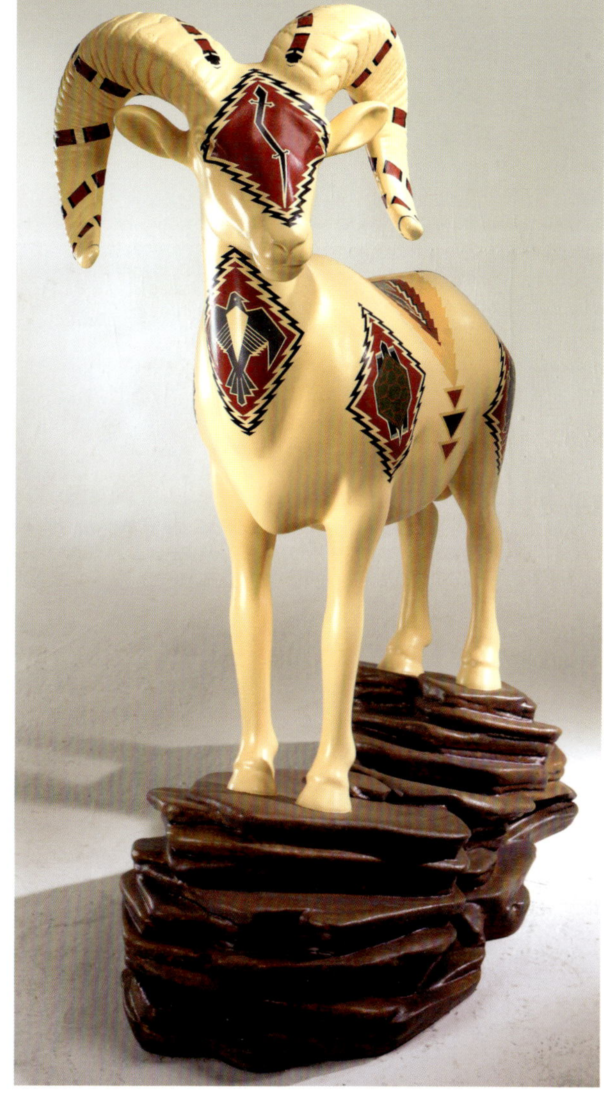

Blue Gold

artist   Chris Sandoval
sponsor   Cabazon Band of Mission Indians
inaugural site   Cabazon Band of Mission
                 Indians Tribal Office

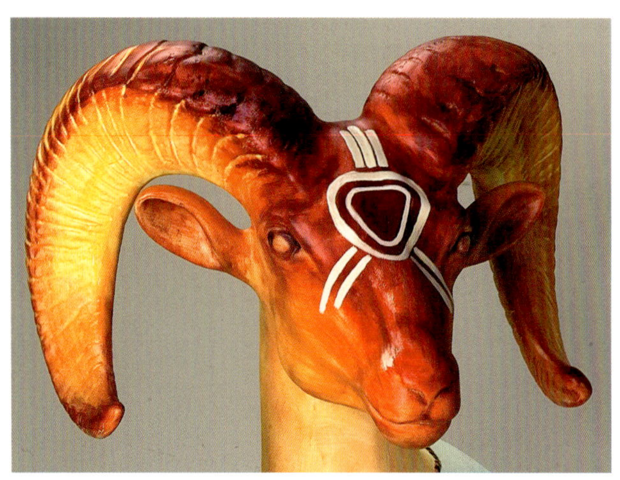

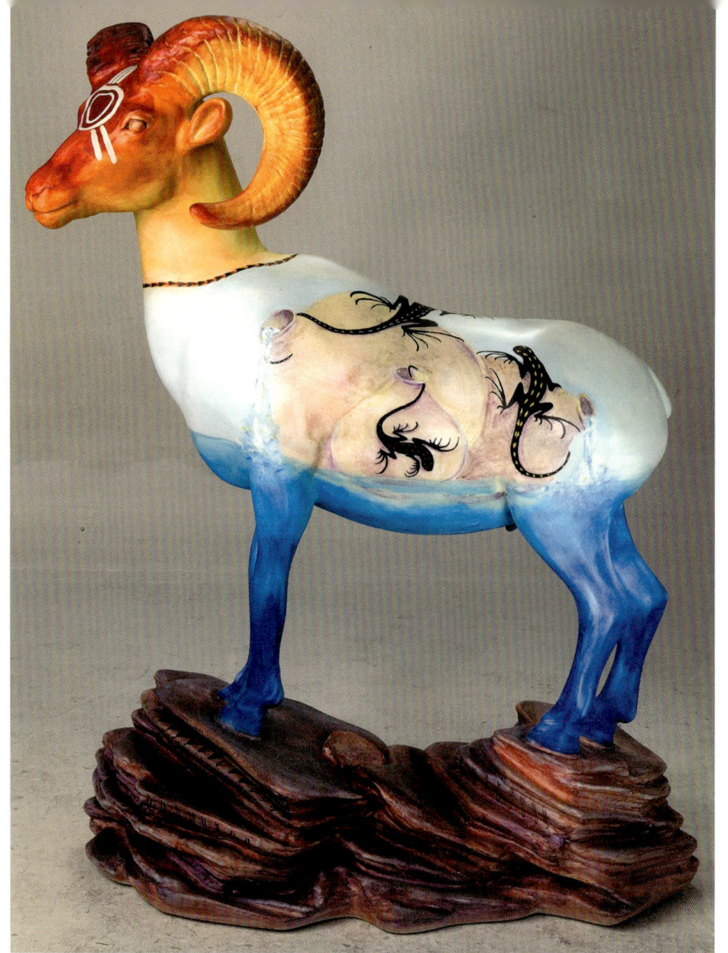

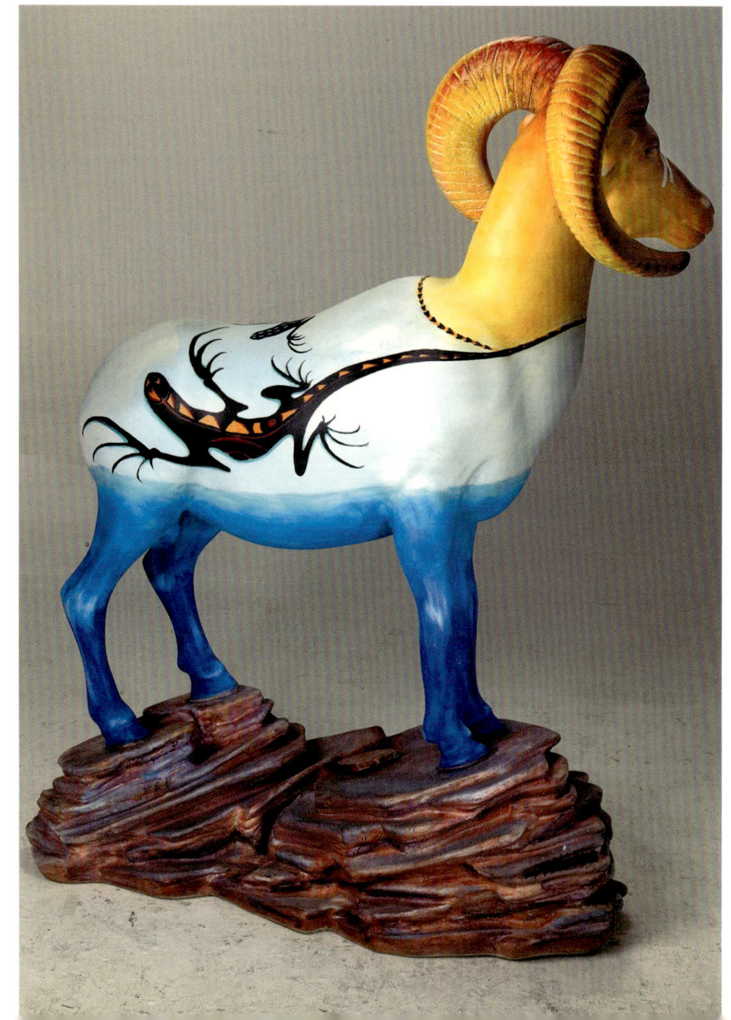

Kokopelli Fun

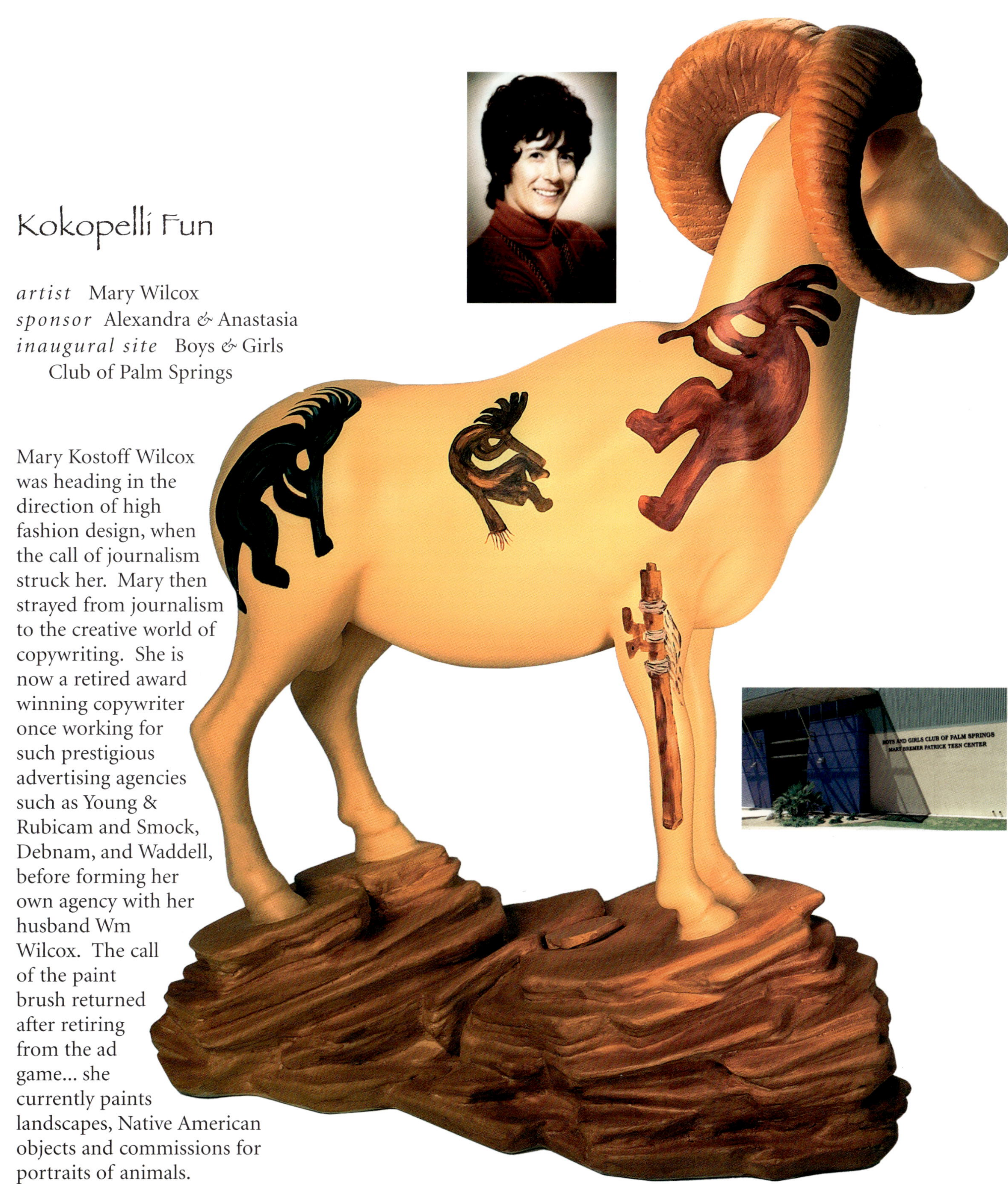

artist Mary Wilcox
sponsor Alexandra *&* Anastasia
inaugural site Boys *&* Girls
    Club of Palm Springs

Mary Kostoff Wilcox was heading in the direction of high fashion design, when the call of journalism struck her. Mary then strayed from journalism to the creative world of copywriting. She is now a retired award winning copywriter once working for such prestigious advertising agencies such as Young & Rubicam and Smock, Debnam, and Waddell, before forming her own agency with her husband Wm Wilcox. The call of the paint brush returned after retiring from the ad game... she currently paints landscapes, Native American objects and commissions for portraits of animals.

Counting Sheep

artist Lisa Patencio
sponsor Alexandra Sheldon
inaugural site Tahquitz Canyon Visitors Center

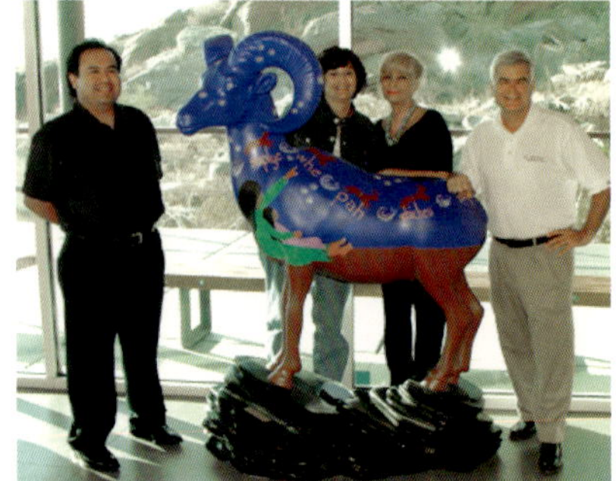

"Counting Sheep" at the unveiling in the Tahquitz Canyon Visitors Center with artist Lisa Patencio (center). Her husband Moraino Patencio stands to her left. Alexandra Sheldon and Michael Hammond Director of Agua Caliente Cultural Museum stand on the right of Lisa.

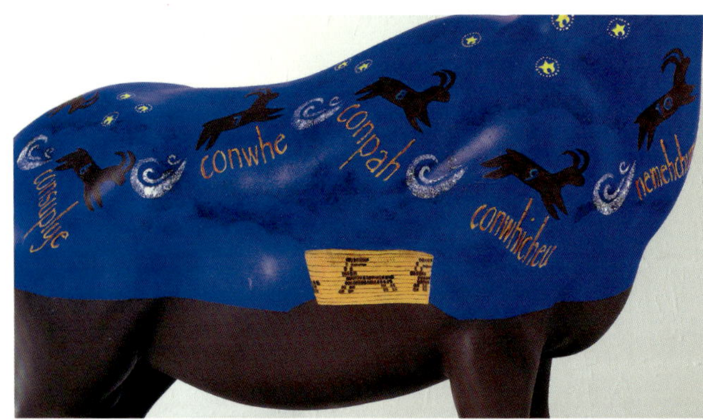

I was flattered beyond words, when Alexandra Sheldon asked me to paint a ram for her. The Path of the Bighorn is a wonderful project to preserve the lives of the bighorn sheep. As anyone who has done a sheep will tell you, it was so hard to let Gary Zornes pick it up and take it away. You really can feel the majestic quiet beauty of these animals while you're painting them.

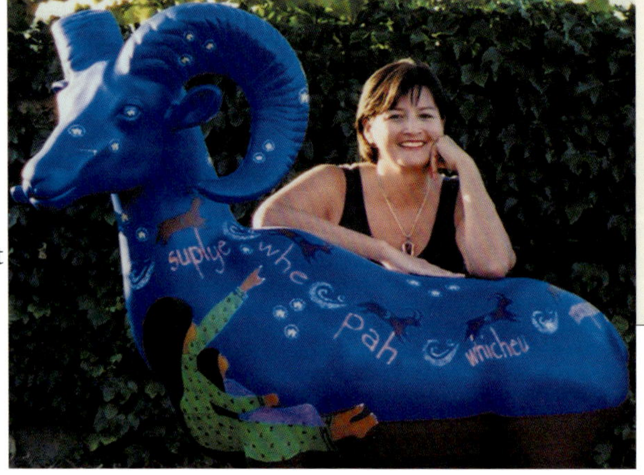

My design concept comes from a basket made by Mrs. Soto of the Augustine Reservation. A Cahuilla mother is counting bighorn sheep to her sleepy daughter. The sheep range across a night sky with the numbers written in Cahuilla below. — Lisa Patencio

Mr. Starry Night

artist Joan Braunstein
sponsor Sheldon's
inaugural site Pacific Mortgage -
    Palm Springs

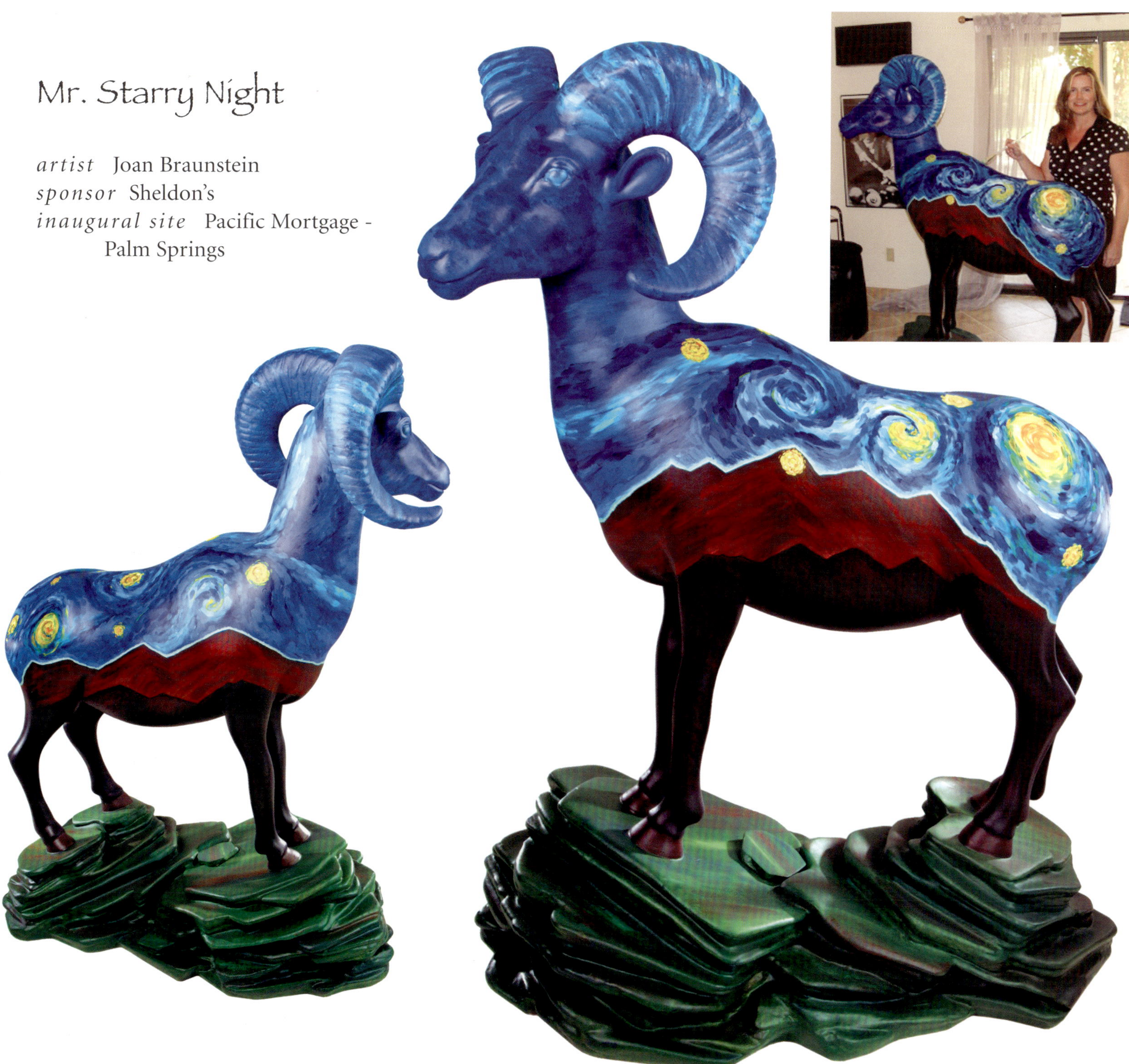

In Honor of Diego Rivera

artist Felipe Hernandez
sponsor Dr. Joel *&* Leslie Hirschberg
inaugural site Tesoros del Pueblo at
The Corridor

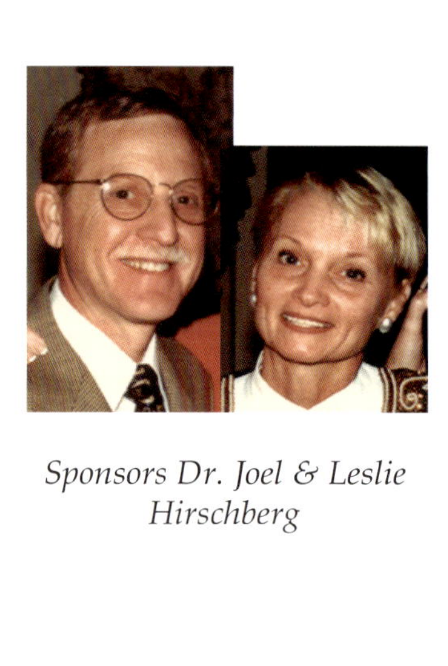

*Sponsors Dr. Joel & Leslie
Hirschberg*

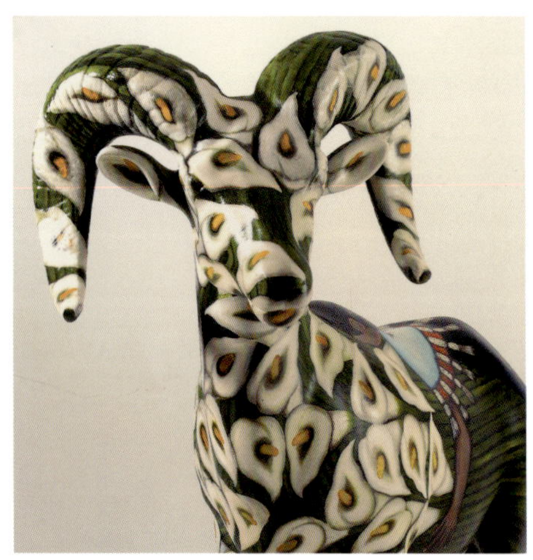

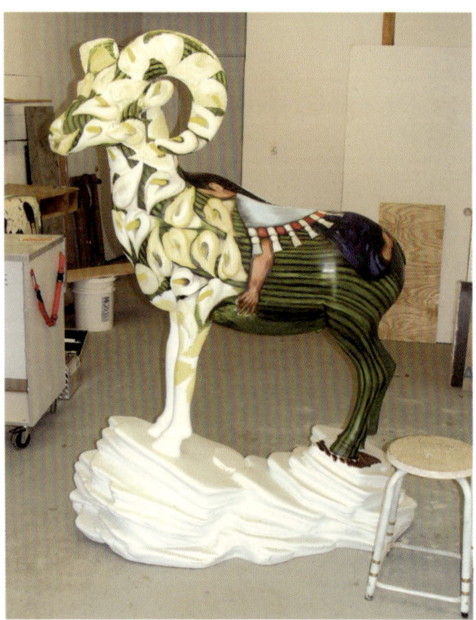

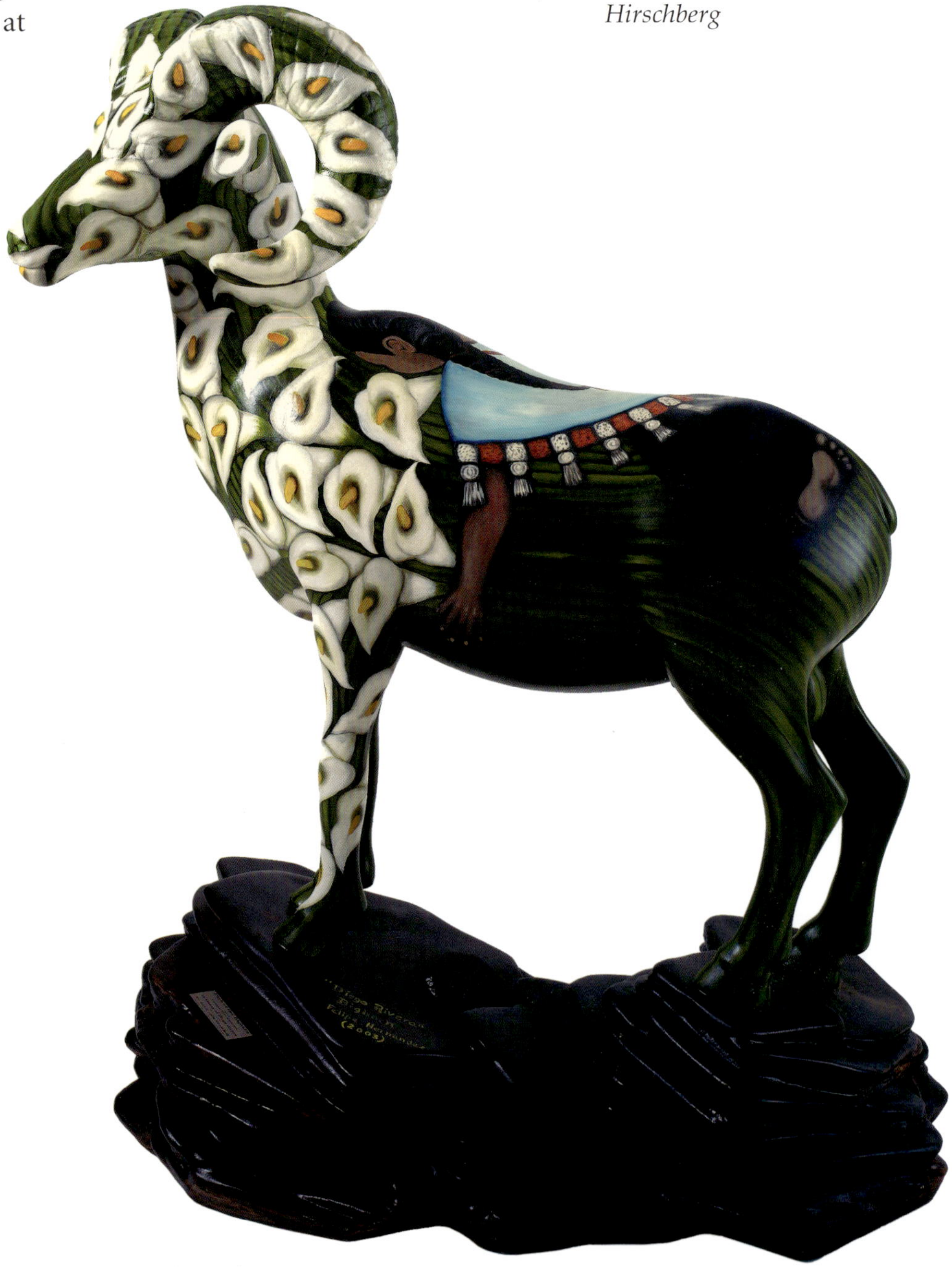

Ram I Am

artist Taylor Robinette
sponsor Sheldon's
inaugural site Marriott
Desert Springs Vacation
Club

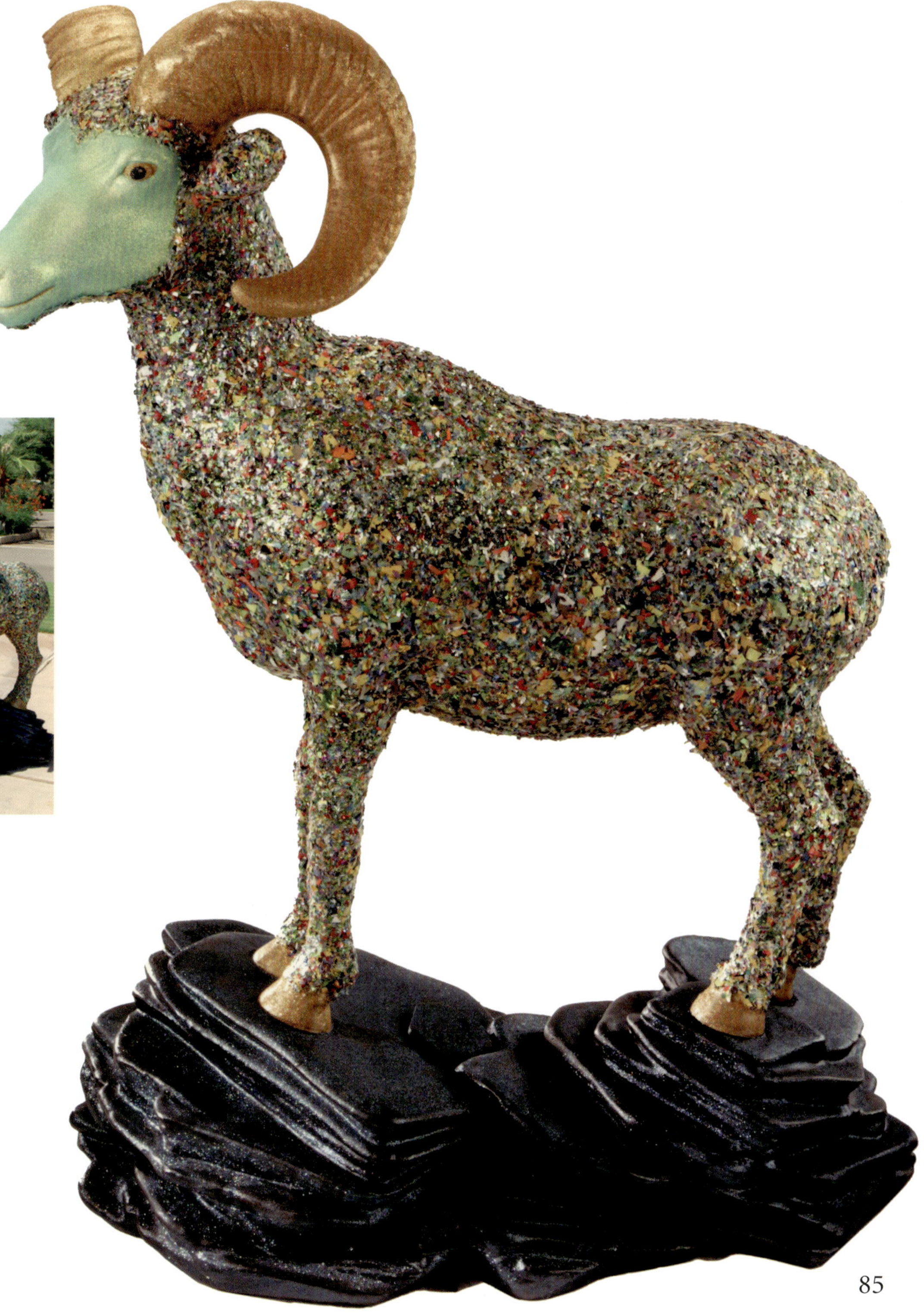

Pasquino

artist   Colin Webster-Watson
sponsor   Mike & Bob Pollock
inaugural site   Palm Springs City Hall

The statue is adorned with poems composed by the artist and written by him on his handmade paper.

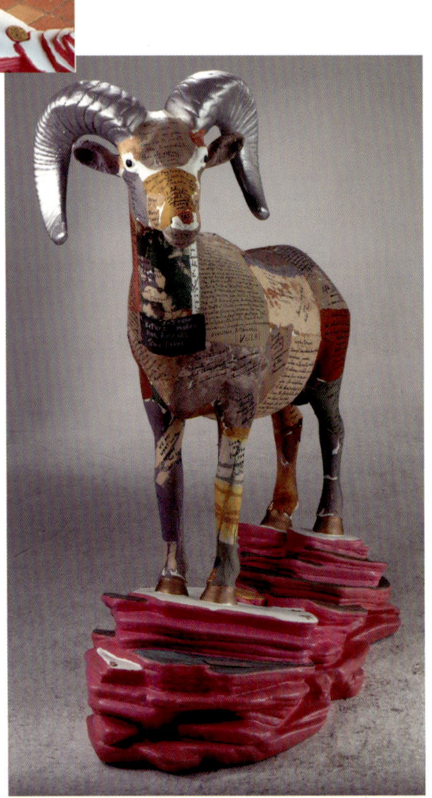

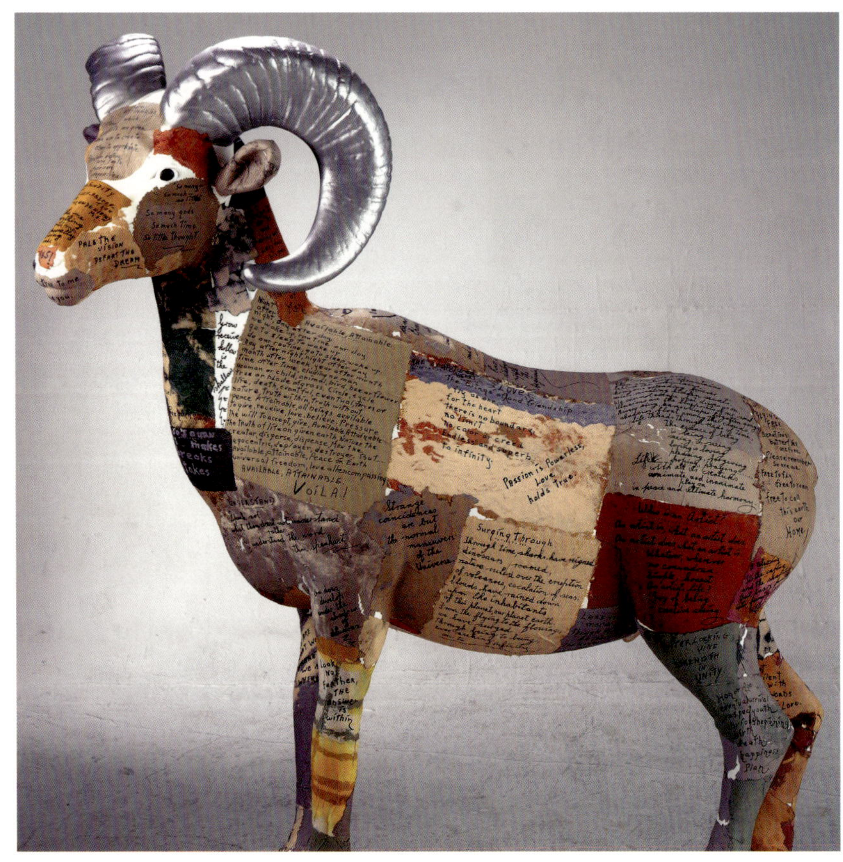

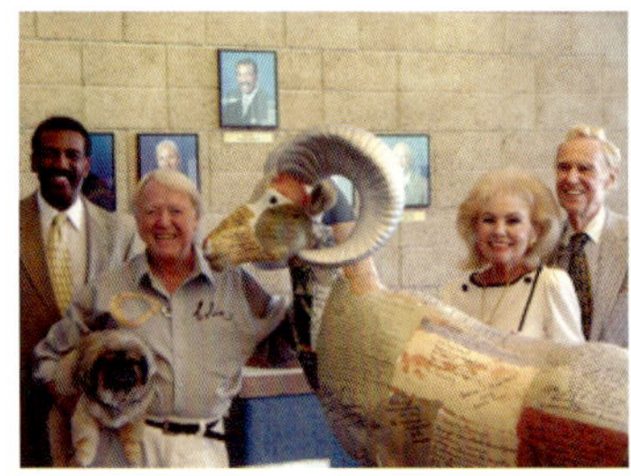

Palm Springs Mayor Ron Oden
Artist Colin Webster-Watson
with sponsors
Mike & Bob Pollock
unveiling ceremony at Palm
Springs City Hall

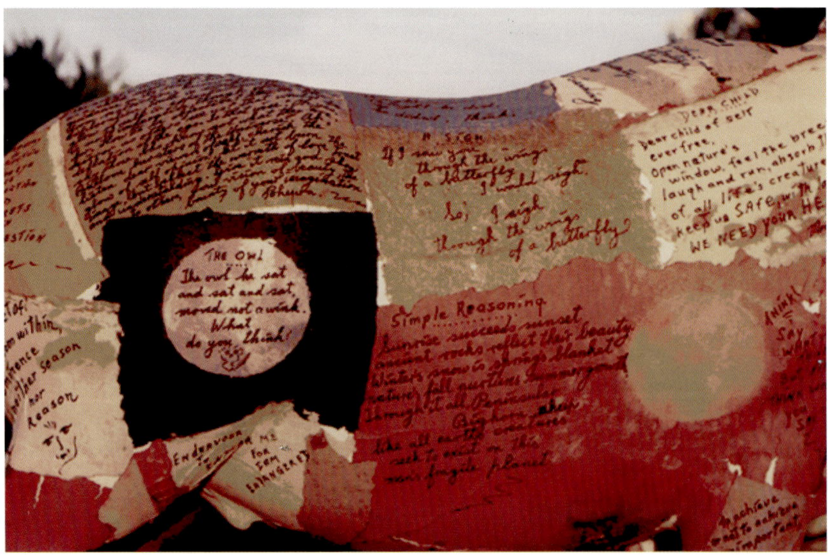

Pathways

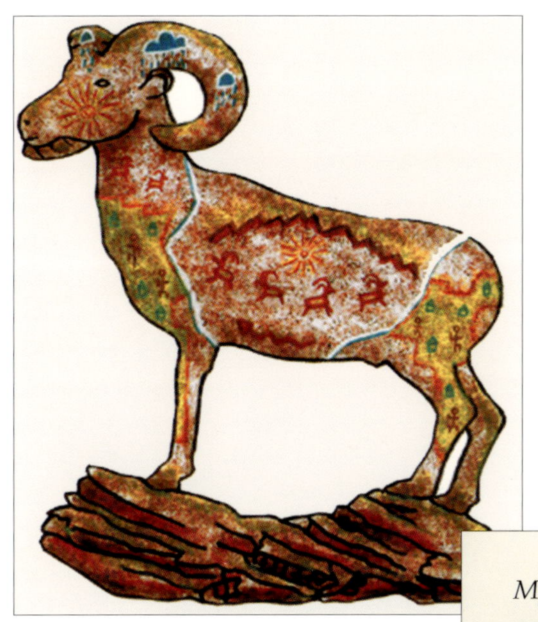

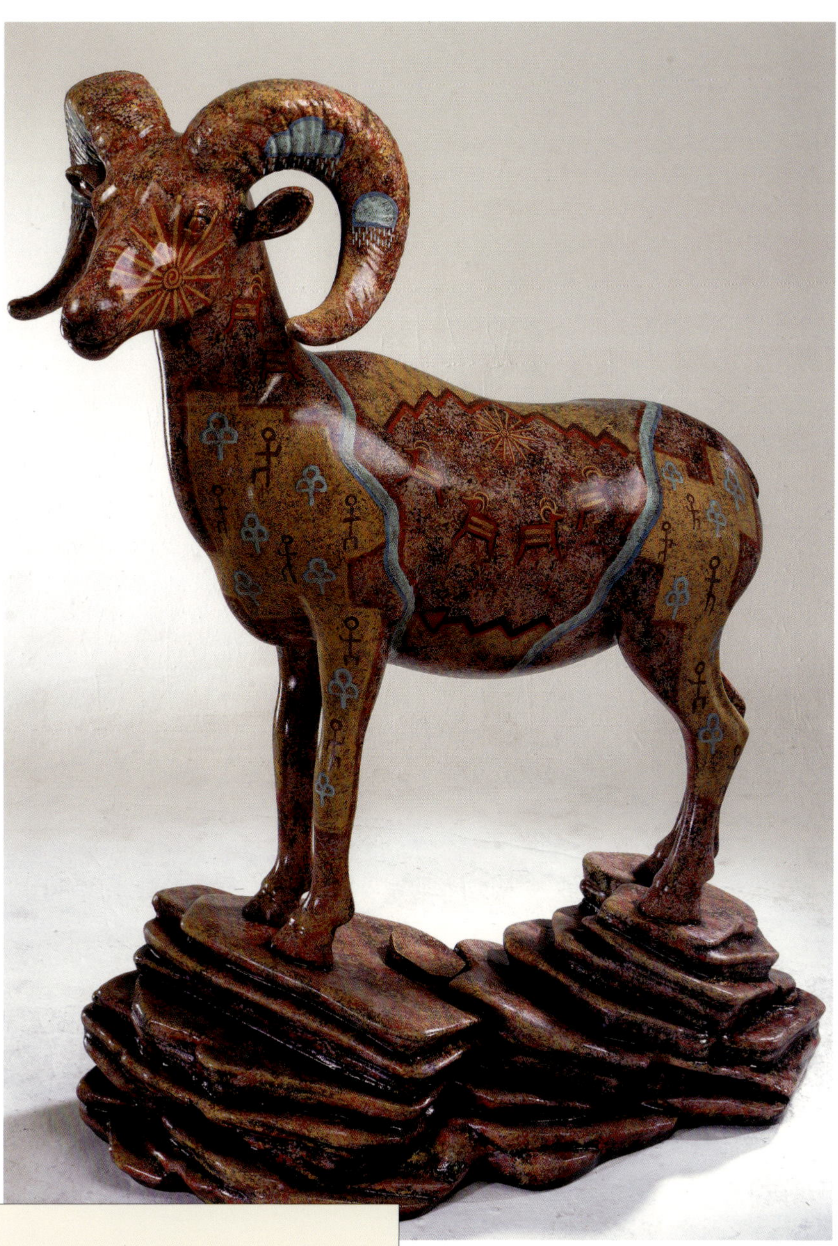

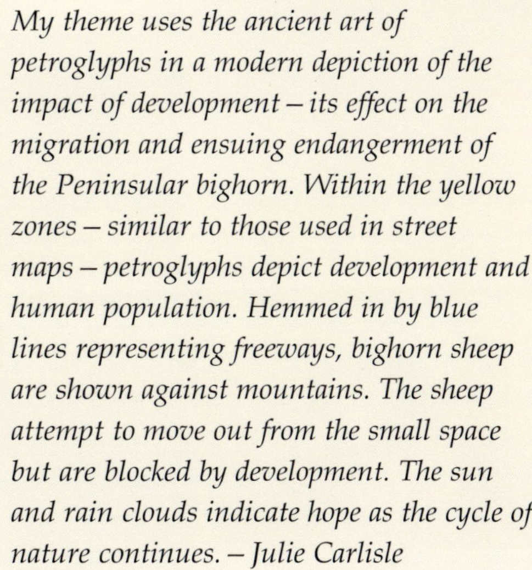

My theme uses the ancient art of petroglyphs in a modern depiction of the impact of development — its effect on the migration and ensuing endangerment of the Peninsular bighorn. Within the yellow zones — similar to those used in street maps — petroglyphs depict development and human population. Hemmed in by blue lines representing freeways, bighorn sheep are shown against mountains. The sheep attempt to move out from the small space but are blocked by development. The sun and rain clouds indicate hope as the cycle of nature continues. — Julie Carlisle

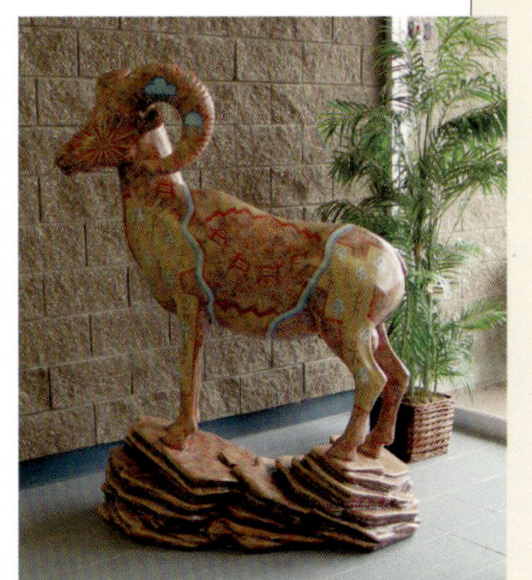

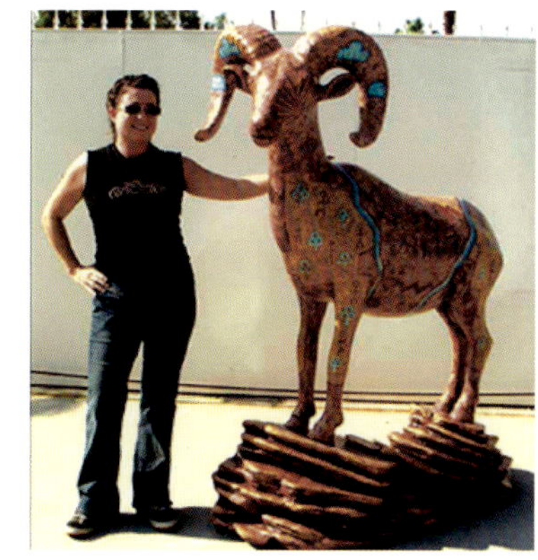

Pemtemwhaha

artist Ojay Venagas
sponsor Agua Caliente Cultural Museum
inaugural site Aqua Caliente Cultural Museum

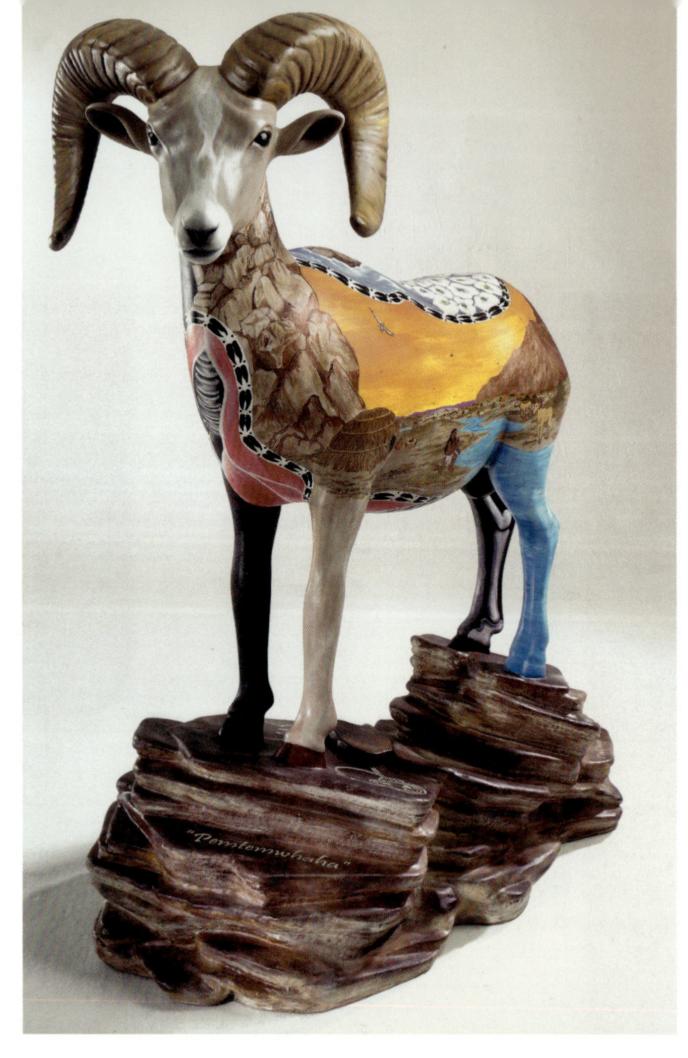

In the Cahuilla culture, Pem-tem-wha-ha, the guardian of hooved animals, is a powerful and respected deity who protects bighorn sheep, antelope, and deer.

The left side of my ram depicts a prehistoric landscape of the Coachella Valley in the daytime, with granite rock representing the San Jacinto Mountains. A Cahuilla hunter stands opposite a ram, symbolic of the ecological relationship between the Cahuilla people and bighorn sheep. In the background, sheep are migrating from the local mountains to the valley floor.

On the right side is a night scene with a mountain Cahuilla family and traditional Bird Singers performing a ceremony honoring Pem-tem-wha-ha. Translucent spirits with ram heads fly out of the fire pit and ascend into the sky.

On the back of the ram are water babies — spirits that live in springs. The water flows down and turns into a bouquet of jimsonweed flowers, plants that are intrinsic to Cahuilla shamanism.

I am grateful to Dr. Lowell Bean, an expert on Cahuilla life, for his assistance with my research, and to Cahuilla elder Alvino Siva, who approved my design.

— O'Jay T. Vanegas

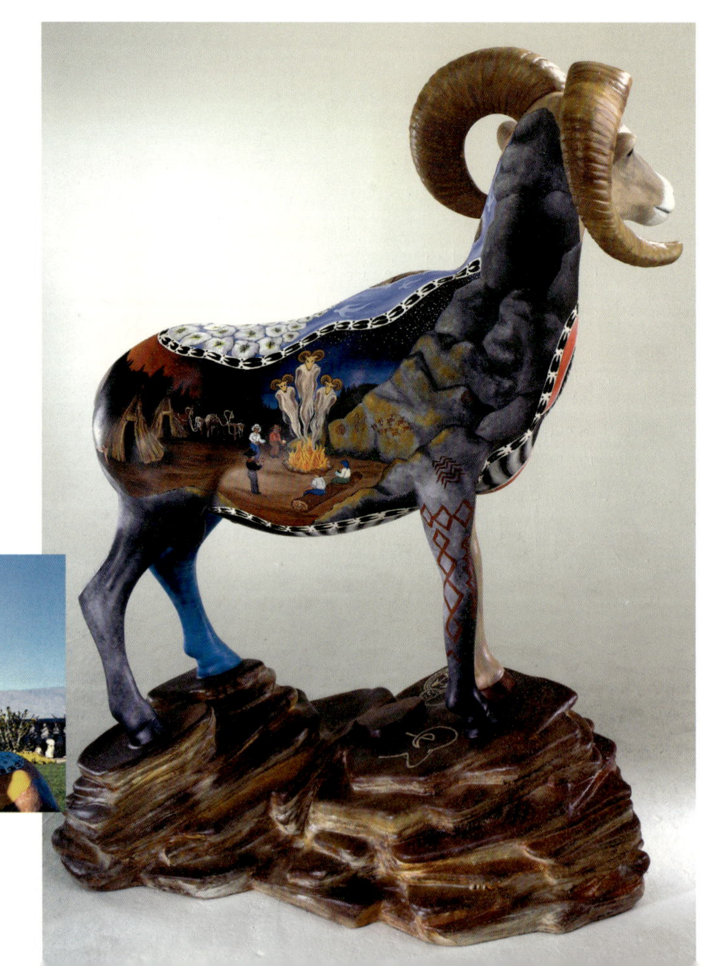

Ramses I

artist Vesna Breznikar
sponsor Tom Zornes
inaugural site Cathedral City City Hall

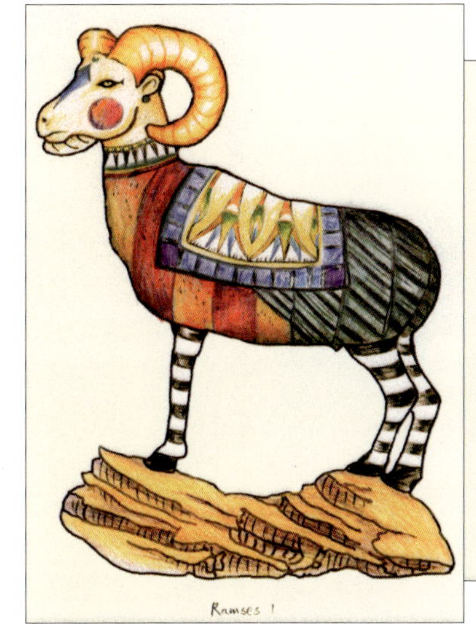

The design is inspired by the Egyptian pharaoh Ramses II. During his reign, he transformed the desert area with his wonderous sculptural architecture. The ancient Egyptians revered the natural world and decorated their buildings with pictures of the surrounding flora and fauna, painted in brilliant colors. (Ramses I celebrates the same spirit in Palm Springs.) — Vesna Breznikar

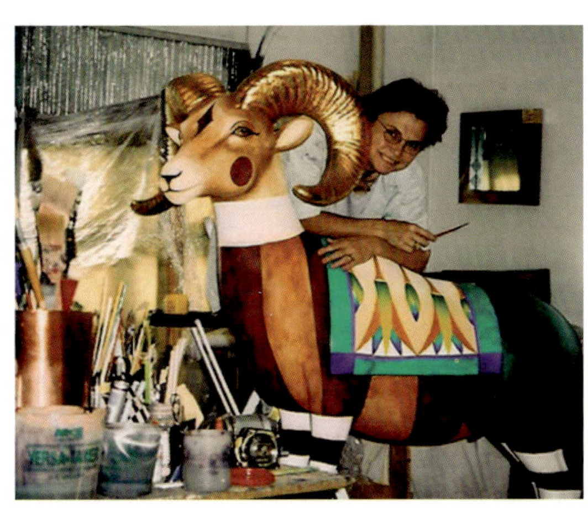

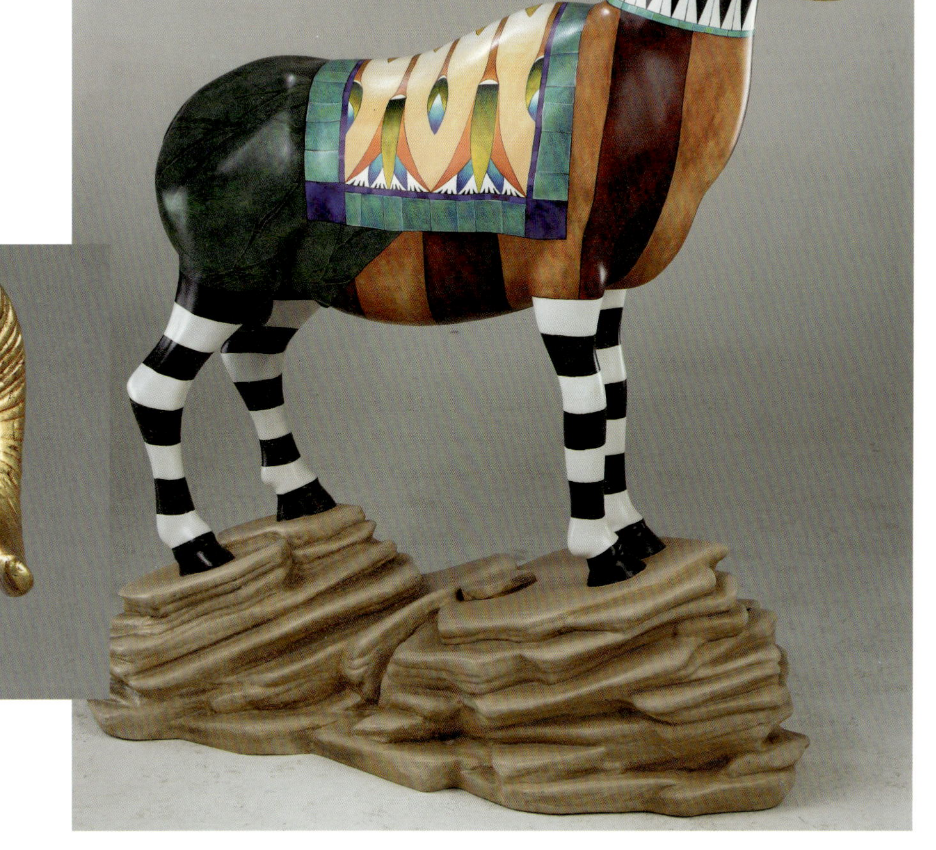

Southwest State of Grace

artist Paul Magloff
sponsor Craig Williams
inaugural site Wyndham Hotel

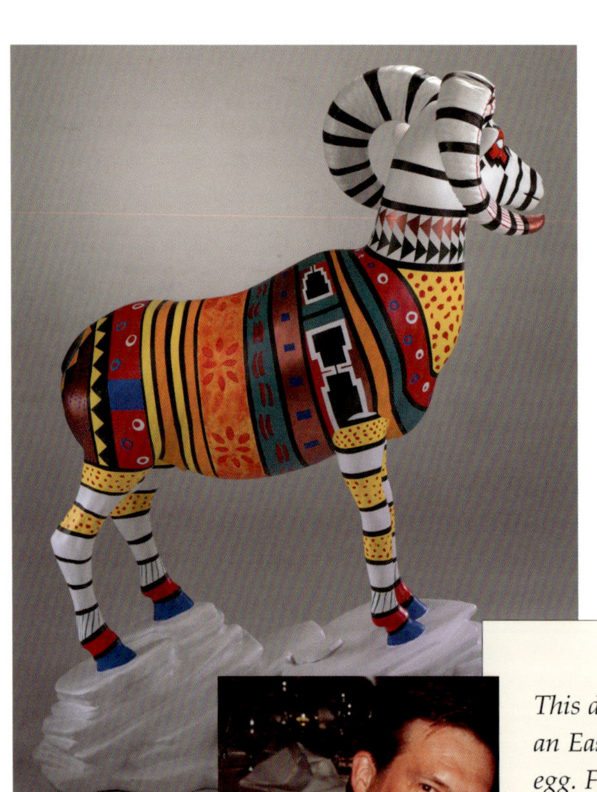

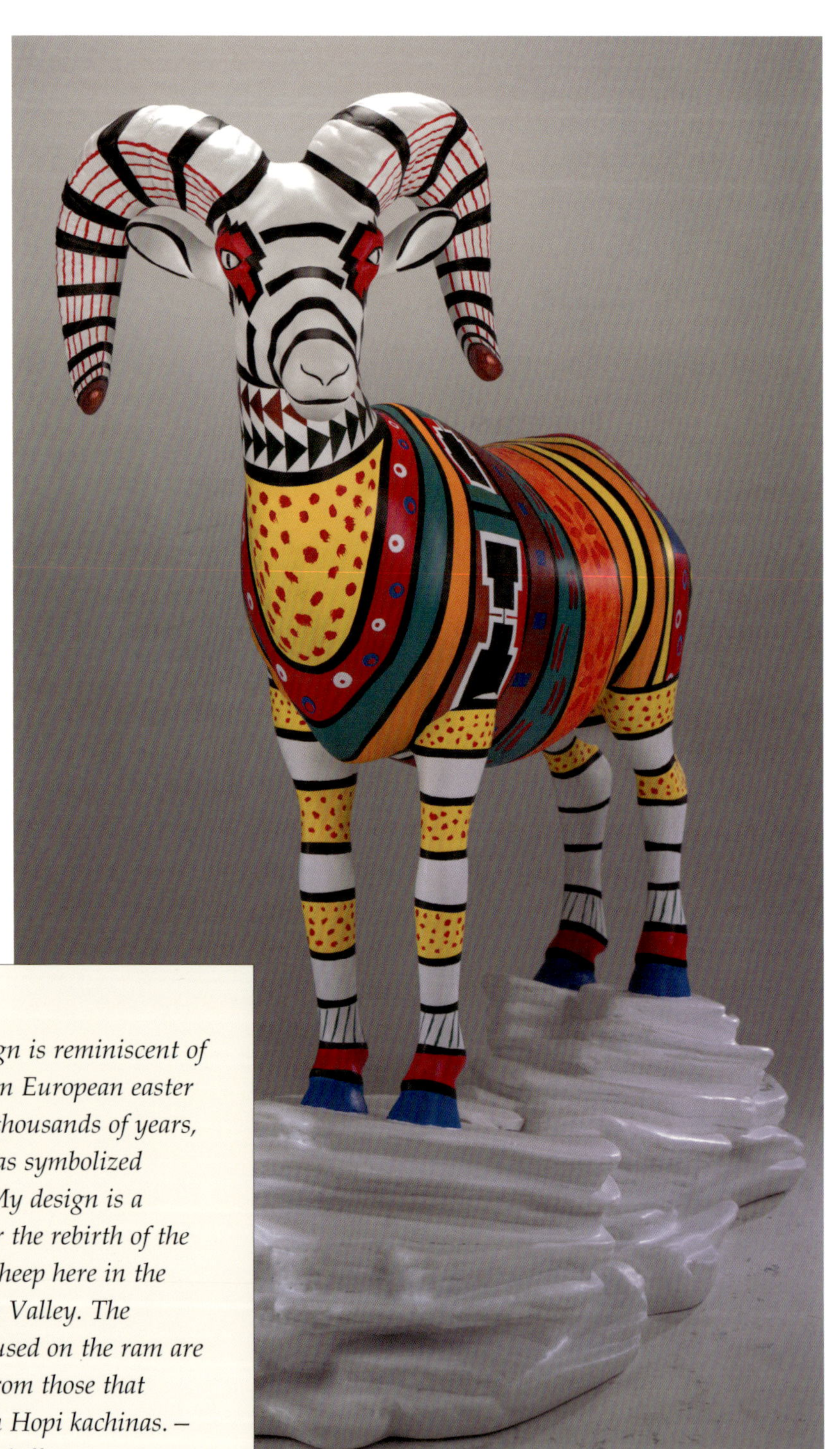

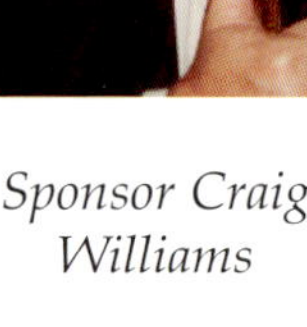

Sponsor Craig
Williams

This design is reminiscent of an Eastern European easter egg. For thousands of years, the egg has symbolized rebirth. My design is a prayer for the rebirth of the bighorn sheep here in the Coachella Valley. The symbols used on the ram are derived from those that appear on Hopi kachinas. — Paul Magloff

Ram through the Ages

artist   D.J. Hall
sponsor   Leonore Annenberg
inaugural site   Palm Springs Desert Museum

D.J. Hall was born in Santa Ana, California. A third-generation Californian, she brings a unique perspective to her portrayals of California life. After earning her BFA from USC in 1973, she has devoted herself to painting full-time ever since. Her works are in numerous public collections, including the Metropolitan Museum of Art. She has exhibited in group shows around the world, and has held solo shows in New York and Los Angeles almost every year since graduation from USC. Currently, she teaches life drawing at Los Angeles' Otis Art Institute.

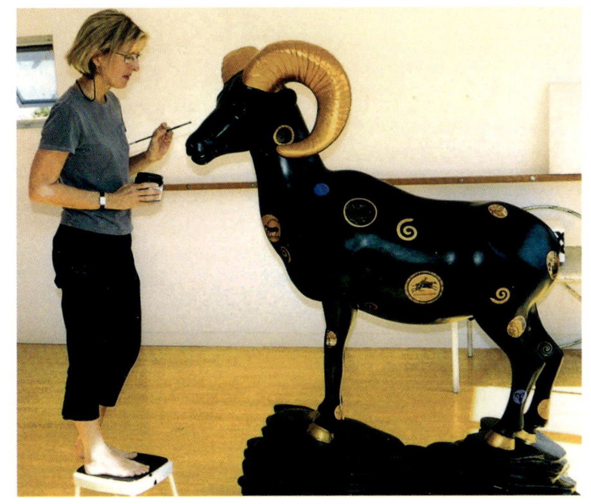

D.J. Hall has won many awards - a few include Archives of American Art, Smithsonian Institution, Washington D.C. 6th Annual Heritage Award, presented by the Santa Monica Heritage Museum, Santa Monica, California for contributions to the cultural heritage of the Santa Monica Bay Community "D.J. Hall Papers", Smithsonian Archives of American Art, Washington D.C.

Spirits of the Santa Rosas

artist Louisa Martin
sponsor Trump 29 Casino
inaugural site Trump 29 Casino

My interest in the history, culture, and art of Native Americans developed while growing up in Colorado and focuses on the Native American women between 1760 and 1920. This was a tragic time of dramatic change, yet Native American women continued in tasks central to daily life and the survival of their families — food was gathered, meals were prepared, children were born, and vast numbers of functional, beautiful objects were fashioned. These objects are valued today not only as artwork, but as a testament to the strength and spirit of these women.
— Louisa Martin

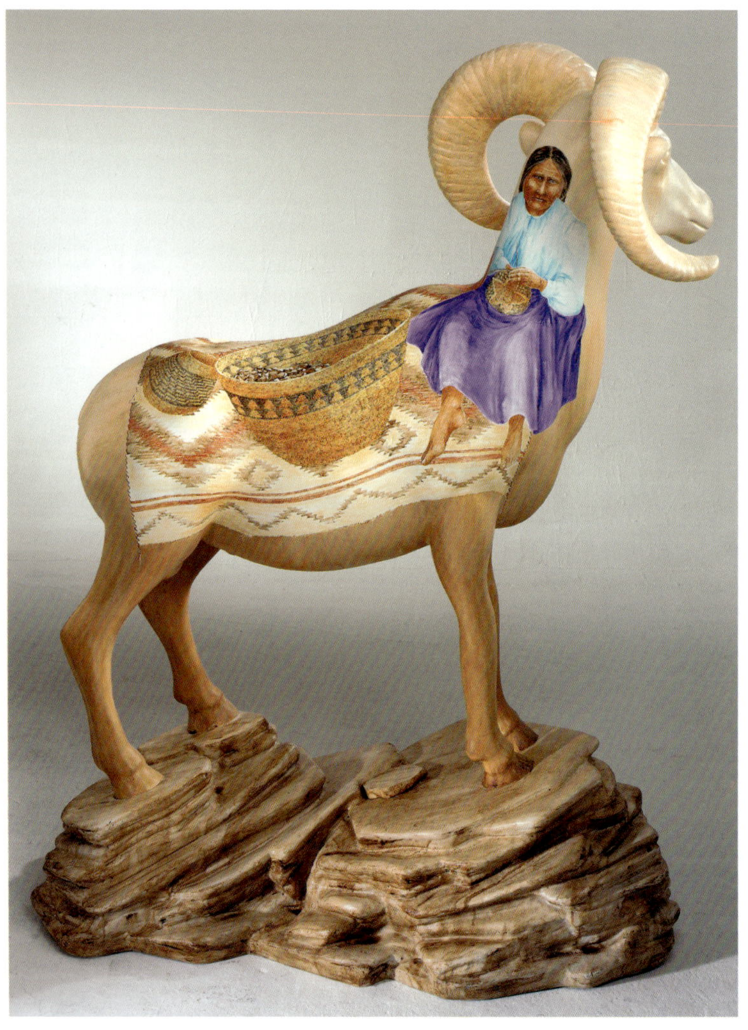

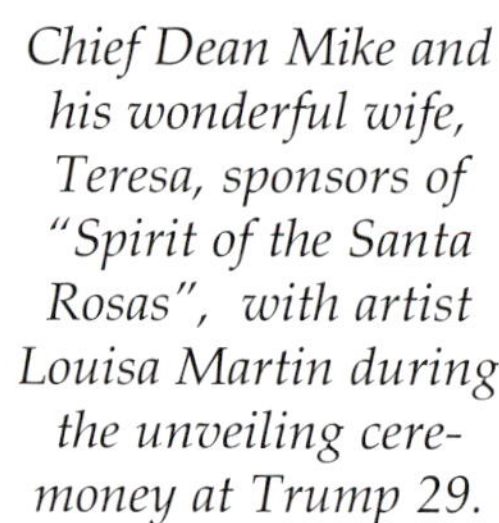

Chief Dean Mike and his wonderful wife, Teresa, sponsors of "Spirit of the Santa Rosas", with artist Louisa Martin during the unveiling ceremoney at Trump 29.

Bird Songs were performed to protect the bighorn sheep

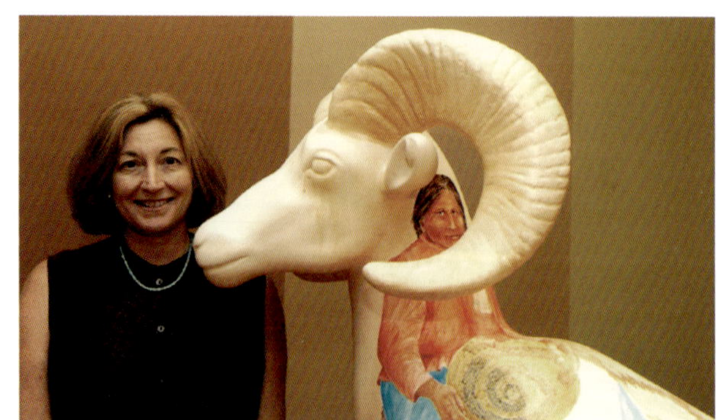

The Guardian

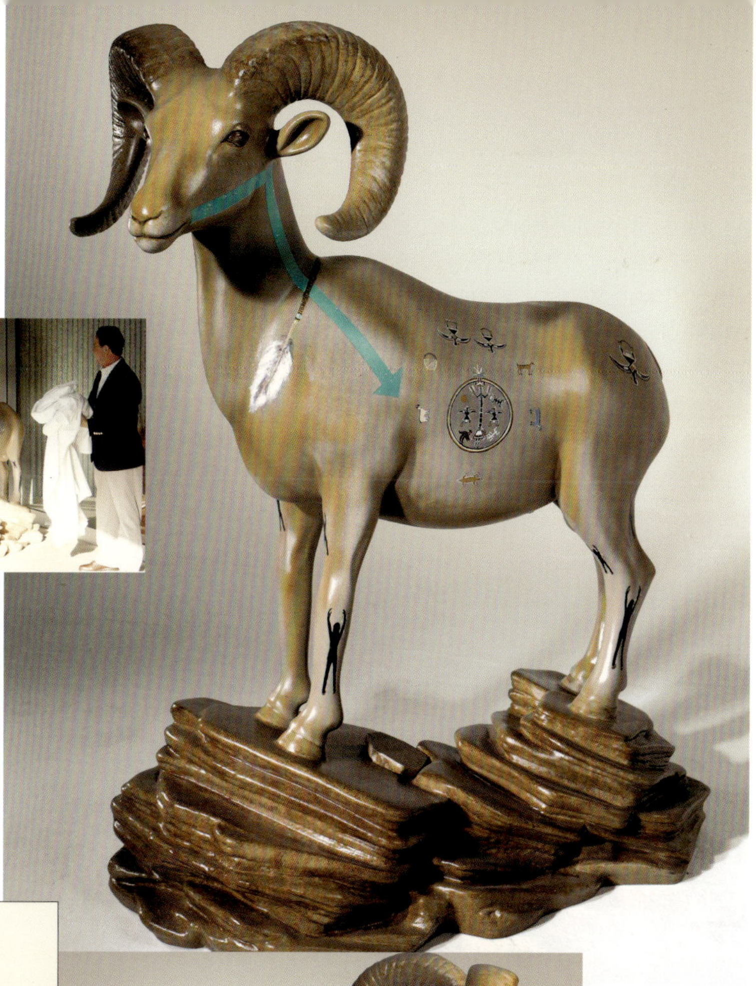

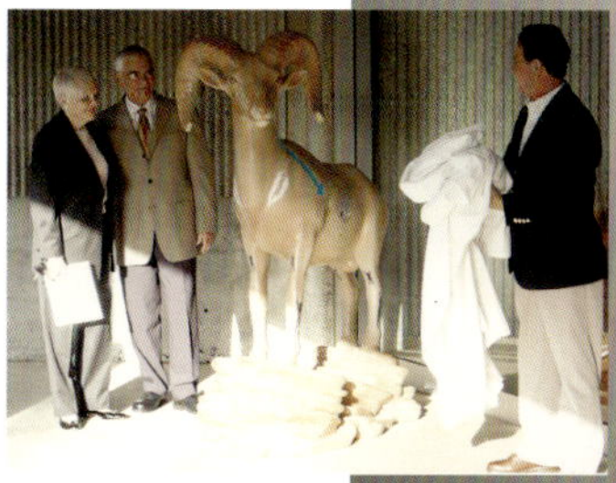

artist Gary Zornes
sponsor Dr. Stuart & Pat Barton
inaugural site Luci Curci Cancer Center

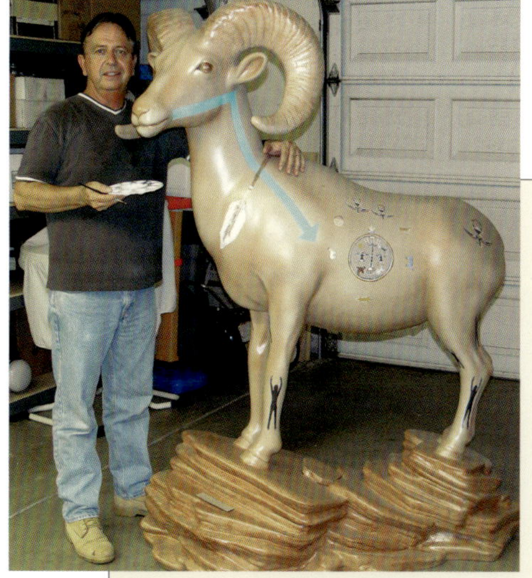

The Native Americans — of whom I am proud to have heritage — held the earth and the animals that inhabited it in great respect. They were the first Guardians, shown here in the form of a protective blanket of sand paintings depicting the protection and nurturing of a young boy. The heart line depicts healing and long life; the two white feathers are in memory of a special friend who is no longer with us. As the once plentiful herds of magnificent Peninsular bighorn sheep began to dwindle to near extinction, new Guardians have stepped forward to take up the gauntlet and carry on a very worthwhile cause. Through the tireless efforts of Bighorn Institute and the wildlife agencies, this proud and cherished animal once again has an opportunity to thrive. — Gary Zornes*
**See Appendix for narrative*

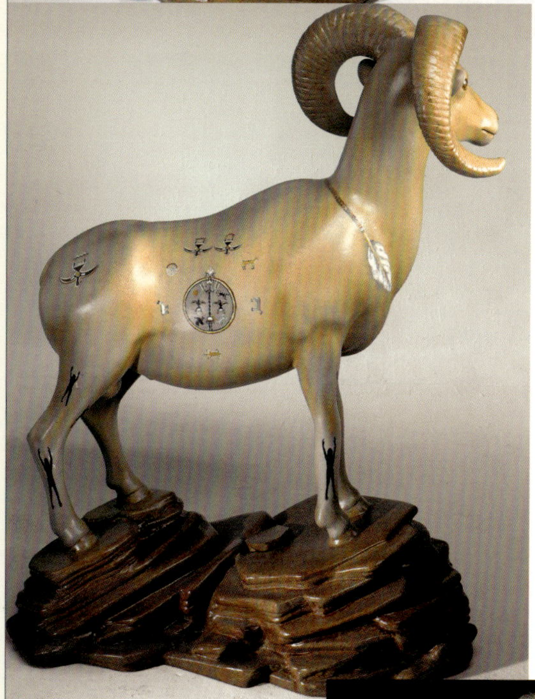

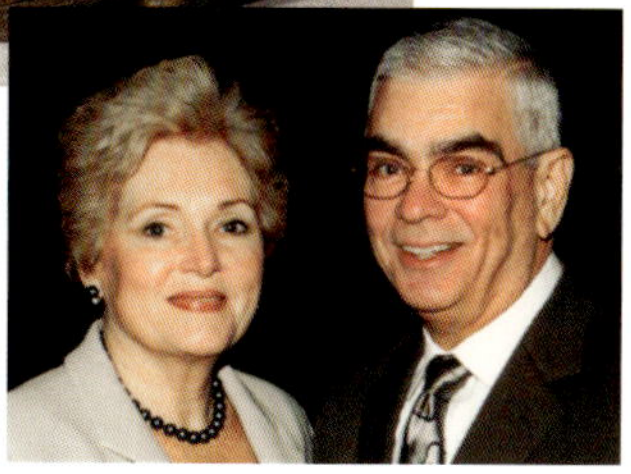

*Sponsors Pat Barton &
Dr. Stuart Barton*

Connecting with Our World

The range of expression seen in these rams speak of the different perspectives, diverse cultures, and rich imagination that abound in the Coachella Valley. Some artists employ detailed realism; some use abstraction. Several artists explore serious issues, while others reveal a delightful sense of humor. Regardless of the style of decoration or the theme chosen, every ram represents the personal voice, talent, and creativity of its maker.

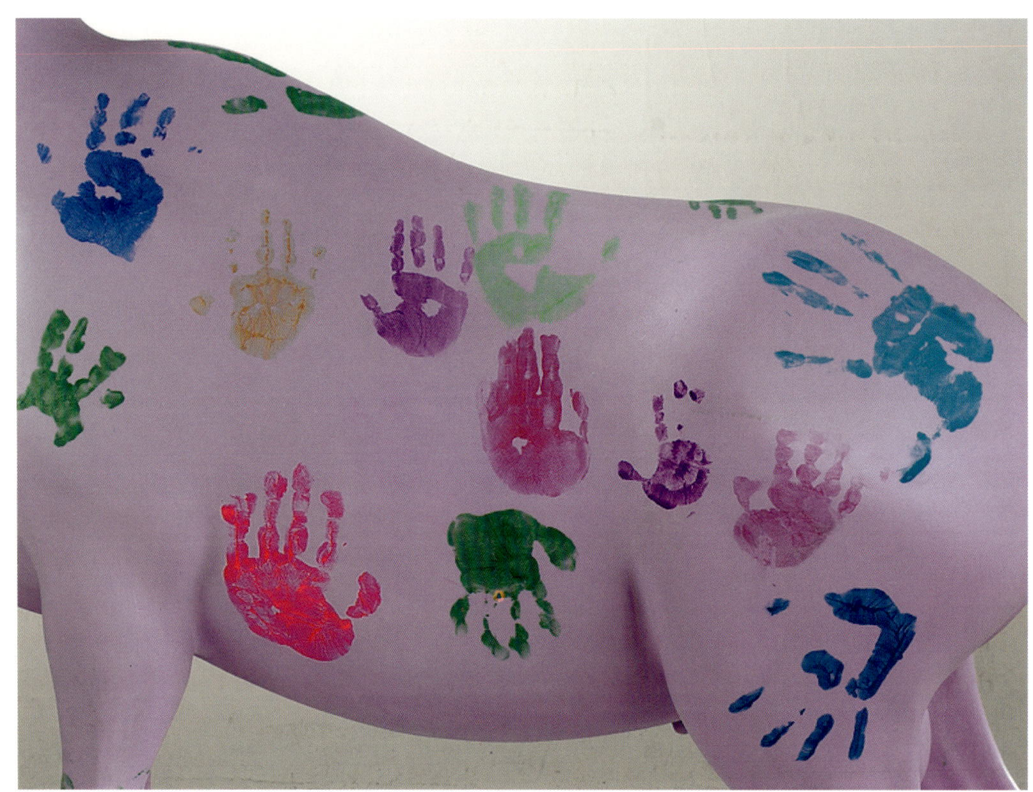

Details from "Helping Hands" ram sculpture painted by Maureen Alsop & children of Cahuilla Elementary School.

And Life Goes On…?

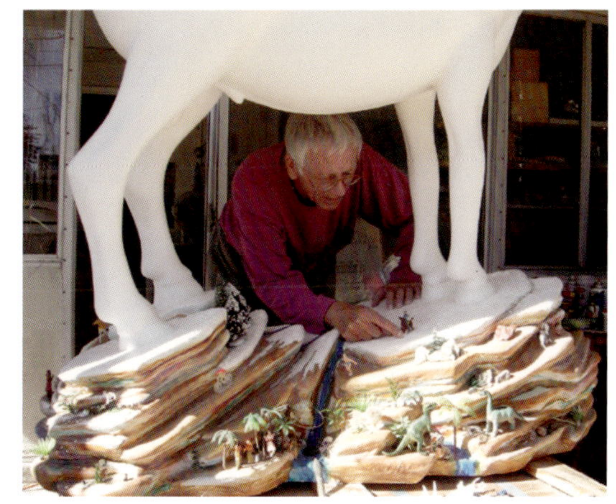

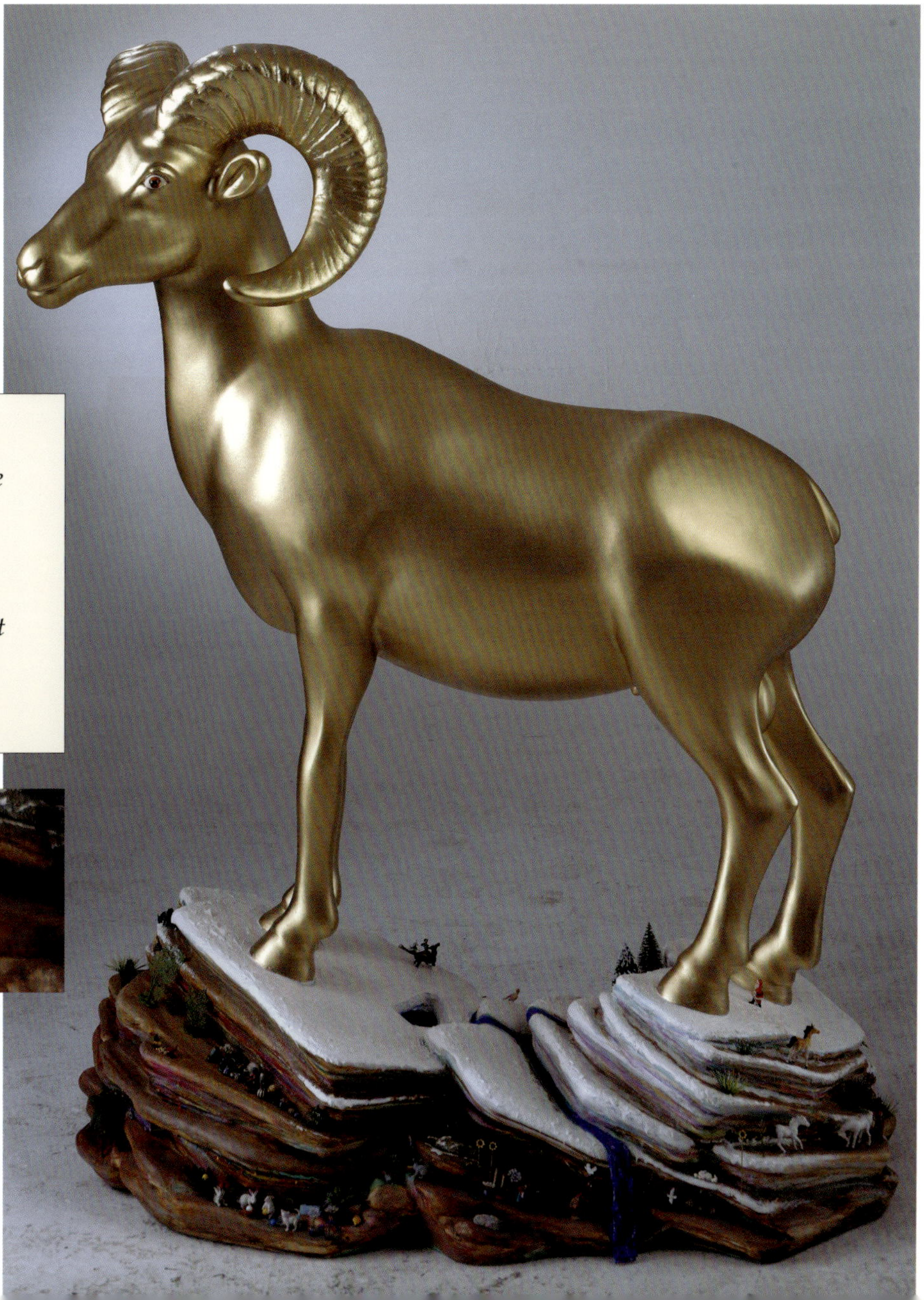

I'm interested in bringing out the form of the ram rather than putting a picture on the side of it. For the color, I decided on gold because of its history of value, worth, and beauty. It also functions when the gold shines at a distance — then you come up to it and see the Lilliputian world under the ram's feet. — Bruce Houston

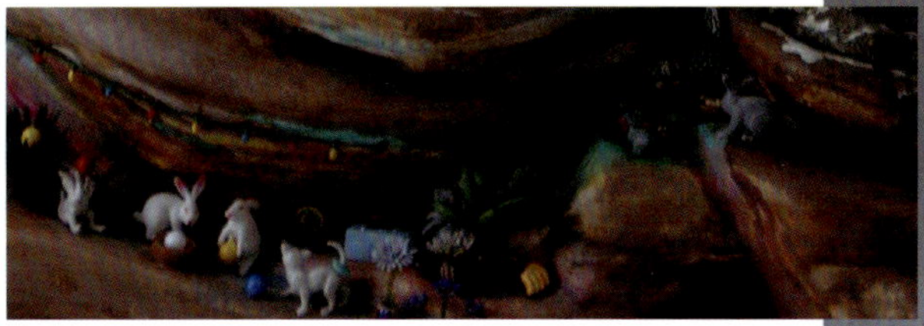

Big Horns for Bighorn

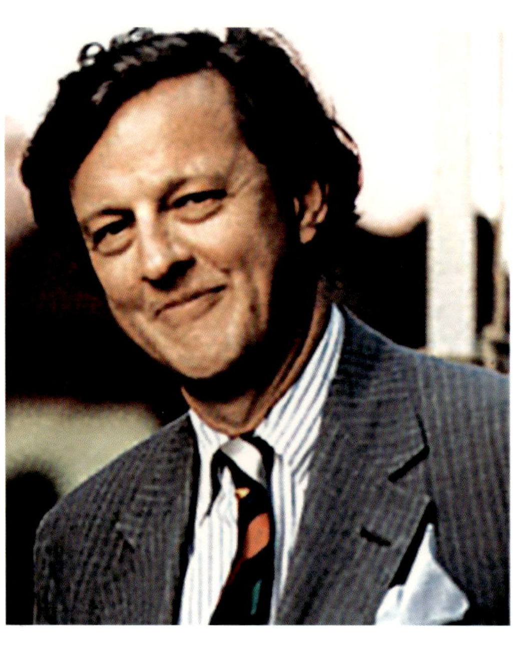

artist Ivan Chermayeff
sponsor David Peet *&* Earl Greenburg
inaugural site Children's Discovery Museum of The Desert

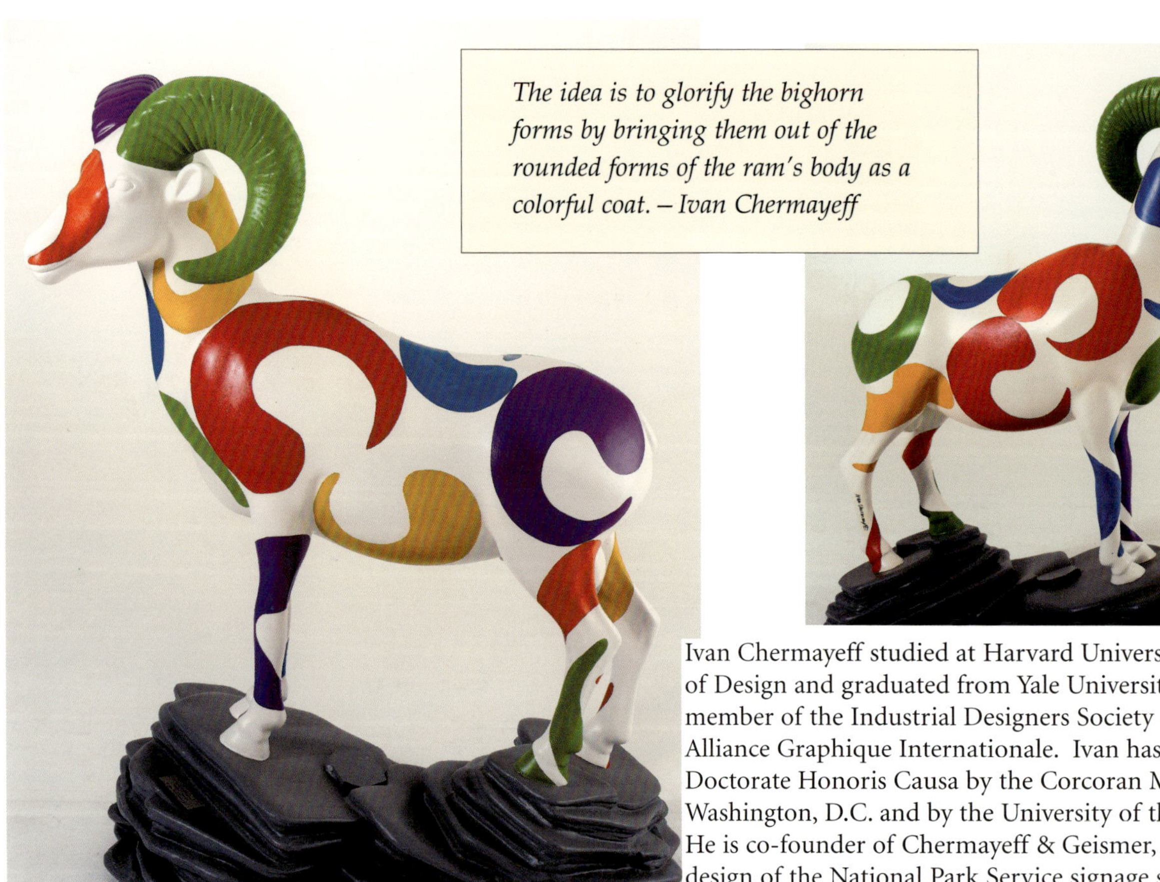

> *The idea is to glorify the bighorn forms by bringing them out of the rounded forms of the ram's body as a colorful coat. — Ivan Chermayeff*

Ivan Chermayeff studied at Harvard University, the Chicago Institute of Design and graduated from Yale University. He is a distinguished member of the Industrial Designers Society of America and the Alliance Graphique Internationale. Ivan has been awarded with a Doctorate Honoris Causa by the Corcoran Museum of Art in Washington, D.C. and by the University of the Arts in Philadelphia. He is co-founder of Chermayeff & Geismer, Inc., responsible for the design of the National Park Service signage system, the logos for the United States Bicentennial celebrations, Chase Manhattan Bank, Xerox Corporation, and Mobil Corporation. He is the author of Observations on American Architecture and Ellis Island

Eclectic Presence

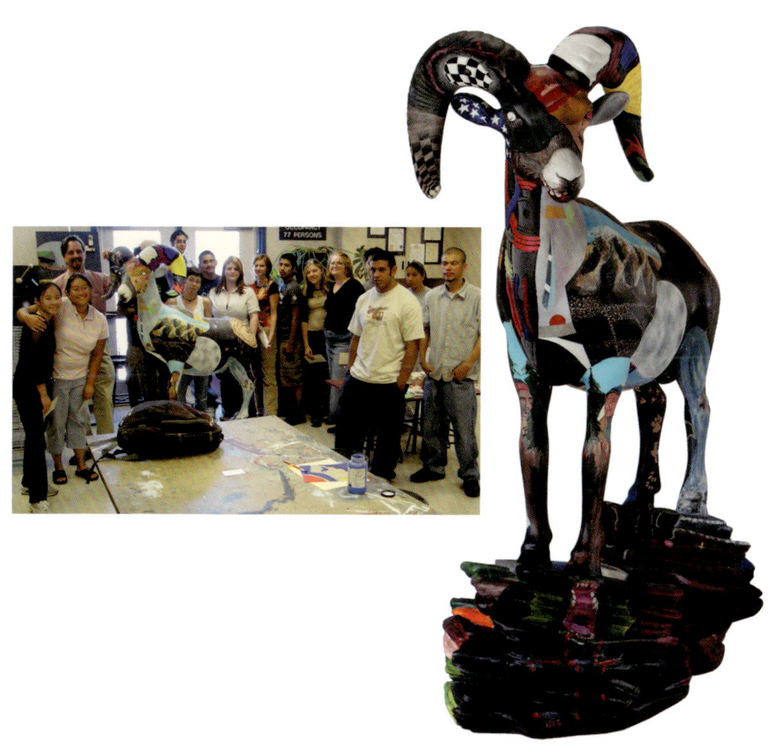

artist   James Taylor & Desert Hot Springs
           High Schools Art Students
sponsor Sheldon's
inaugural site   Desert Hot Springs High School

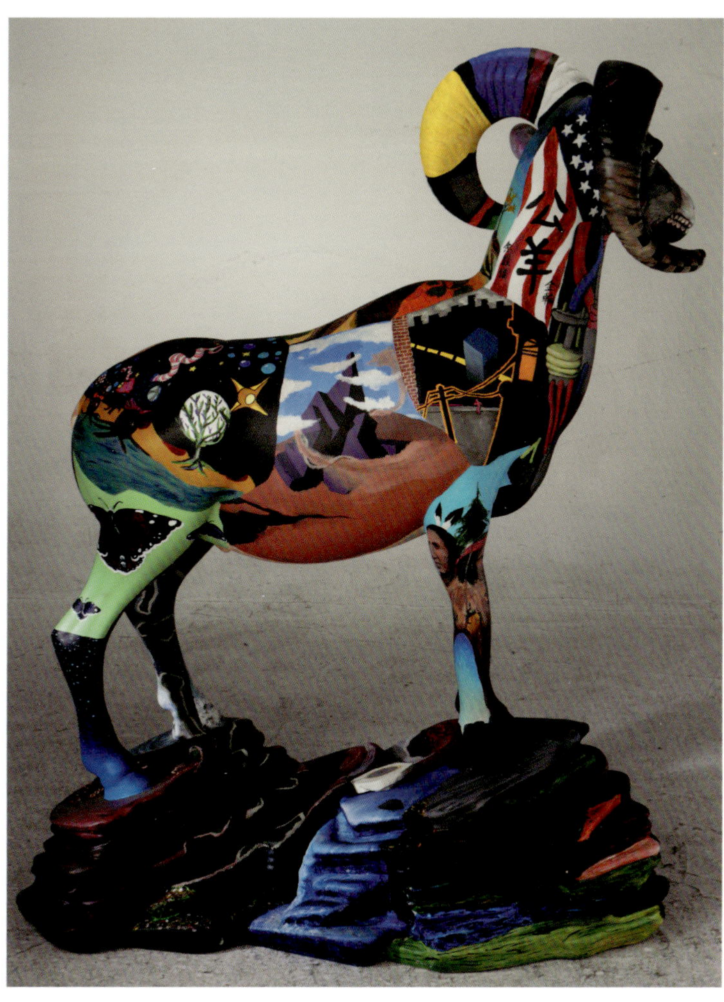

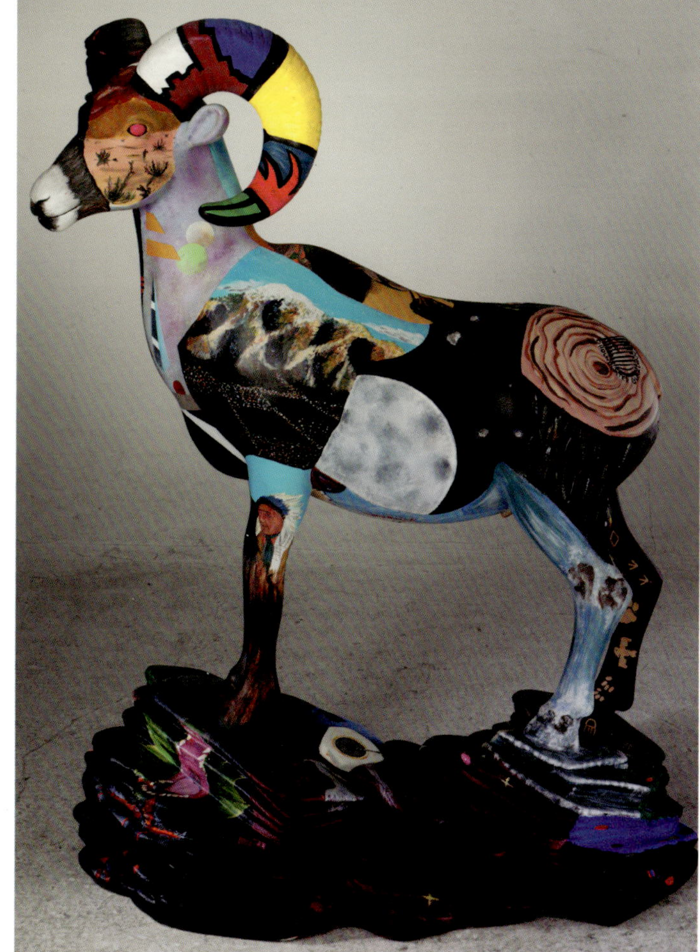

Helping Hands

artist Maureen Alsop *&* Kids
sponsor Alexandra *&* Sidney Sheldon
inaugural site Cahuilla Elementary School

The handprints are from pre-kindergarten through 5th grade students enrolled in Cahuilla Elementary School's Life Skills Program. This special education project emphasizes communication, survival, and self-help skills for children with mild to moderate delays. In addition to school-wide classroom units that incorporated lessons on the bighorn's plight into science classes, participants were able to become tangibly involved in the protection of an endangered species through a demonstration of creativity and spirit.

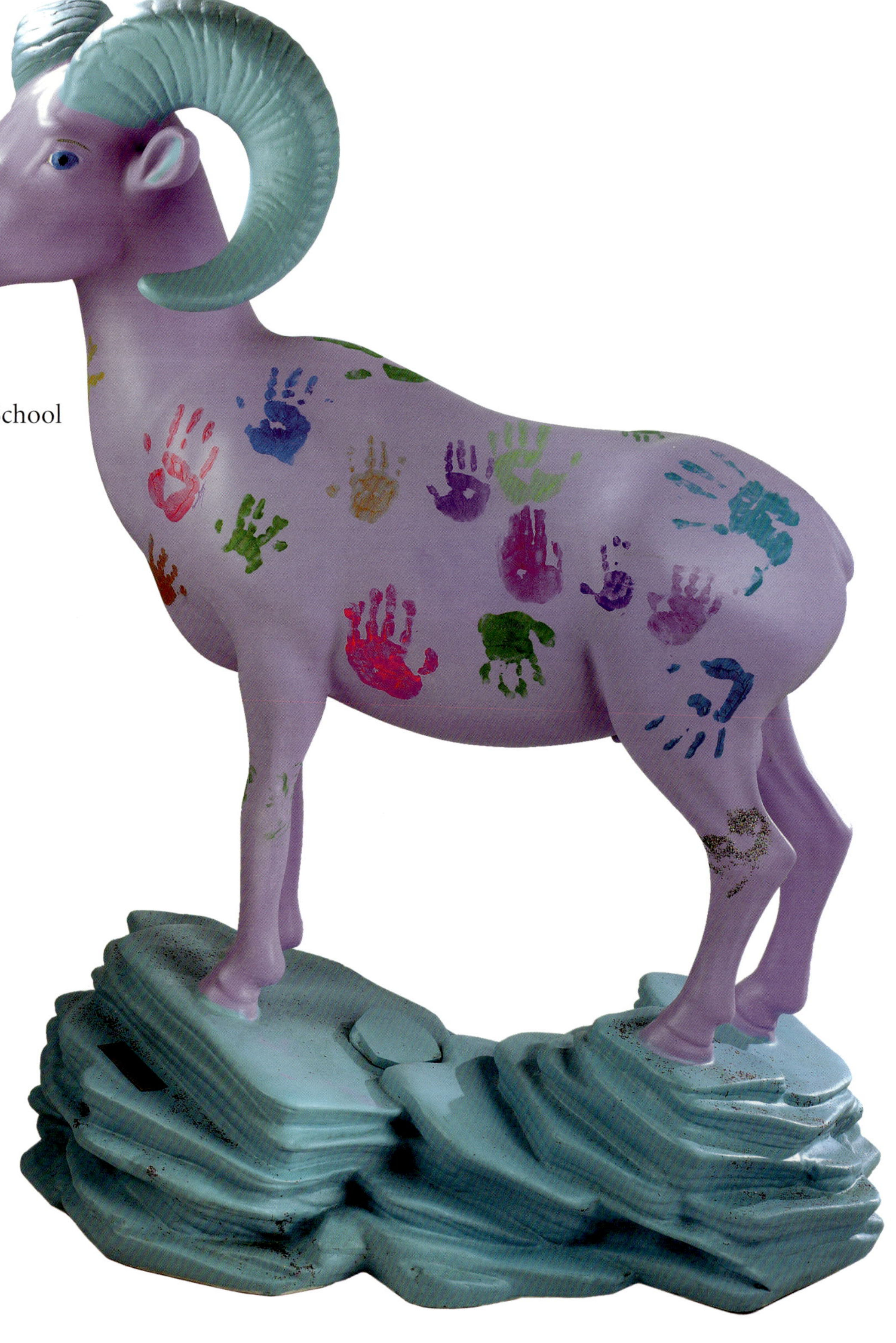

Liberty

artist Jayne Behman *&* Students
sponsor Alexandra *&* Sidney Sheldon
inaugural site Marywood Country Day School

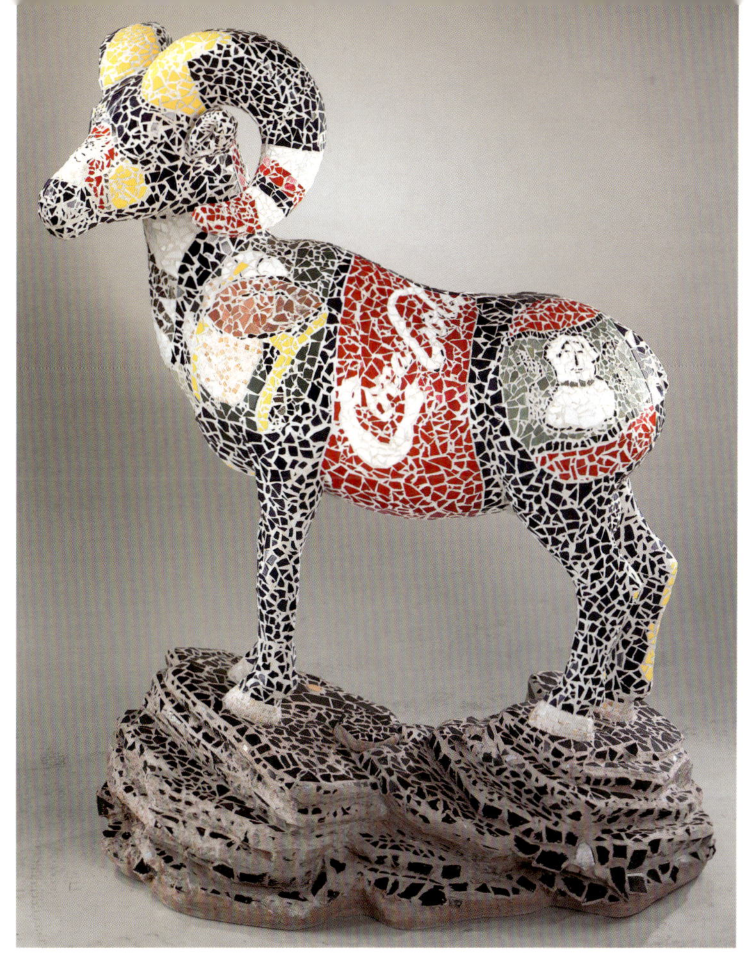

The theme of Liberty incorporates icons of the American way of life and of freedom, such as sports, George Washington, the Twin Towers, and the Stars and Stripes. Students from grades 2, 3, 5, and 8 worked on this bighorn, including design, breaking and applying the tiles by hand, and the finish cleaning. The process included lengthy discussions regarding this endangered animal and what it represents.

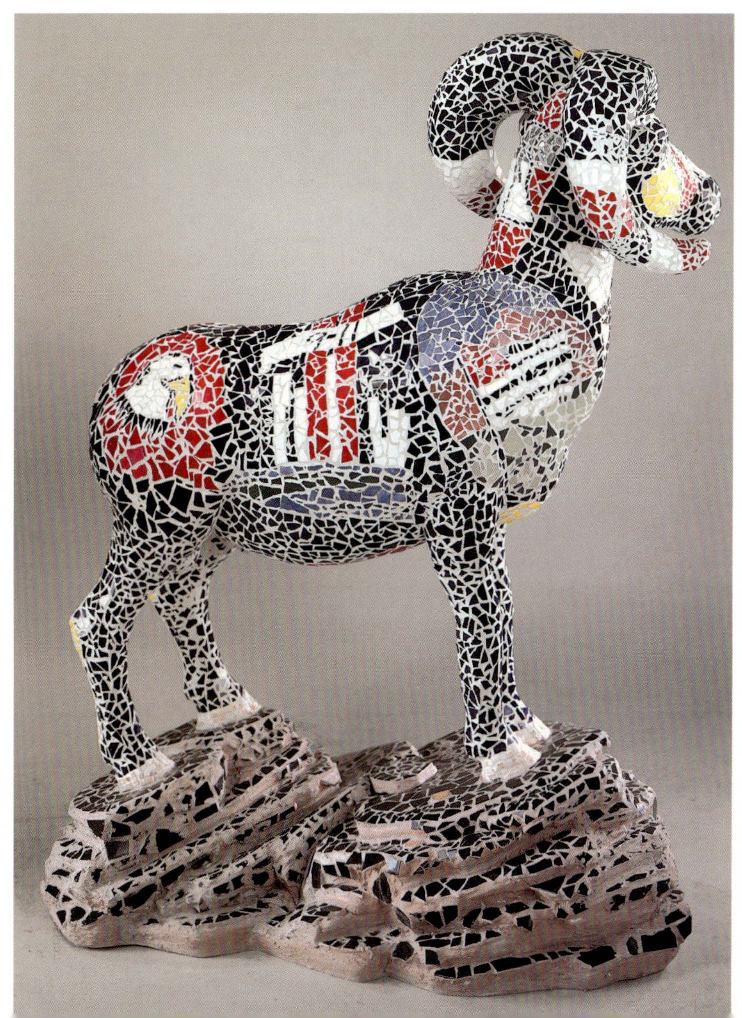

Isle of Ewe

artist Richard Meyers
sponsor Carole & Seb Sterpa
inaugural site Wyndham Hotel

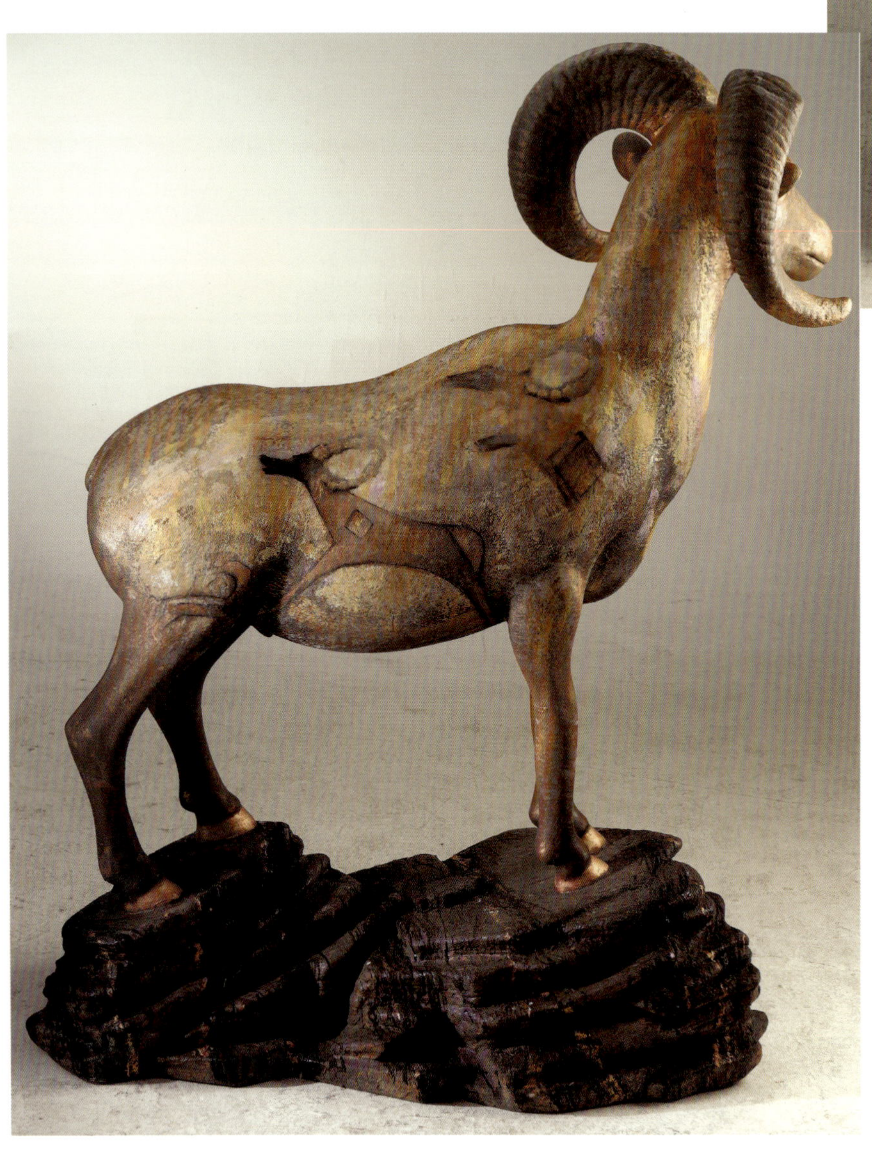

Monarch of the Mountains

artist Delos Van Earle
sponsor Dr. Lawrence & Mary Cone
inaugural site The Living Desert

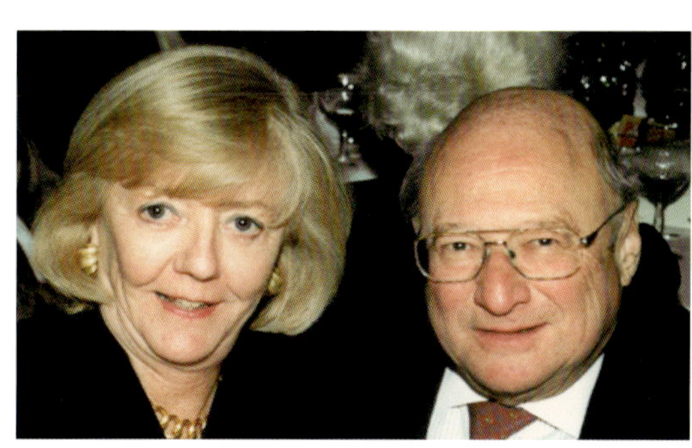

*Sponsors
Mary and Dr.
Lawrence Cone*

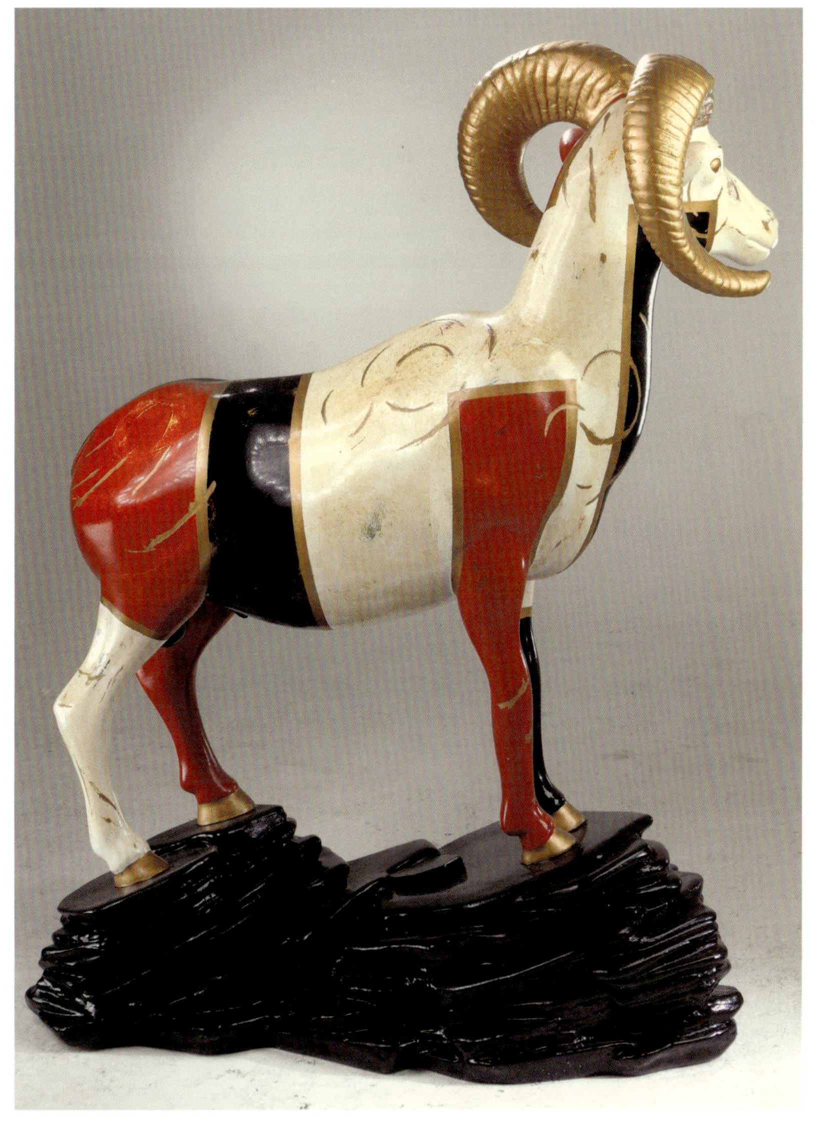

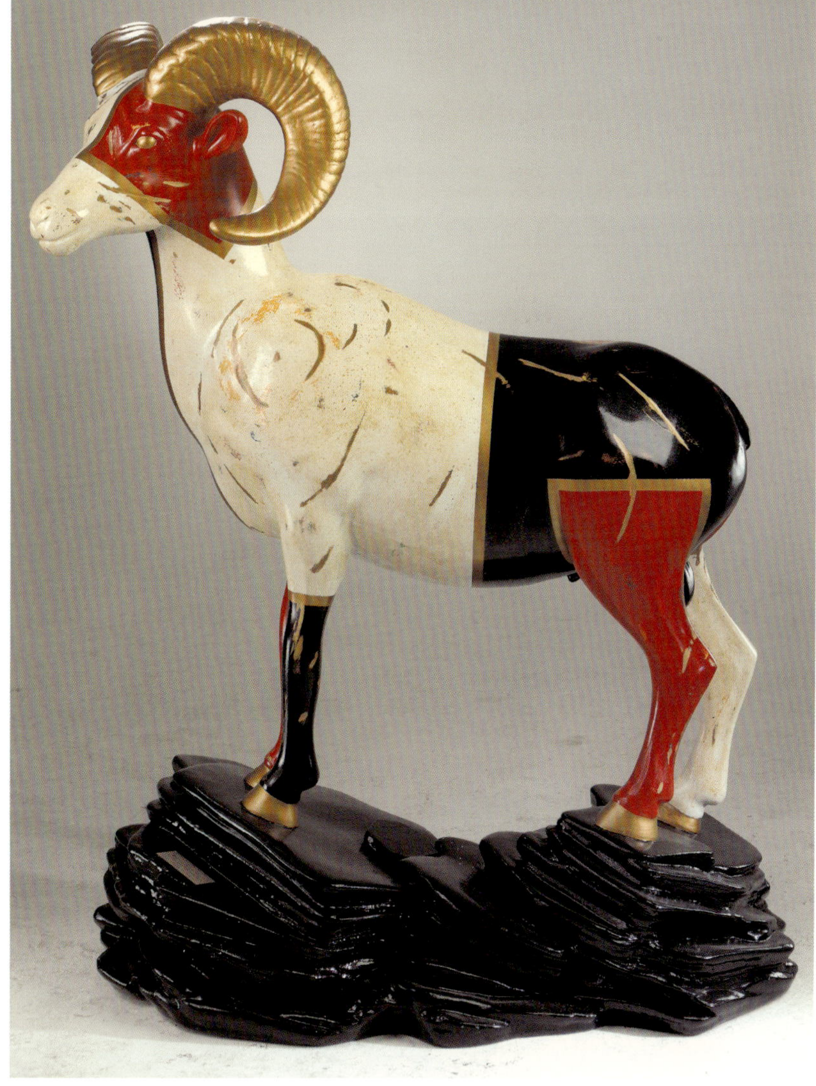

Palm Springs Nights

artist Penelope Merrell
sponsor Eloise & Richard Agee
inaugural site Palm Springs Aerial Tramway

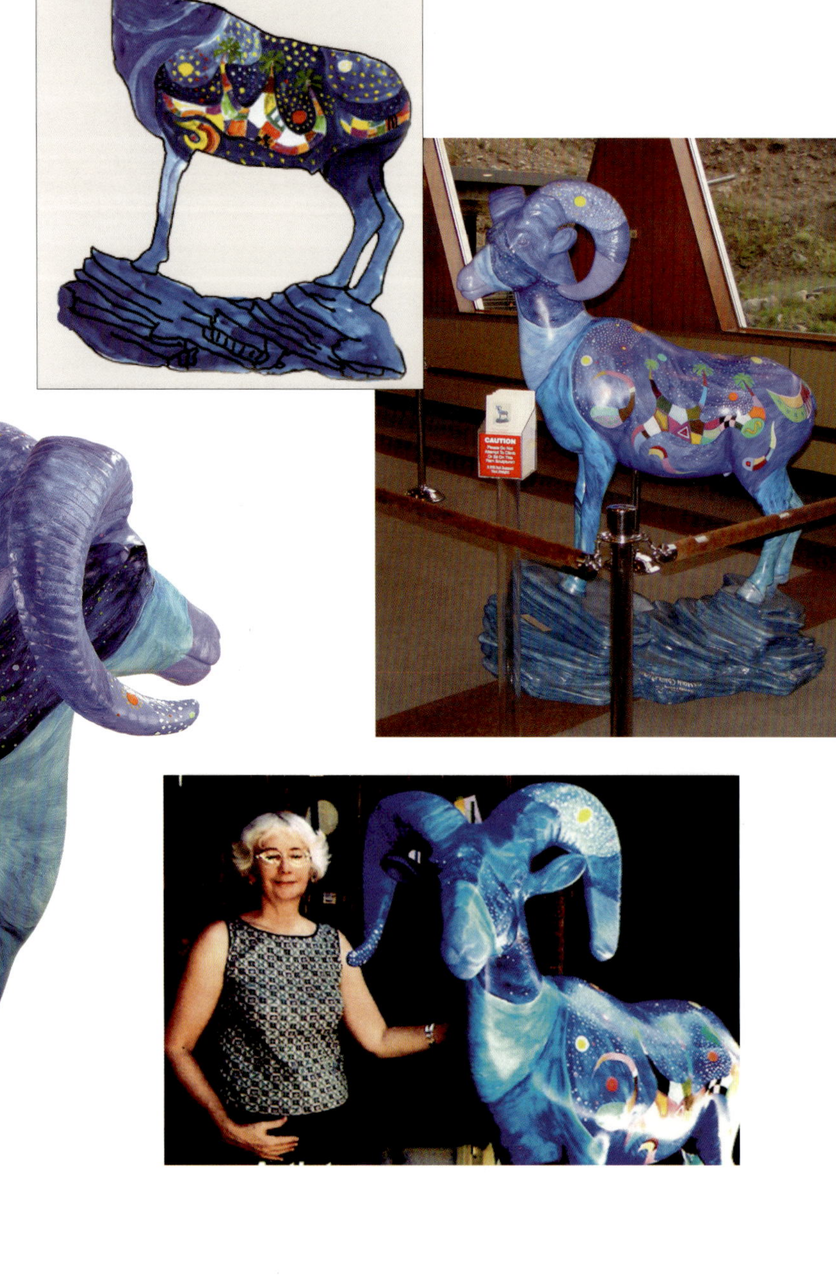

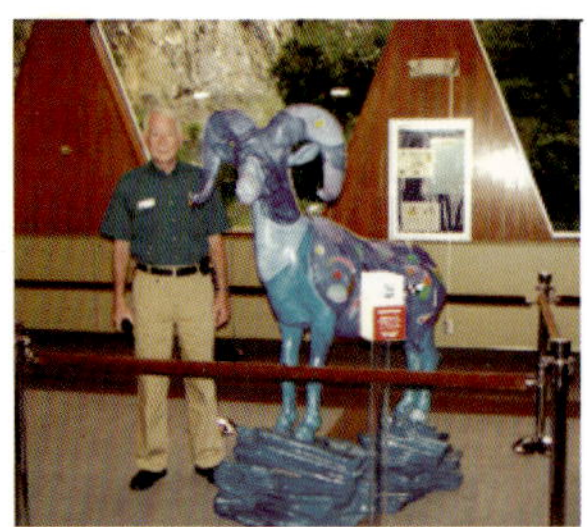

Rob Parkins Director of the Palm Springs Aerial Tramway proudly stands by "Palm Springs Nights" in its location spot at the lower tram station.

Past & Present

artist Kelly Smith
sponsor Betty & Richard Sheldon
inaugural site Wells Fargo Bank

In the past, the bighorn sheep's path was wide and vast. They were free to roam all over the Coachella Valley. Through the years, as more people came to live in the valley, the bighorn's path became thinner and thinner. What was rock is now concrete, what was dirt is now turf. Thankfully, there are organizations such as Bighorn Institute to help in the preservation of wildlife. Face it: the valley would be very dull without our wildlife. — Kelly S. Smith

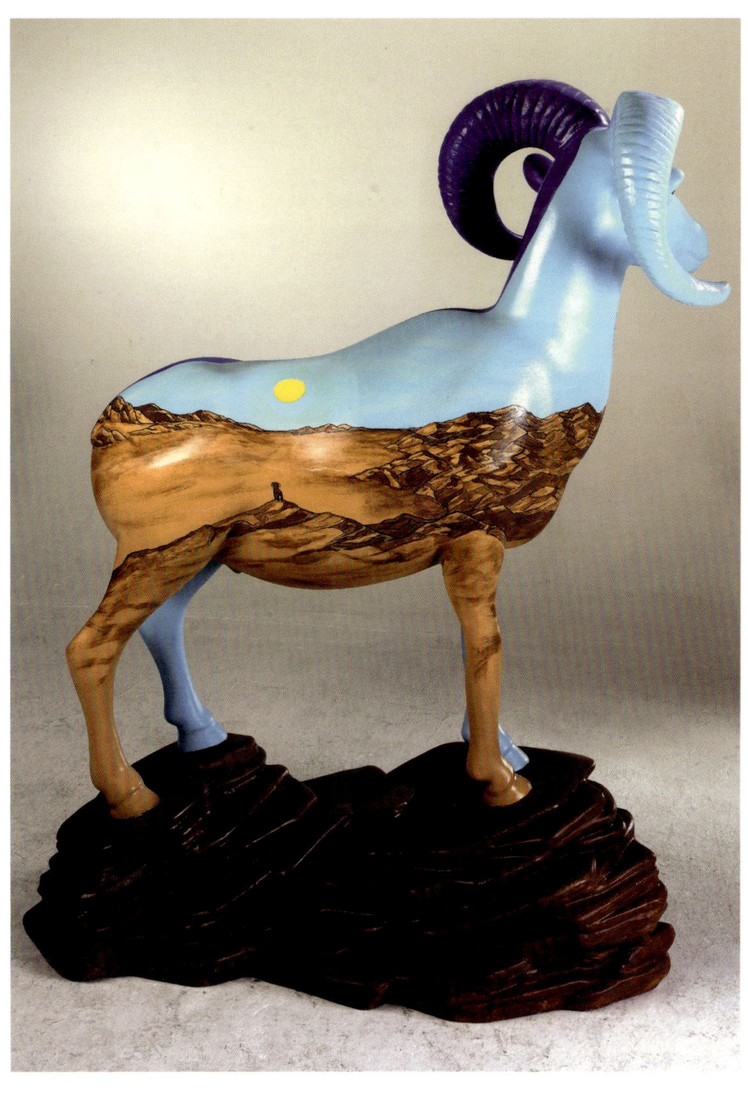

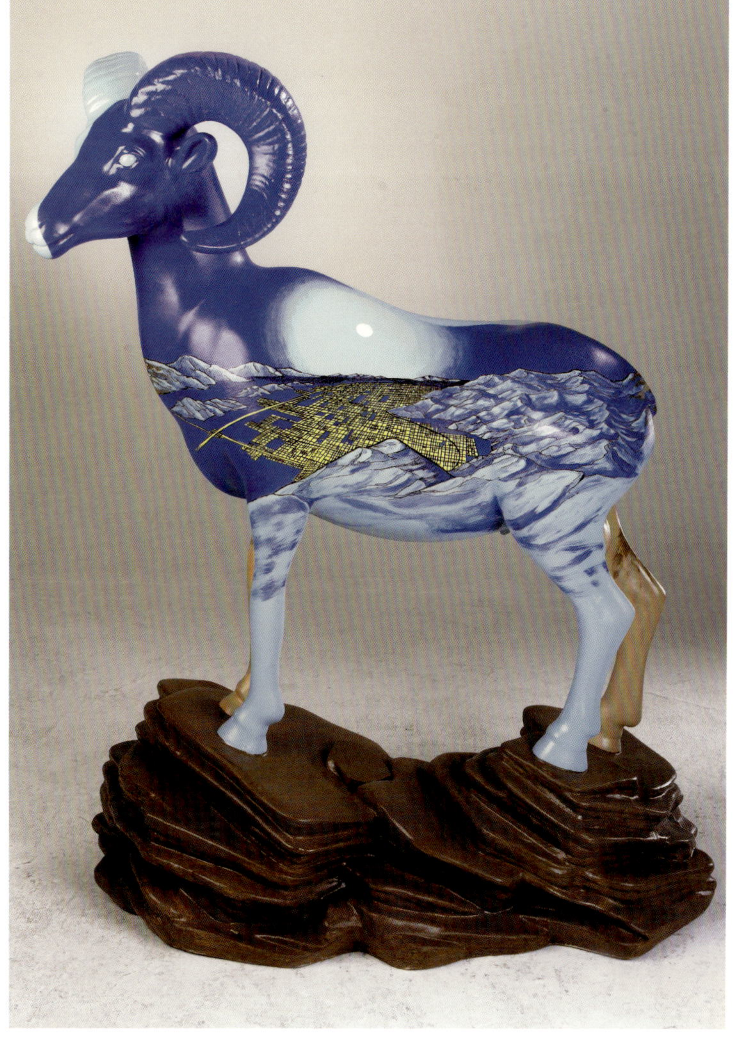

Paradox

artist Gary Zornes
sponsor Sheldon's
inaugural site Palm Springs Hilton Resort

Just as contradictory as heavy marble being supported by clouds is the existence of the Peninsular bighorn sheep. While possessing a rugged beauty as they leap from rocky ledges and romp with ease along rough mountain trails, this beautiful creature is in delicate balance with man and nature. Only the dedicated work of organizations like Bighorn Institute has prevented these natural wonders from being moved from the Endangered Species List (where they currently reside) to the Extinct List. Do not be deceived by their rugged exteriors. These magnificent animals need our dedicated efforts to survive and to remain the icons of the Coachella Valley that they have rightfully become. — Gary Zornes

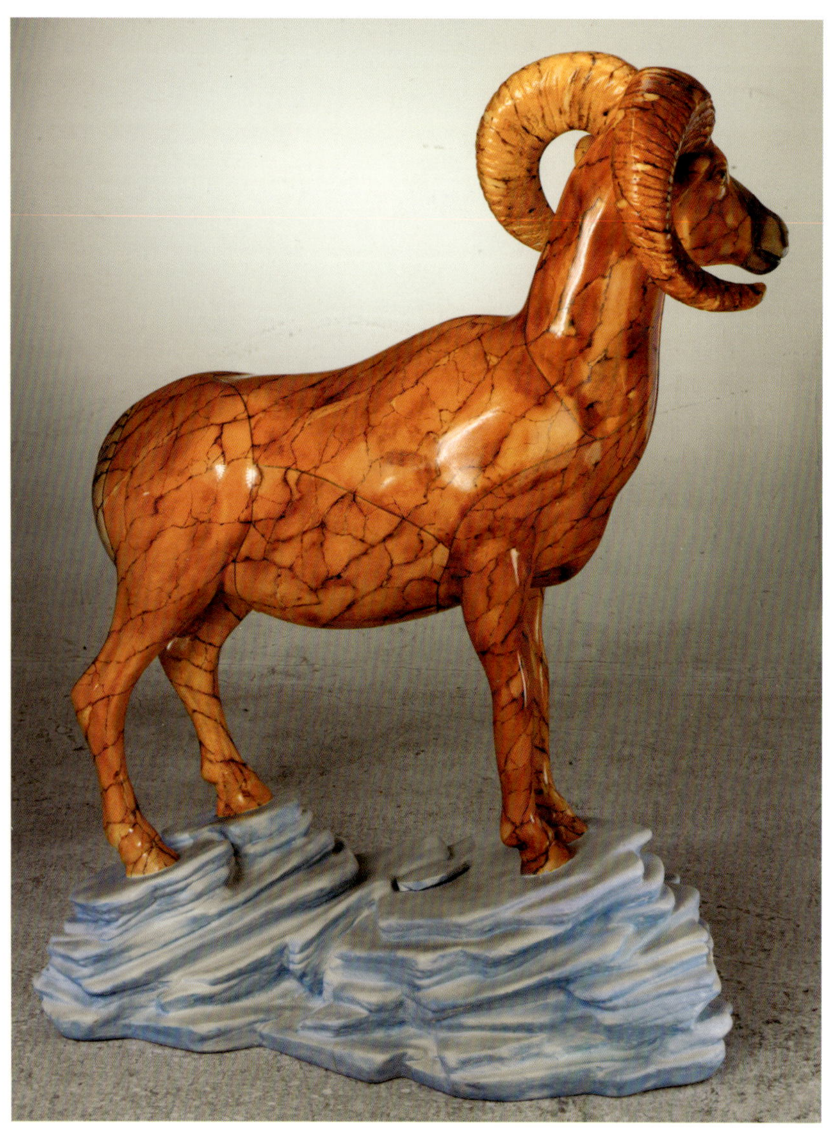

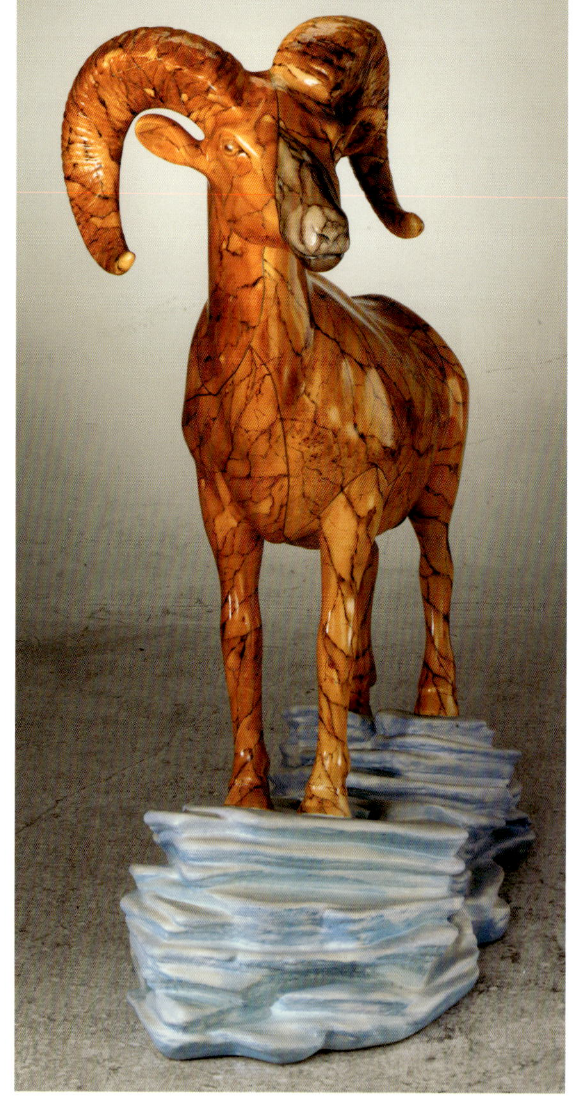

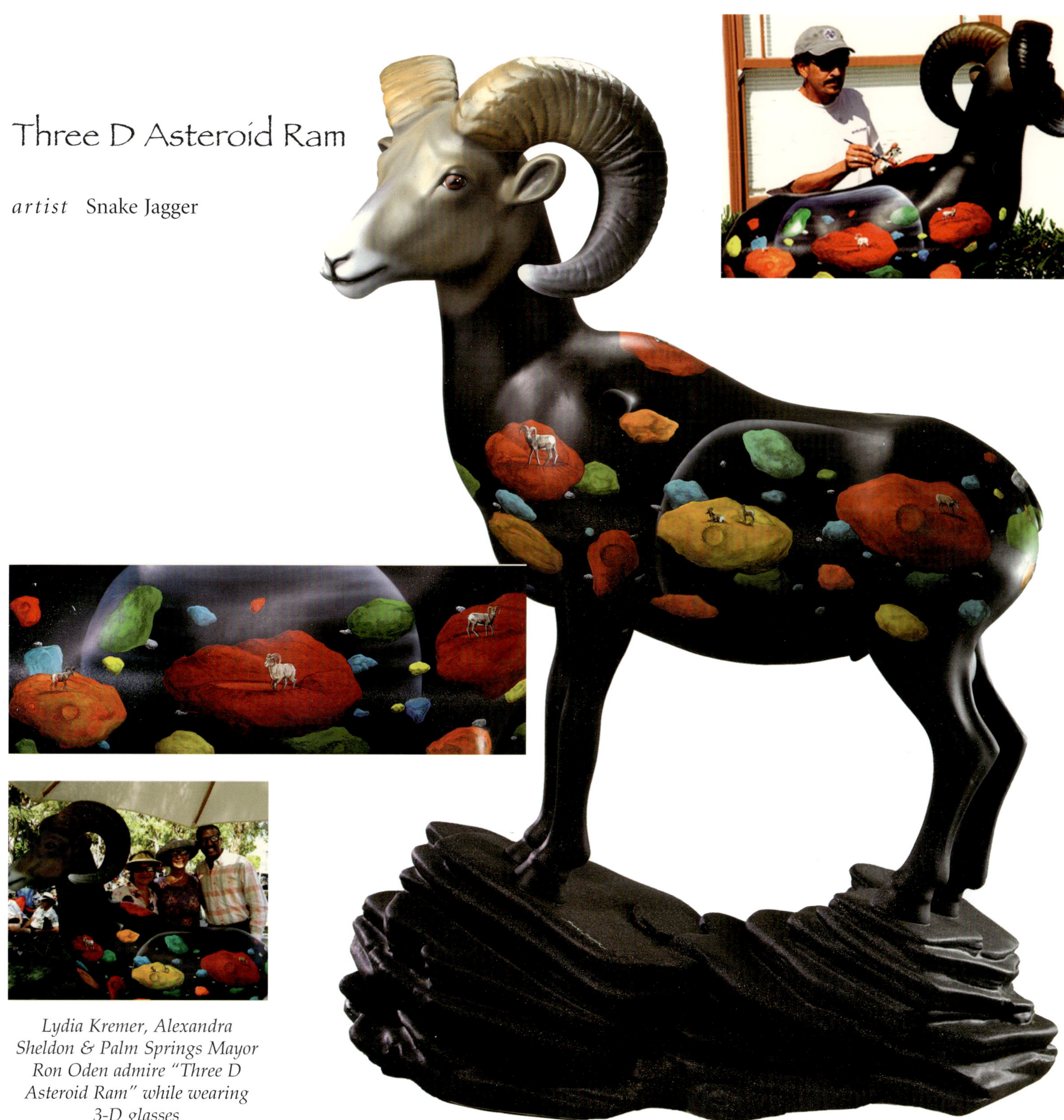

Three D Asteroid Ram

artist   Snake Jagger

*Lydia Kremer, Alexandra
Sheldon & Palm Springs Mayor
Ron Oden admire "Three D
Asteroid Ram" while wearing
3-D glasses*

Putting on the Ritz

artist   Michael Milauskas
sponsor   Dr. Albert *&* Dorothy Milauskas
location   Milauskas Eye Institute

Because I grew up in Palm Springs, bighorn sheep are a familiar part of my life. Although the Ritz Carlton Hotel is no more, "Putting on the Ritz" is a fun allusion to the statue in front of the building. The bighorn is a bit retro with spats on his hooves and his "slick" horns call to mind the shiny slicked-back men's hairstyles of the 1920s and 1930s.
— Michael Milauskas

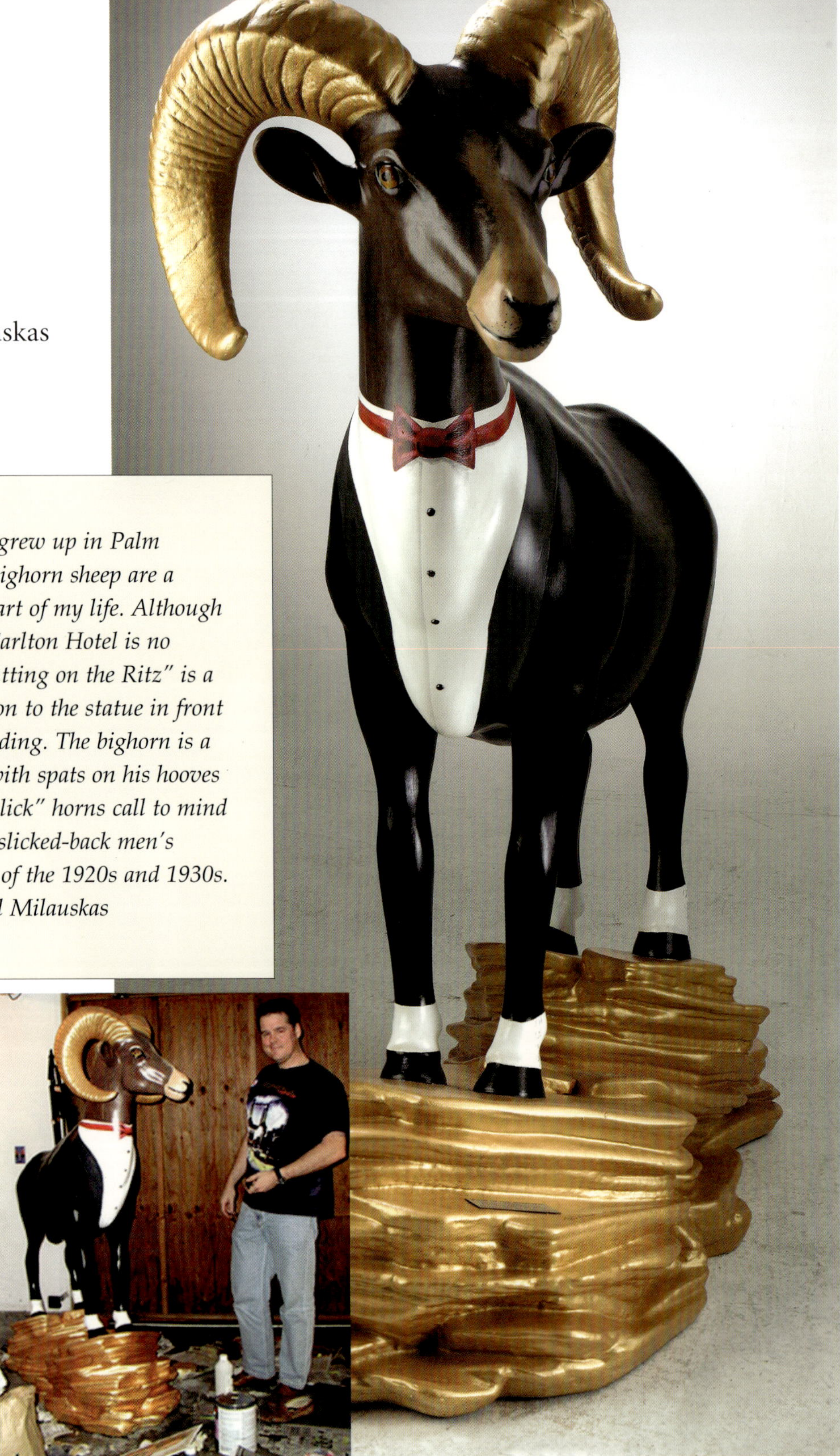

Patriot

artist Brenda Johnson
sponsor President Gerald & Betty Ford
location Palm Desert Sheriff's Station

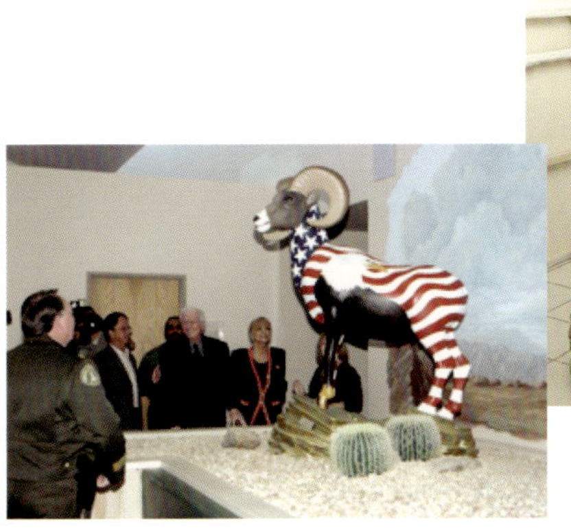

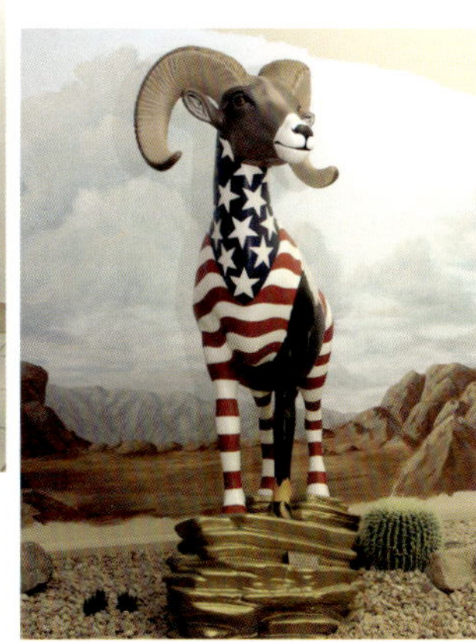

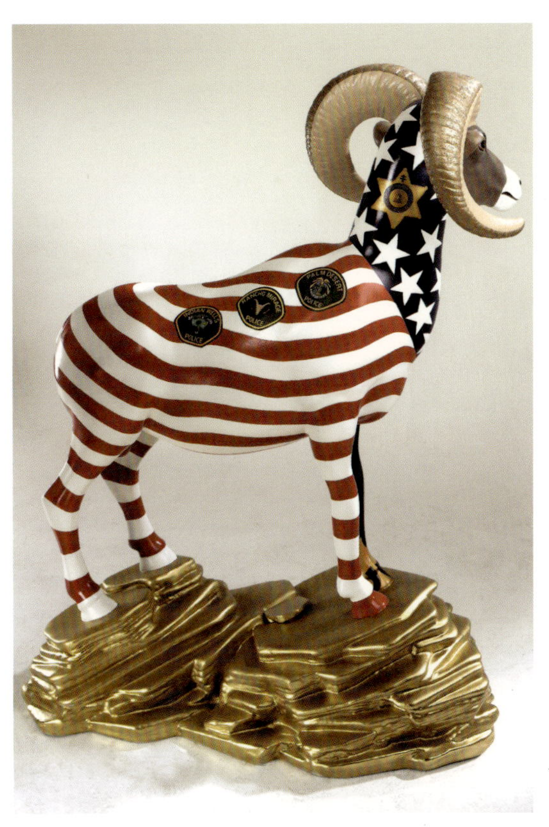

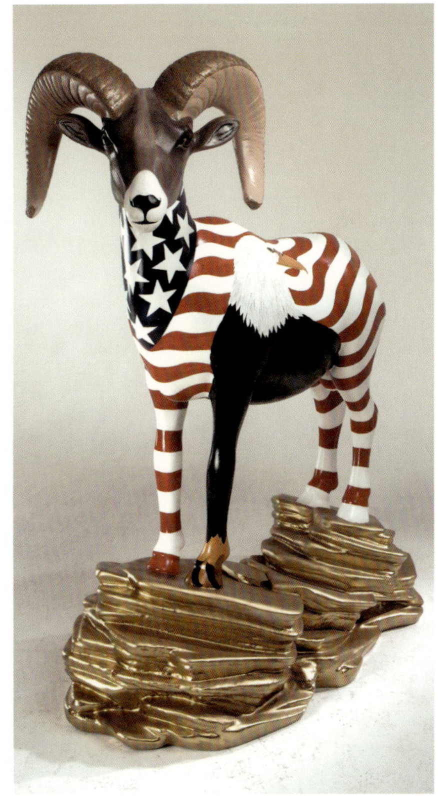

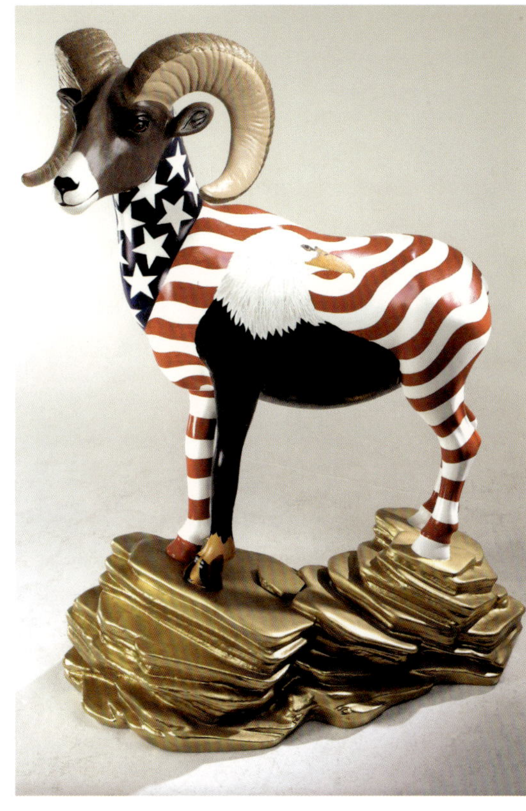

Reaching out to the Bighorn Sheep

artist Second Grade Class, Cielo Vista Elementary School
sponsor Arlene Rosenthal
inaugural site Cielo Vista Elementary School

*Over three hundred protective handprints,
from children attending second grade at
Cielo Vista Elementary, decorate their ram
"Reaching out to the Bighorn Sheep".*

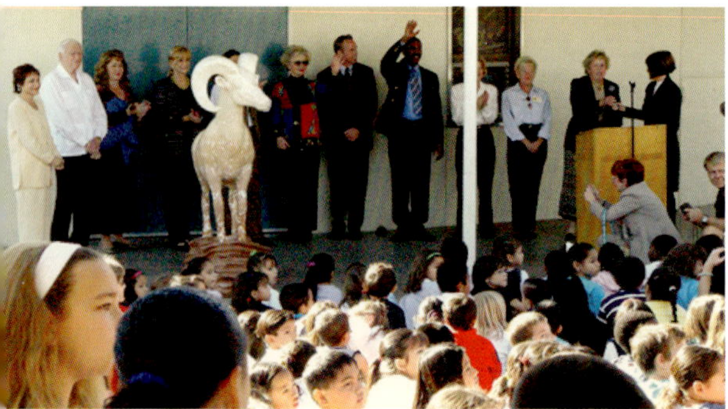

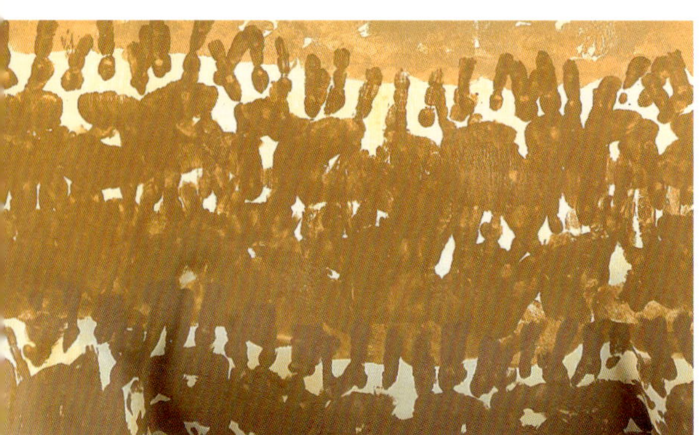

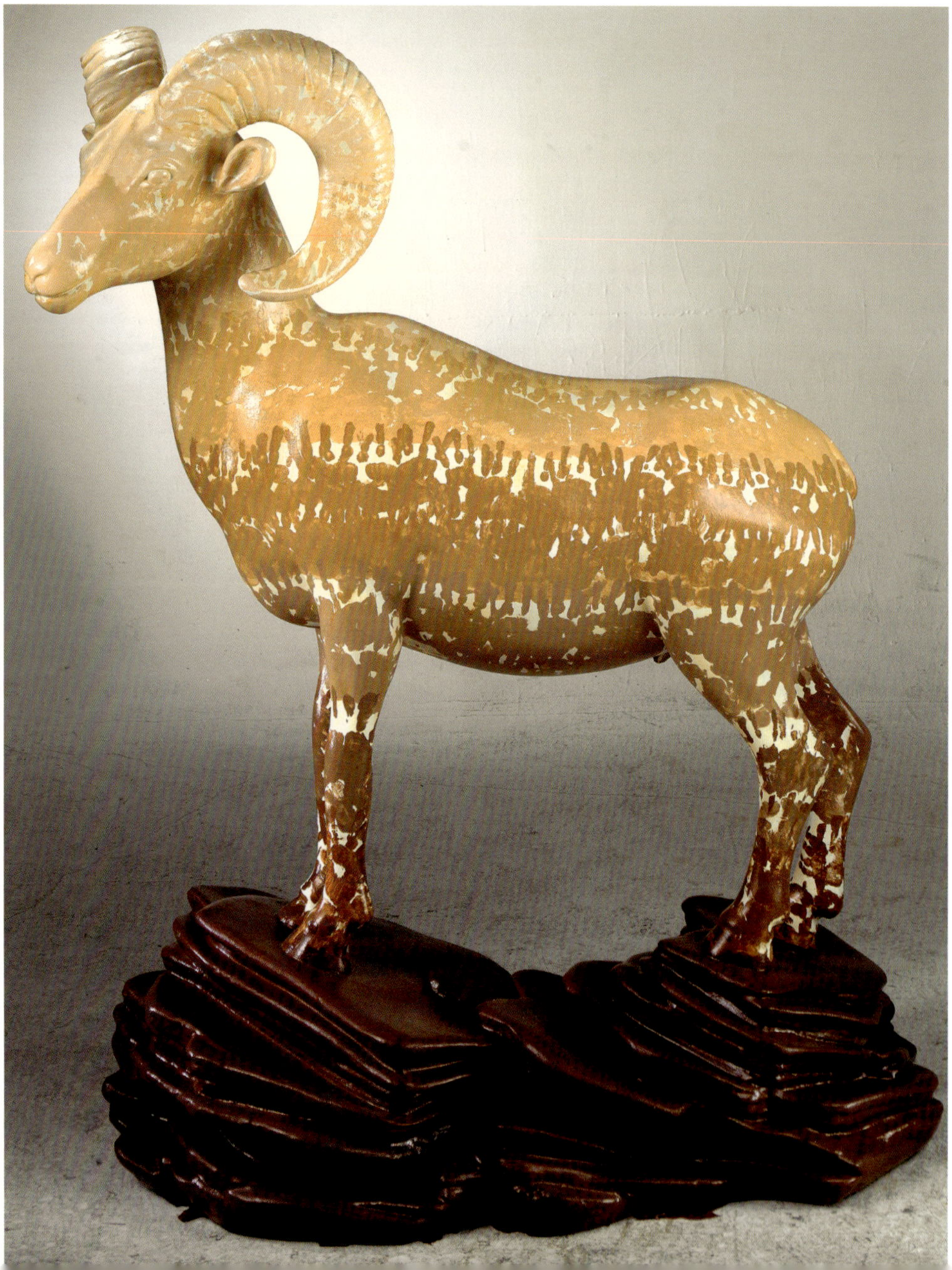

Rebirth

artist Ron Chespak
sponsor The Desert Sun
inaugural site The Desert Sun

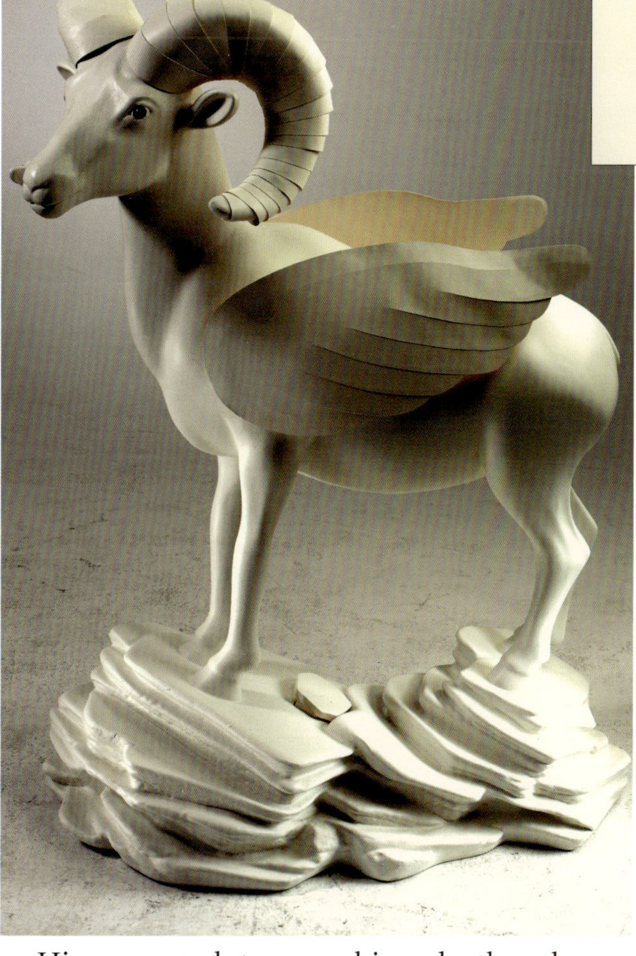

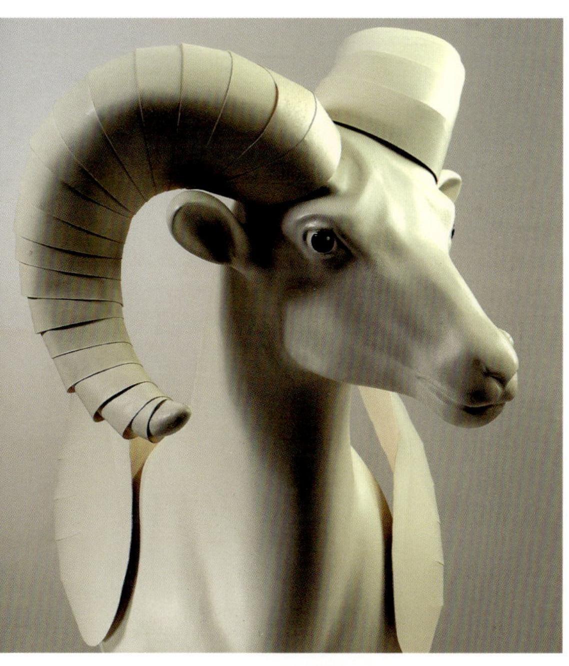

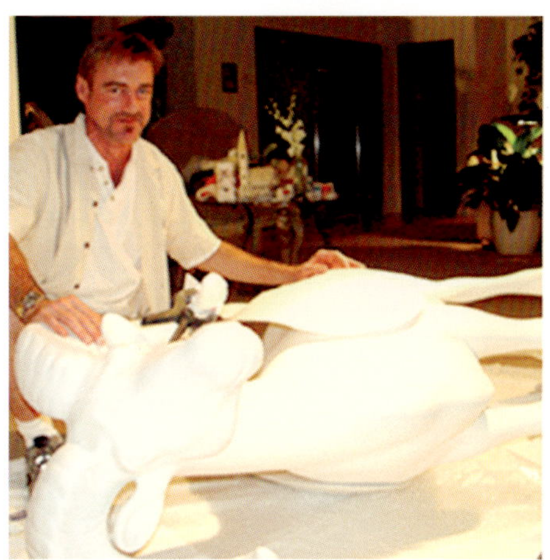

Ron Chespak is one of the only celebrated artists working in the unusual medium of paper sculpture. He earned his Bachelor of Fine Arts Degree from California State University, Fullerton in 1982. Following that he worked as Senior Art Director and Creative Director for two of the world's top advertising agencies. After this success, he decided to leave Madison Avenue to pursue his passion.

His paper sculpture combines depth and composition with stark white objects, strong vivid color and graduated hues that emerge with a texture of sophisticated elegance. The artist's accolades include awards, national museum exhibitions and inclusion in numerous magazines and art history textbooks. He has also been featured on several television shows and specials.

In 1999, he opened the Ron Chespak Paper Sculpture Gallery in Palm Springs, a venue where he showcases his art exclusively. In the past decade, he has earned worldwide recognition as one of the foremost artists working in paper sculpture today. Together with his galleries, children's art museum and publishing company, he continues to inspire a new generation of the art-loving public. He also raises money and consciousness for several national charitable organizations.

Sonic Bloom

artist Isabella Fiore
sponsor Saks Fifth Avenue
inaugural site Saks Fifth Avenue

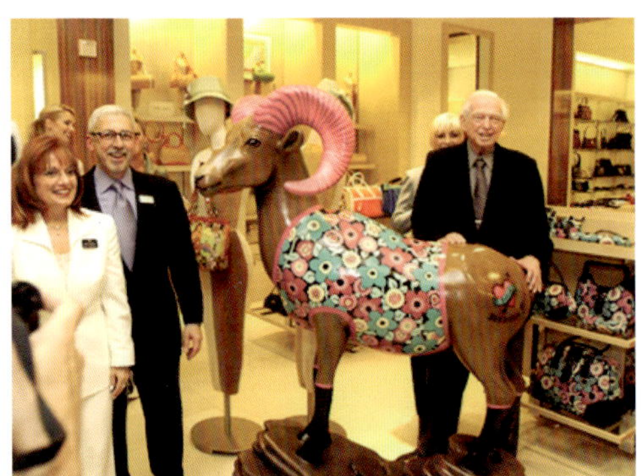

Sponsors from Saks Fifth Avenue Pam Riccio & John Columbo at the unveiling of Isabella Fiore's painted ram "Sonic Bloom" at Saks Fifth Avenue, Palm Desert. Behind the ram Sidney & Alexandra Sheldon enjoy the festivities.

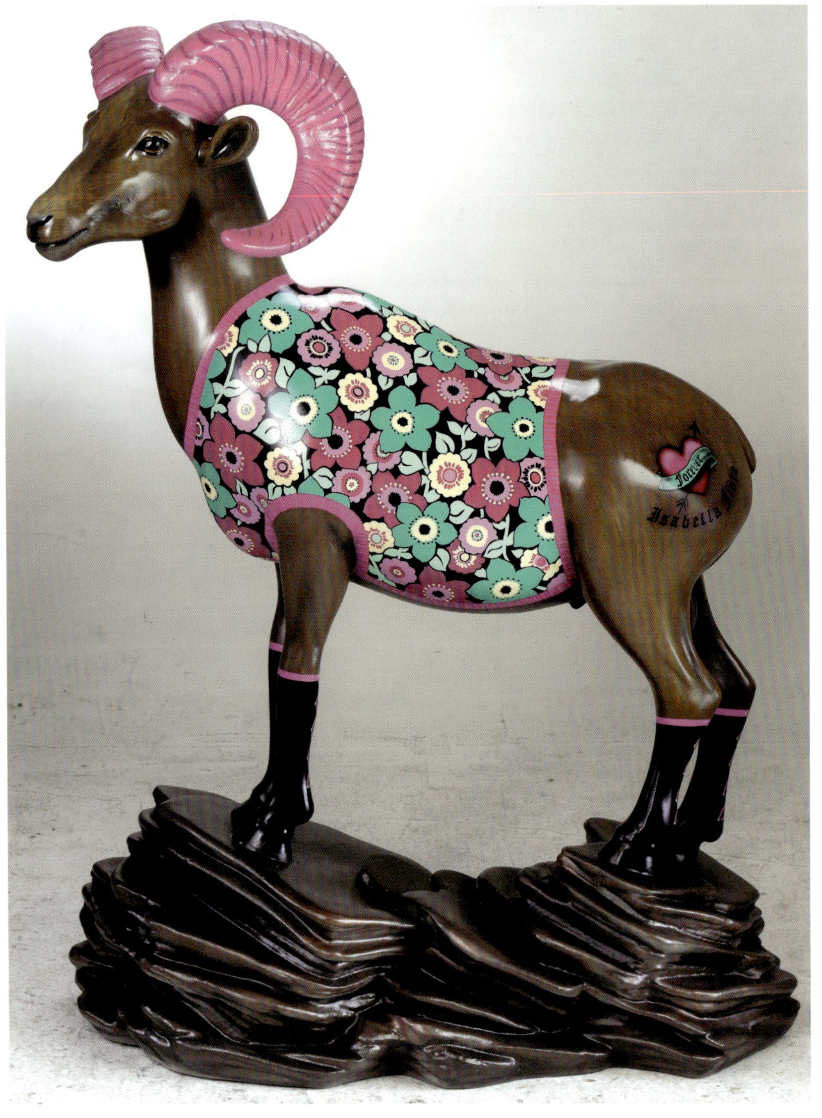

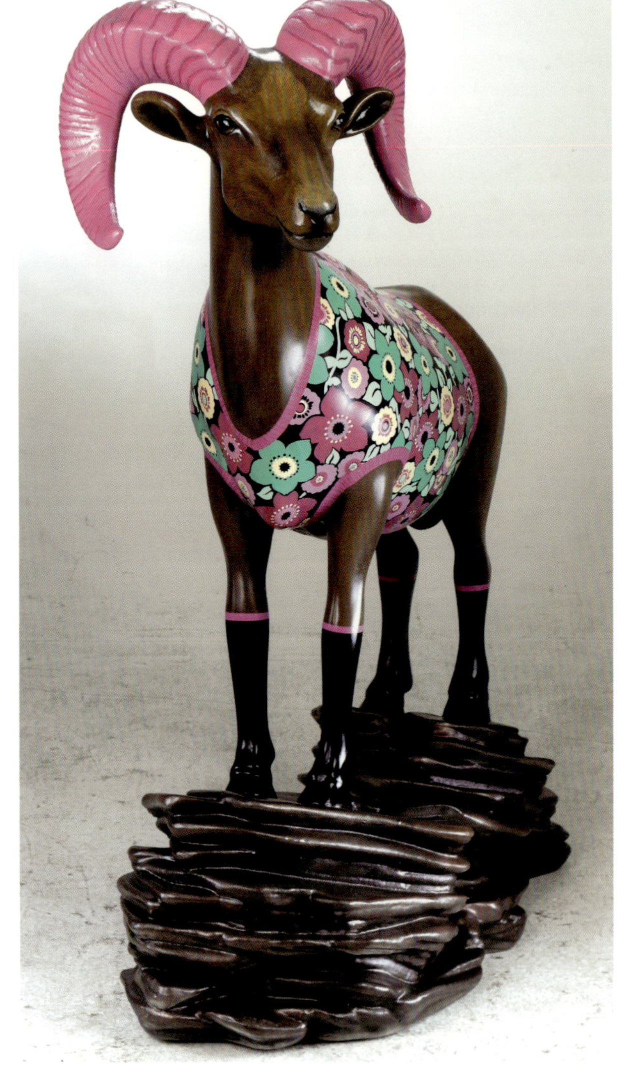

Springtime

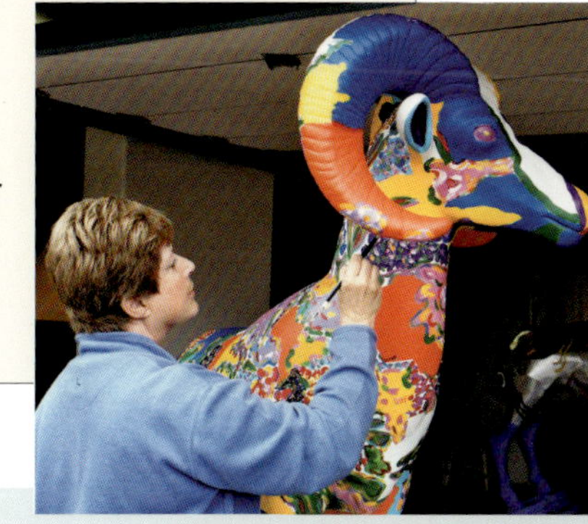

artist   Yvonne Maloney
sponsor   Women in Film
inaugural site   The Gardens on El Paseo

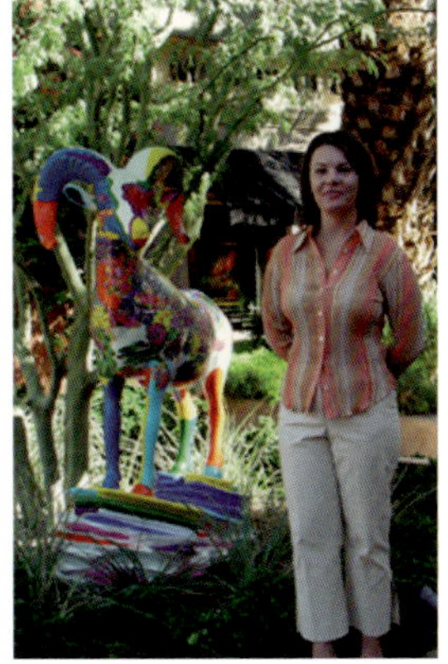

Melinda Byrd, at the Gardens on El Paseo admires "Springtime".

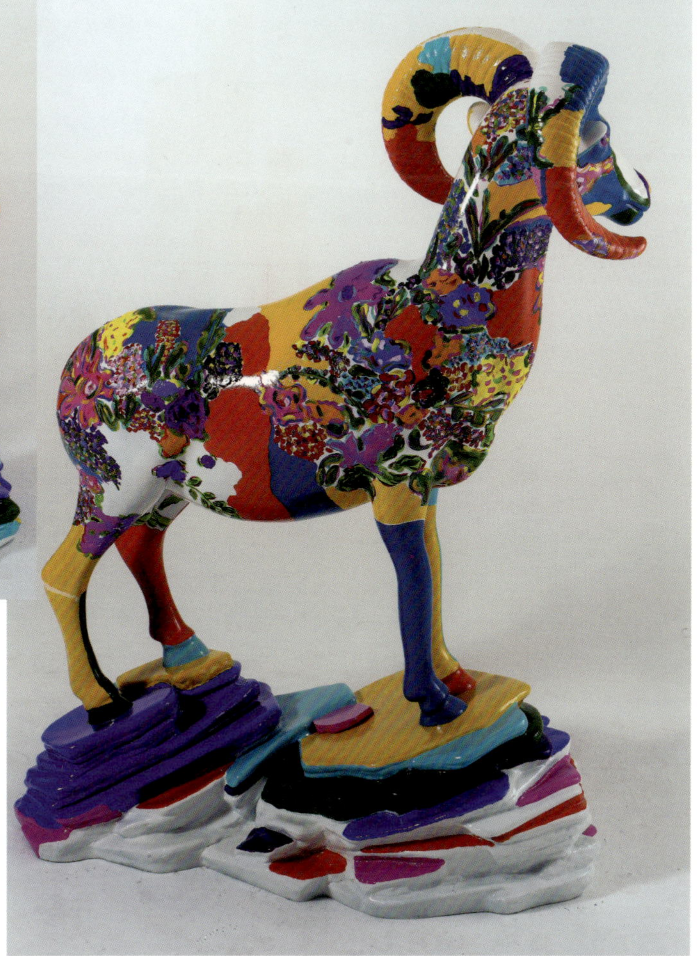

"Yvonne Maloney's painting of elegant ladies and flowers set forth a mood of days gone by. They are bold beautiful and full of color." Born in Malta, Yvonne Maloney spent her early childhood on the island before immigrating with her family to Canada and then to the United States. The arts of Matisse and Modigliani have influenced the artist and served as her inspiration. Among her exhibitions are those at Scripps Cancer Center/Scripps Green Hospital in La Jolla, California, the Foundation for the children of the Californias in their Hospital Infantil de las Californias in Tijuana, Mexico and the Palm Springs Desert Museum. KPBS's Online Magazine featured her artwork on its magazine cover two times in 2003 and her work "Lydia in Green" was auctioned at Sotheby's in New York for the benefit of the New York Academy of Art. Collectors from Beverly Hills and Rancho Santa Fe, California, Grosse Point, Michigan, Canada, England, Mexico and Malta have purchased her paintings.

International Ram

artist La Quinta High School Art & Ceramic Club
sponsor Elaine & Leonard Silverstein
inaugural site Desert Sands Unified
Administration Office

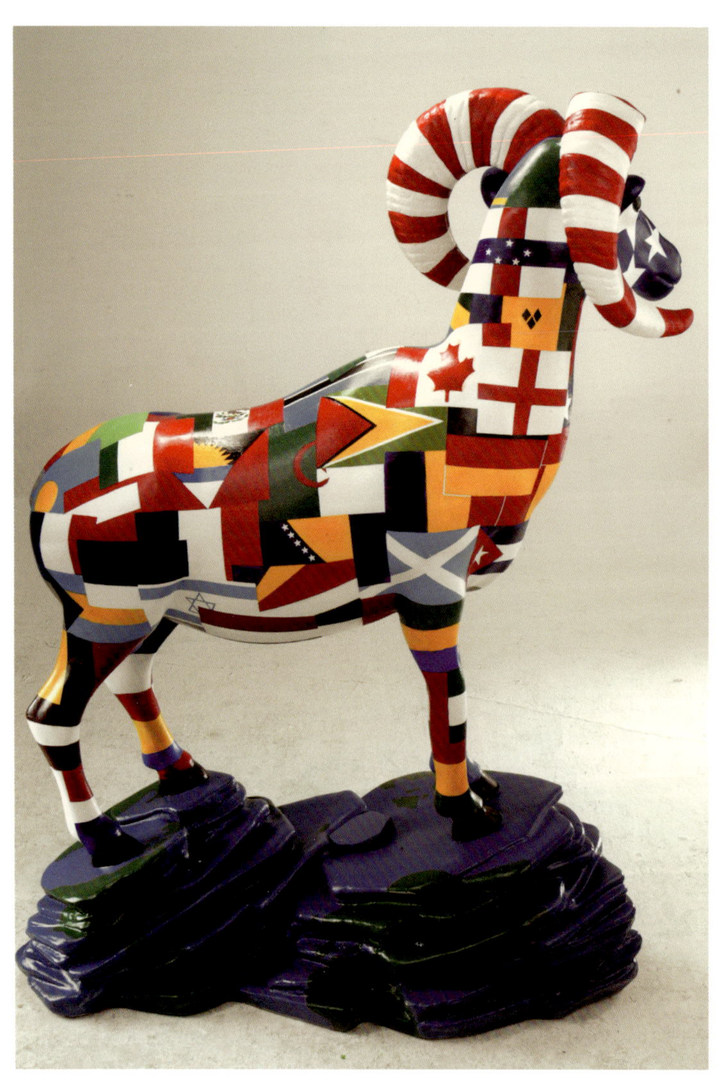

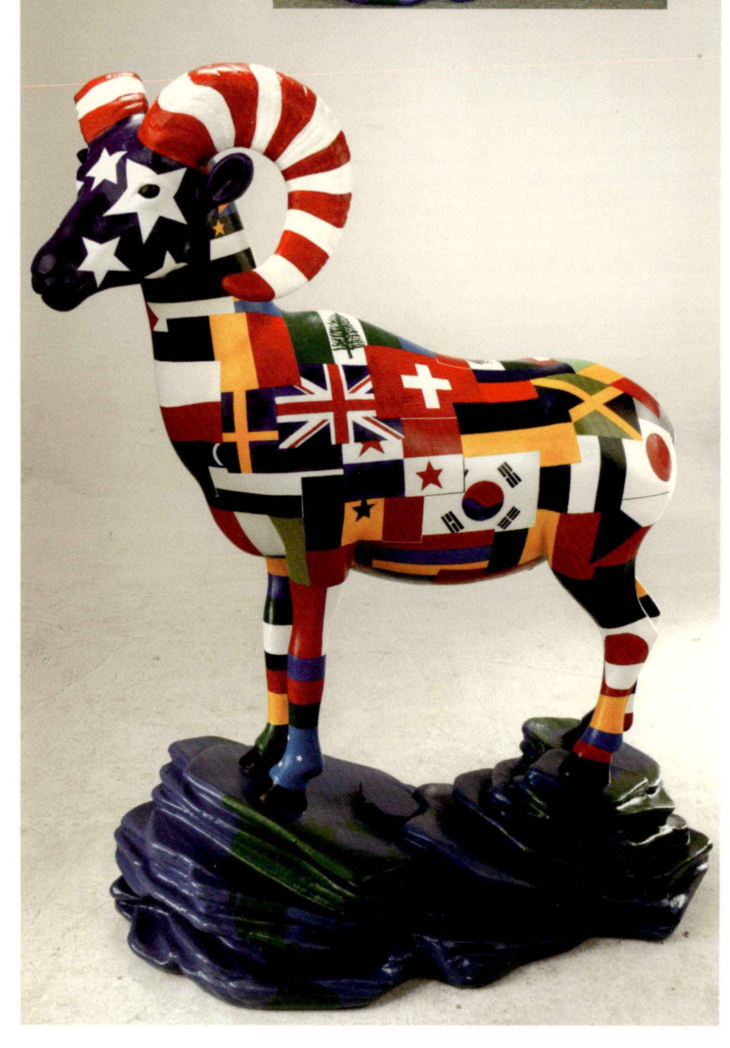

This Is a Record of the Time

artist   Palm Springs Desert Museum
        Junior Docents coordinator, Xavier Cortez
sponsor   Bighorn Institute
inaugural site   Palm Springs Desert Museum

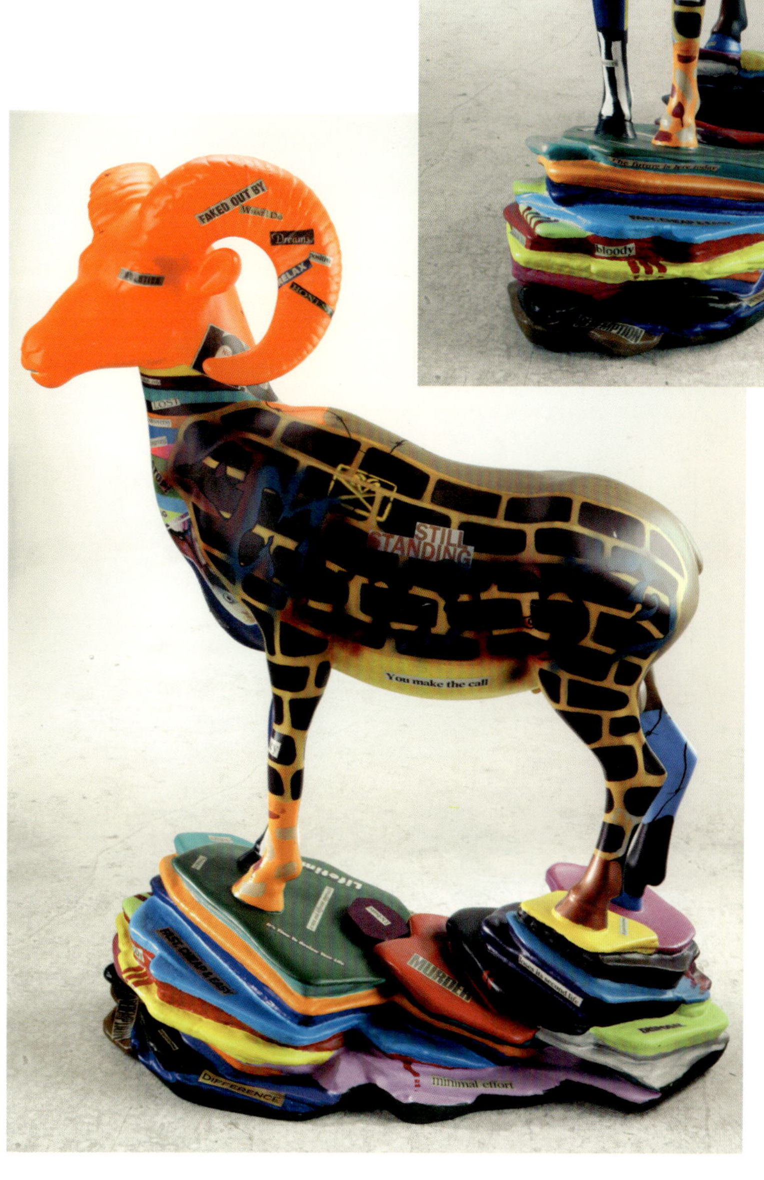

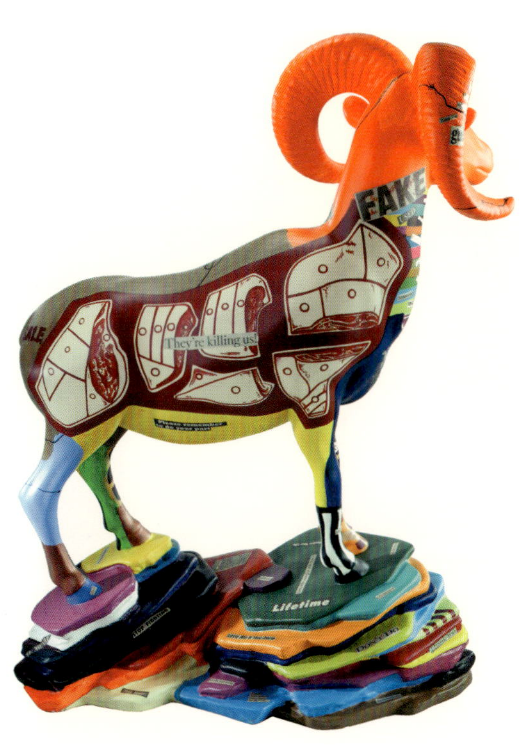

Welcome to Palm Springs

artist Joe Wertheimer
sponsor Jackie Lee & Jim Houston
inaugural site Palm Springs International Airport

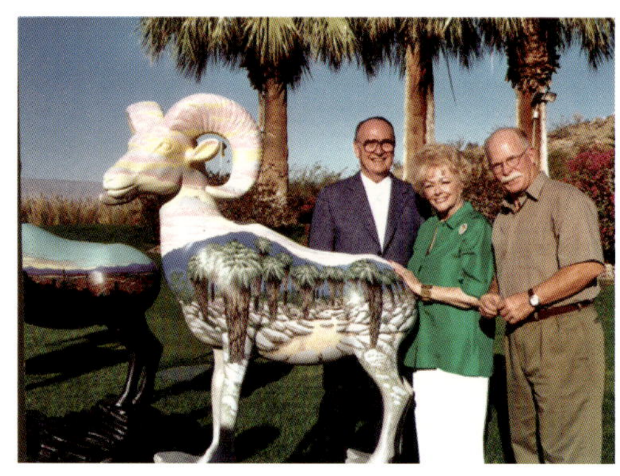

*Sponsors Jackie Lee & Jim Houston with
artist Joe Wertheimer (right)*

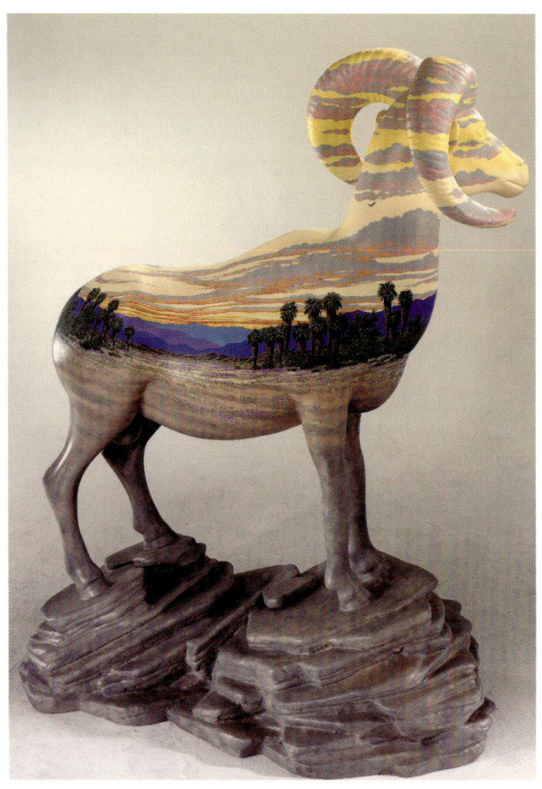

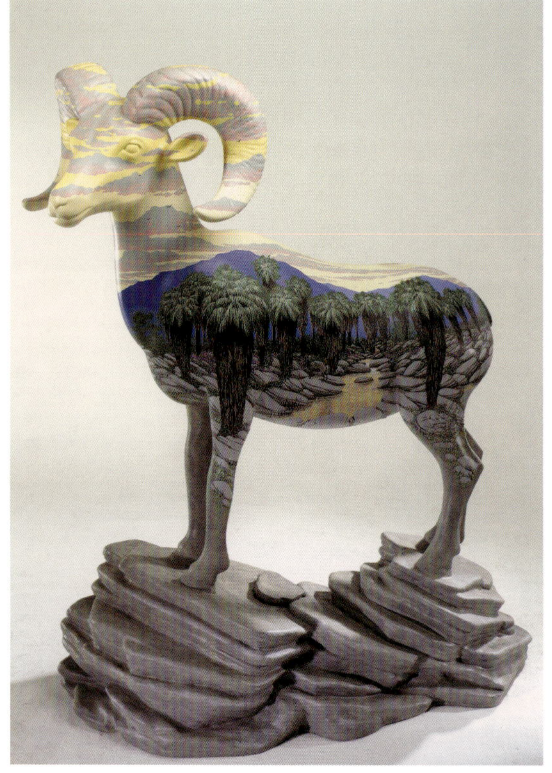

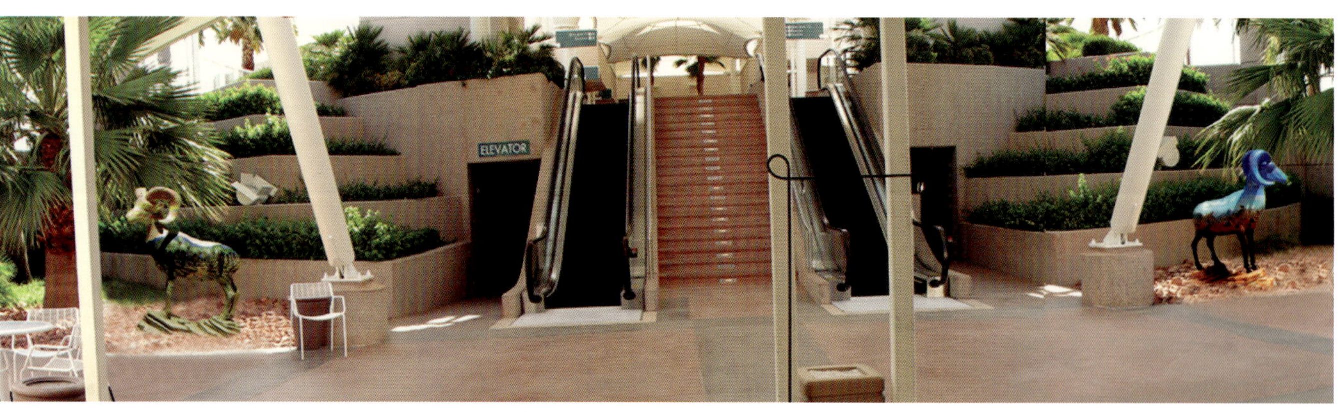

Windpower at Dusk

artist   Joe Wertheimer
sponsor   Jackie Lee & Jim Houston
inaugural site   CBS 2 News

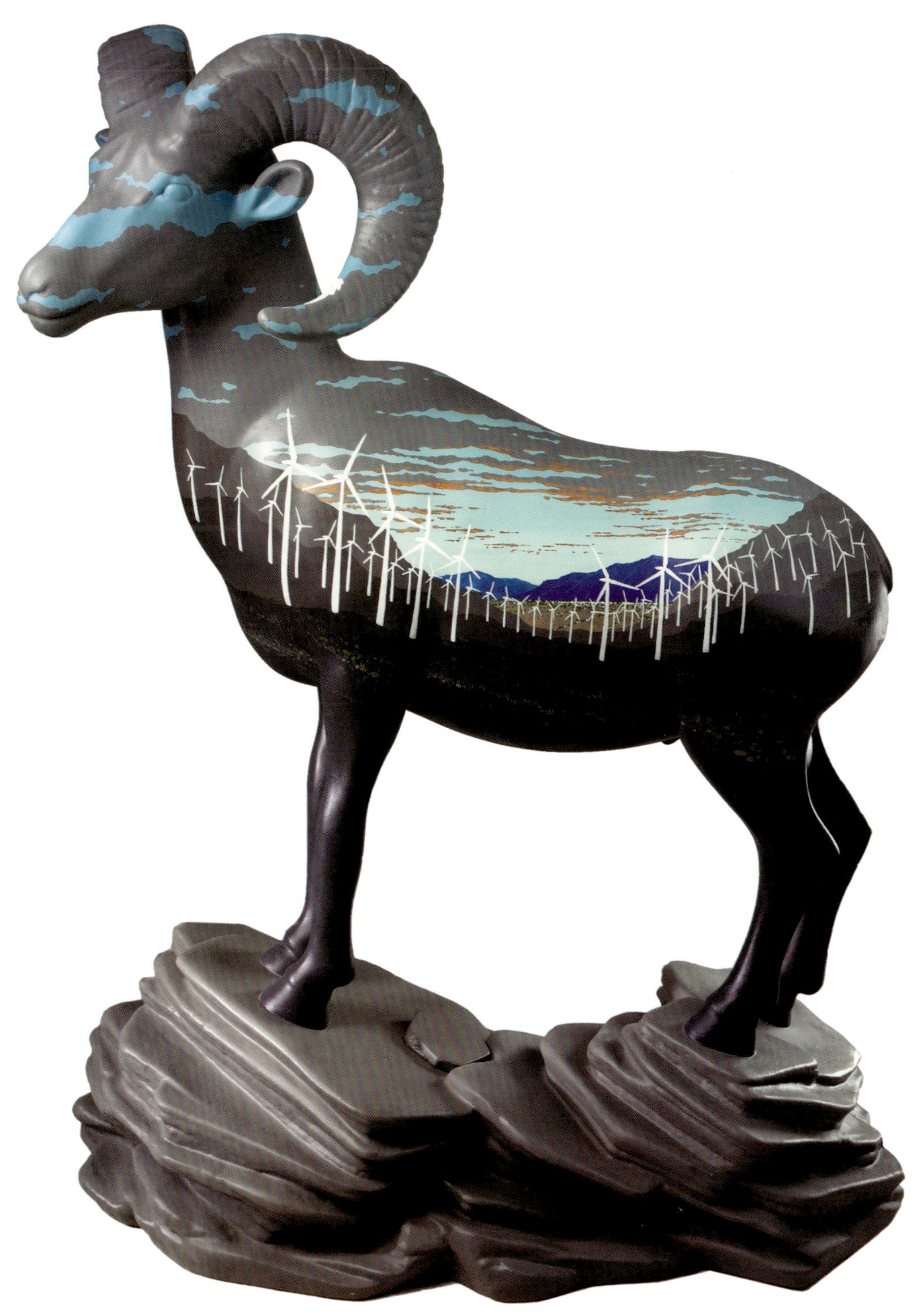

In the Shadow of Mt. San Jacinto

artist Terry Masters
sponsor Rozenne & Ric Supple
inaugural site Camelot Theater

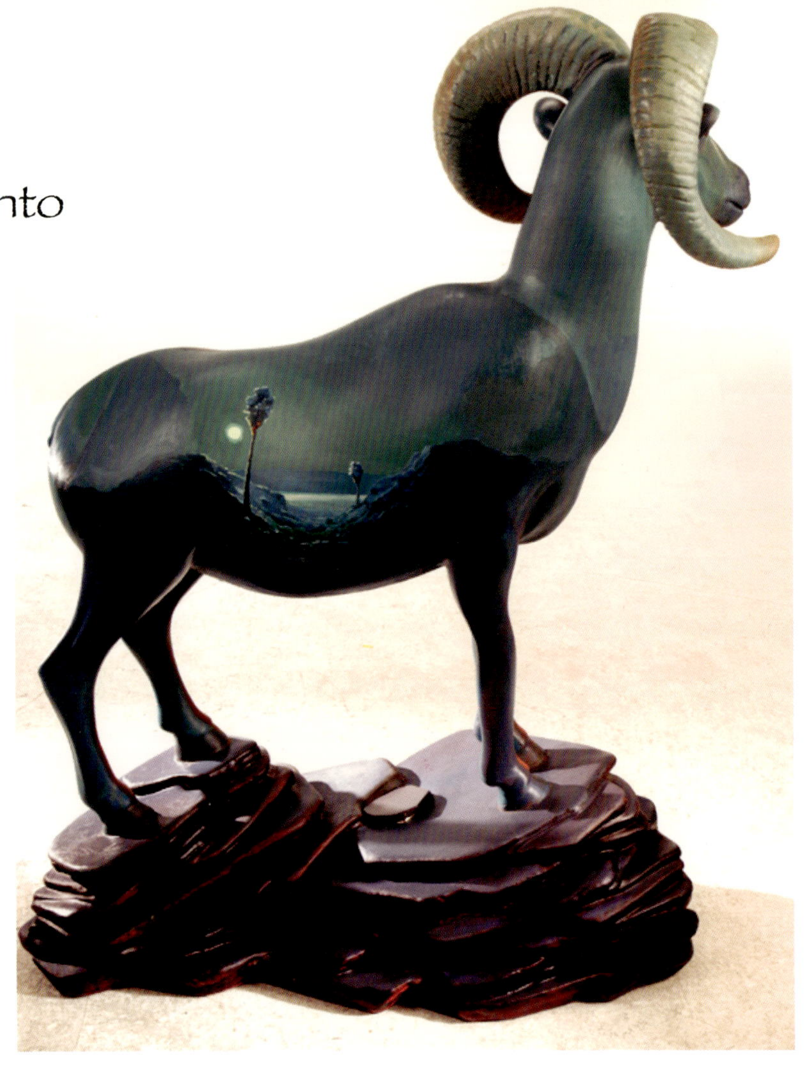

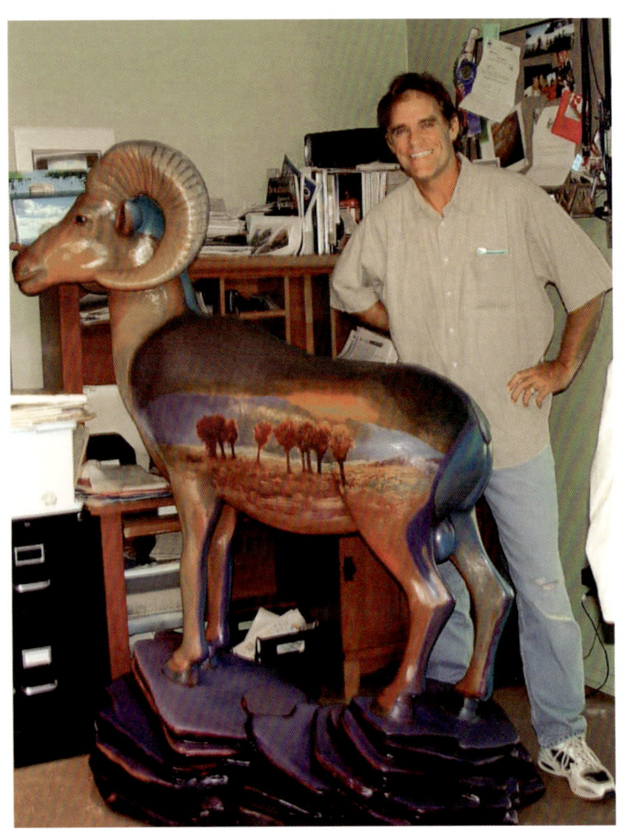

A Plein-air painter, Terry Masters focuses on the Southwest desert with a goal of capturing the majesty and intricacies of light on the desert. He has his studio in Palm Springs, California. Masters is largely self taught, but has studied with Jeremy Lipking at the California Art Institute as well as having received instruction from Ken Auster, Dan Gerhartz and Mark Kerckhoff. He is a native Californian, born in Sacramento in 1955. Masters is an artist member of the California Art Club, the Laguna Plein Air Painters Association and the Tucson Plein Air Painters Society.

Painting the Bighorn for Knowledge

artist Visitors to Children's Discovery Museum of the Desert
sponsor Bighorn Institute
inaugural site Children's Discovery Museum of the Desert

It gives me such pleasure to watch the ram change colors every day as the children paint him. This is the mission of our museum — to teach young people about our environment in a creative way.
— Betty Barker, Chairman

Connecting with Celebrities

Since the 1930s, the Palm Springs area has been a frequent destination for figures in the public eye. Its proximity to Los Angeles coupled with its relaxed tempo of life has made it popular with actors, writers, and other celebrities as a site for homes, vacations, and retreats. Many have a special appreciation of the privacy that is available to them here.

Their painted rams and drawings speak eloquently of the generosity of spirit of these special friends and are testimony that the magnitude of their talent is often matched by the magnitude of their heart.

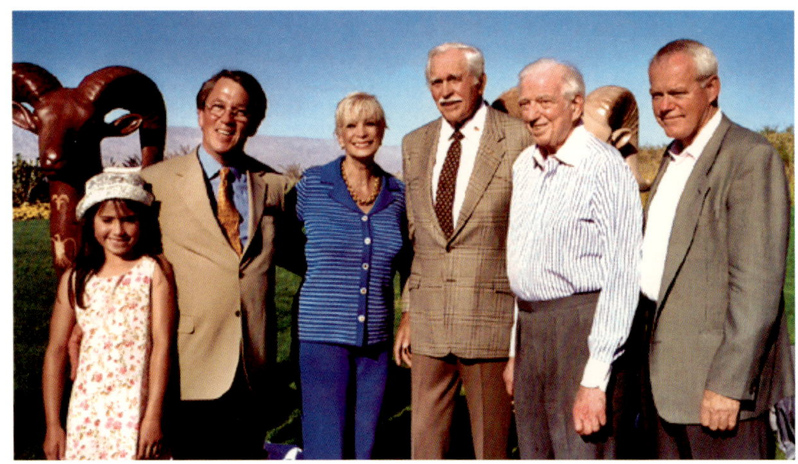

Very special freinds to the Path of the Bighorn and the endangered Peninsular bighorn sheep - Herbert Spiegel, Managing Director of the Lodge at Rancho Mirage, with his daughter Alexandra, and Alexandra Sheldon, Howard Keel, Sidney Sheldon and Jim DeForge during the unveiling ceremony of the first six painted rams held at The Lodge at Rancho Mirage. All of the celebrity actor rams were on display at this beautiful hotel, in kind thanks to the wonderful and very special friendship with Herbert Spiegel.

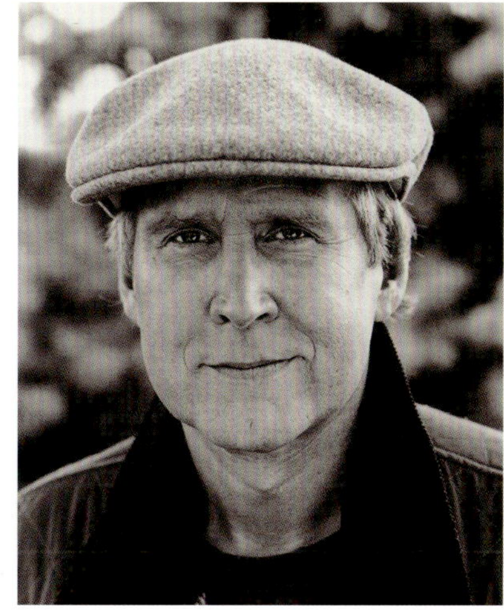

Chevy Chase

artist Chevy Chase
sponsor Mary & Bob VanDusen
inaugural site The Lodge at Rancho Mirage

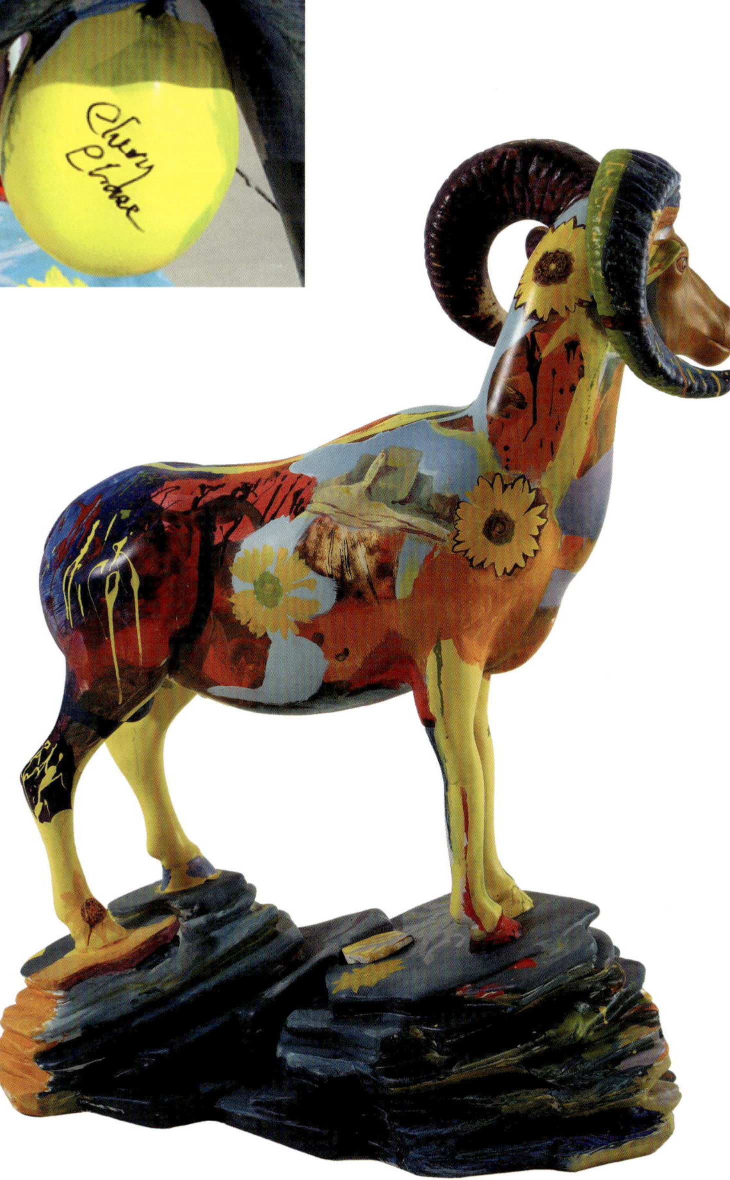

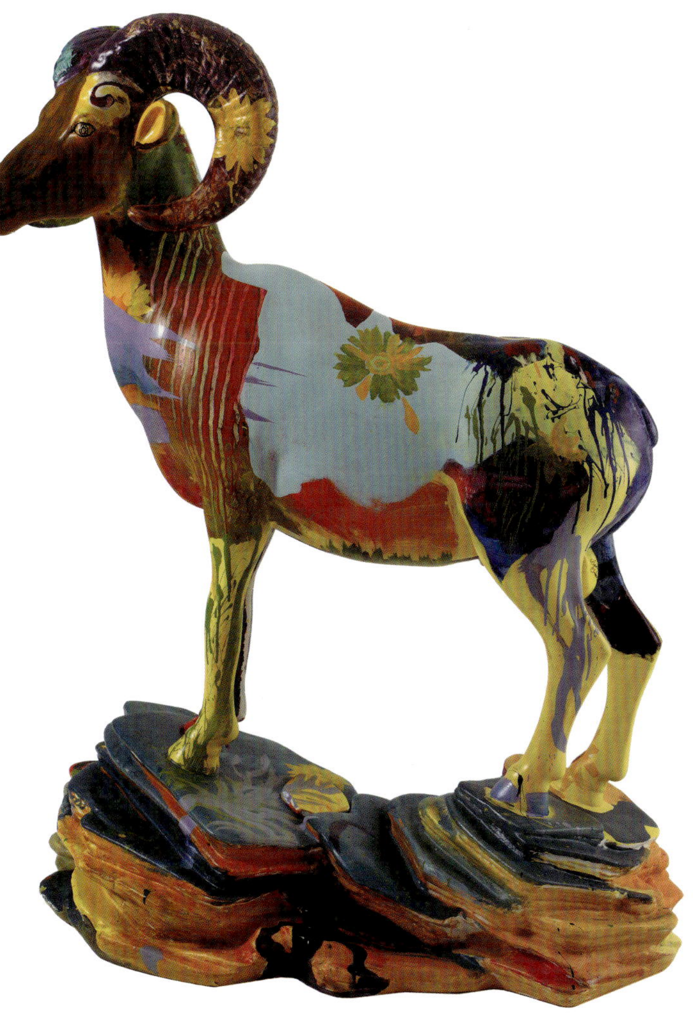

Born Cornelius Crane Chase, he changed his name to Chevy Chase, joined the Saturday Night Live crew, and embarked on a highly successful movie career. Chase scored in the eighties with hits such as Caddyshack, the National Lampoon movies and the Fletch movies. All his films show his talent for deadpan comedy.

Angels at Bat for Bighorn

artist   Ken Zornes & J.R. Best Signs
sponsor   Anaheim Angels
inaugural site   Big League Dreams Sports Park

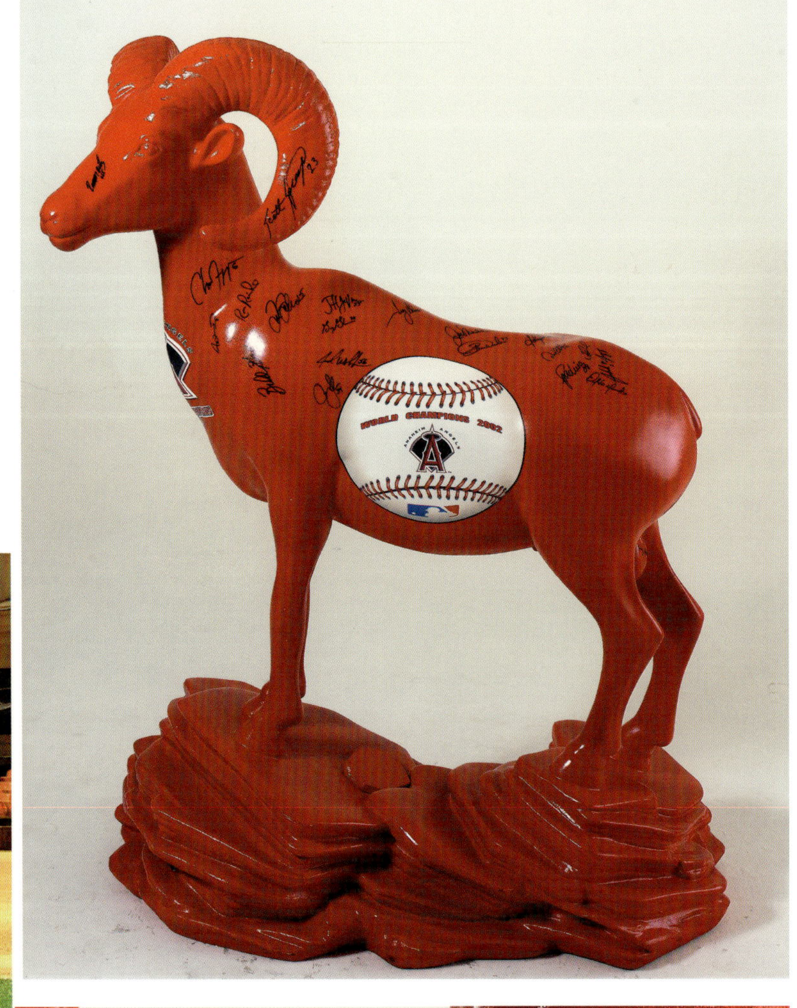

The Angels painted ram was signed by the team after they won the 2002 World Championship. It has graced the premises of Big League Dreams Sport Park in Cathedral City, California. A place where young baseball players come to play in hopes of realizing their dreams of being in the Big League.

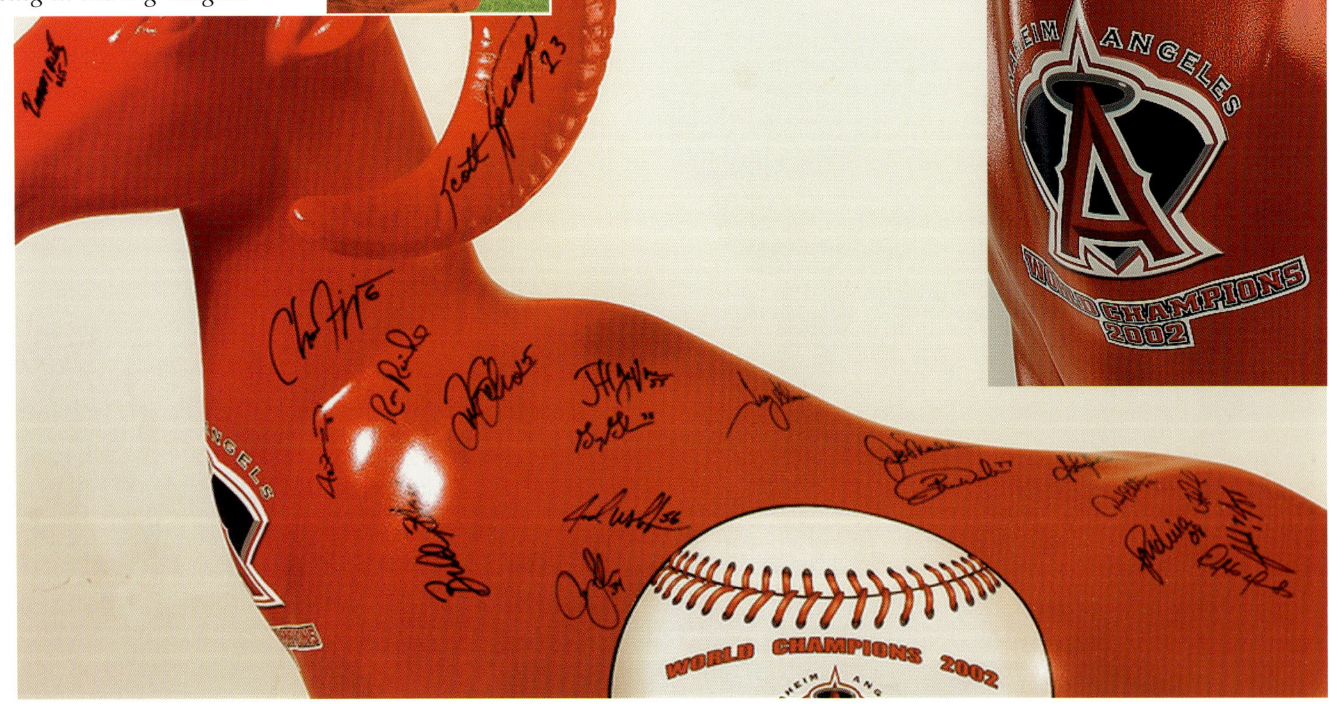

Dodgers at Bat for Bighorn

artist Ken Zornes *&* J.R. Best Signs
sponsor Los Angeles Dodgers
inaugural site Big League Dreams Sports Park

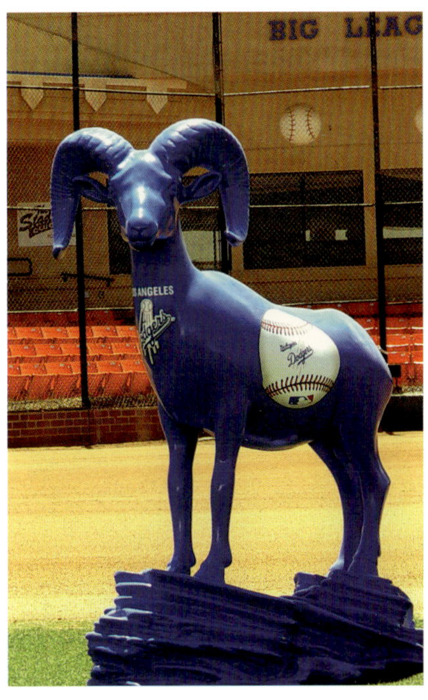

The Los Angeles Dodgers painted ram was signed during a special event... the 2004 RBI dinner... for inner city youth to be able to learn and have a place to play baseball with the players of the Los Angeles Dodgers, and other major league teams. This ram has also graced Big League Dreams Sports Park in Cathedral City, California.

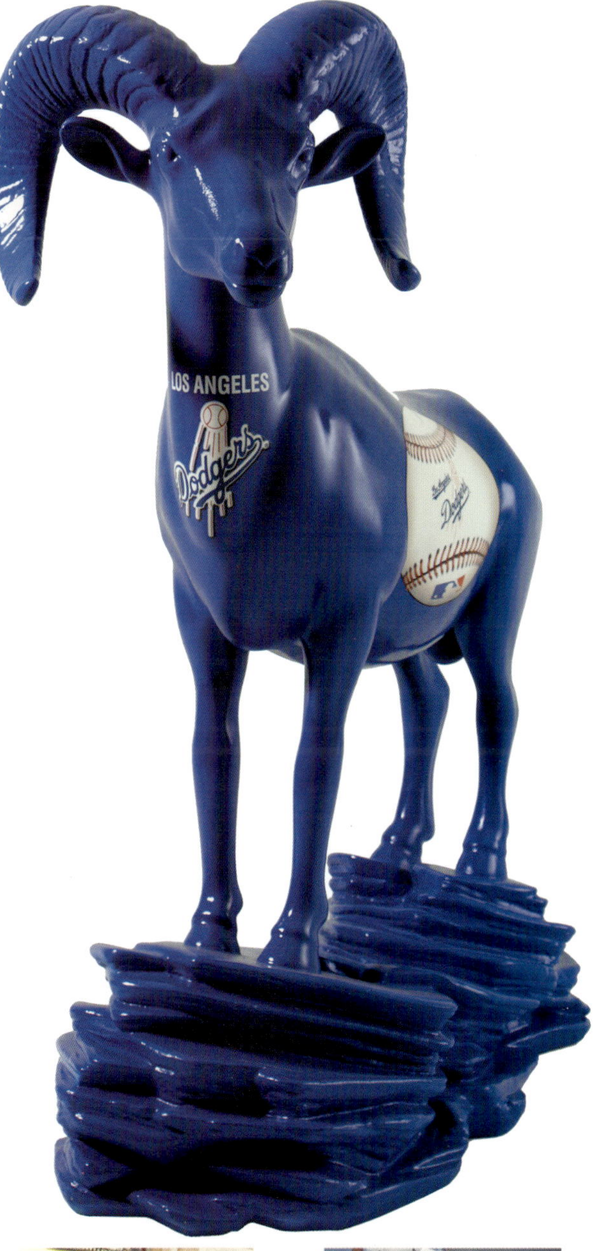

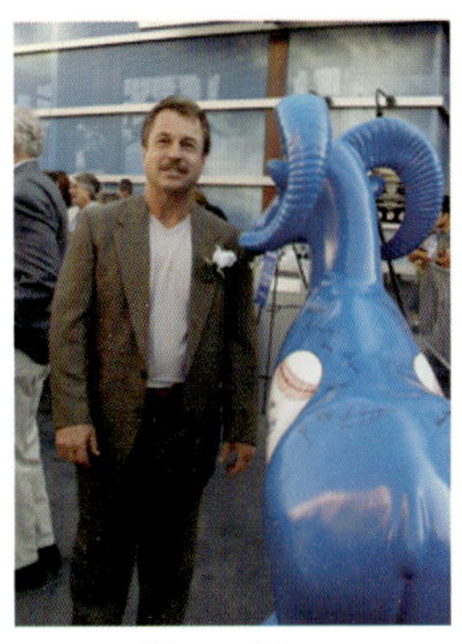

Ron Cey

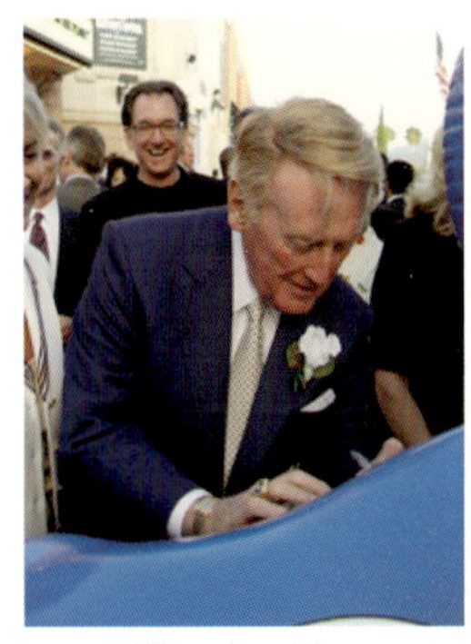

Vin Scully

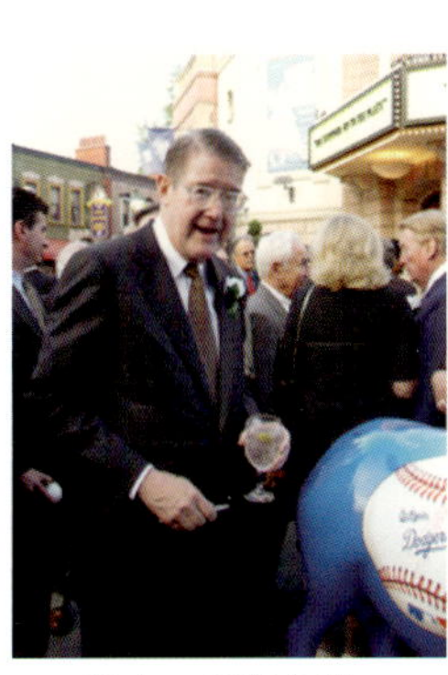

Peter O'Mally

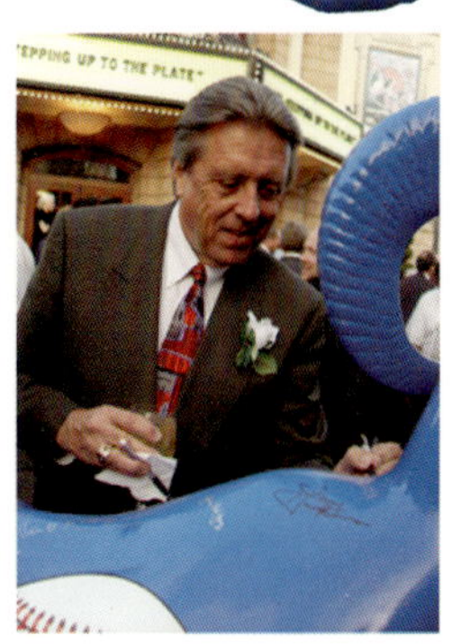

Rick Monday

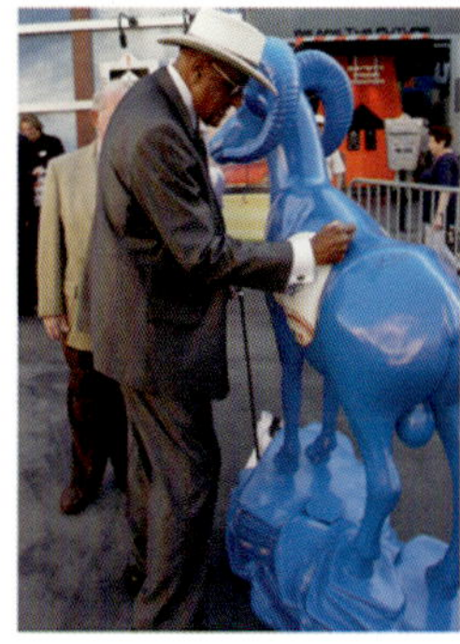

Don Newcombe

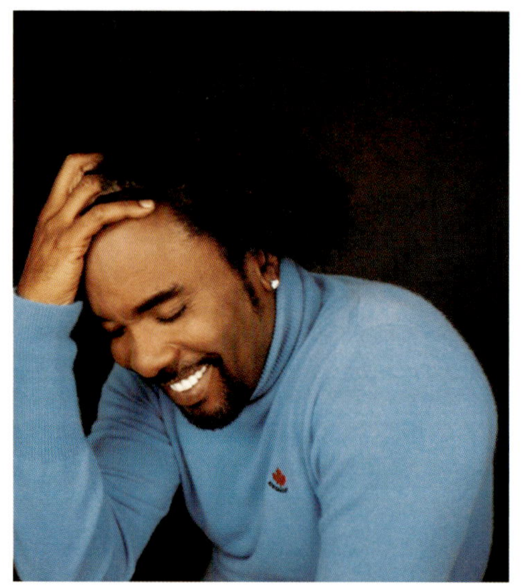

Cabaret

artist Lee Daniels
sponsor The Mann's & the Sheldon's
inaugural site The Lodge at Rancho Mirage

Lee Daniels is an actor, and the producer of - Monsters Ball starring Halle Berry and Billy Bob Thornton; The Woodsman starring Kevin Bacon, Kyra Sedgwick - release date December 24, 2004 and is premiering as a director, with the movie Shadowboxer, starring Cuba Gooding Jr. Lee created his painted and decorated ram sculpture "Cabaret" during the filming of Shadowboxer in Philadelphia... this glittering ram appears in the movie.

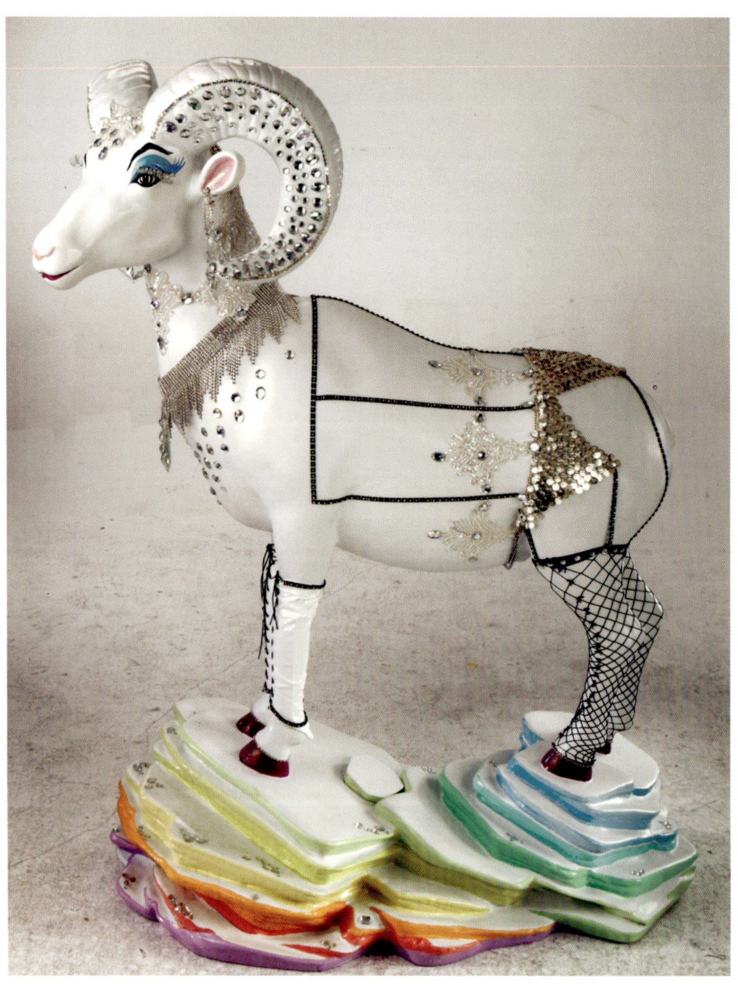

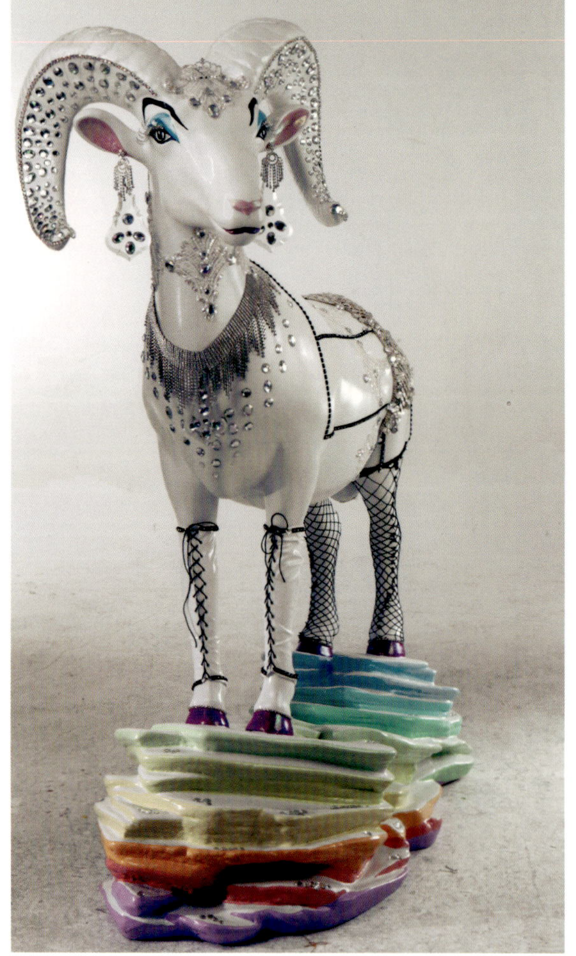

Fish Out of Water

artist   Sally Struthers
sponsor   Mary & Sam Langford
inaugural site   The Lodge at Rancho Mirage

Actress Sally Struthers is a multi-faceted actress starring and appearing in everything from All in the Family, Gilmore Girls, and many guest appearances to being a spokesperson for the Christian Children's Fund.
"By the time I painted my ram I'd had time to see what everyone else had done and I wanted to do something completely different. I thought about the ram as a species and its evolution and how many thousands of years it had roamed the desert. Those deserts were once under water and if you believe Darwin's theories, then the ram's inception began as some sort of fish. So I called it 'Fish out of Water'."

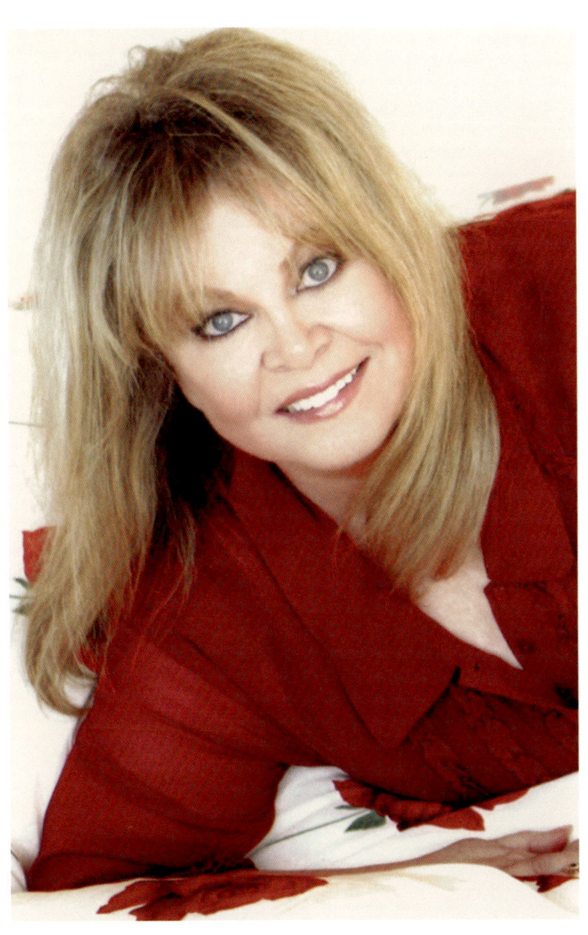

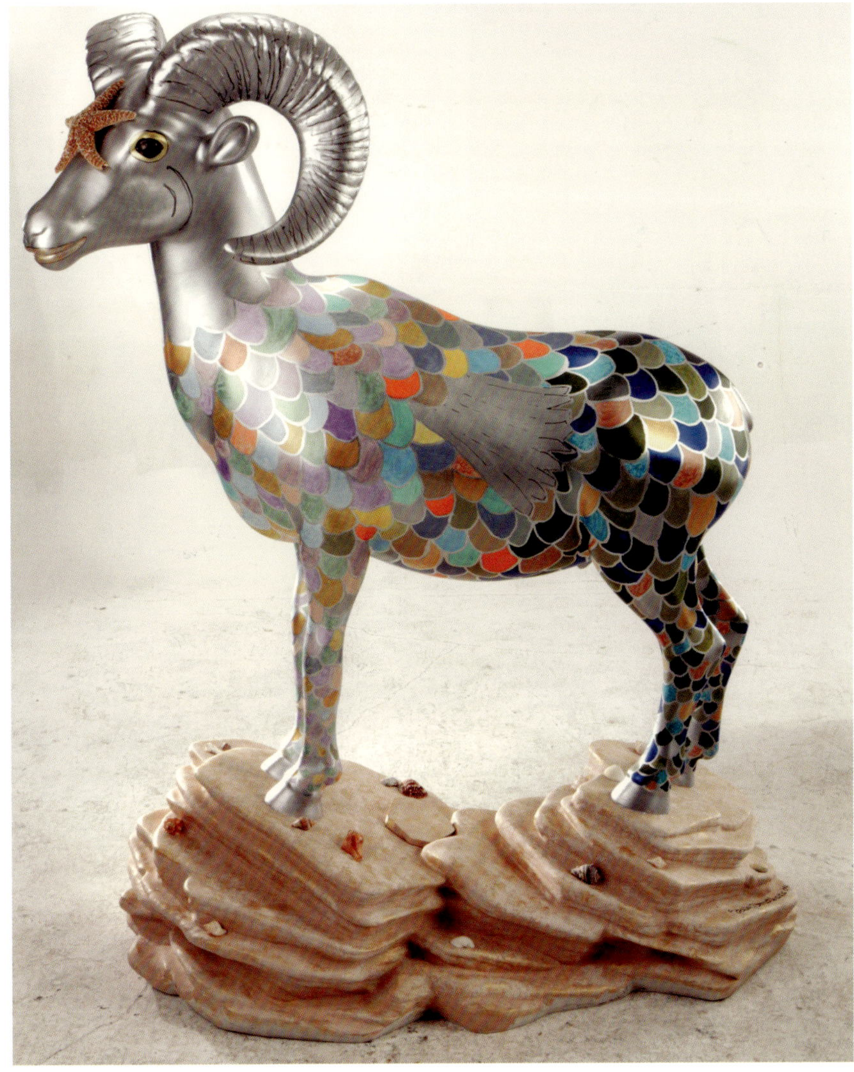

Morning Walk with Friends

artist Alexandra & Sidney Sheldon
sponsor Renoir & Sasha
inaugural site The Lodge at Rancho Mirage

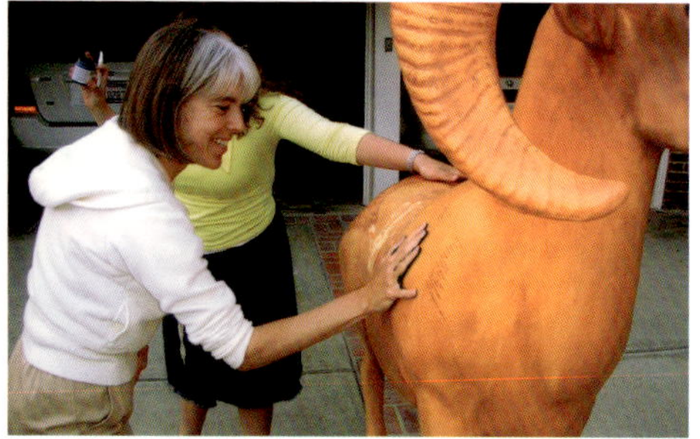

Sidney's daughter Mary

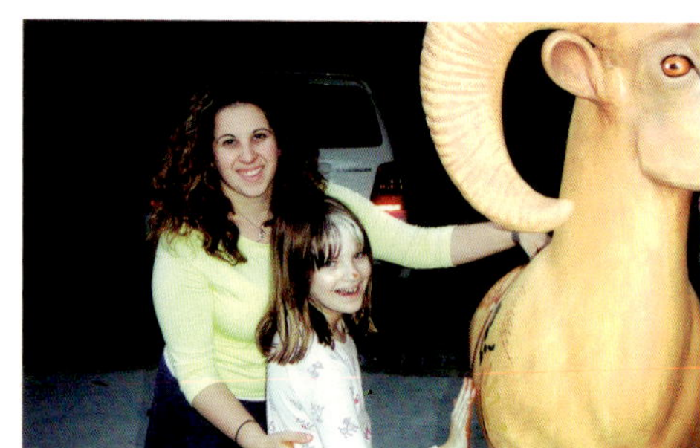

Grandchildren Lizy & Rebecca

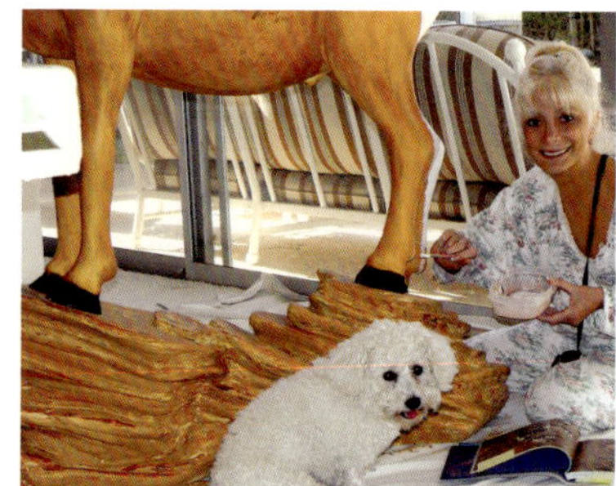

Alexandra with help from Sasha

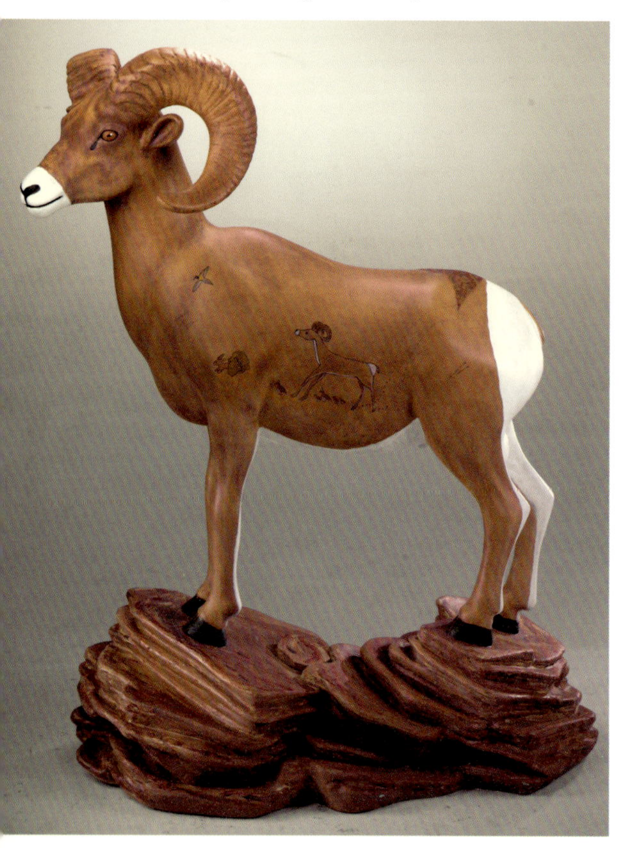

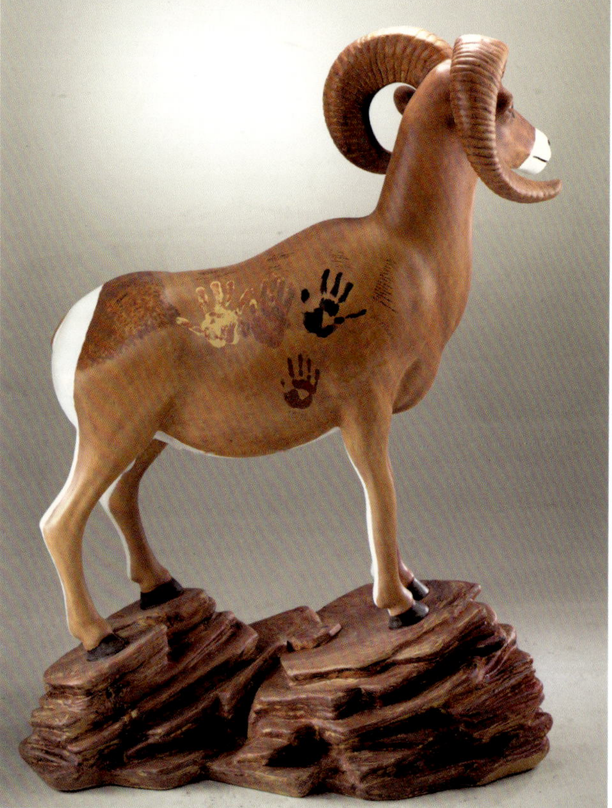

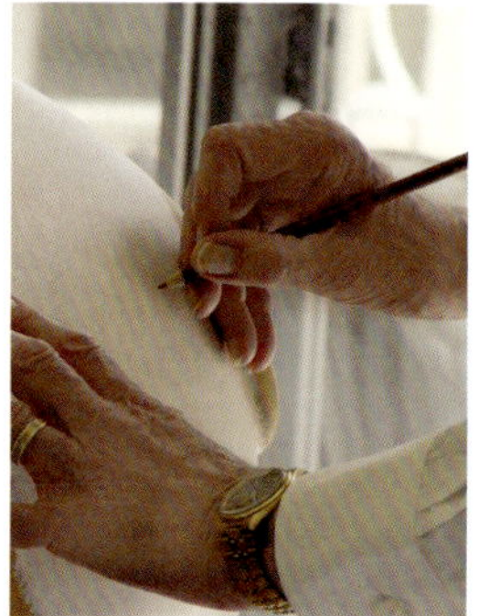

Sidney creates with words and paint

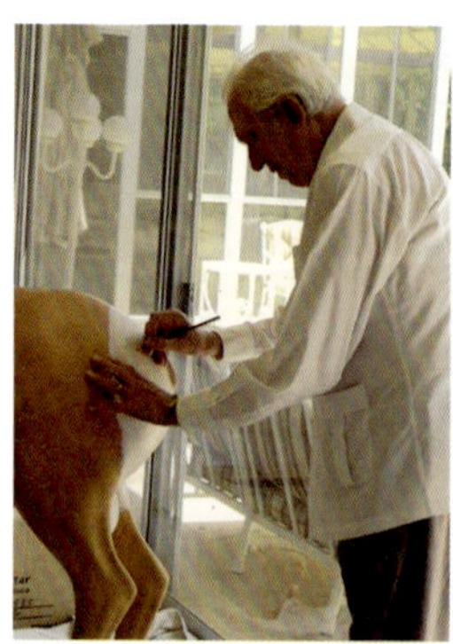

The Storyteller

artist Alexandra & Sidney Sheldon
sponsor Corniche Travel
inaugural site Palm Springs Public Library

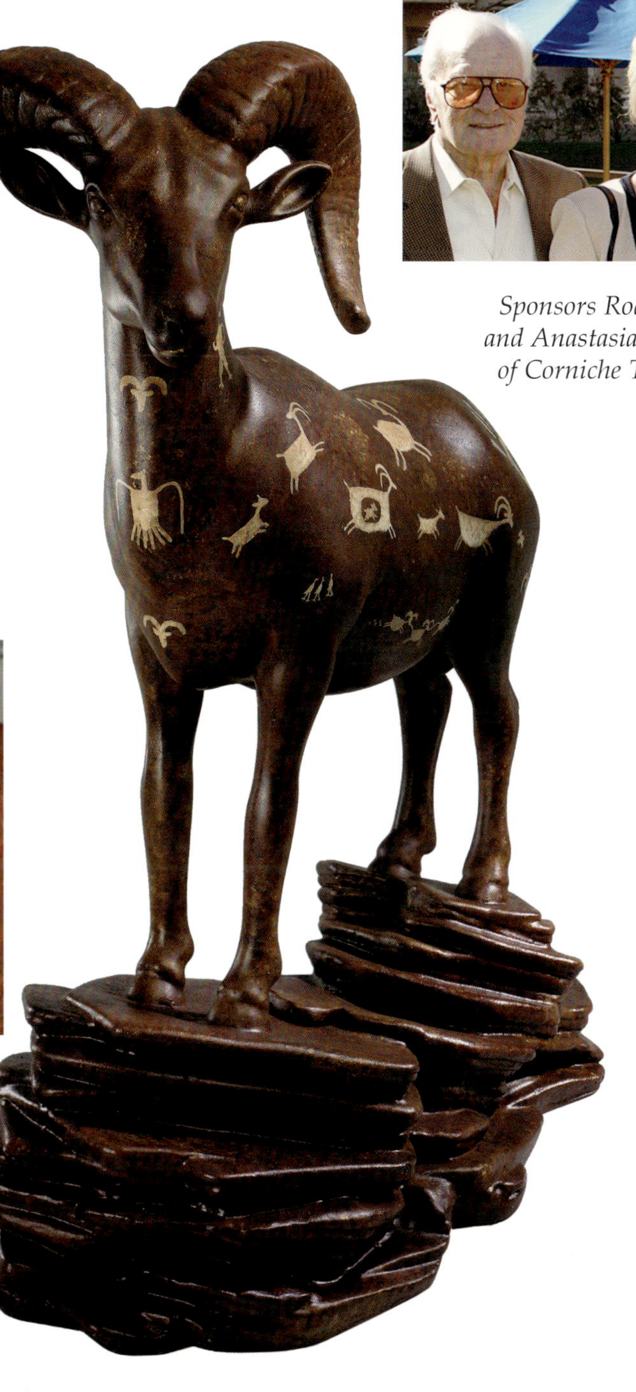

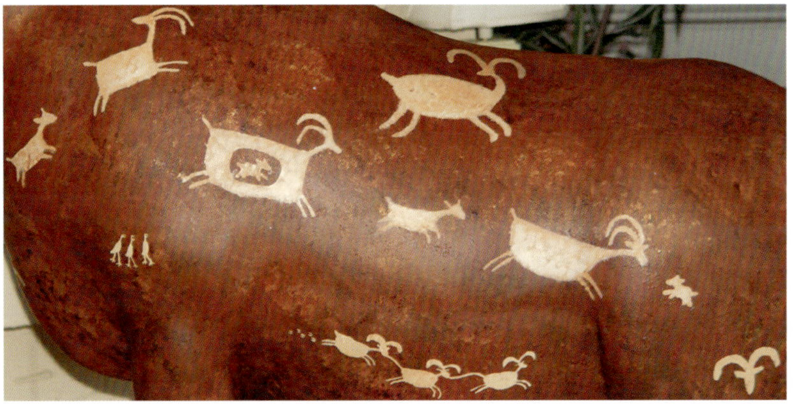

A master storyteller, Sidney Sheldon has garnered international praise and recognition the world over. The winner of an Oscar, a Tony and an Edgar Allan Poe Award, Sheldon has over 200 television scripts, 25 major motion pictures, 6 Broadway plays and 18 novels (which have sold over 300 million copies) to his credit, ranking him as one of the world's most prolific writers. With each of his books having hit #1 on the New York Times bestsellers list, Sheldon is one of three best-selling authors alive today.

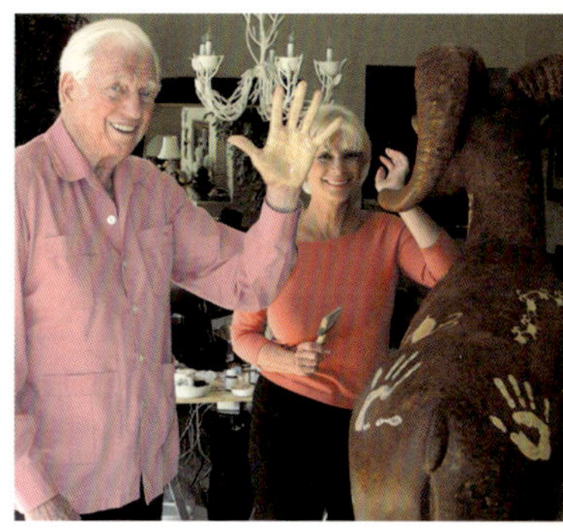

Sponsors Roderick and Anastasia Mann of Corniche Travel

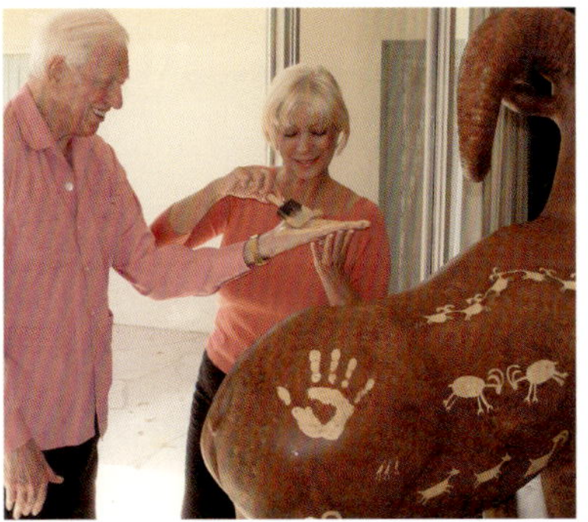
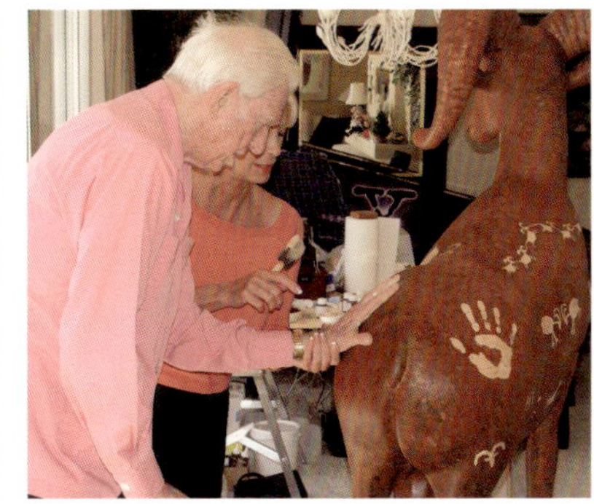
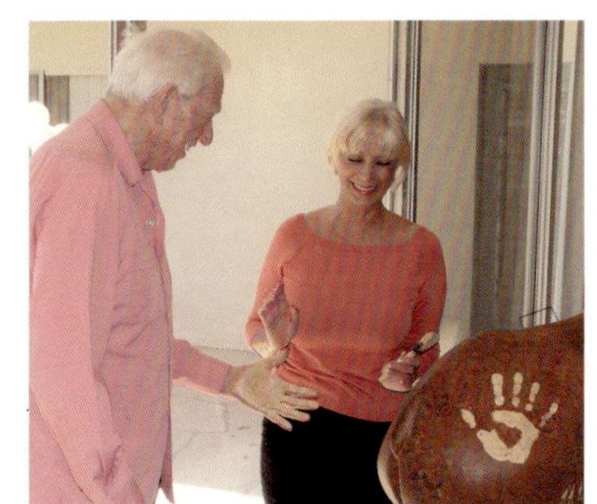

Quagga

artist   Stefanie Powers
sponsor   Sidney Sheldon
inaugural site   The Lodge at Rancho Mirage

Stefanie Powers is a veteran of over 200 television appearances as well as the star of ABC's 80's hit, "Hart to Hart" (1979). In addition to her international fame as Jennifer Hart, Stefanie was also the star of such T.V. series as "The Girl from U.N.C.L.E.", (1966), "Feather and Father Gang"(1977) and "Maggie". In 1974, Stefanie formed a friendship with actor William Holden. Through many similarities and interests, their relationship blossomed into one of romance that would last until the sudden death of Holden in 1981. Stefanie is also President of the William Holden Wildlife Foundation, Director of the Mount Kenya Game Ranch and international speaker on wildlife preservation.

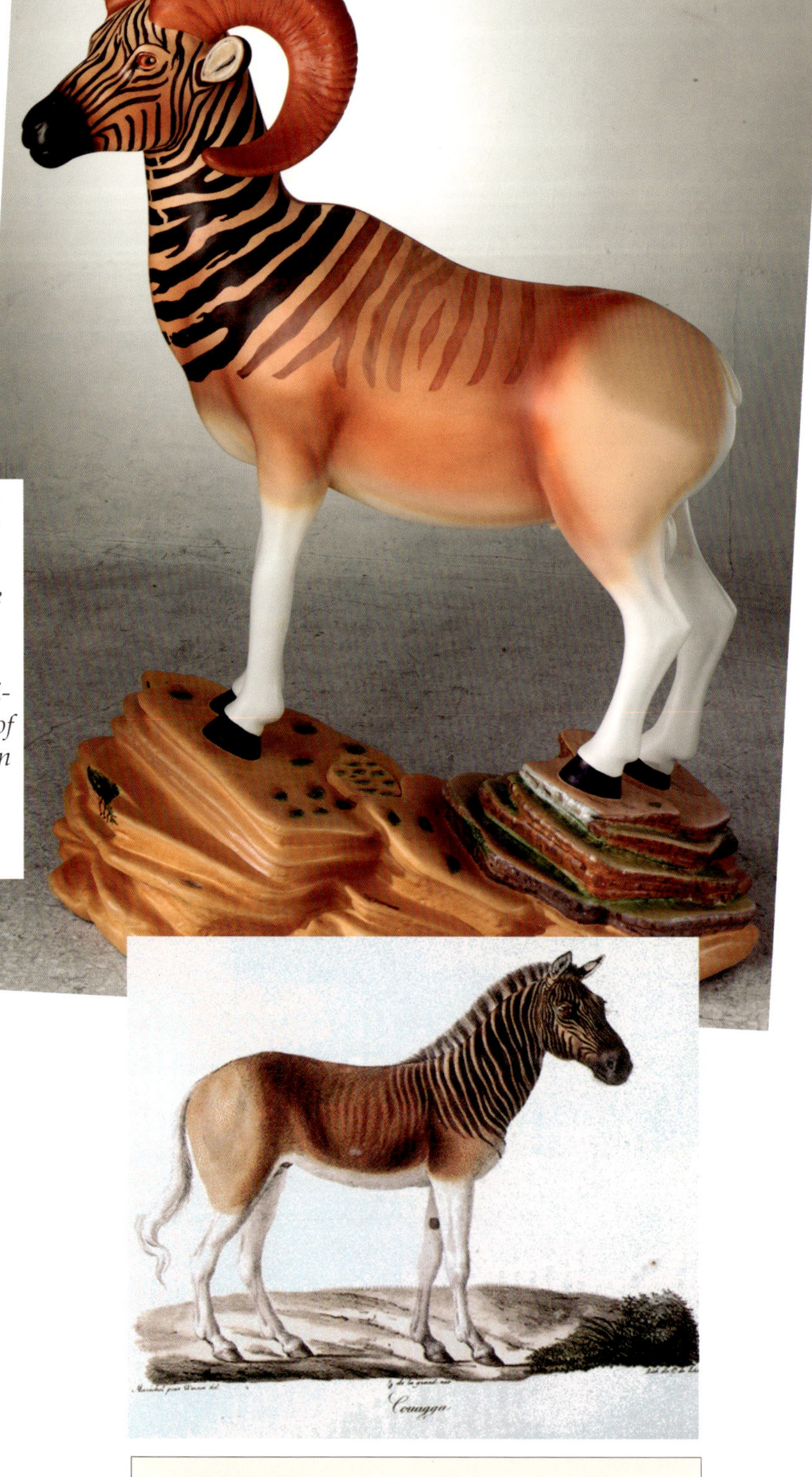

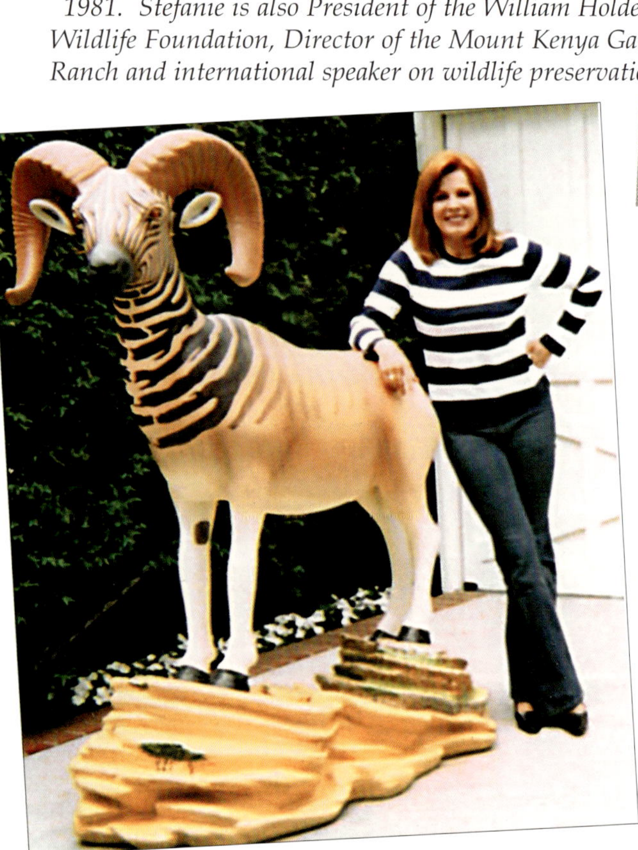

Stefanie Powers painted her ram sculpture based on the extinct zebra, Quagga. Her message to everyone is "Please do not let the Peninsular bighorn sheep go the way of the Quagga."

Still Dreamin'

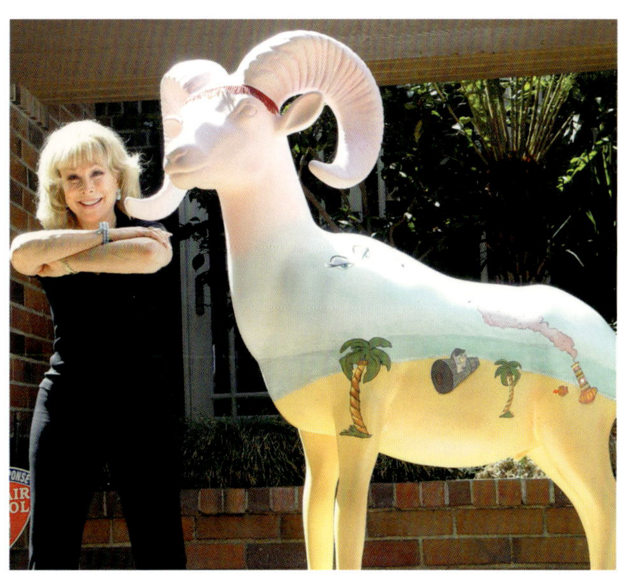

artist Barbara Eden
sponsor Sidney Sheldon
inaugural site The Lodge at Rancho Mirage

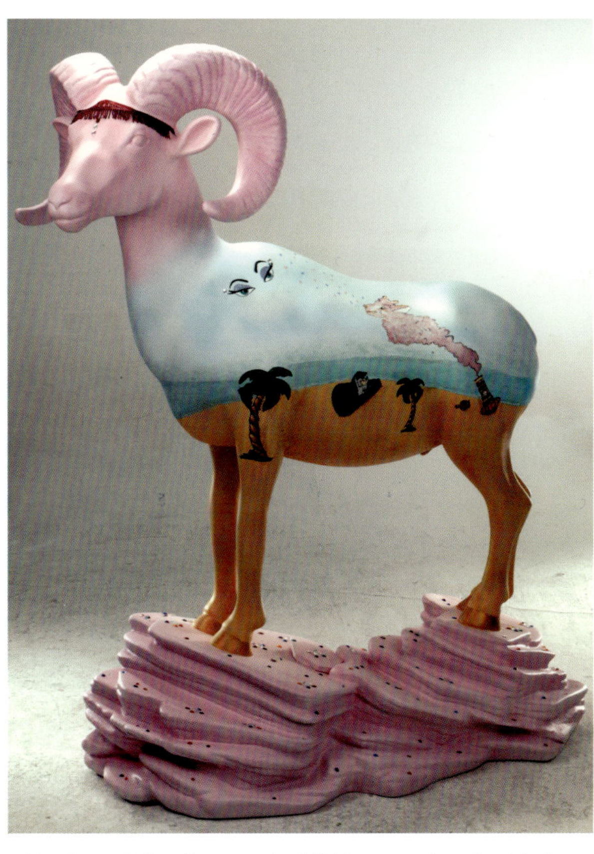

Barbara Eden is most indelibly associated with her role as the genie in the bottle in the long-running T.V. sitcom "I Dream of Jeannie" (1965), co-starring Larry Hagman. Her first film role was in "Back from Eternity" (1956). In 1957, she starred on T.V. in "How to Marry a Millionaire" and she starred in "Harper Valley P.T.A."

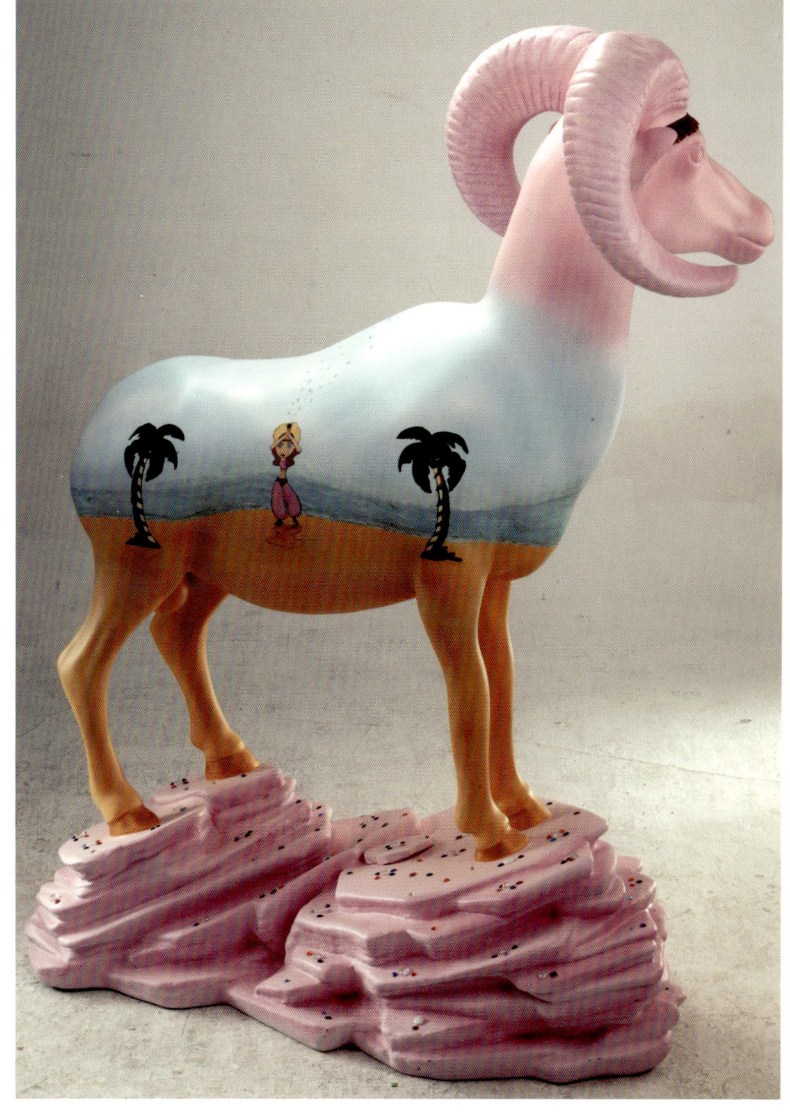

Sam the Ram

artist Phyllis Diller
sponsor Bob & Dolores Hope
inaugural site The Lodge at Rancho Mirage

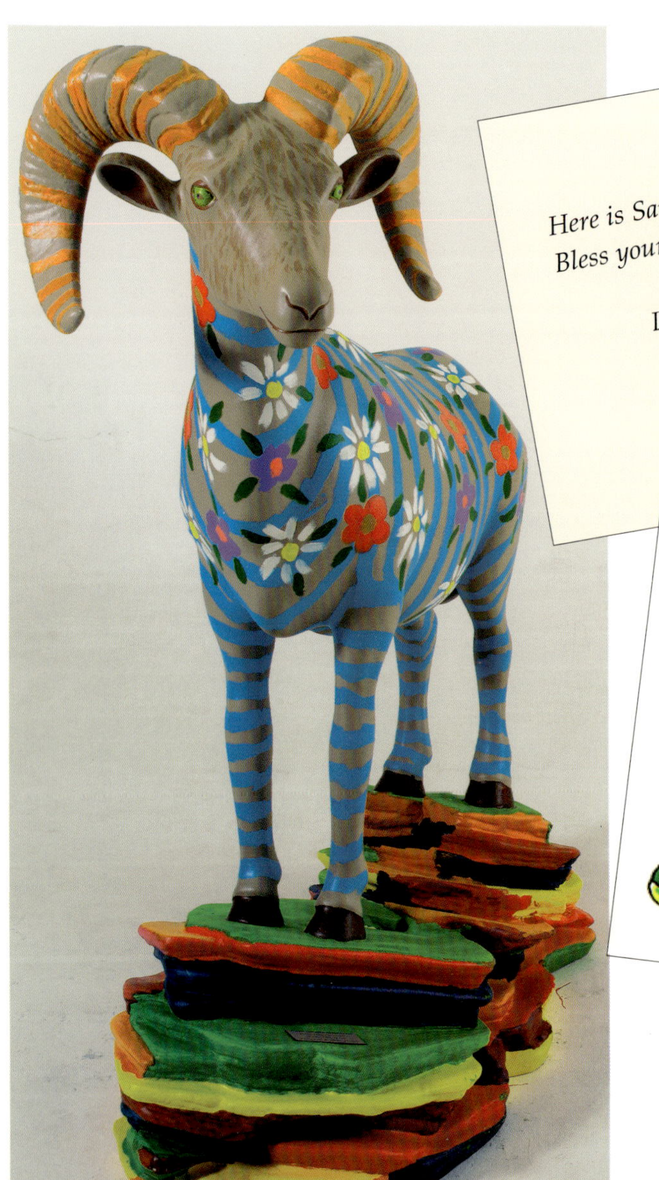

Here is Sam the Ram!.
Bless your work.

LOVE,
Phyllis

Comedienne Phyllis Diller is famed for her stand-up routine where she talks about her fictional husband "Fang". Phyllis briefly served as an honorary mayor in the affluent town of Brentwood, California. She studied at Chicago's Sherwood Music Conservatory. As of 2000, Phyllis had appeared as a piano soloist with 100 symphony orchestras across the United States. She received her star on the Hollywood Walk of Fame in 1993. She describes her comedy as "tragedy revisited".

Sugar

artist Tony Curtis
sponsor The Lodge at Rancho Mirage
inaugural site The Lodge at Rancho Mirage

Tony Curtis, was born in the Bronx and started his career in the movies in 1949 coming from the theatre, using at first the name James Curtis and later Anthony Curtis. He has been in such wonderful movies such as: "Sweet Smell of Success", "The Defiant Ones" (earning an Oscar nomination as an escaped convict chained to Sidney Poitier), "Some Like it Hot" (1959, partnered with Jack Lemmon, as a crossdressing musician, who tries to woo Marilyn Monroe), and "Operation Petticoat", "Spartacus", "The Great Imposter", "The Outsiders" (1961, as Native American war hero Ira Hayes). Later he confined himself to lightweight comedies like "Forty Pounds of Trouble" (1963), "Goodbye Charlie", "Sex and the Single Girl" and "The Great Race". Tony starred with his late wife Janet Leigh in the fanciful bio-pic "Houdini". Tony's painted ram sculpture "Sugar" is based on Marilyn Monroe's part from the movie "Some Like it Hot".

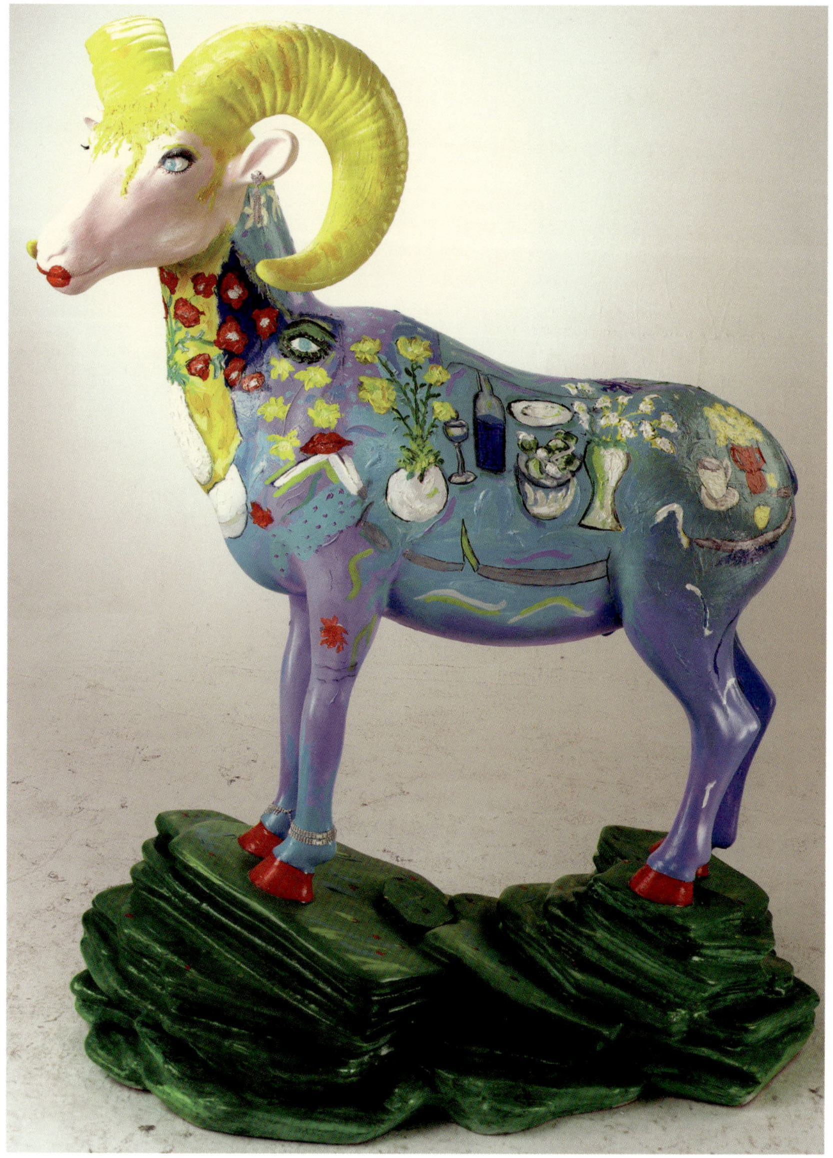

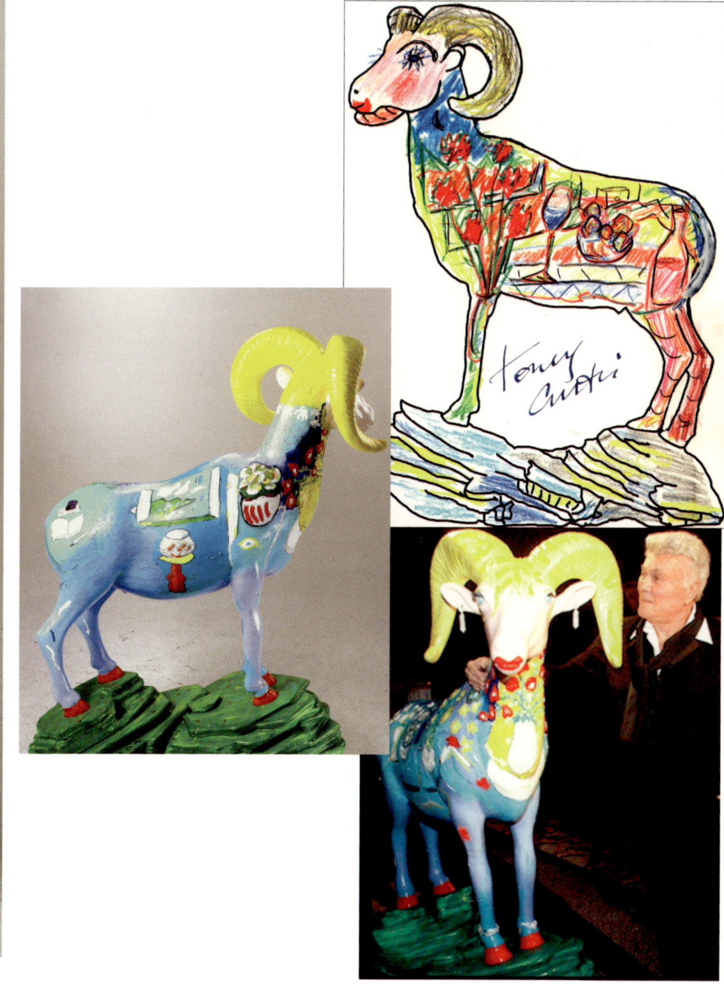

Ramses

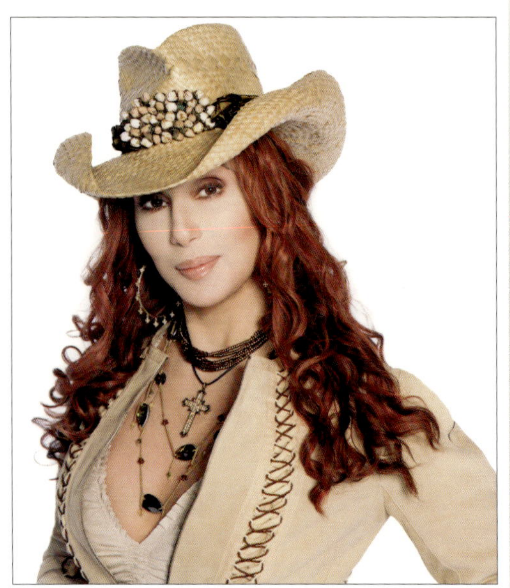

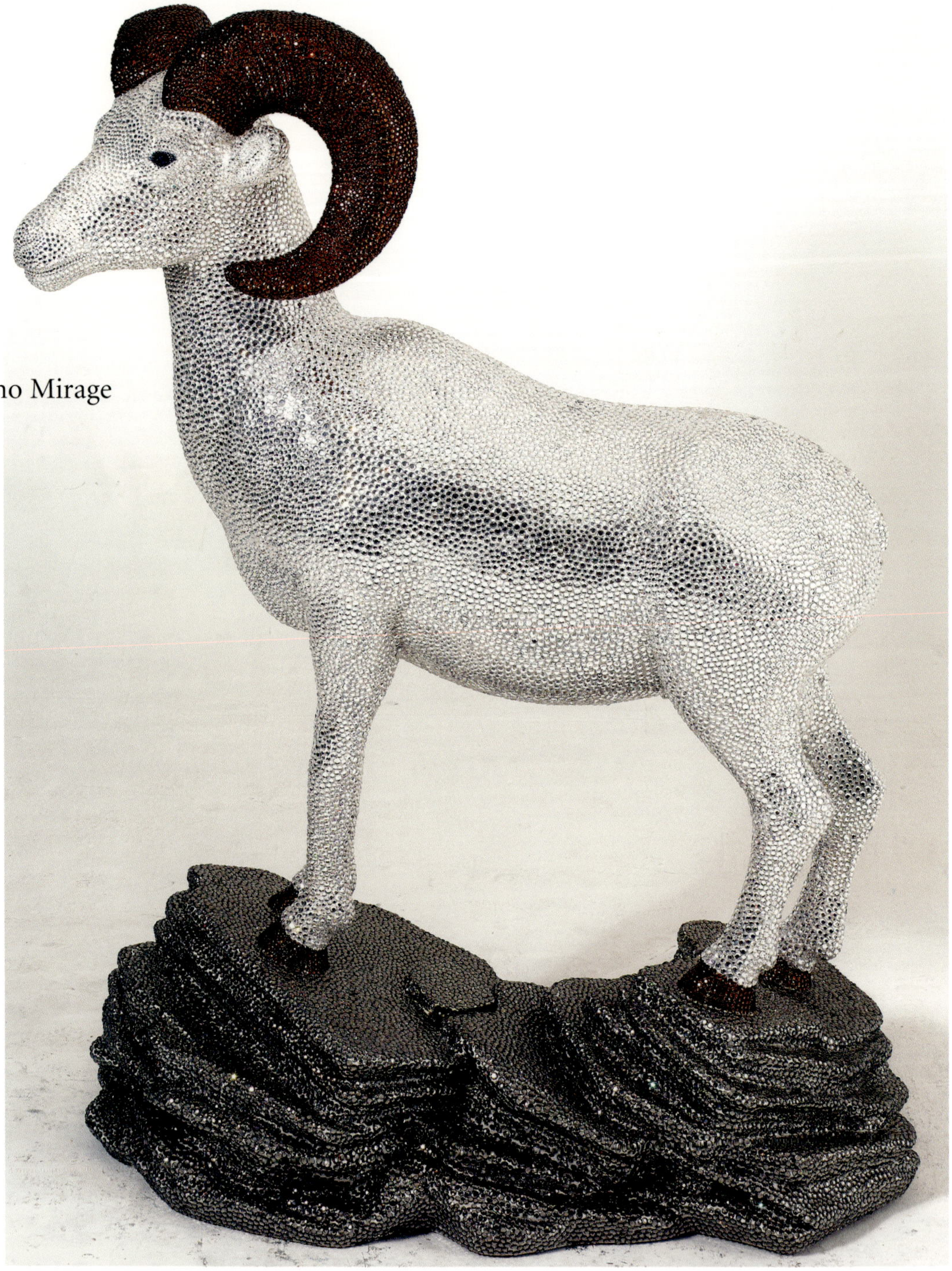

Cher's top television series with then-husband Sonny Bono in the 1960's and 1970's made Cher a pop culture icon before she ever hit the silver screen. While she is known world-wide for her singing, acting is her preferred medium, in her own words..."it is so much deeper". Cher has appeared in a number of films such as: "Come Back to the Five and Dime", "Jimmy Dean, Jimmy Dean" and "Good Times" (1967, with Sonny) and "Mask". Cher was nominated for a Best Supporting Actress Academy Award for a strong performance in "Silkwood". The Oscar that she coveted did not elude her for long; she won the 1987 Best Actress Academy Award for her performance in "Moonstruck". Cher's beautiful ram sculpture "Ramses" is created out of thousands of Austrian crystals.

Yukon Gold

artist Anjelica Huston
sponsor Alexandra & Sidney Sheldon
inaugural site The Lodge at Rancho Mirage

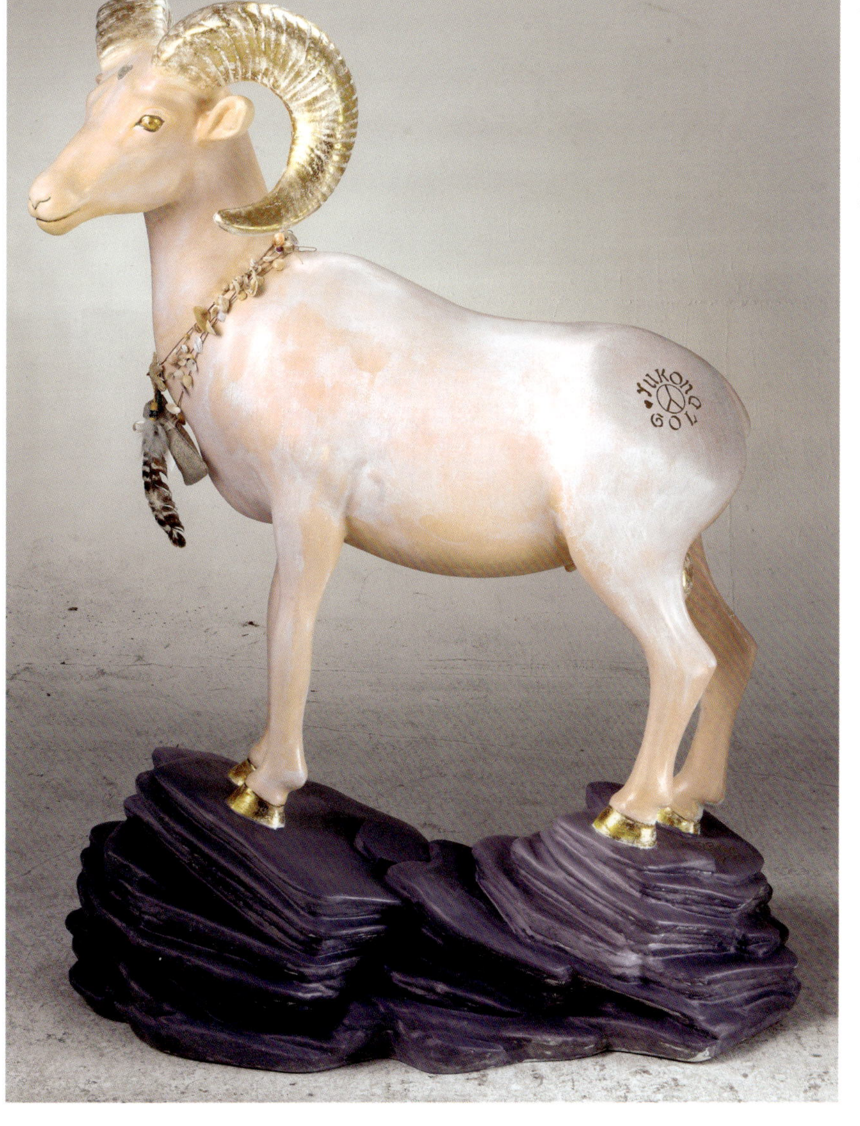

Anjelica Huston's brilliant acting shone brightly in the black comedy "Prizzi's Honor", which won her a Best Supporting Actress Oscar. She earned additional Academy Award nominations as Ron Silver's long-lost wife in "Enemies", "Love Story", and as John Cusack's amoral mom in "The Grifters". She was also perfectly cast as the sinister but svelte Morticia Addams in "The Addams Family" and its 1993 sequel, "Addams Family Values". She teamed up with Jack Nicholson for "The Crossing Guard". Some of her other films are: "Swashbuckler", "The Last Tycoon", "The Postman Always Rings Twice" (starring long time flame Jack Nicholson), "Frances", "The Ice Pirates", "This Is Spinal Tap", "Gardens of Stone", "The Dead" (The latter John Huston's final directorial effort), "Mr. North" (1989), "Crimes and Misdemeanors" and "The Witches". Anjelica's painted ram is based on the Robert Service poem "Yukon Gold"...a copy of that poem is tucked away in the little pouch around "Yukon Gold's" neck.

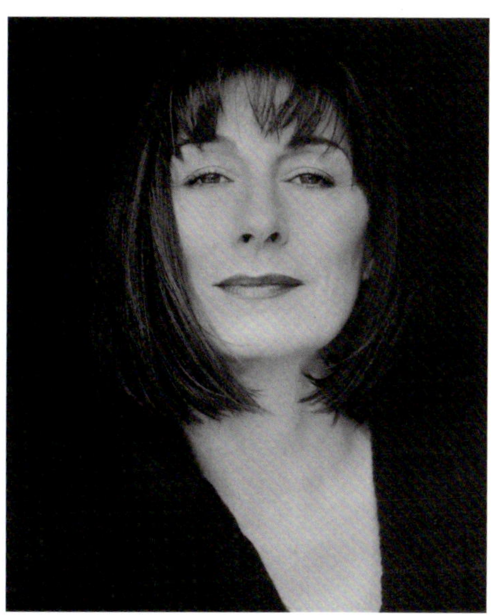

Path of the Bighorn has been blessed with the support and creative inspiration by so many celebrities whose beautiful work is showcased on the preceding pages. They generously took time from their busy careers to join our effort in drawing attention to the conservation of endangered Peninsular bighorn sheep. However, many others wanted to participate in the project but their demanding schedules made it difficult for them to paint a life-sized sculpture.

That's when we thought of a solution: we asked them to use their imaginations to draw a sketch of a bighorn sheep. More than 70 notable names in the fields of music, film, television and sports submitted a colorful drawing. The sketches that follow prove their creative talents run deep and well beyond their chosen professional fields.

We think you'll agree.

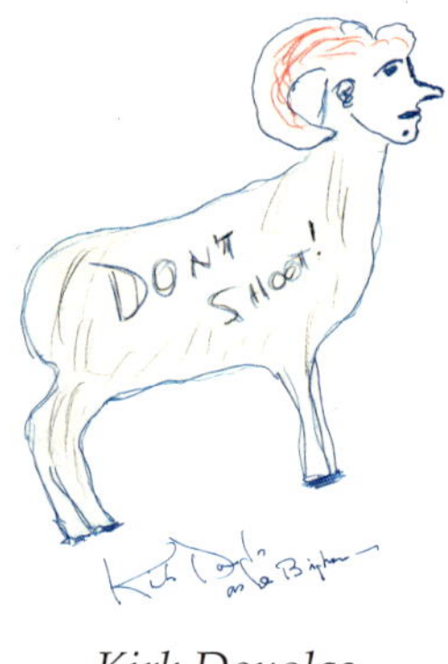

Kirk Douglas

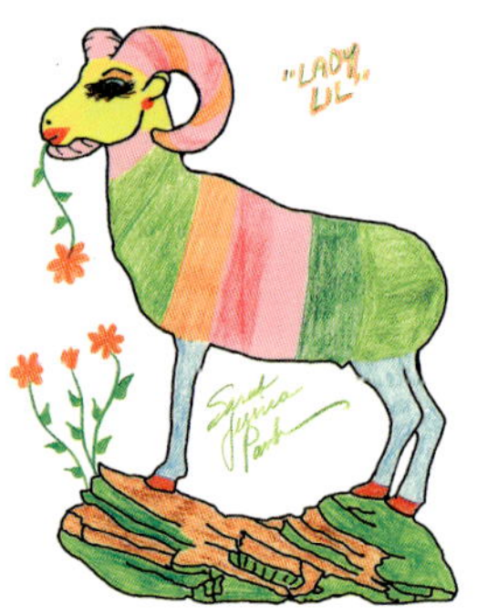
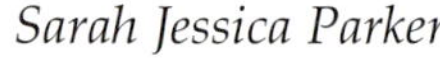

Sarah Jessica Parker

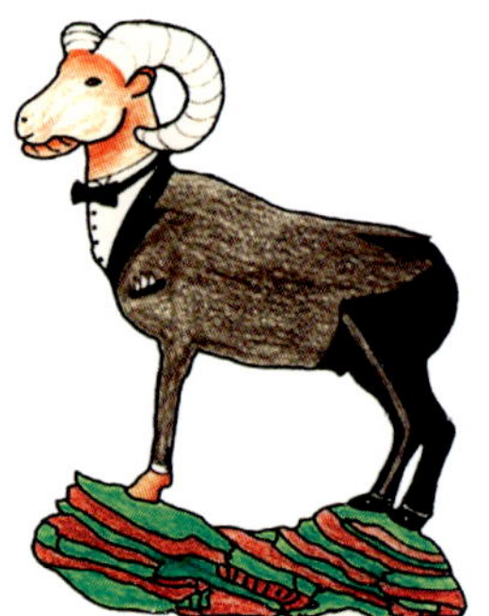

Johnny Mathis

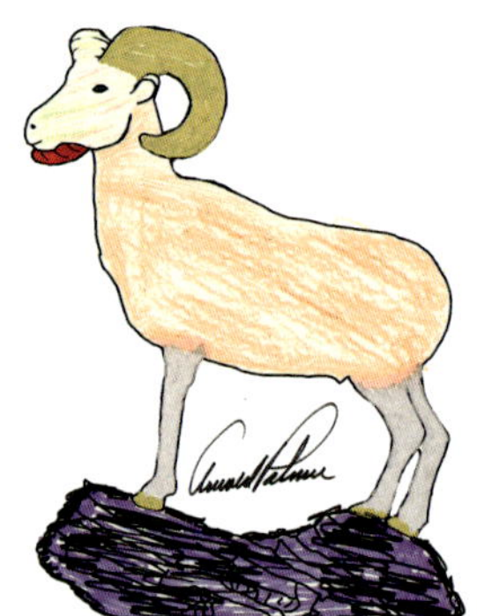

Arnold Palmer

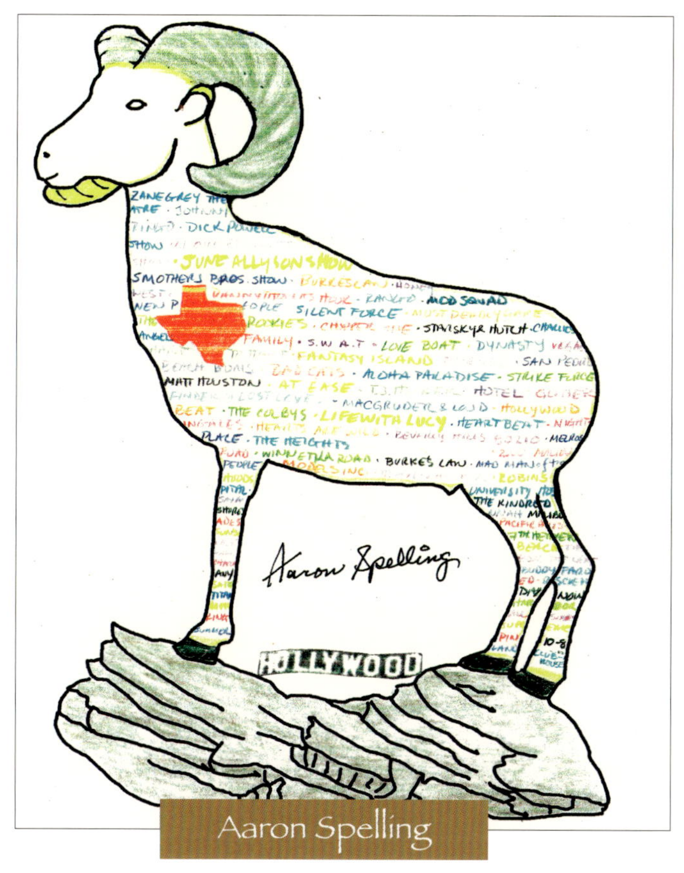

Aaron Spelling

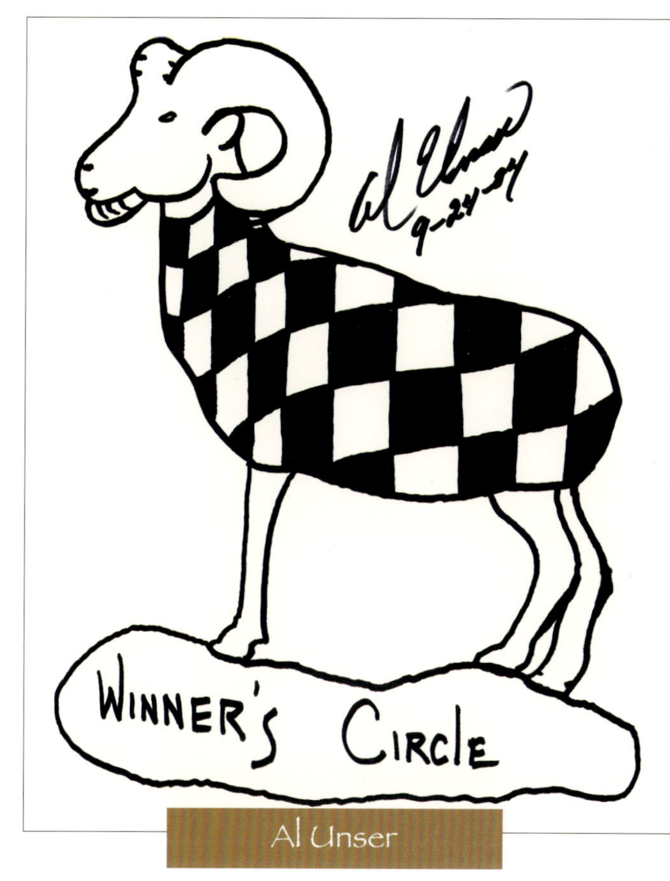

Al Unser

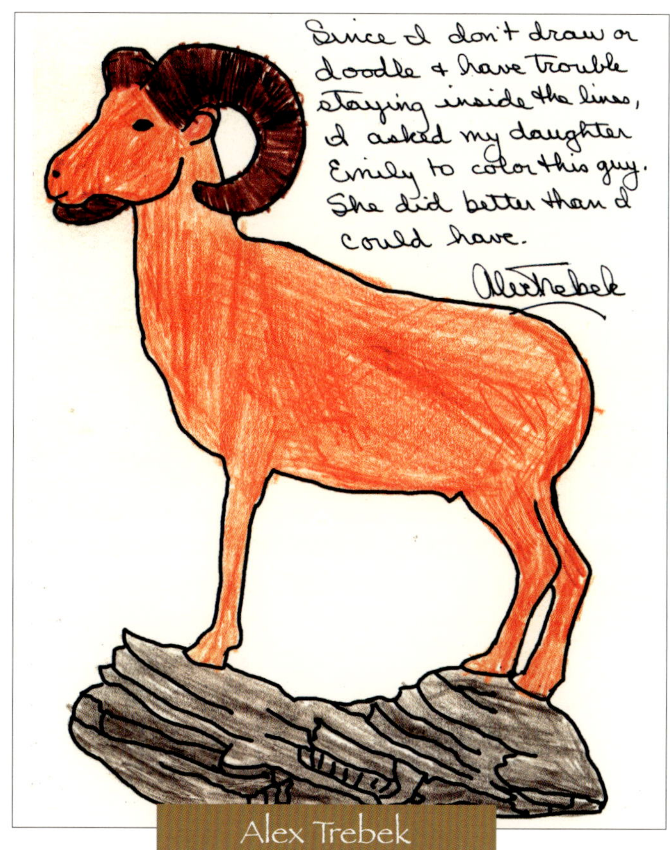

Alex Trebek

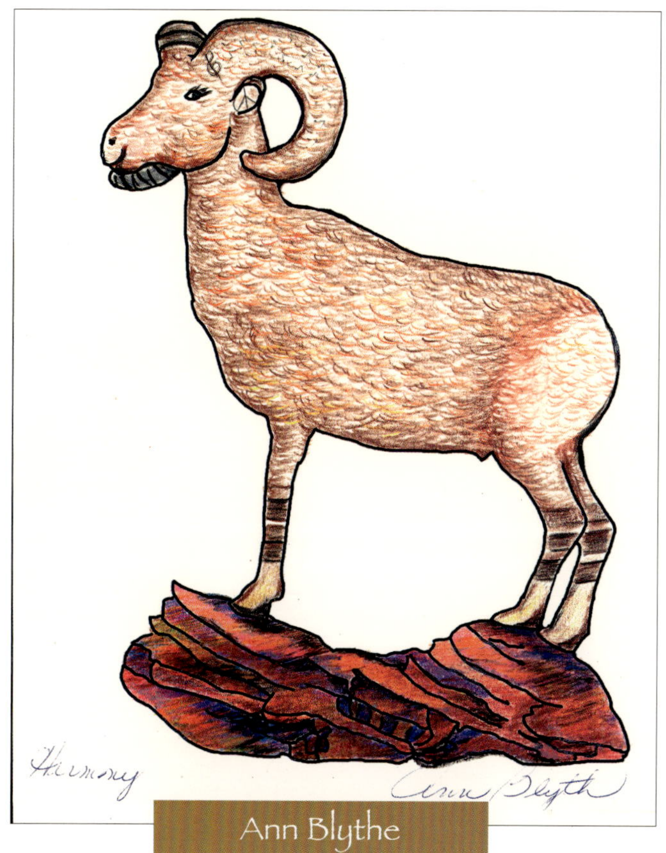

Ann Blythe

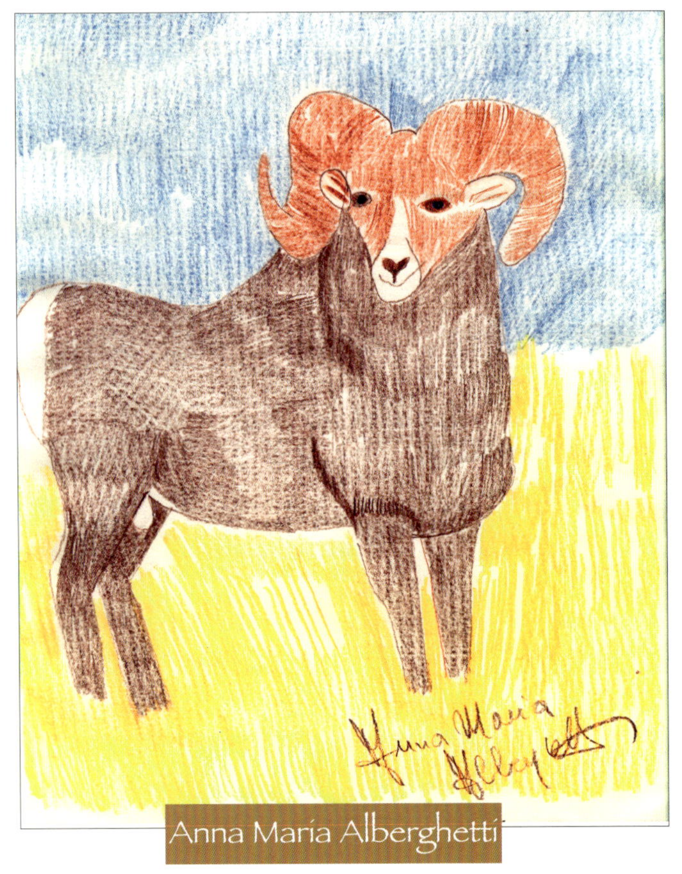

Anna Maria Alberghetti

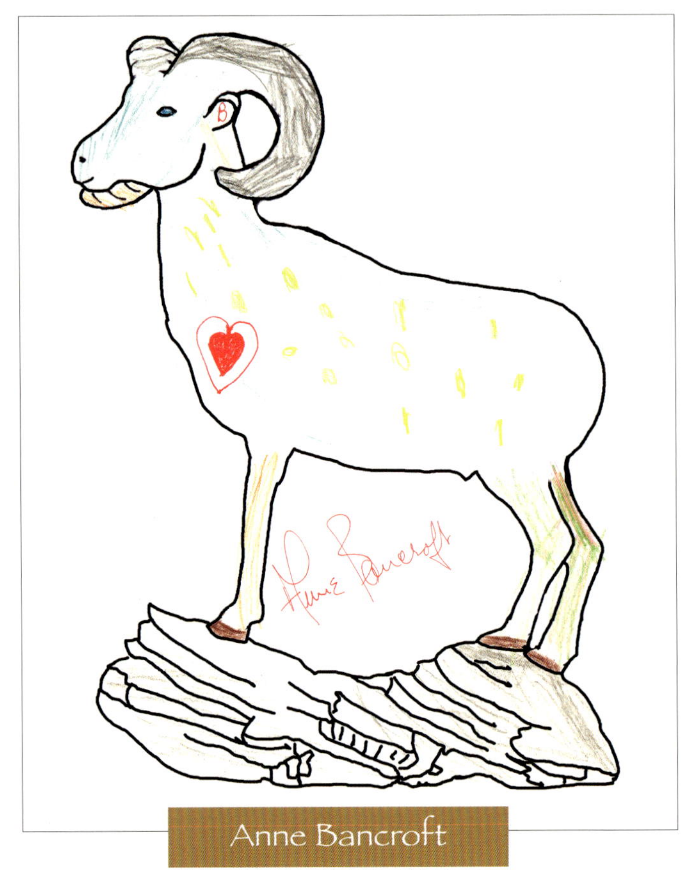

Anne Bancroft

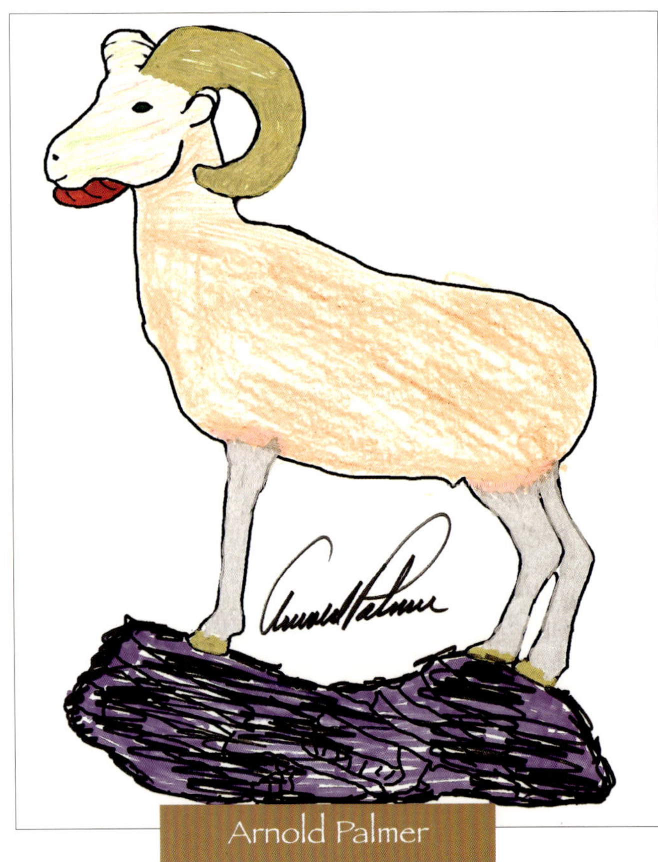

Arnold Palmer

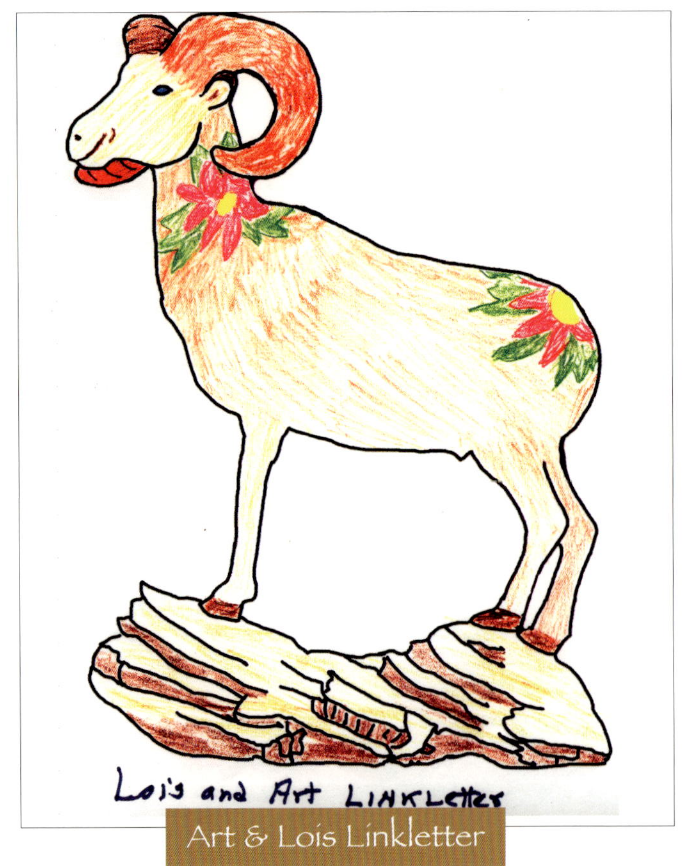

Art & Lois Linkletter

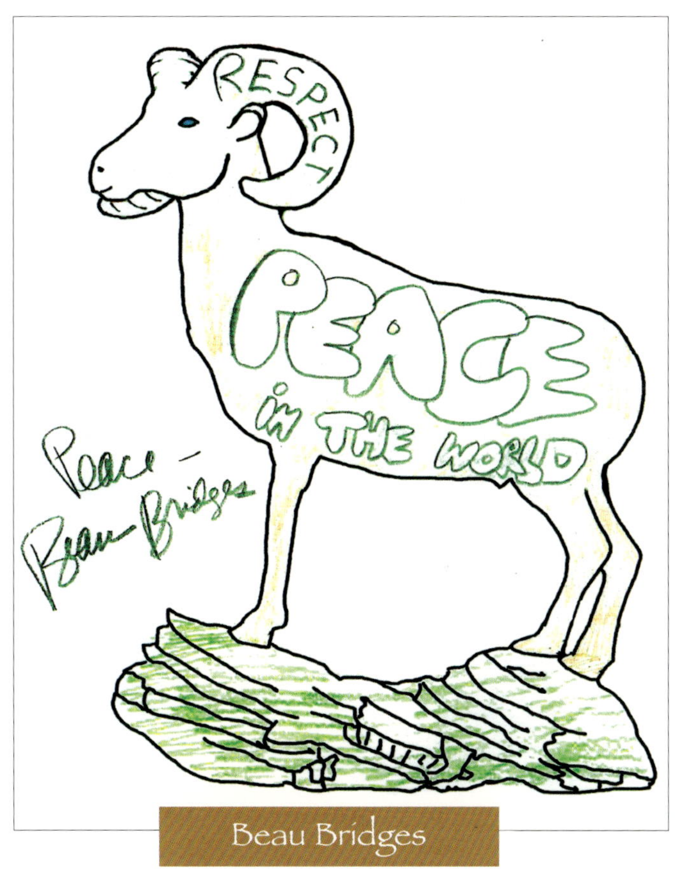

Beau Bridges

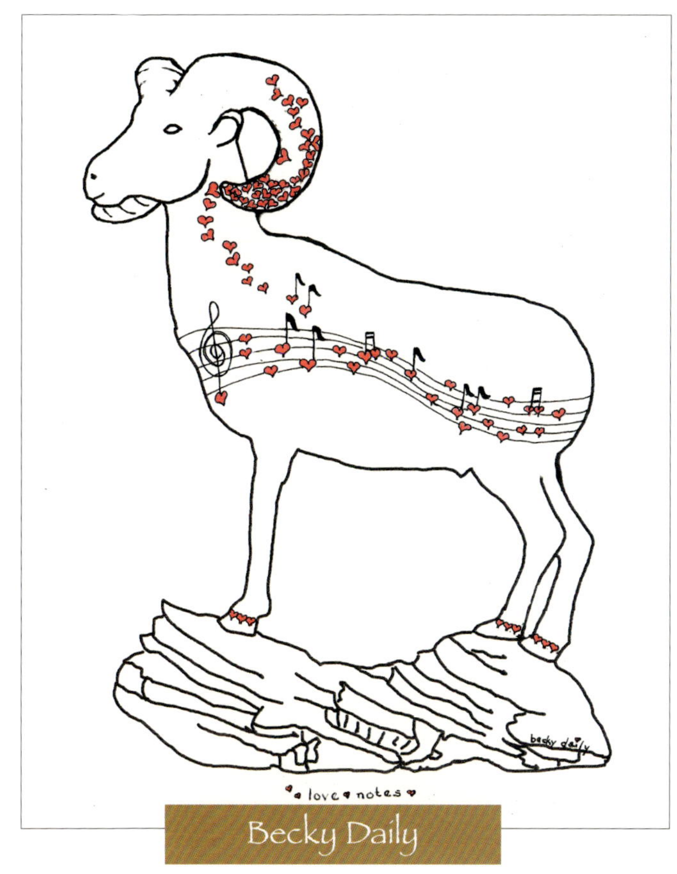

Becky Daily

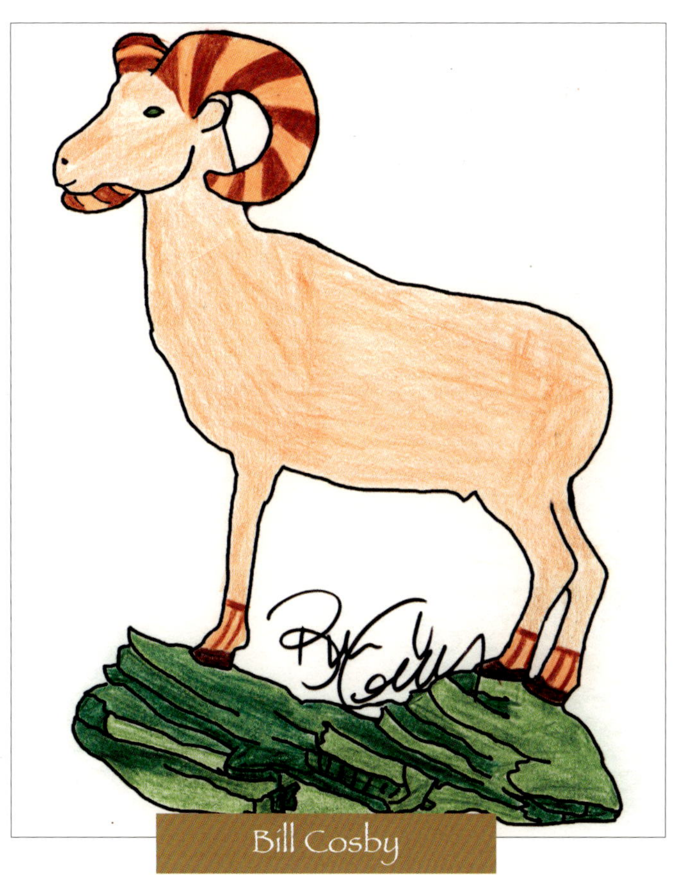

Bill Cosby

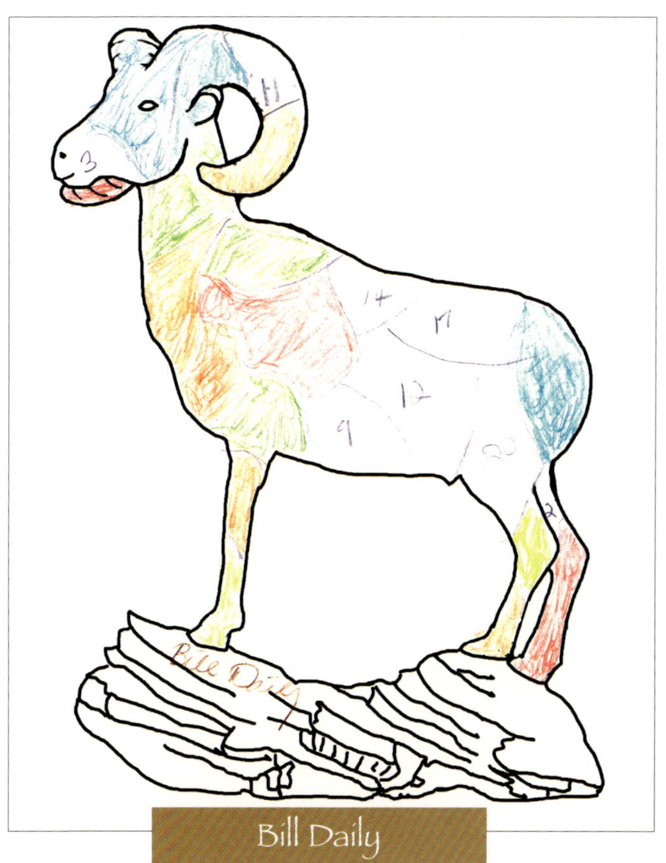

Bill Daily

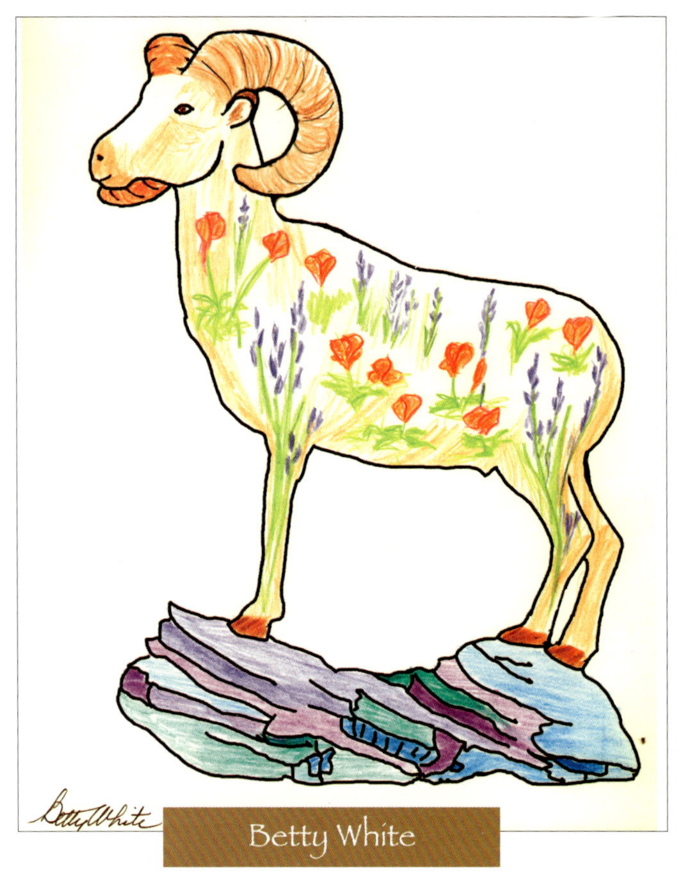

Betty White

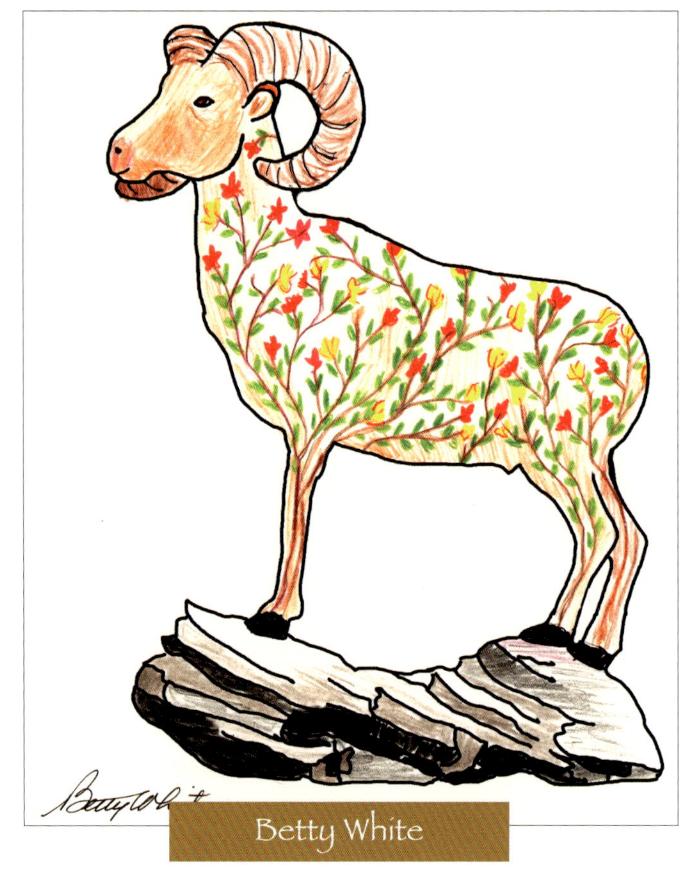

Betty White

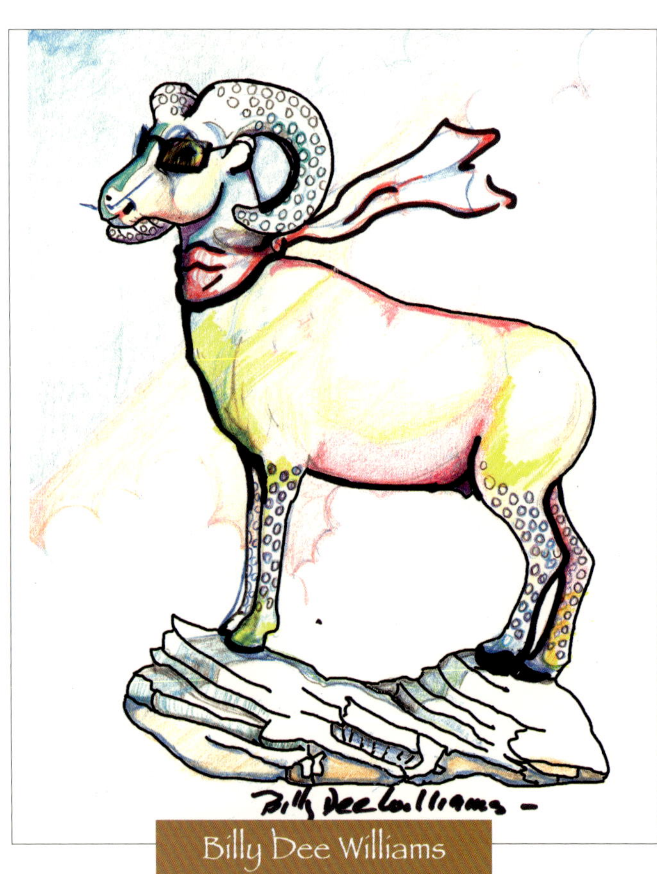

Billy Dee Williams

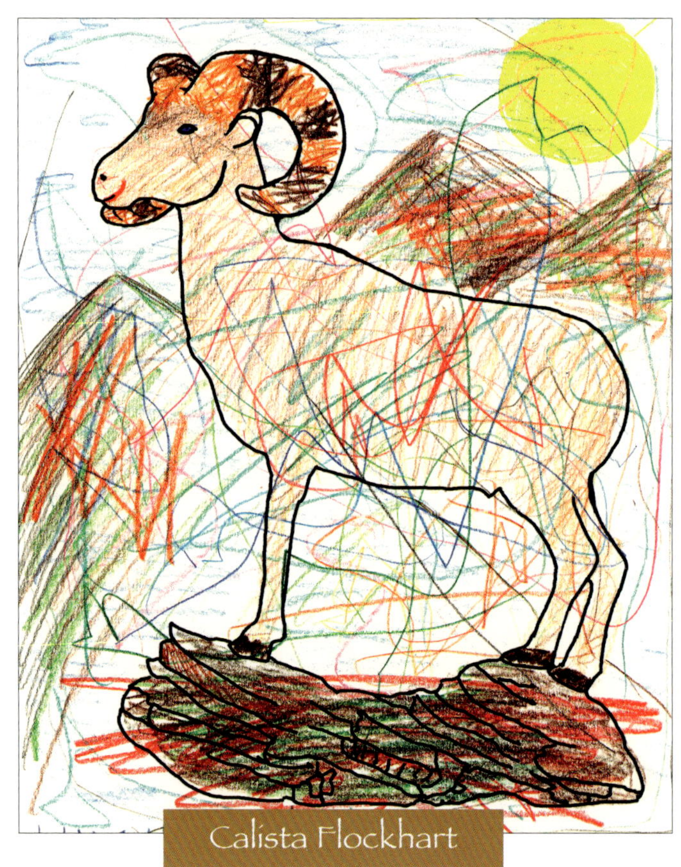

Calista Flockhart

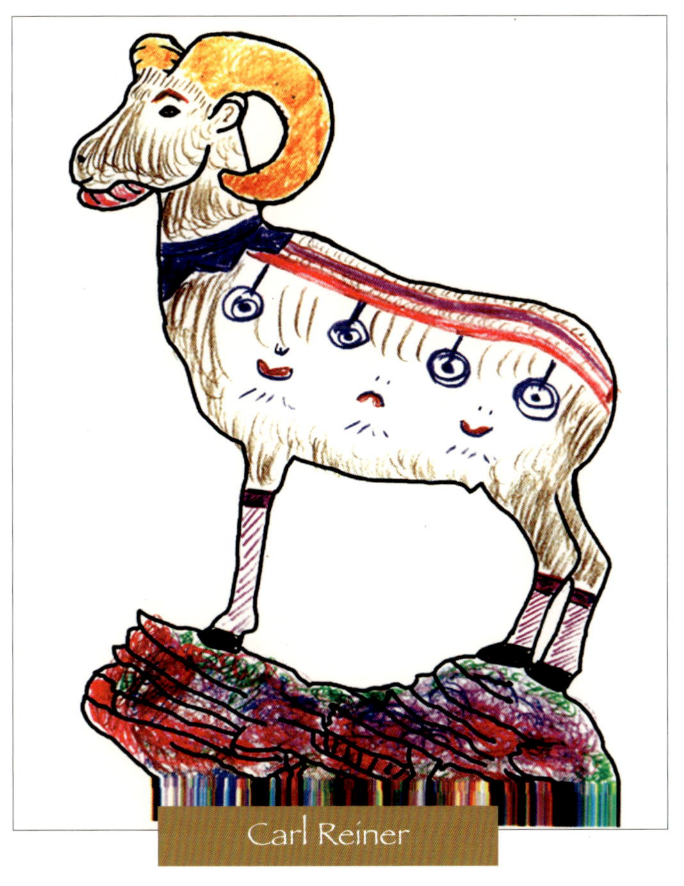

Carl Reiner

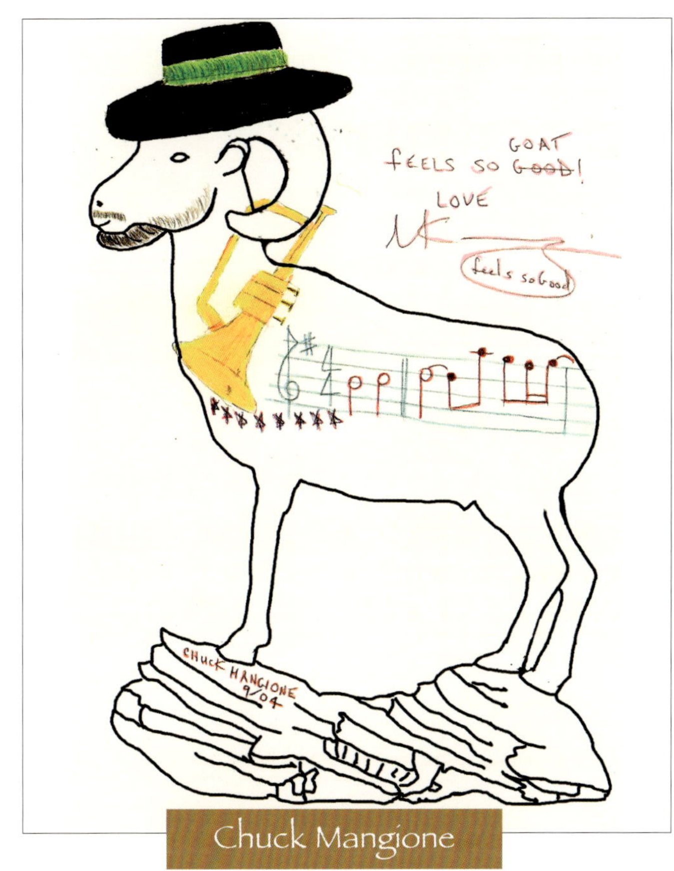

Chuck Mangione

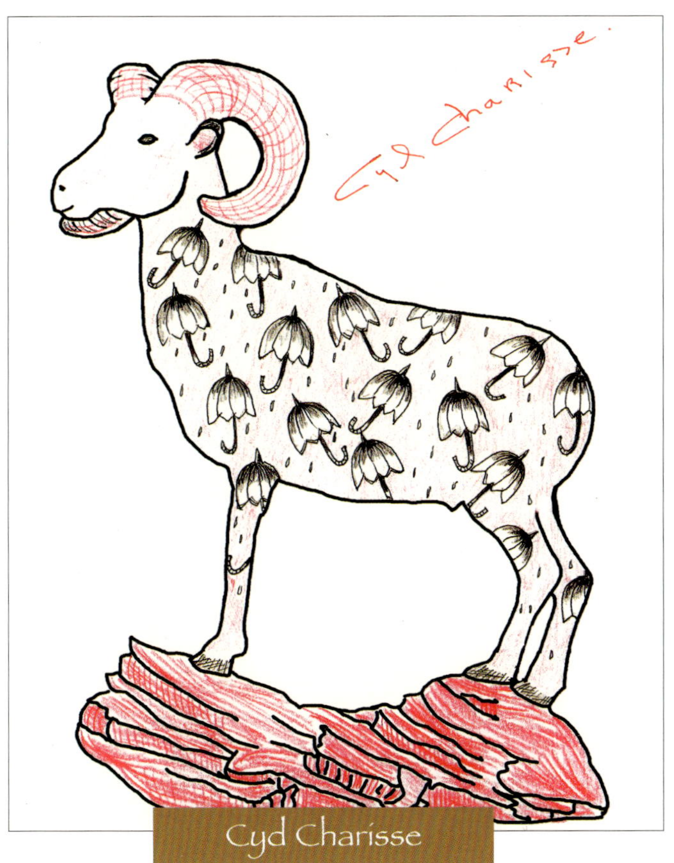

Cyd Charisse

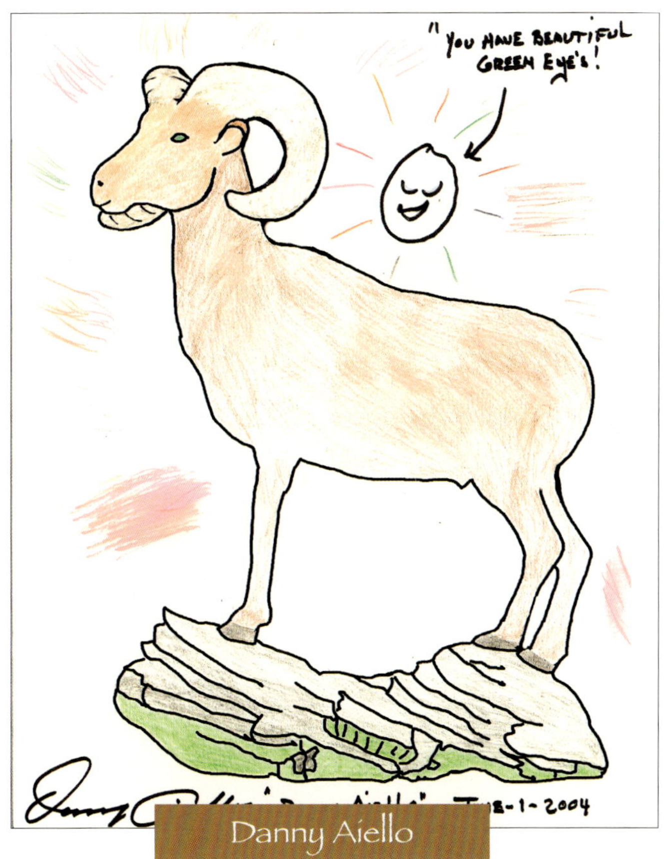

Danny Aiello

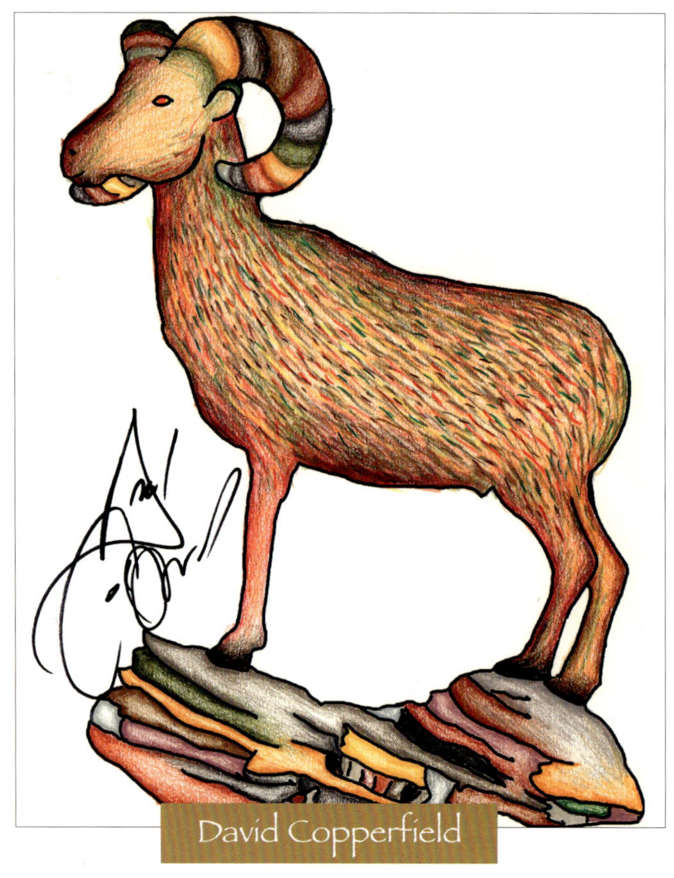

David Copperfield

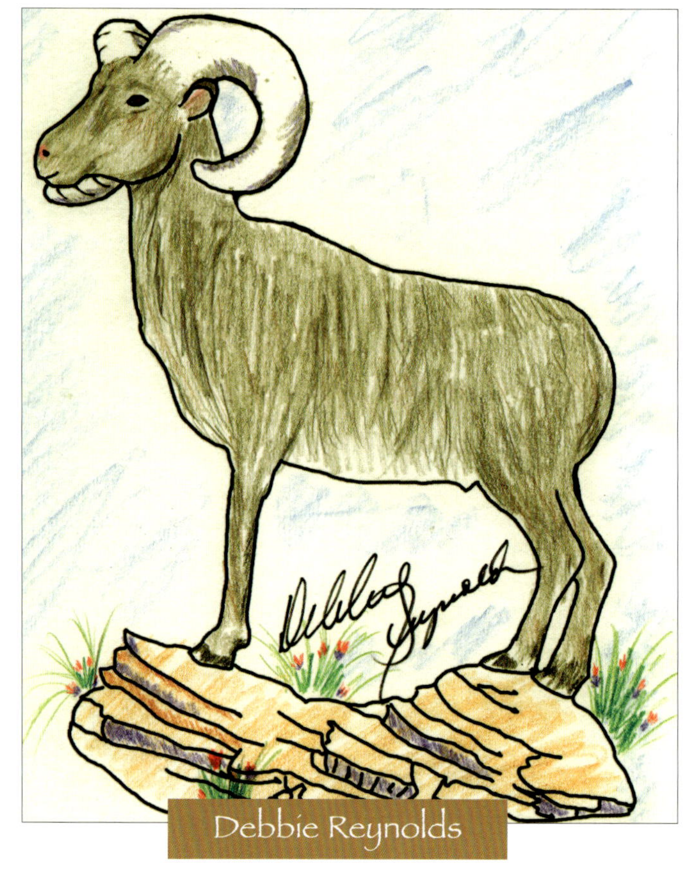

Debbie Reynolds

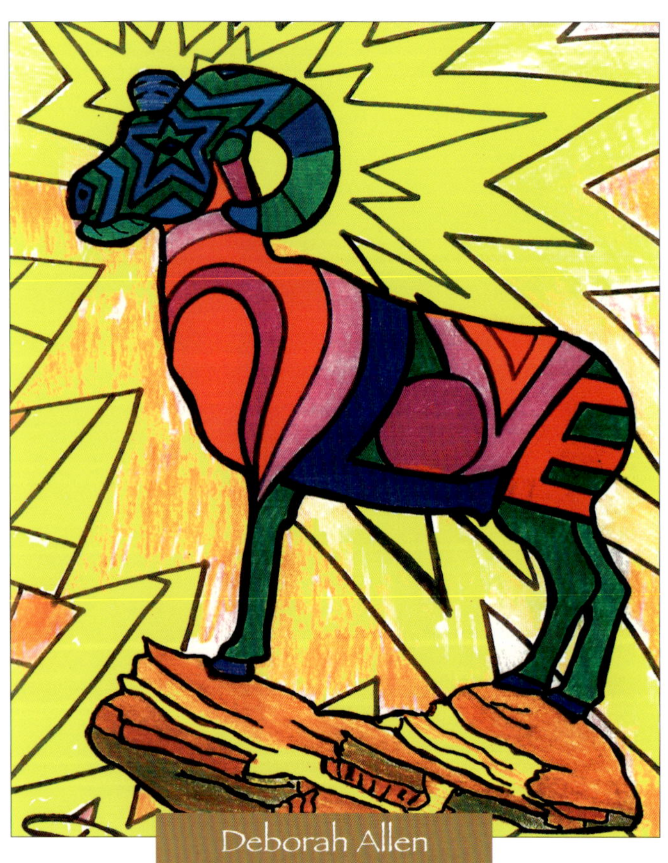

Deborah Allen

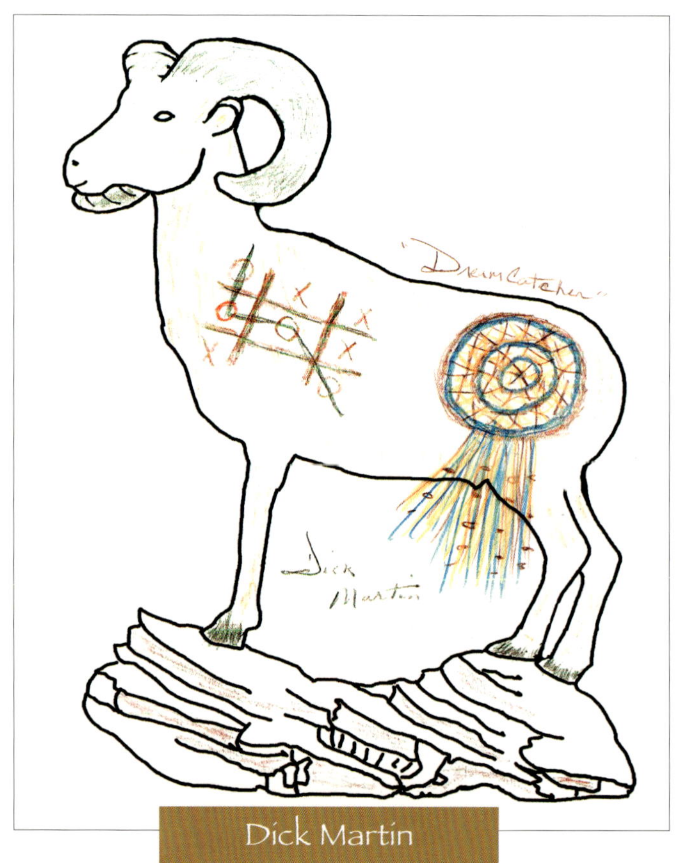

Dick Martin

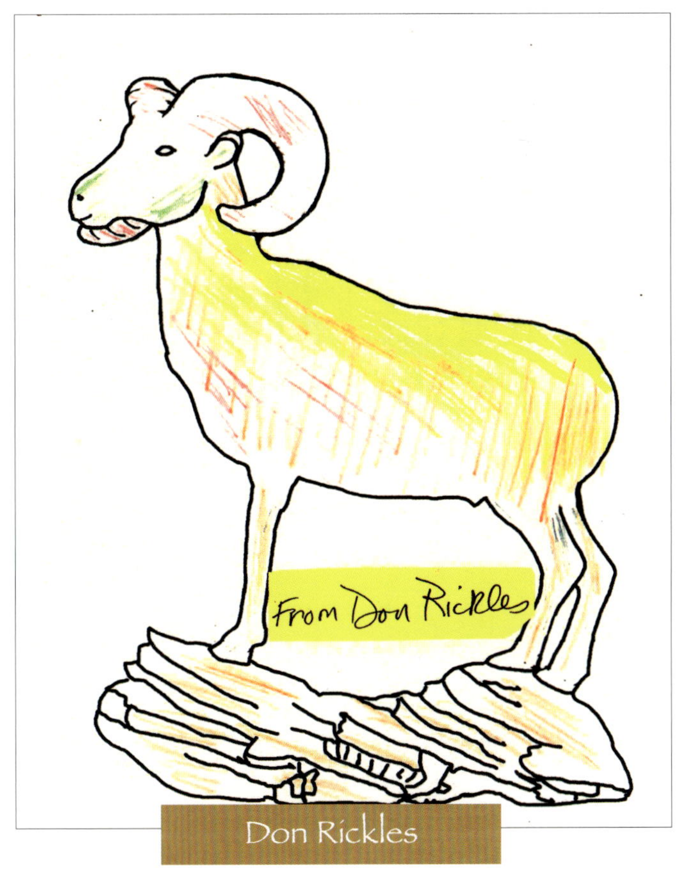

Don Rickles

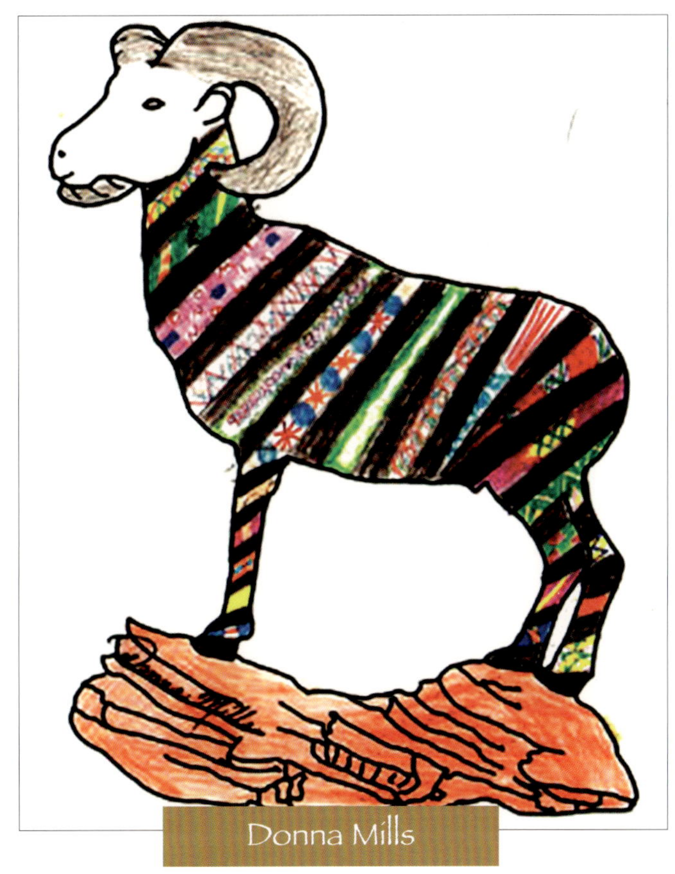

Donna Mills

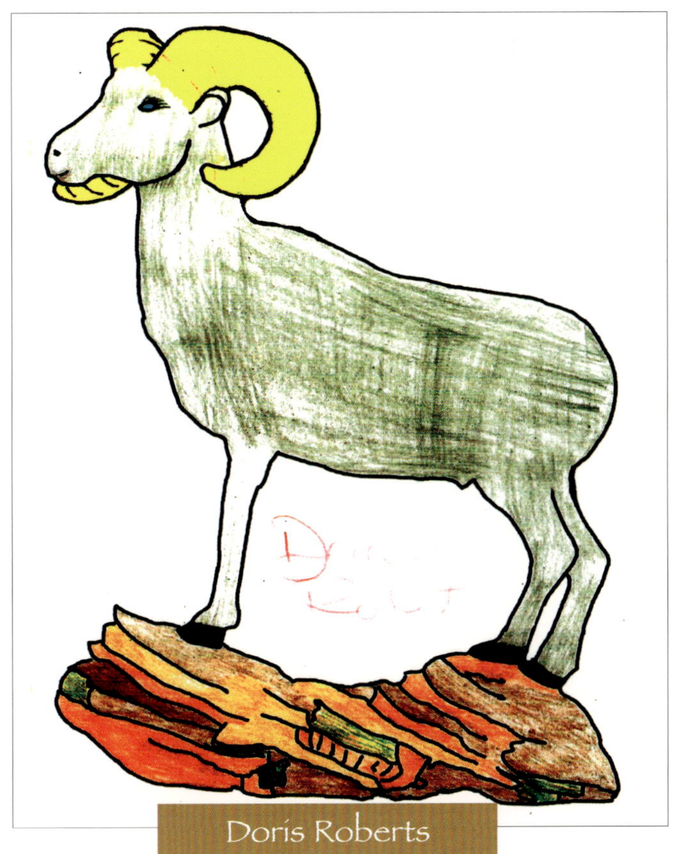

Doris Roberts

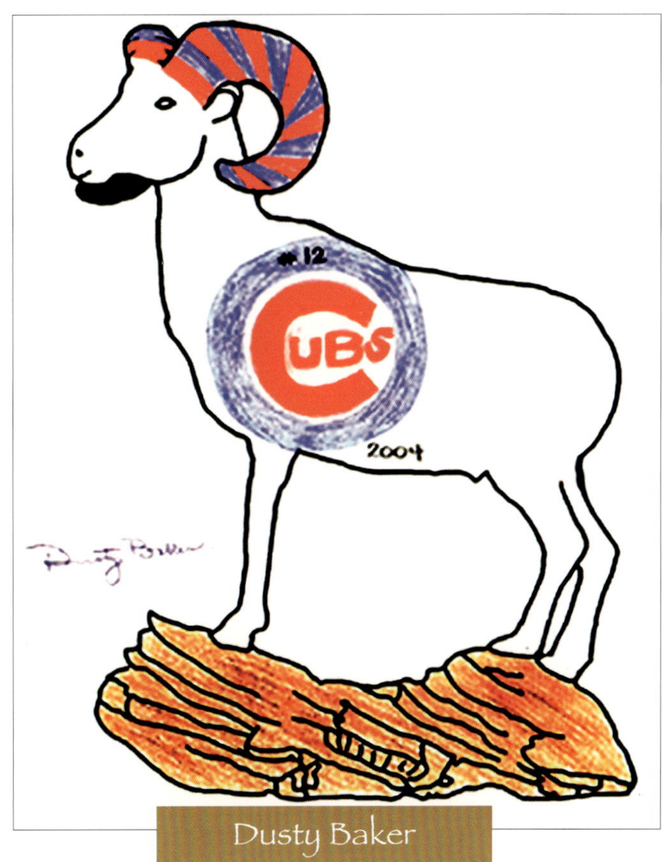

Dusty Baker

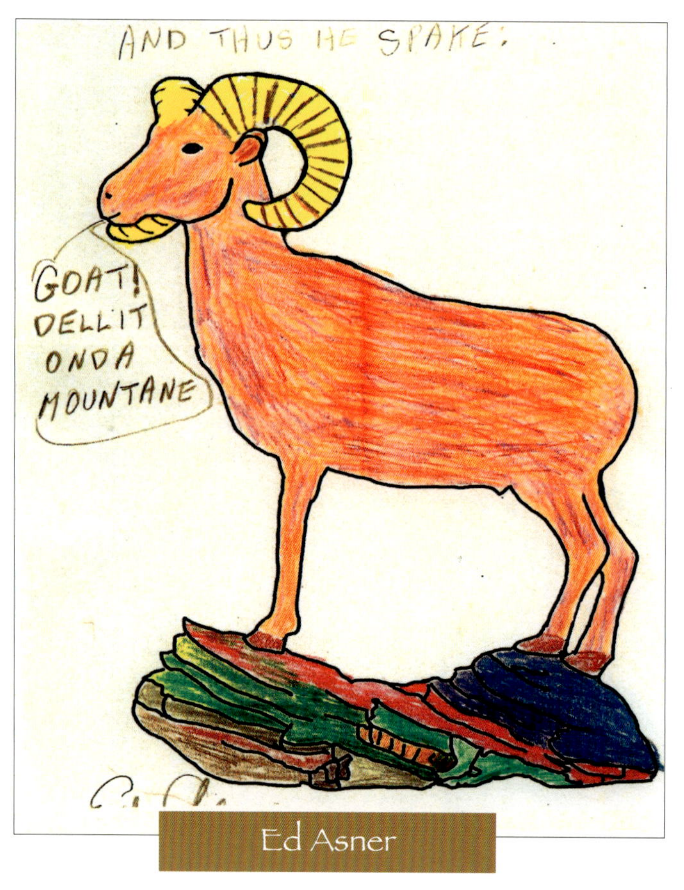

Ed Asner

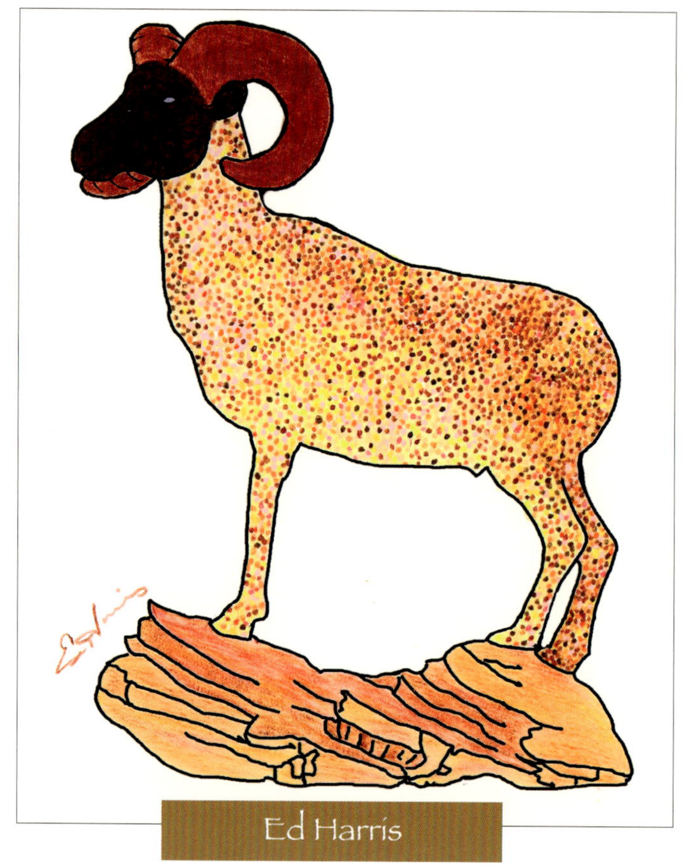

Ed Harris

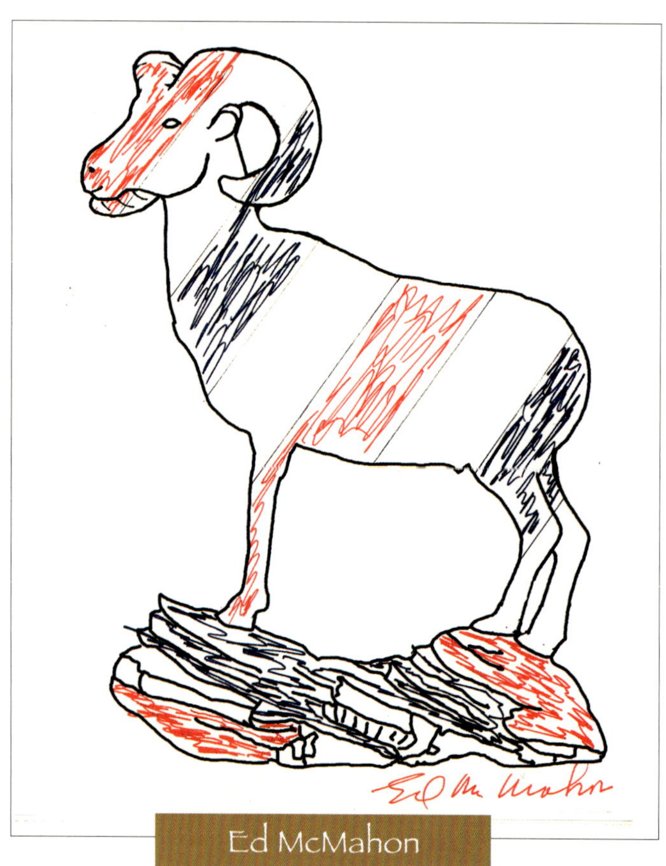

Ed McMahon

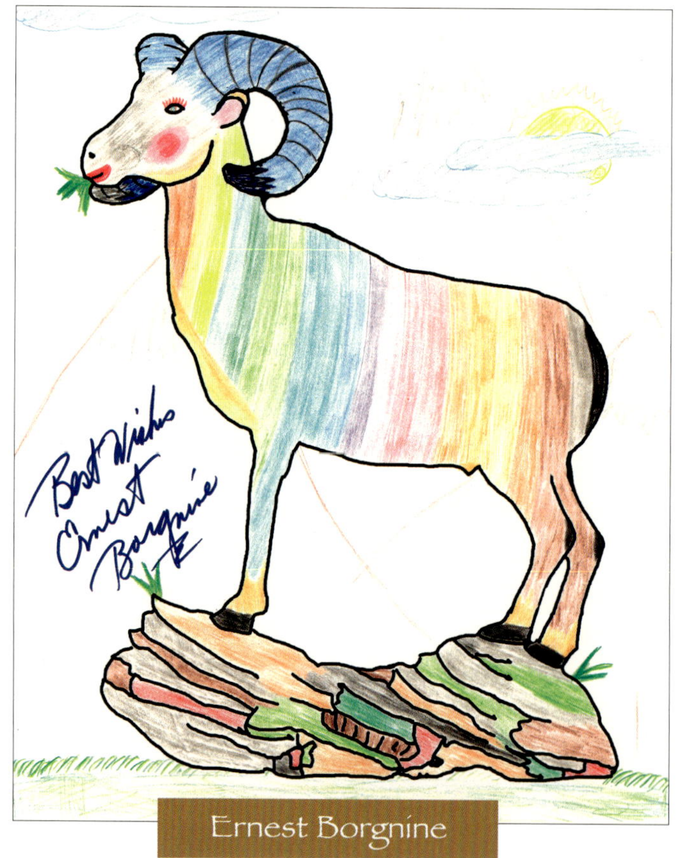

Ernest Borgnine

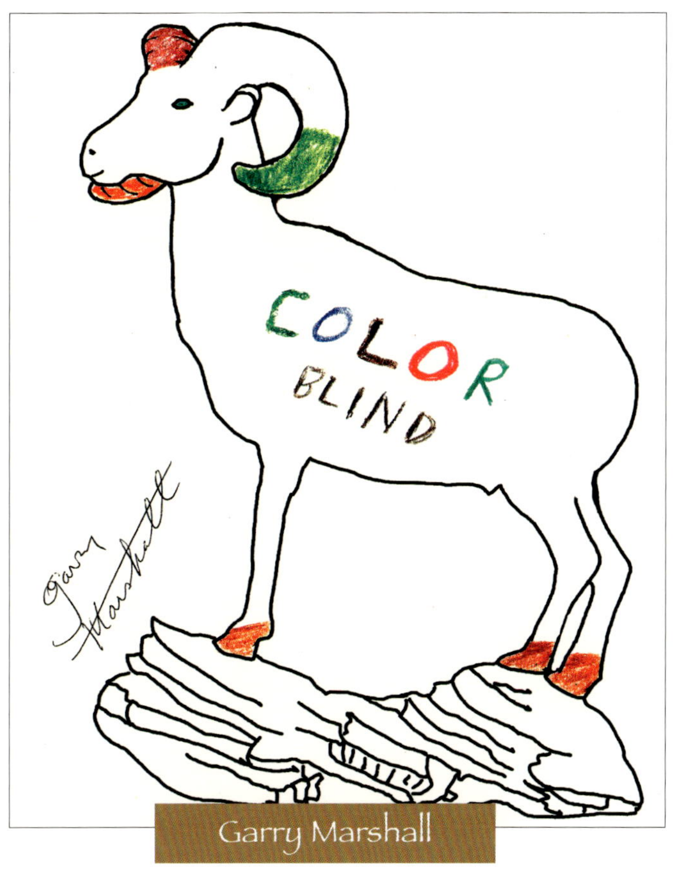

Garry Marshall

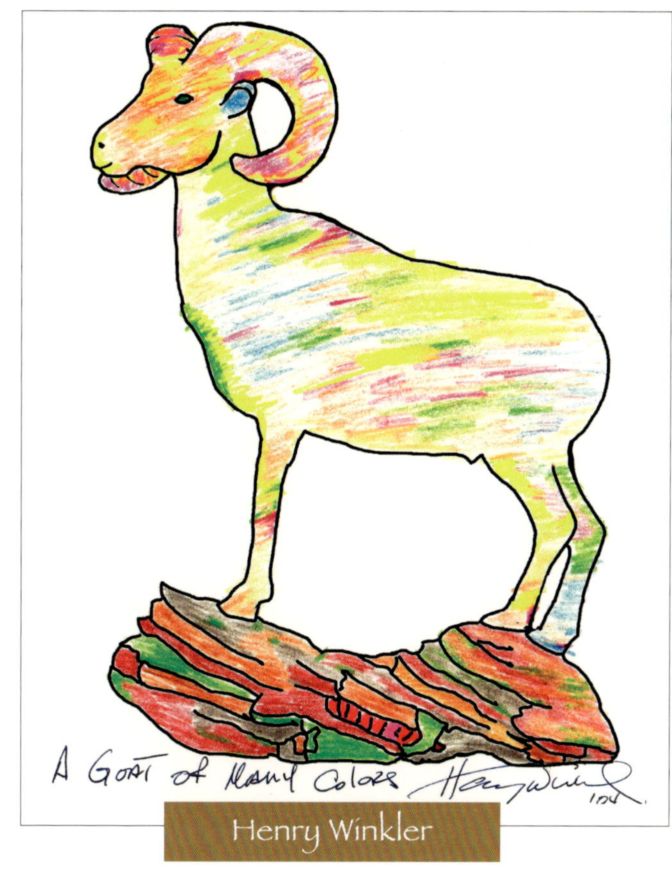

Henry Winkler

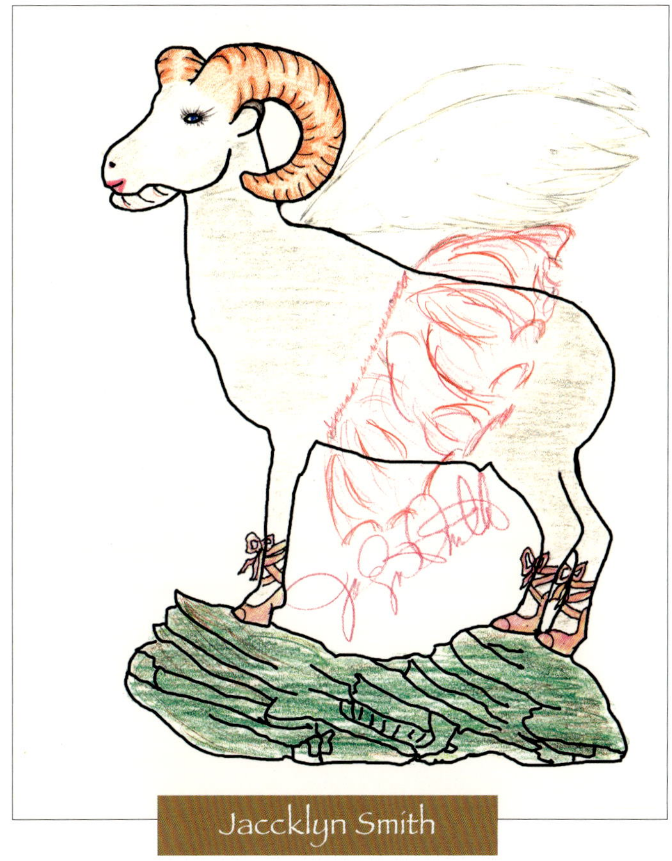

Jaccklyn Smith

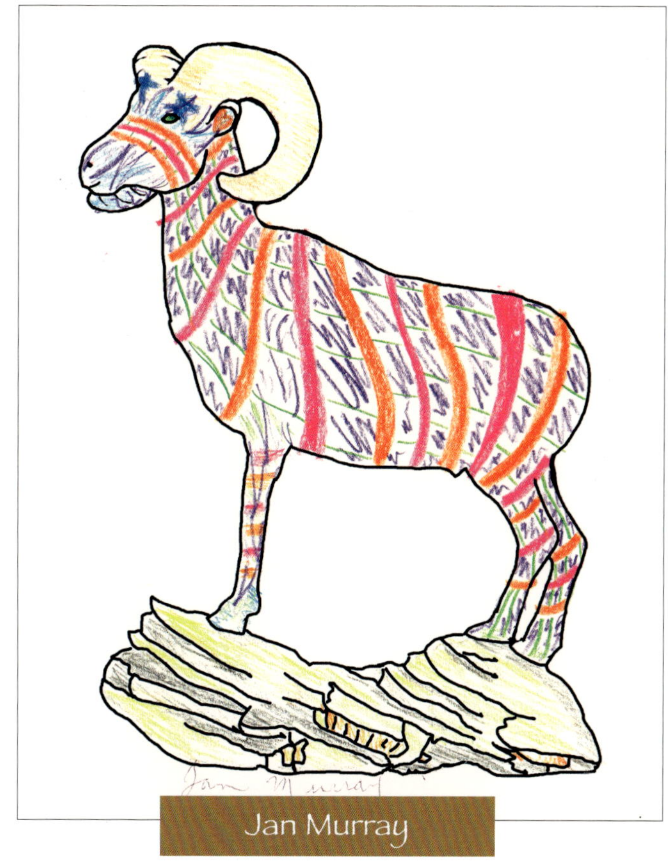

Jan Murray

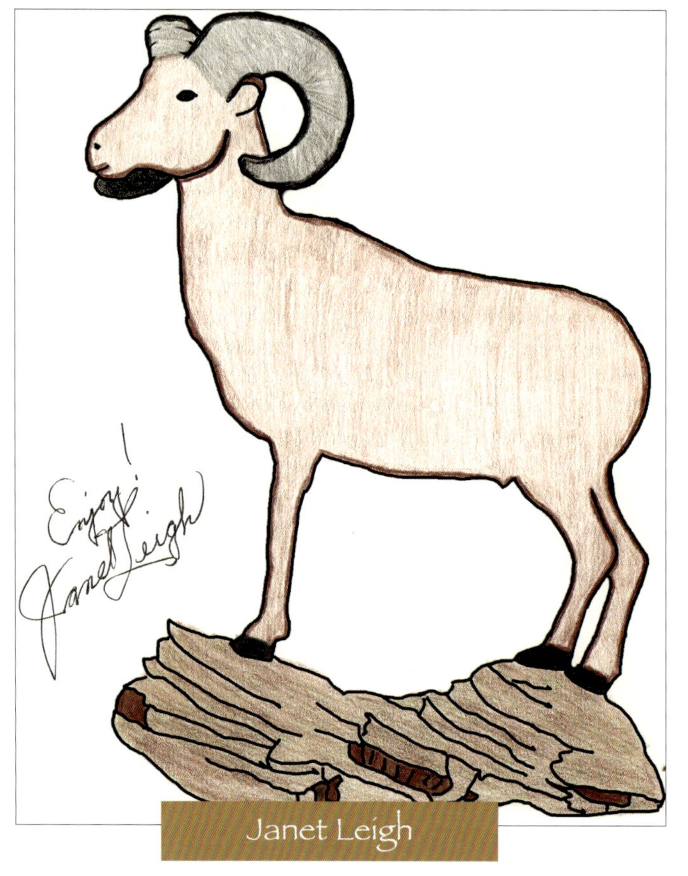

Janet Leigh

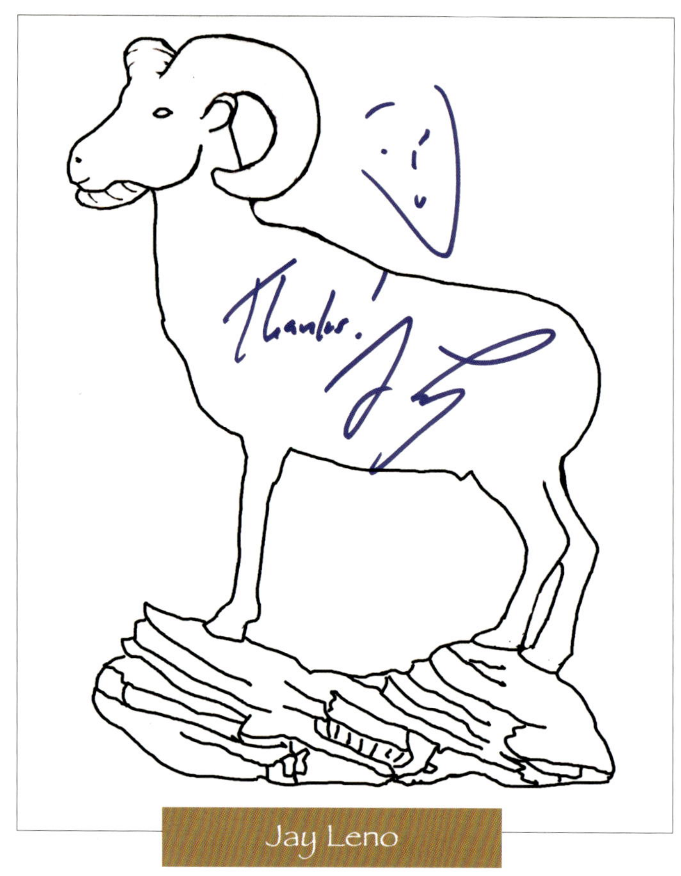

Jay Leno

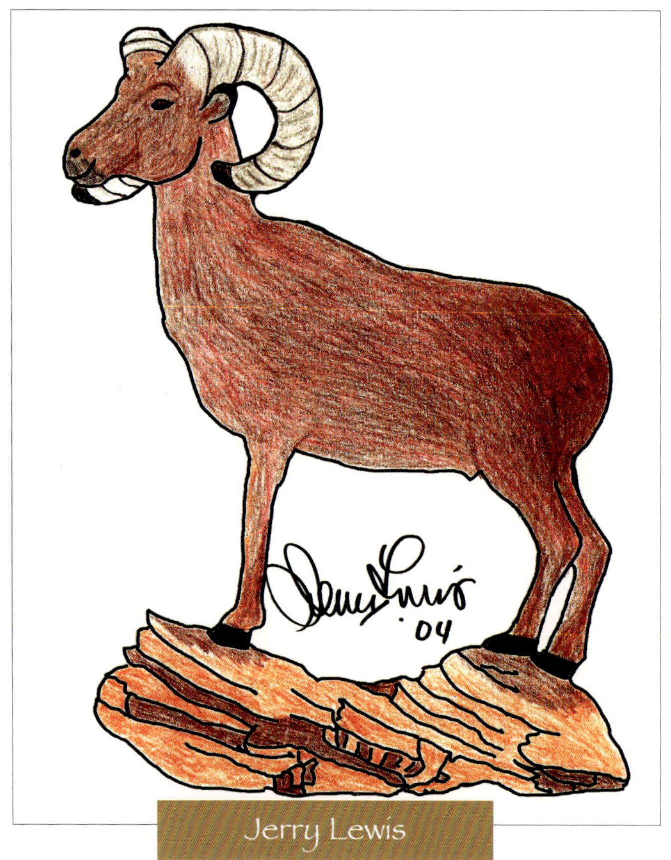

Jerry Lewis

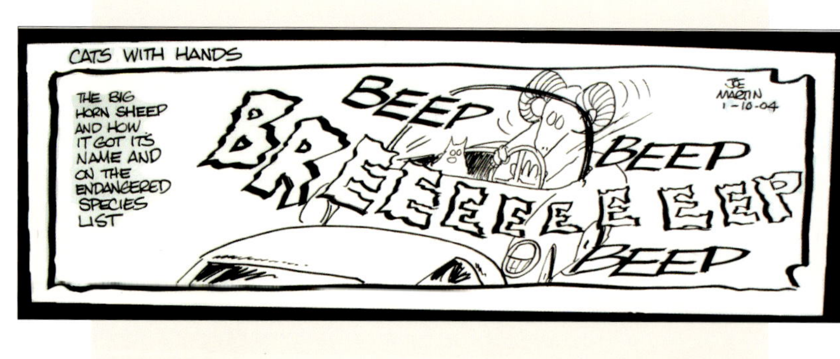

Joe Martin

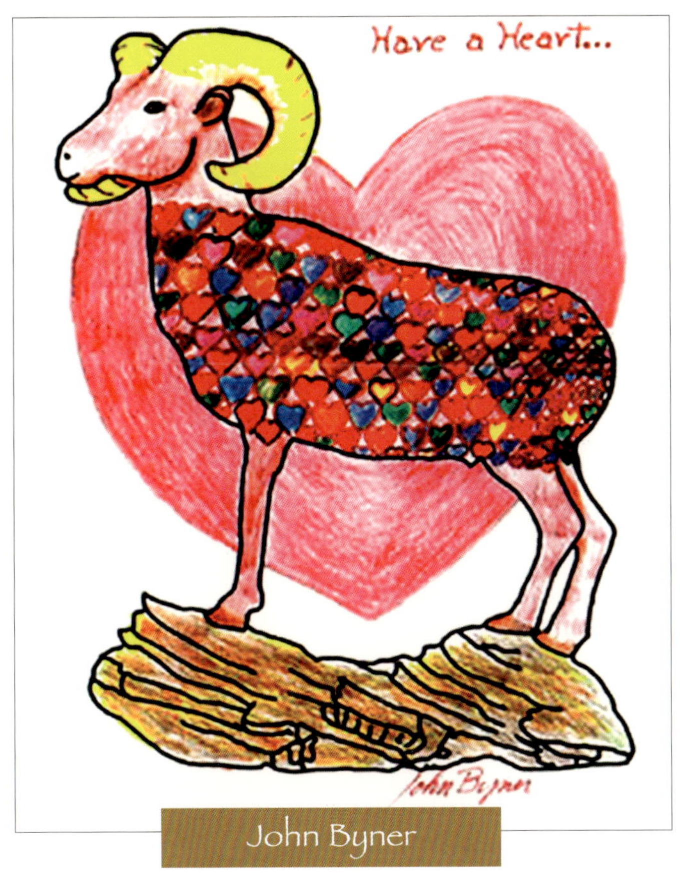

John Byner

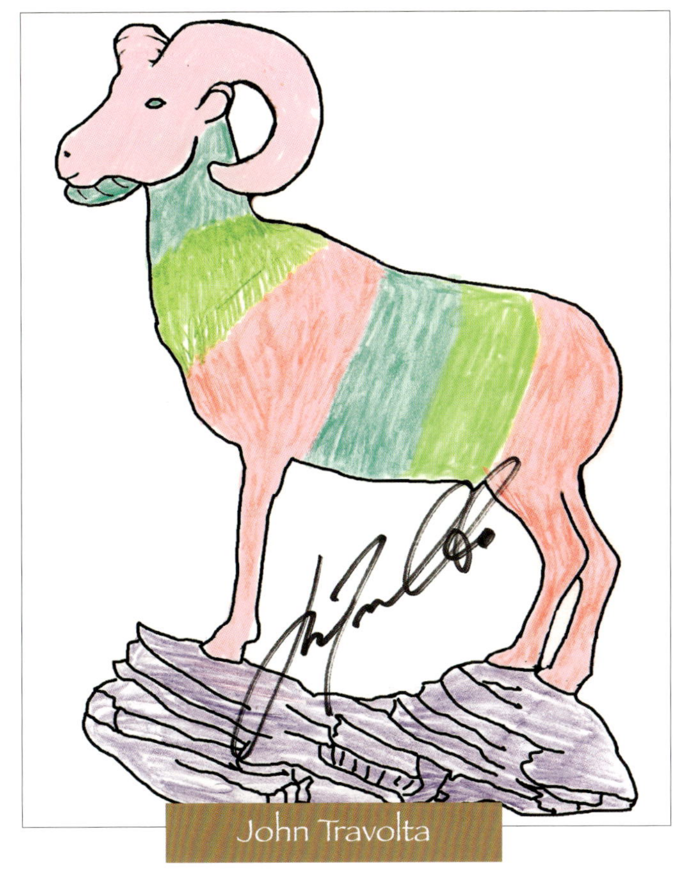

John Travolta

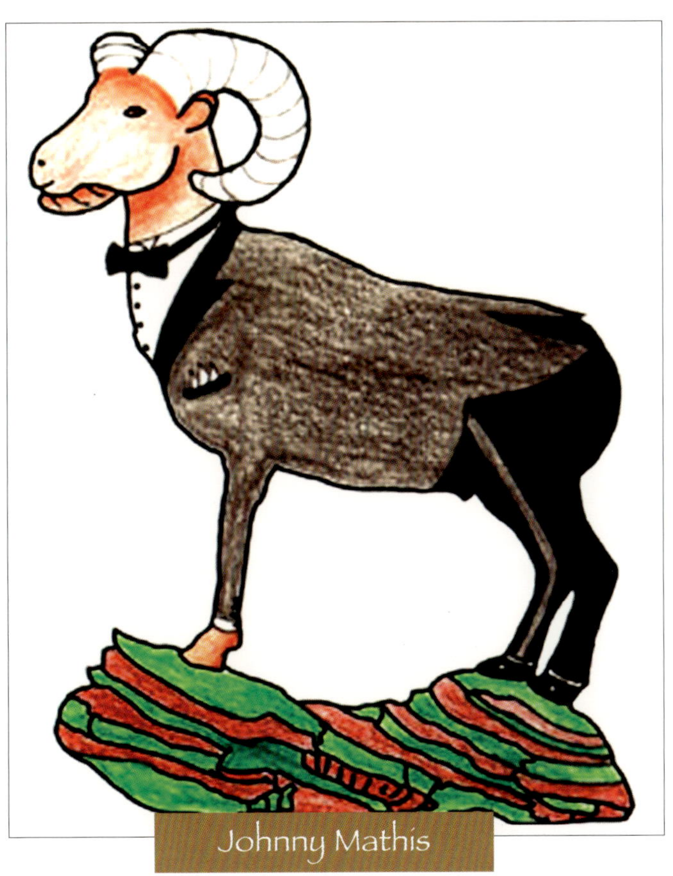

Johnny Mathis

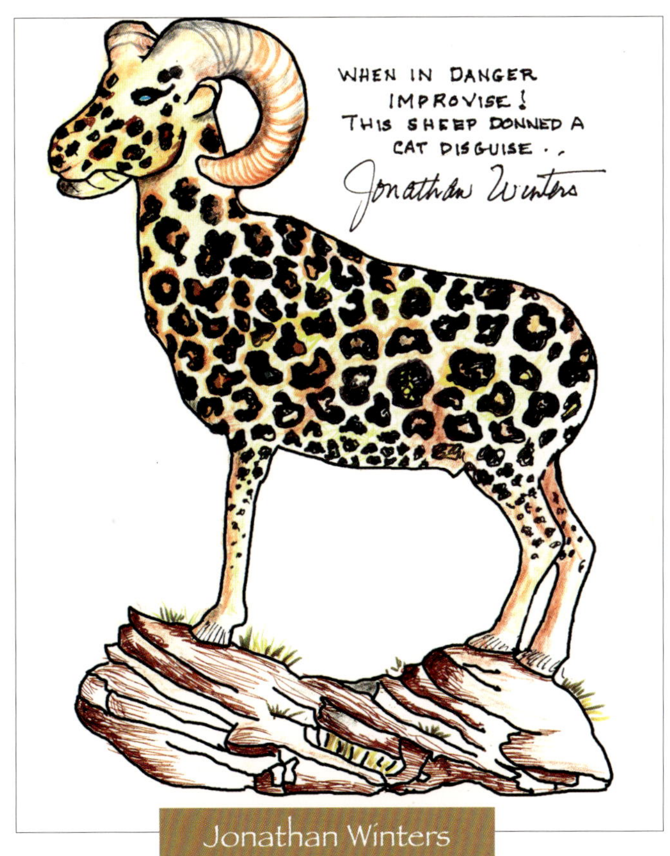

Jonathan Winters

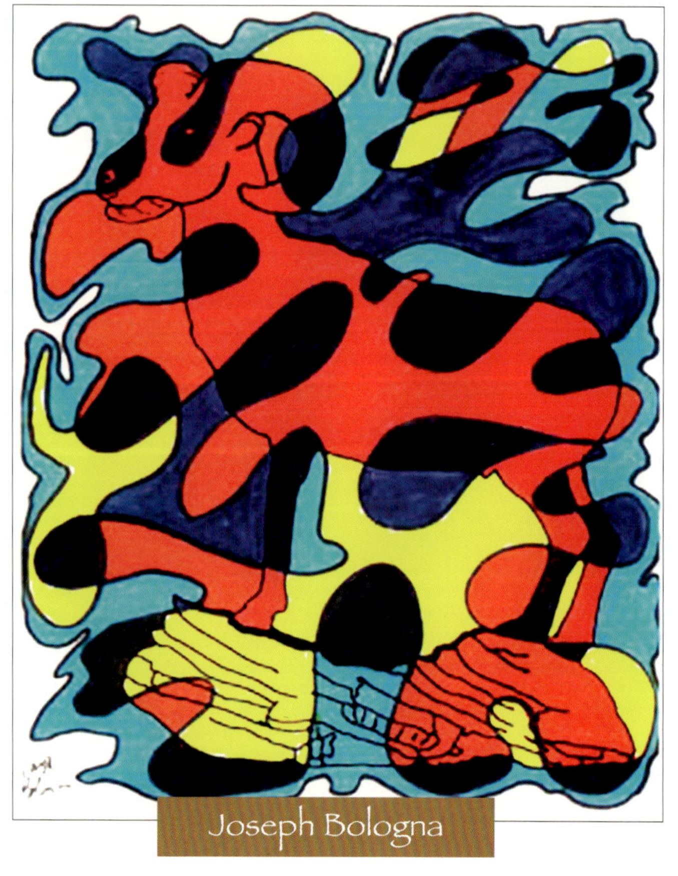

Joseph Bologna

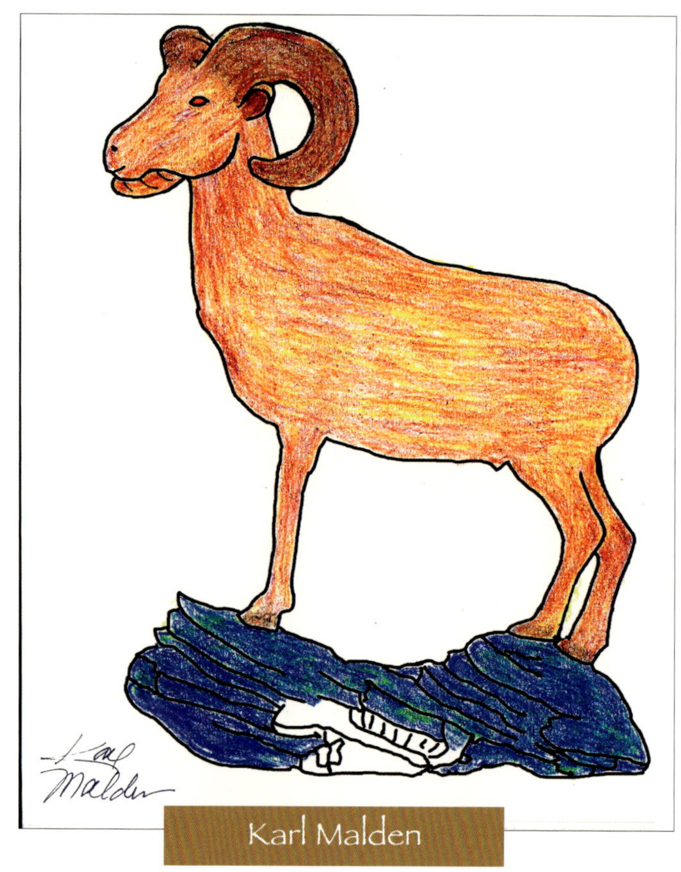

Karl Malden

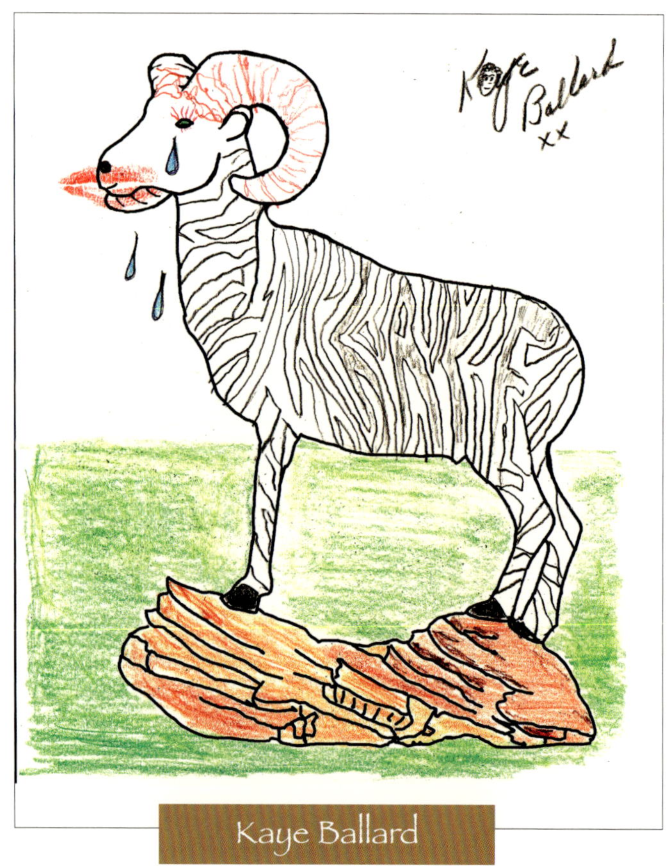

Kaye Ballard

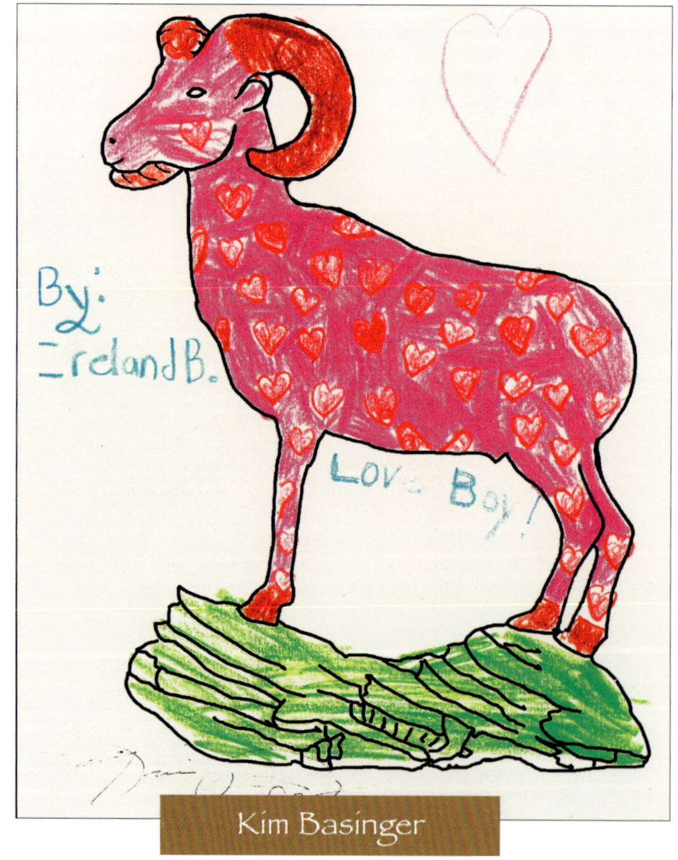

Kim Basinger

144

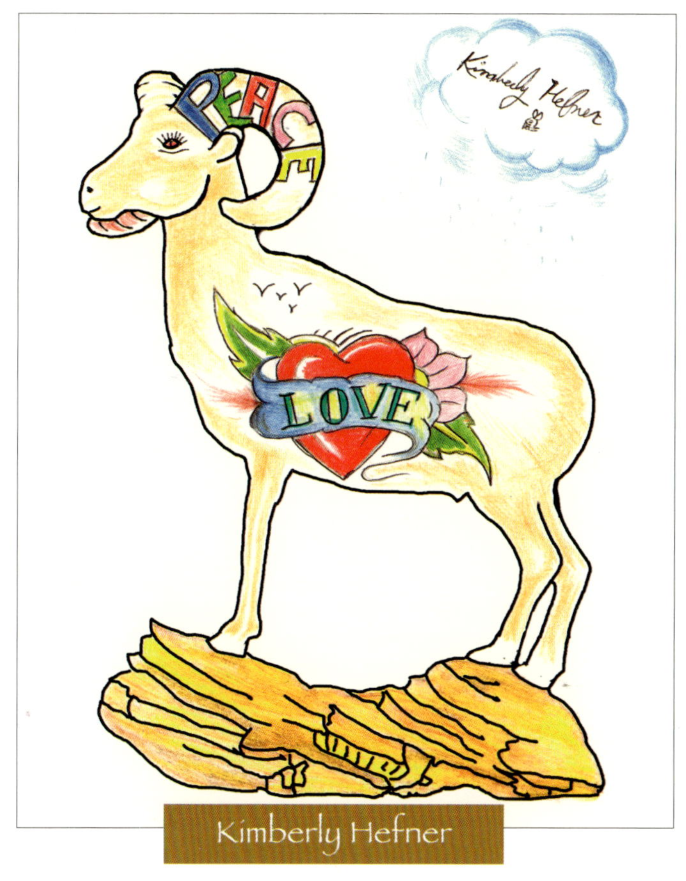

Kimberly Hefner

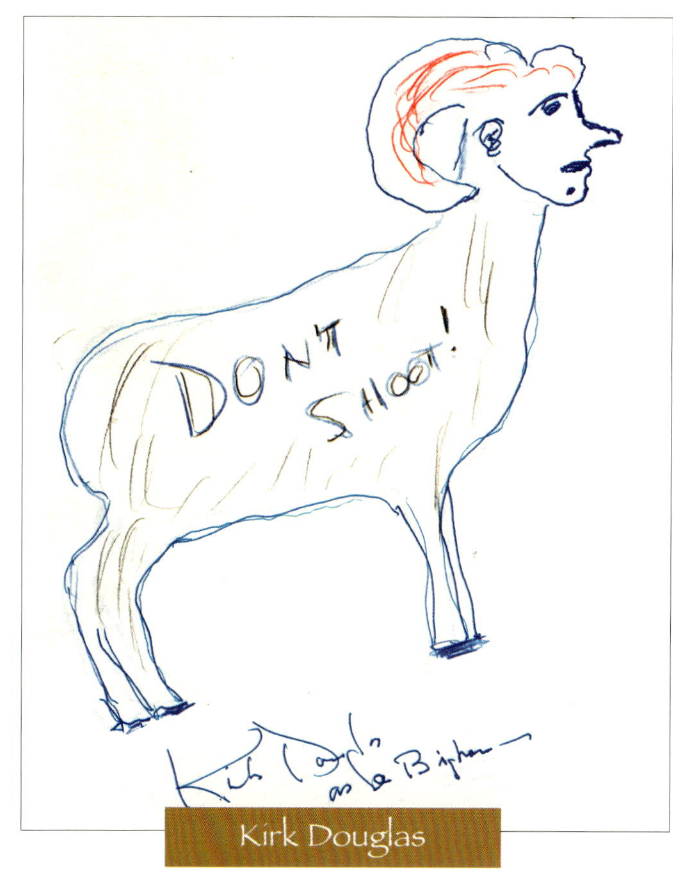

Kirk Douglas

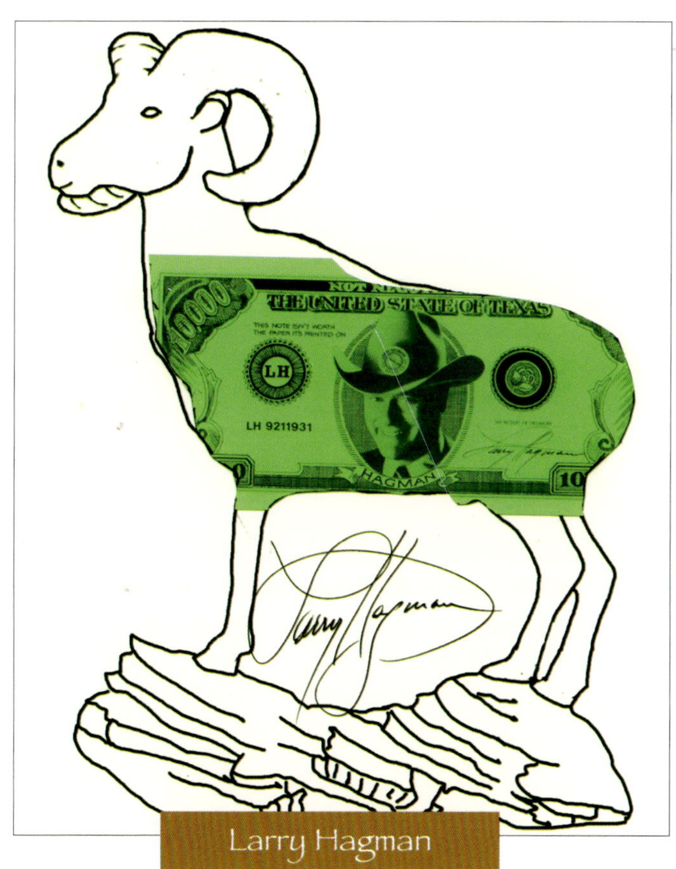

Larry Hagman

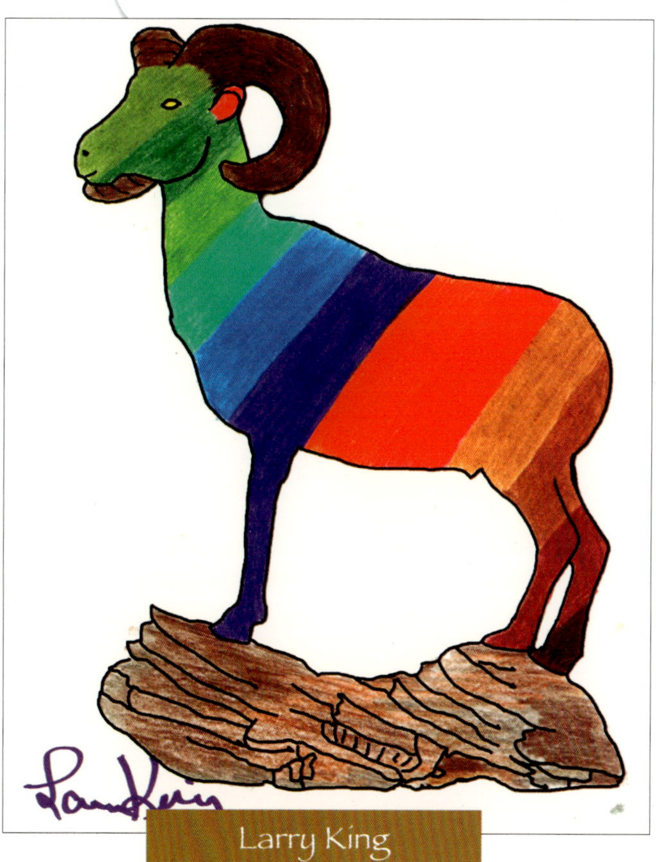

Larry King

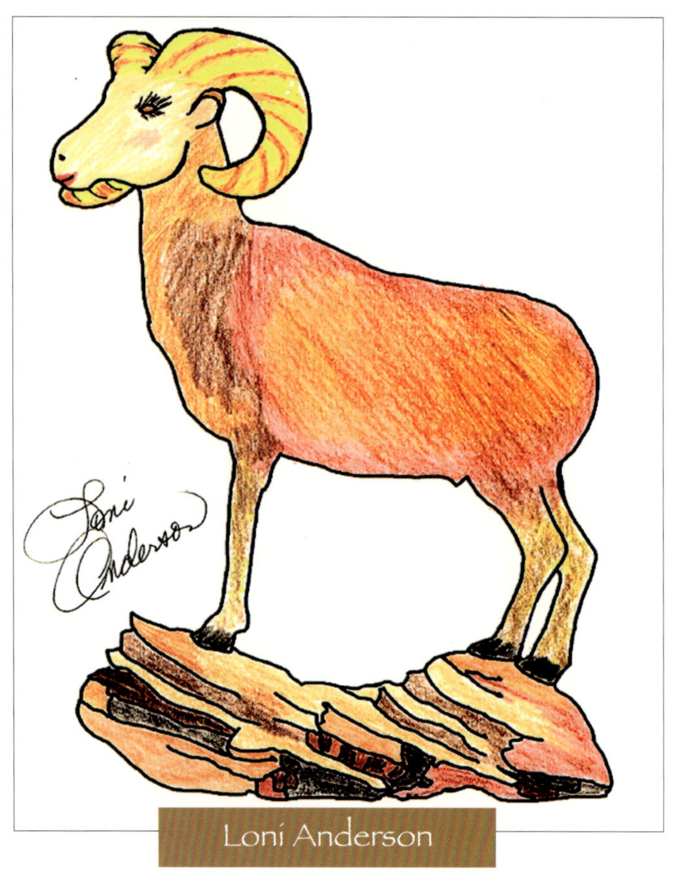

Loni Anderson

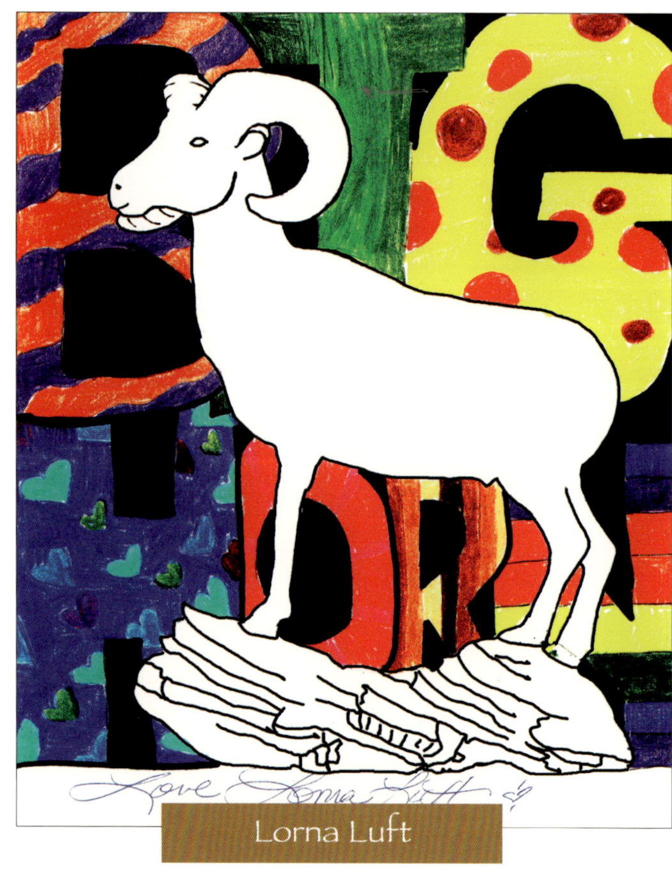

Lorna Luft

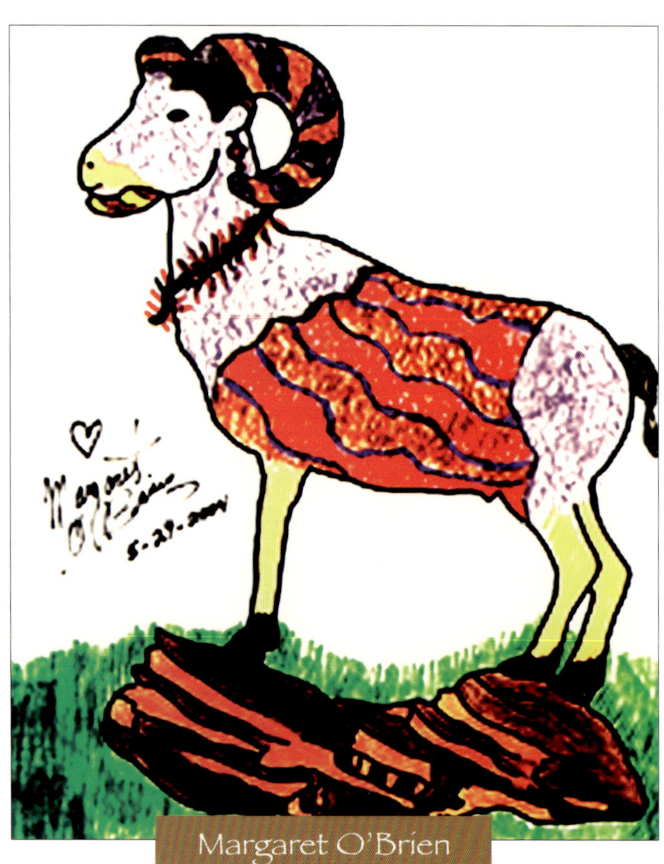

Margaret O'Brien

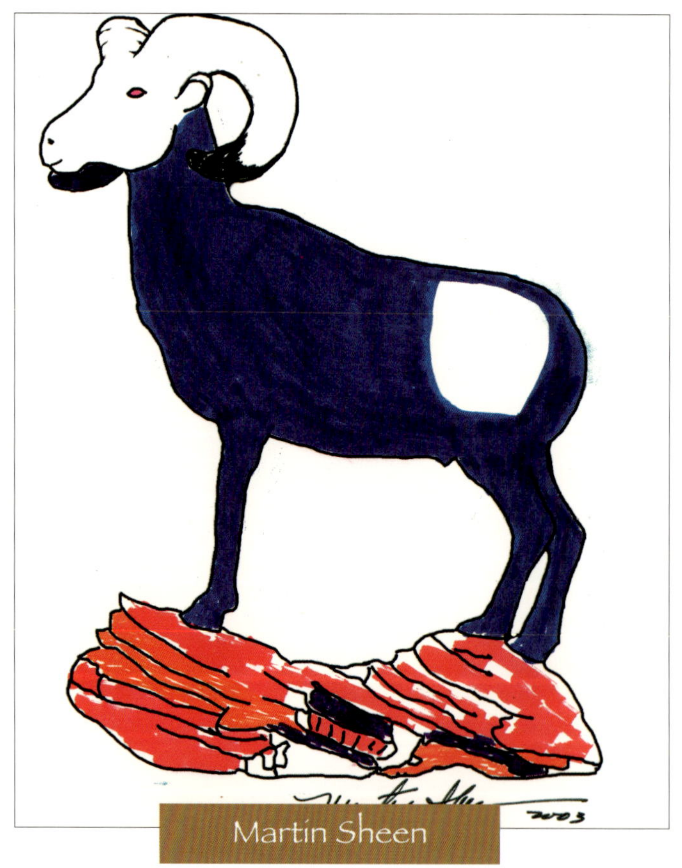

Martin Sheen

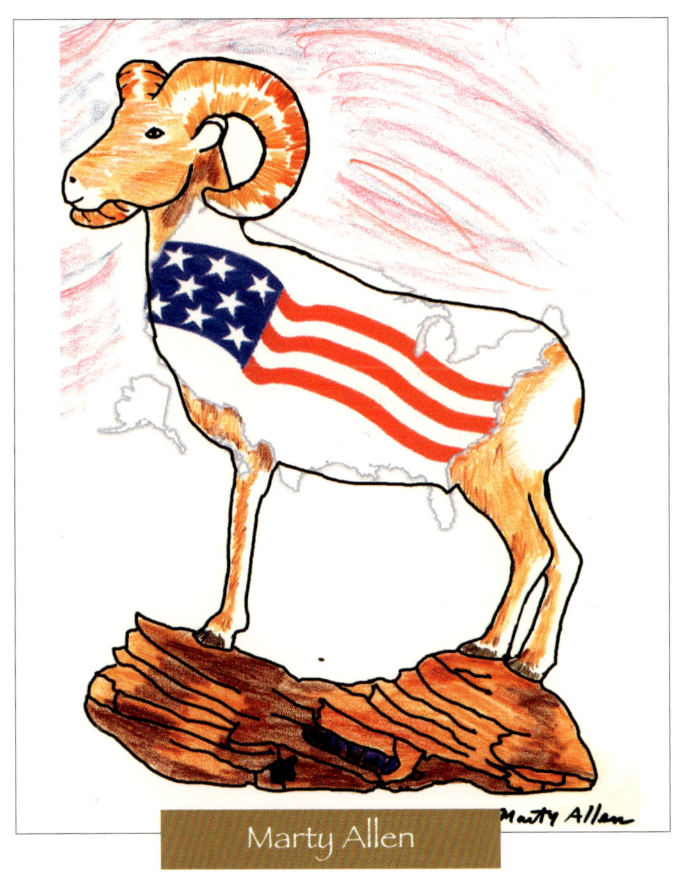

Marty Allen

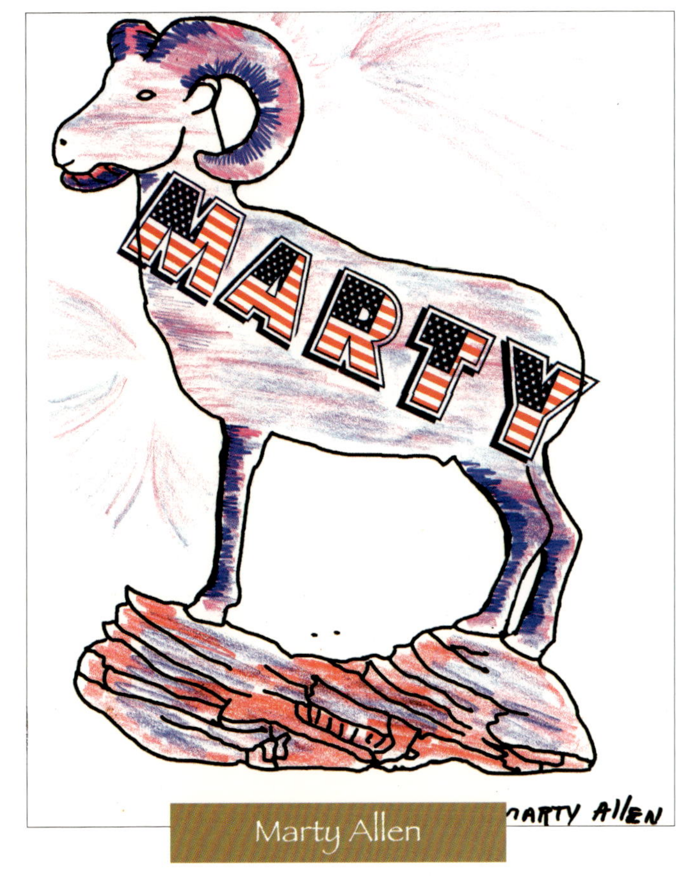

Marty Allen

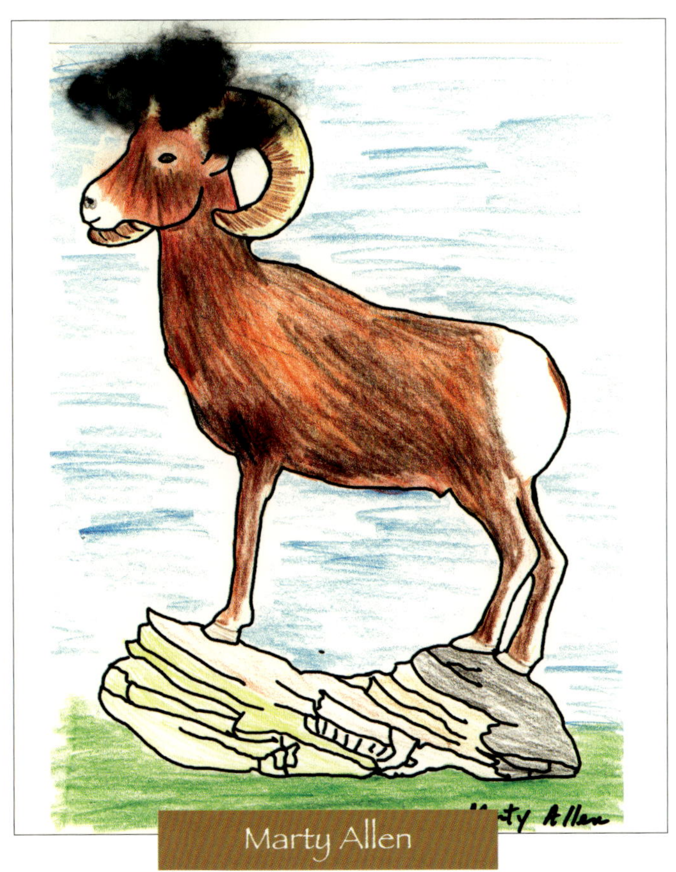

Marty Allen

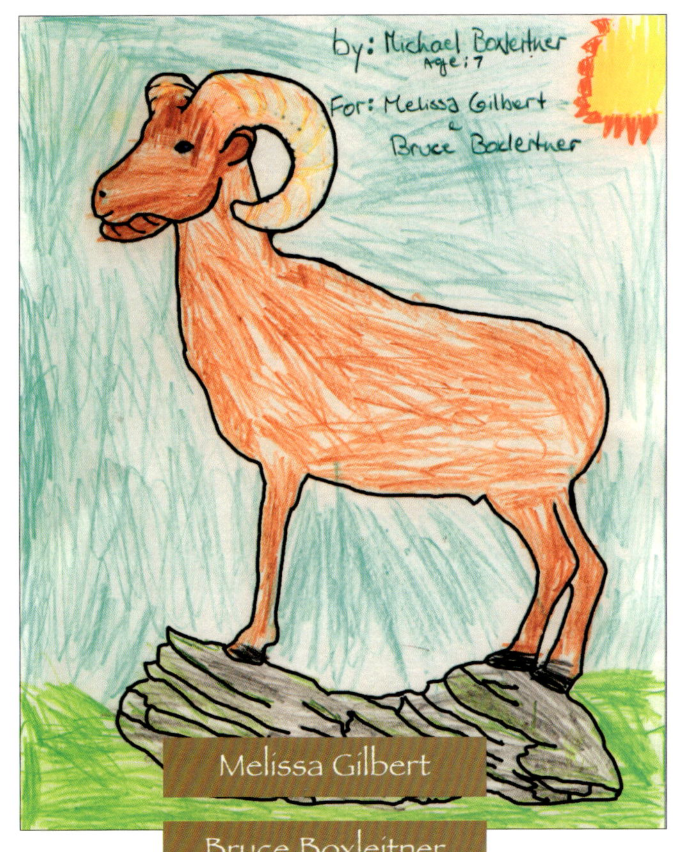

Melissa Gilbert

Bruce Boxleitner

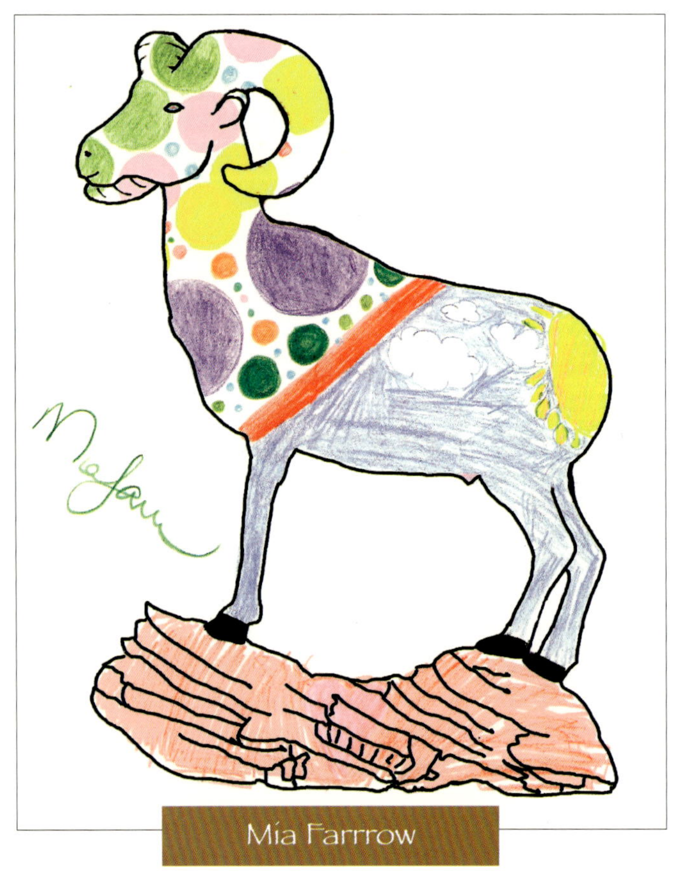

Mia Farrrow

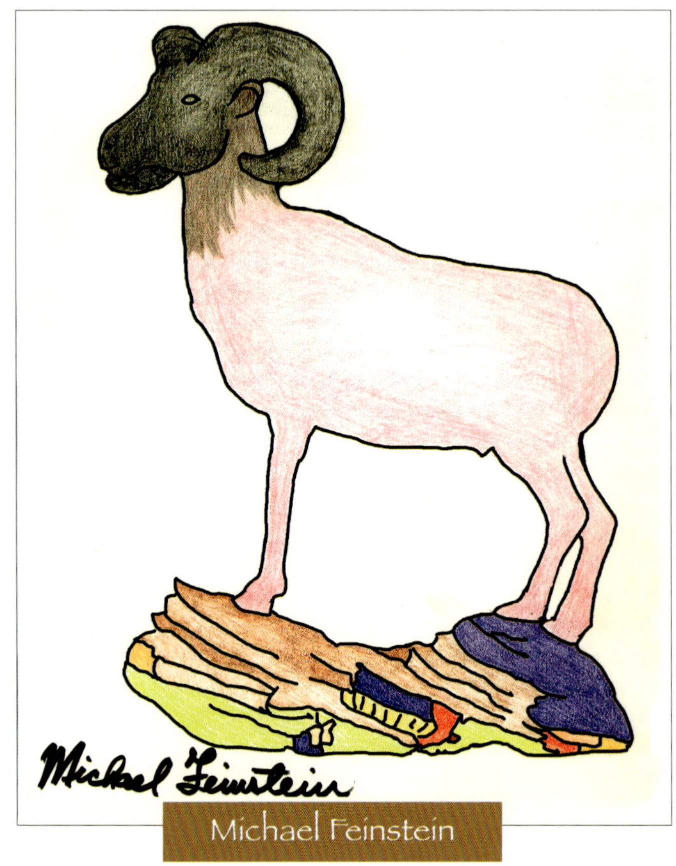

Michael Feinstein

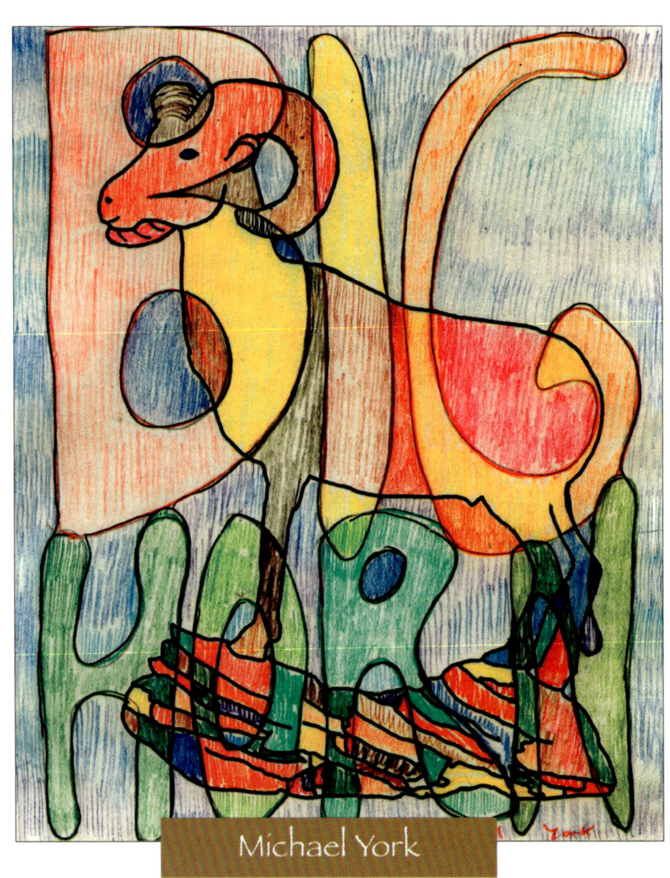

Michael York

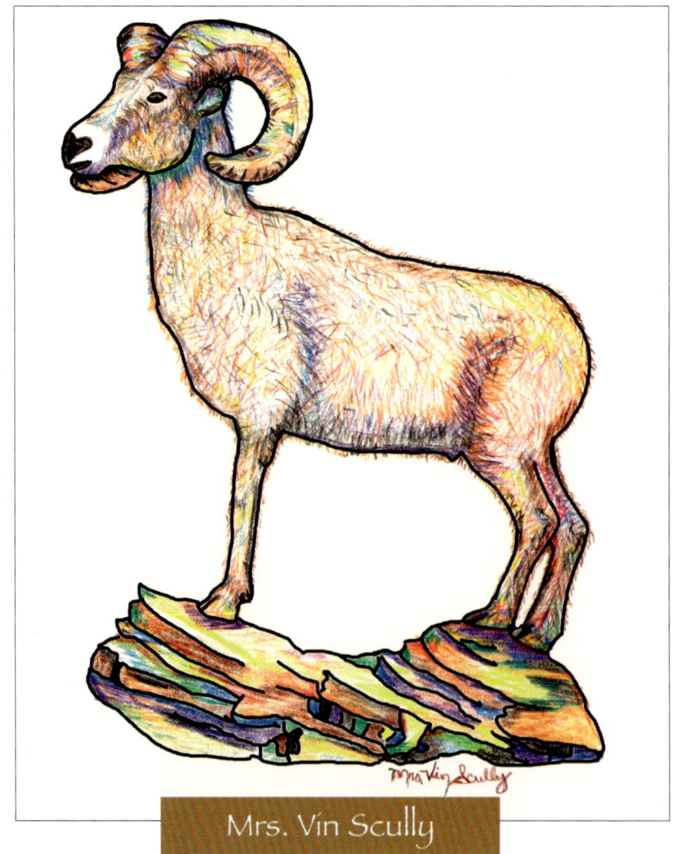

Mrs. Vin Scully

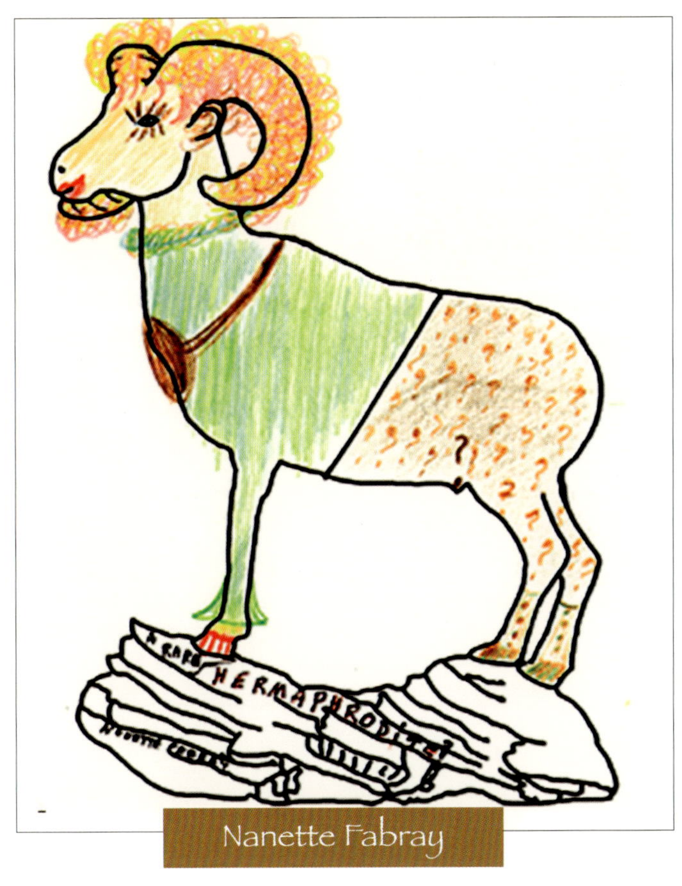

Nanette Fabray

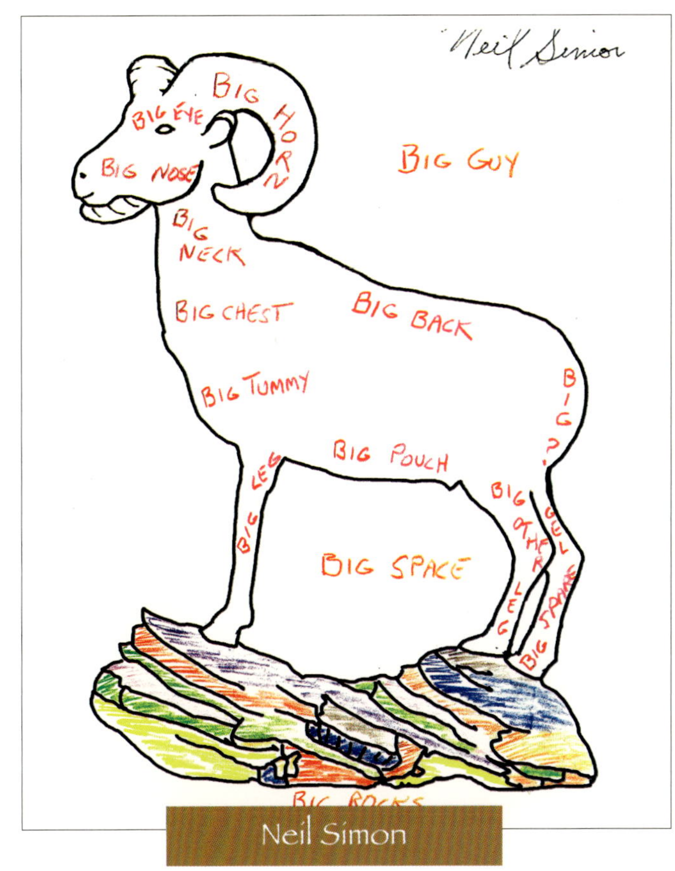

Neil Simon

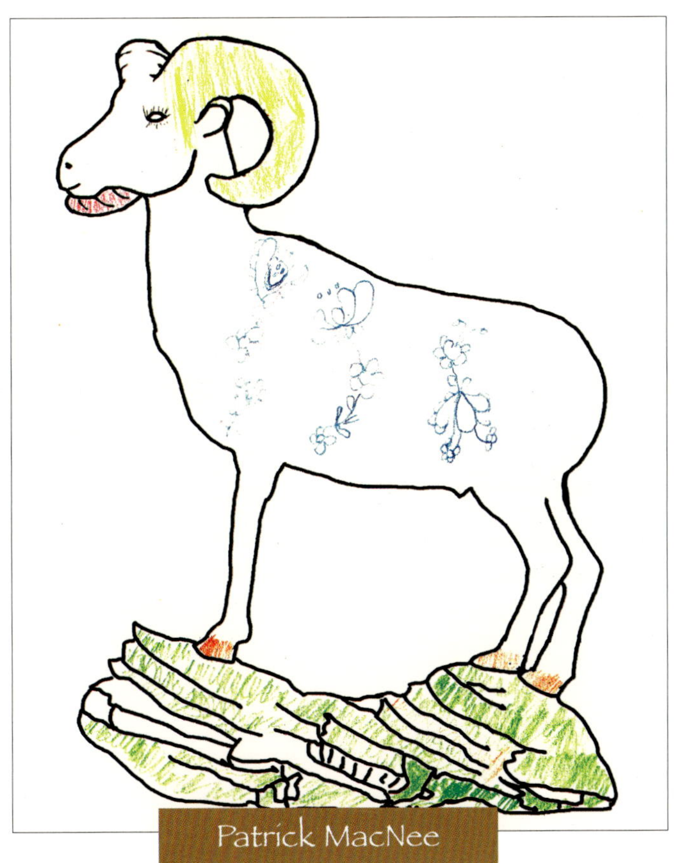

Patrick MacNee

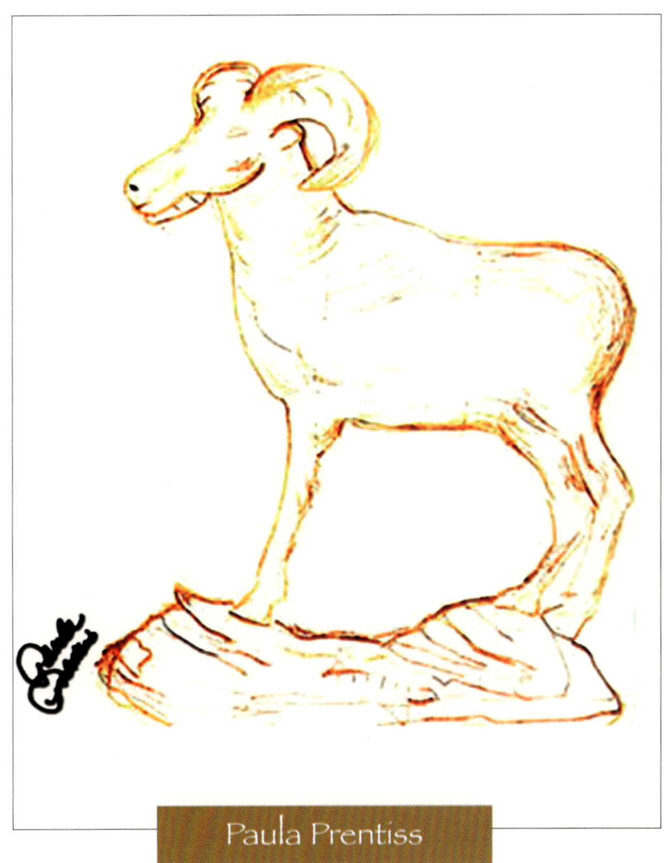

Paula Prentiss

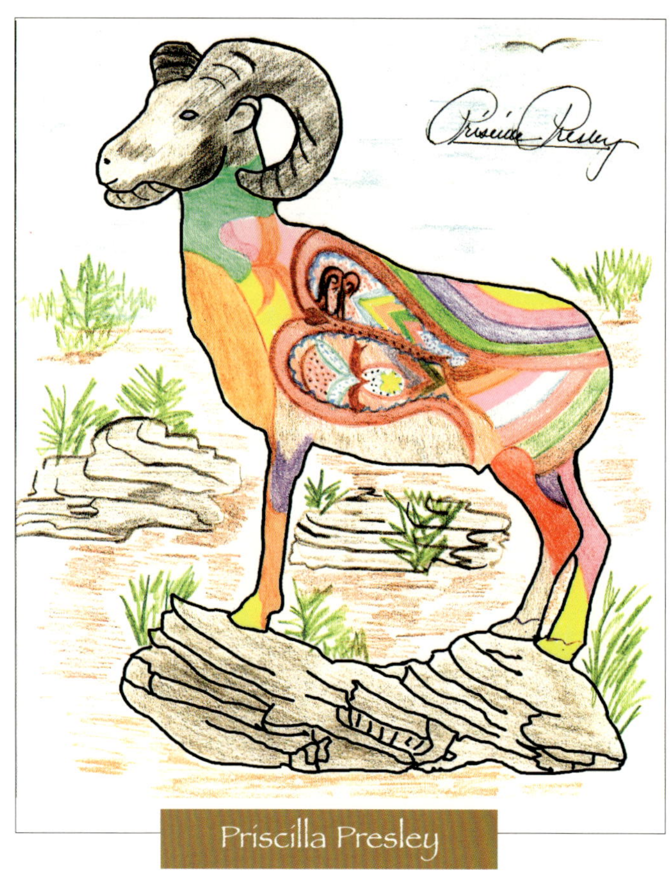

Priscilla Presley

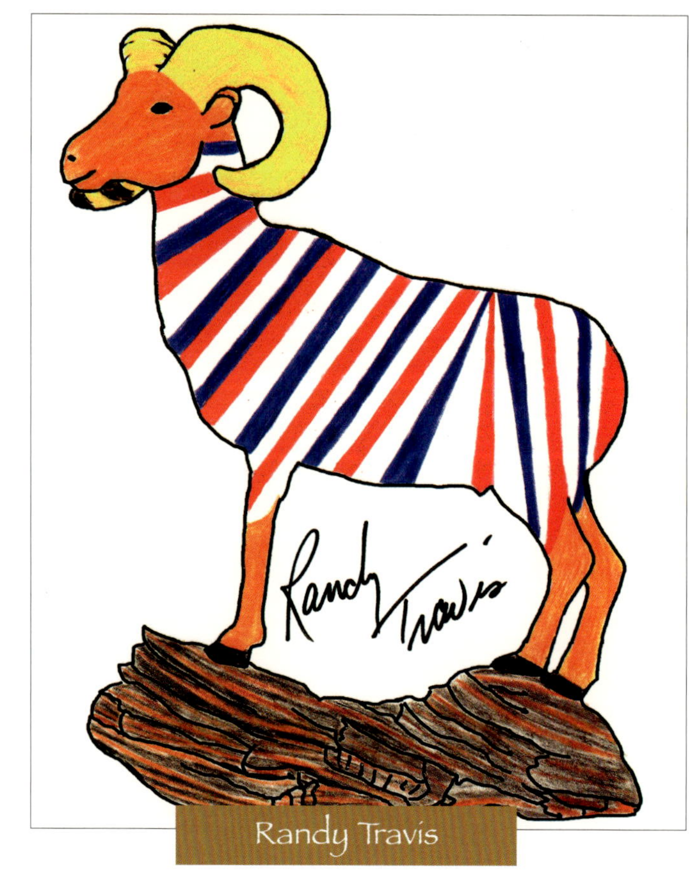

Randy Travis

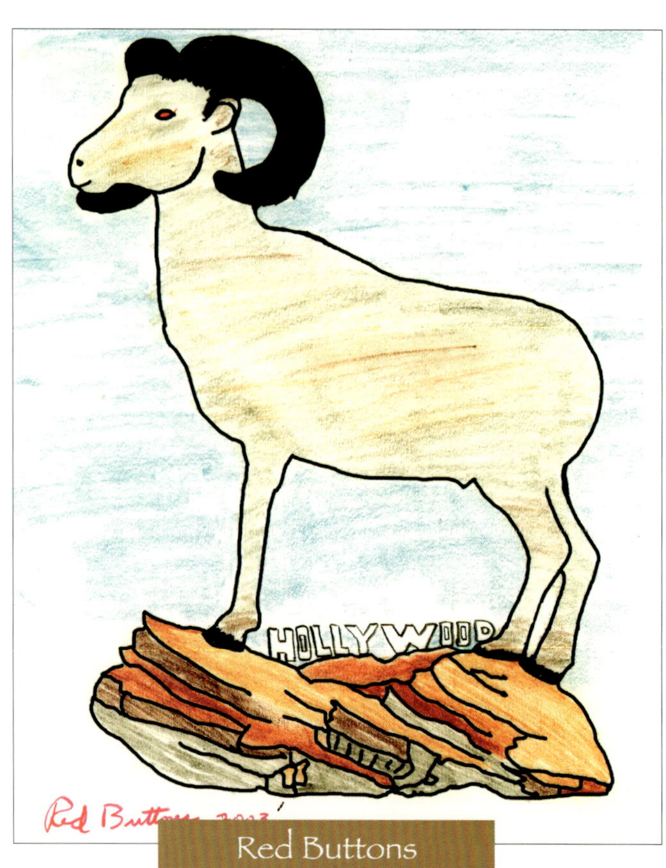

Red Buttons

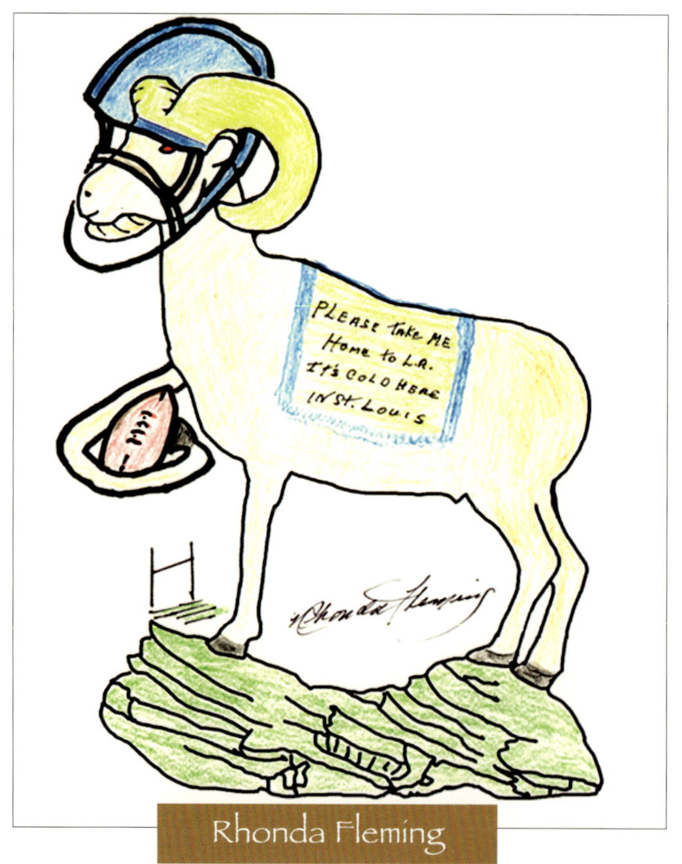

Rhonda Fleming

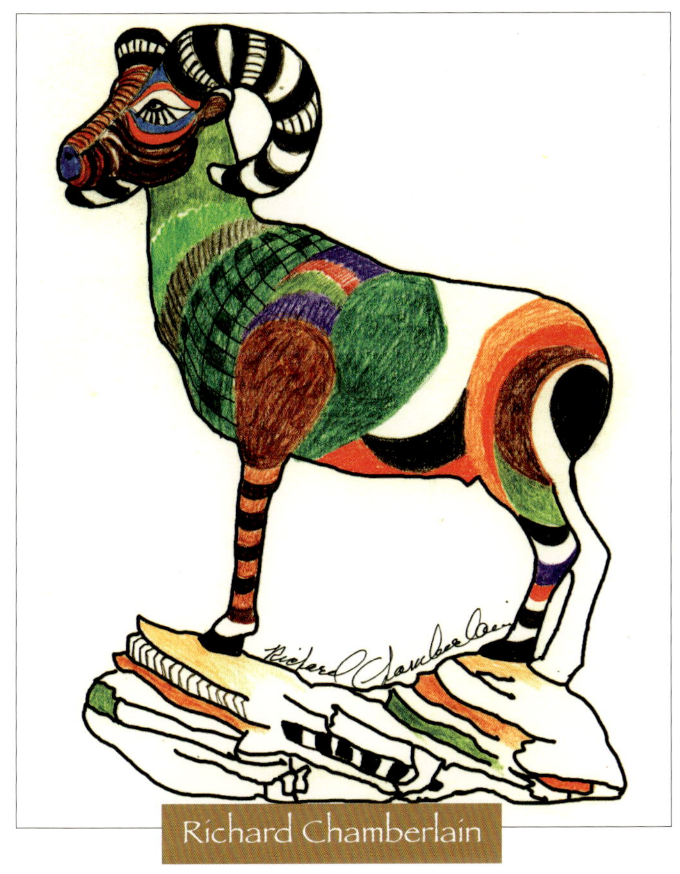

Richard Chamberlain

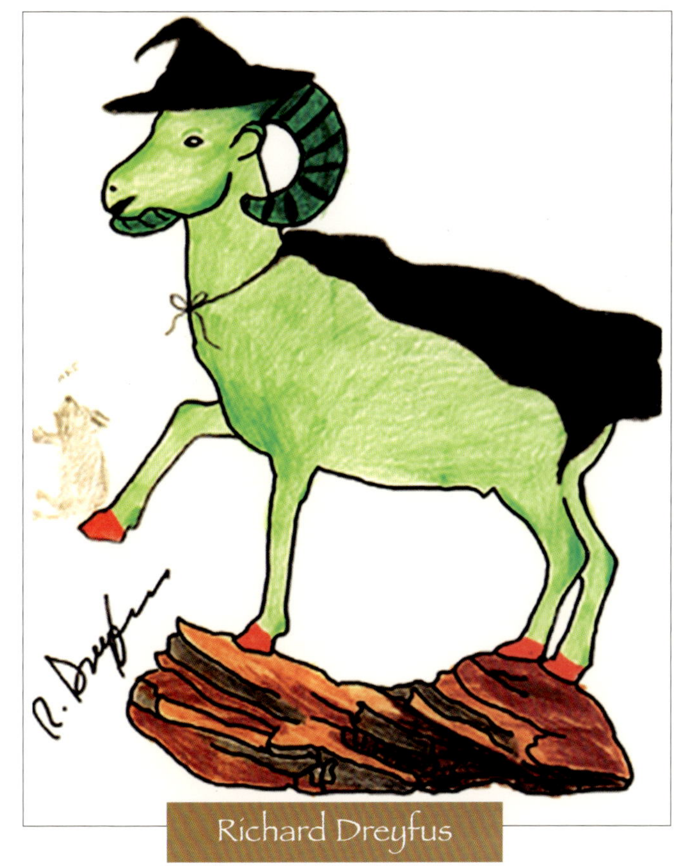

Richard Dreyfus

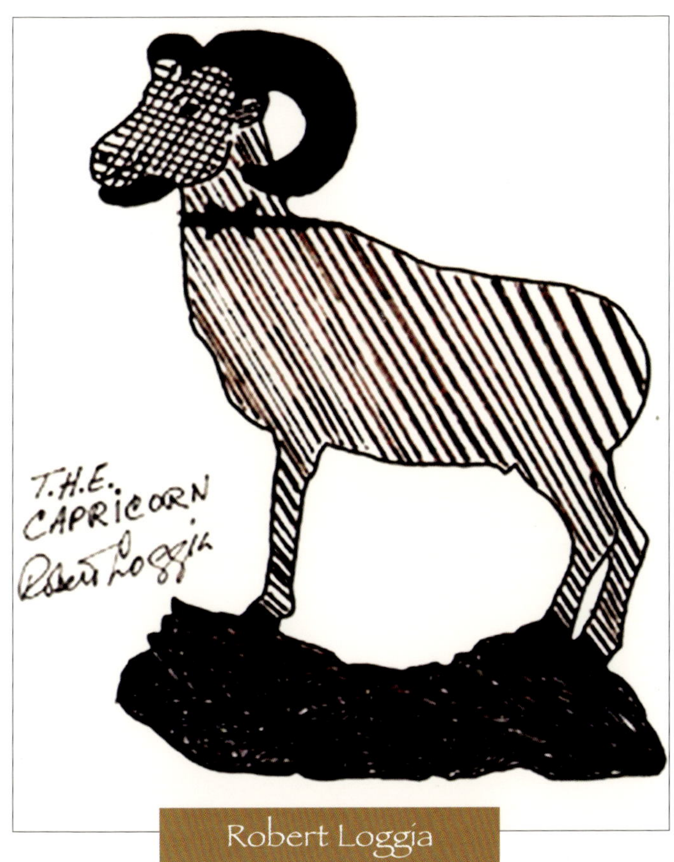

Robert Loggia

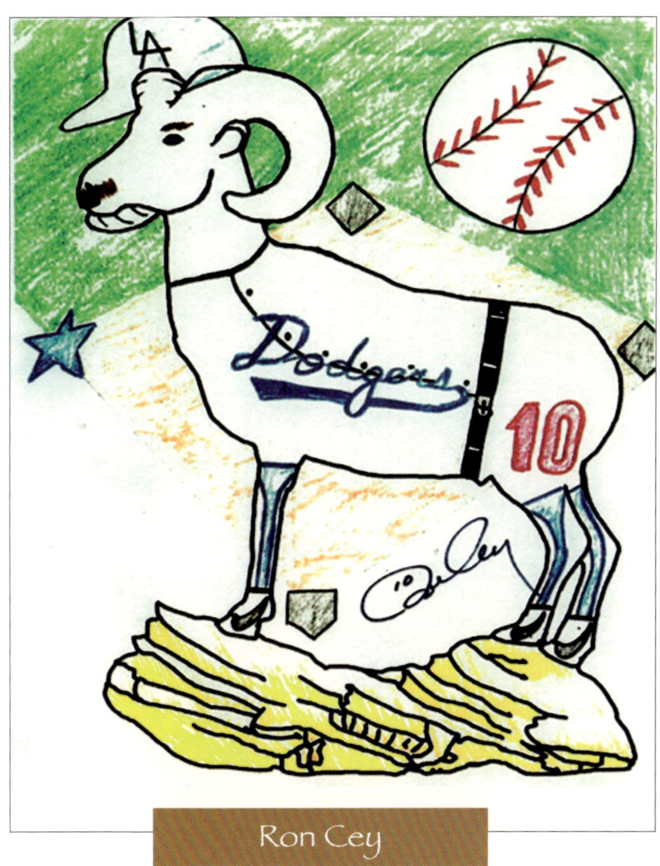

Ron Cey

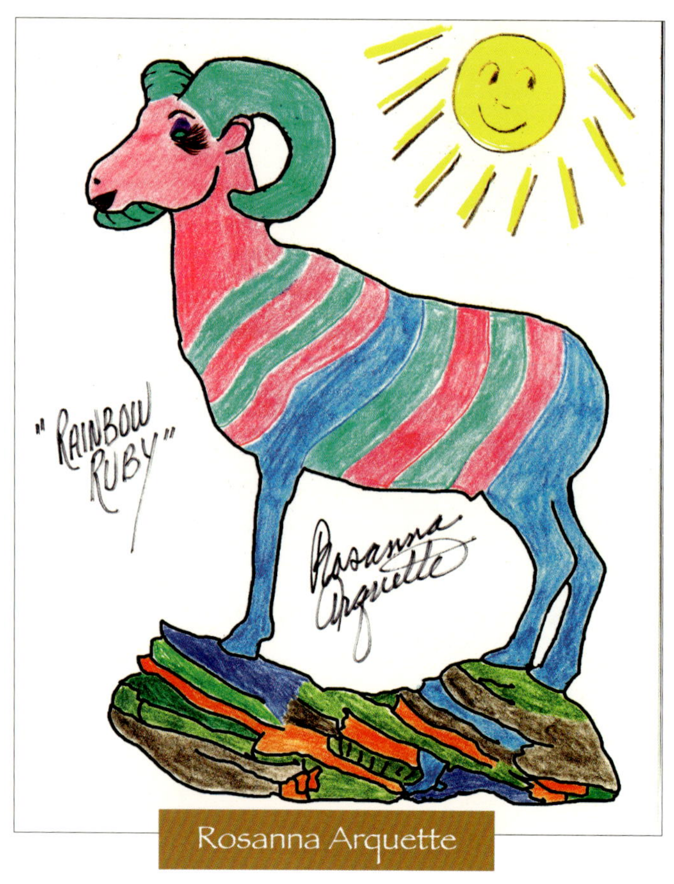

Rosanna Arquette

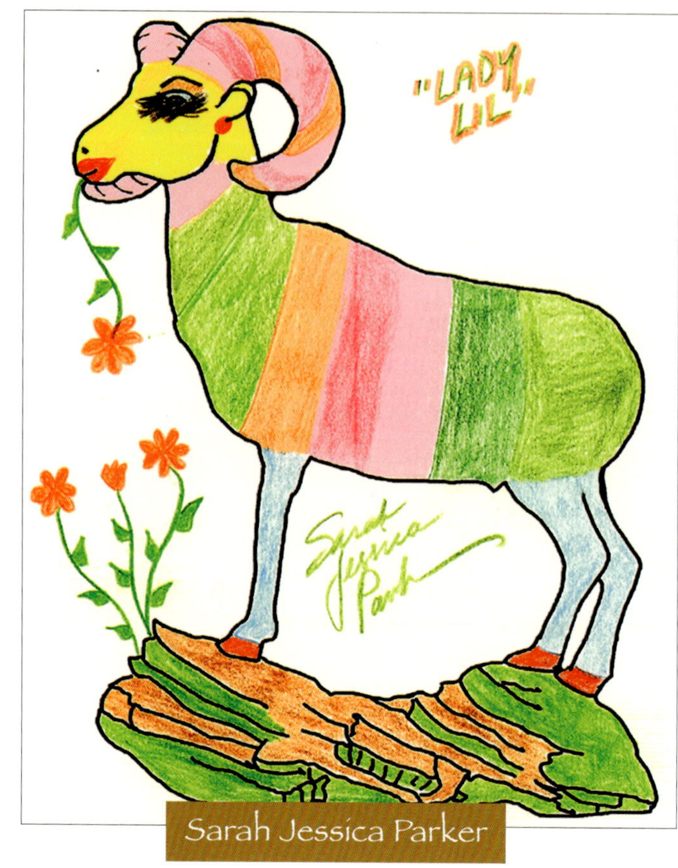

Sarah Jessica Parker

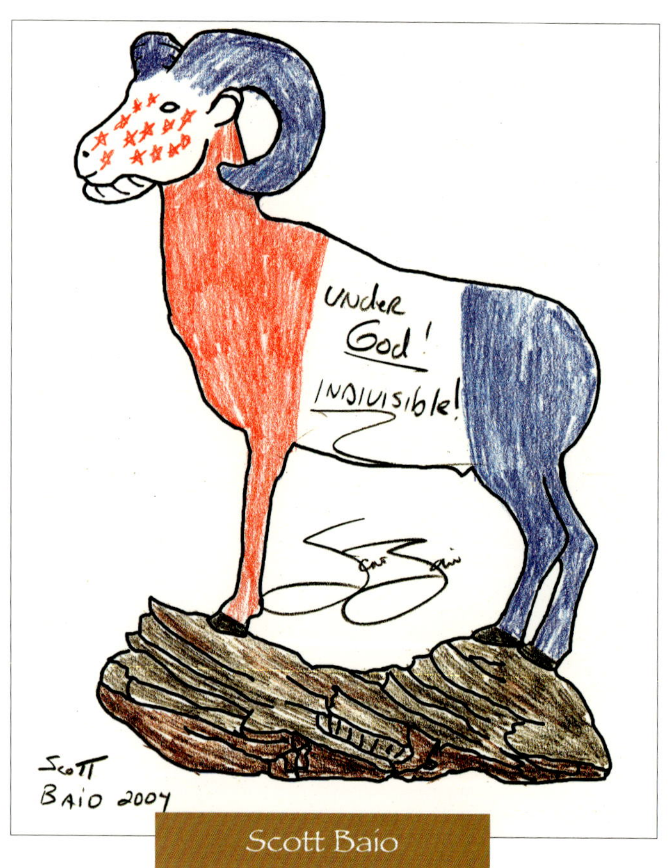

Scott Baio

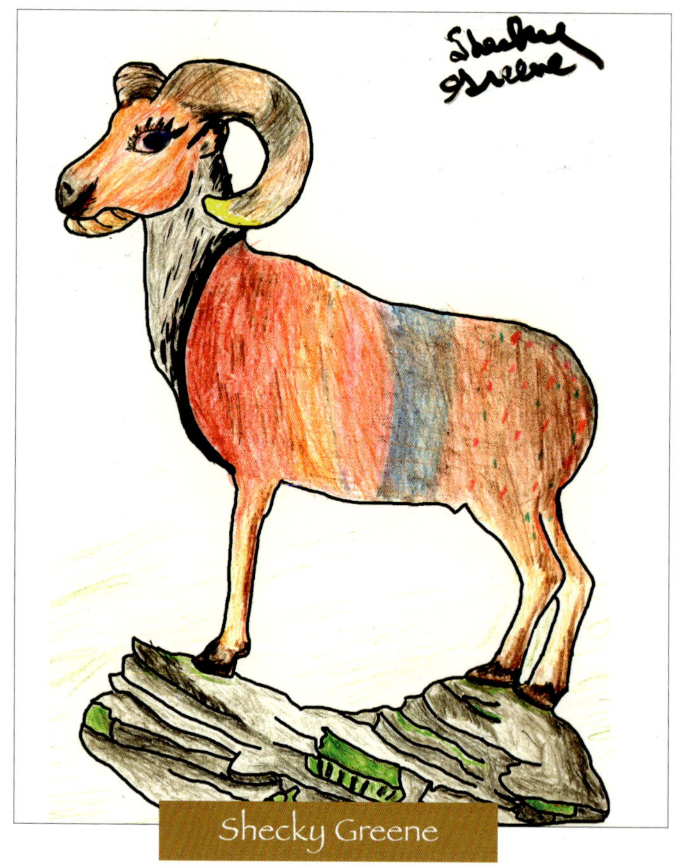

Shecky Greene

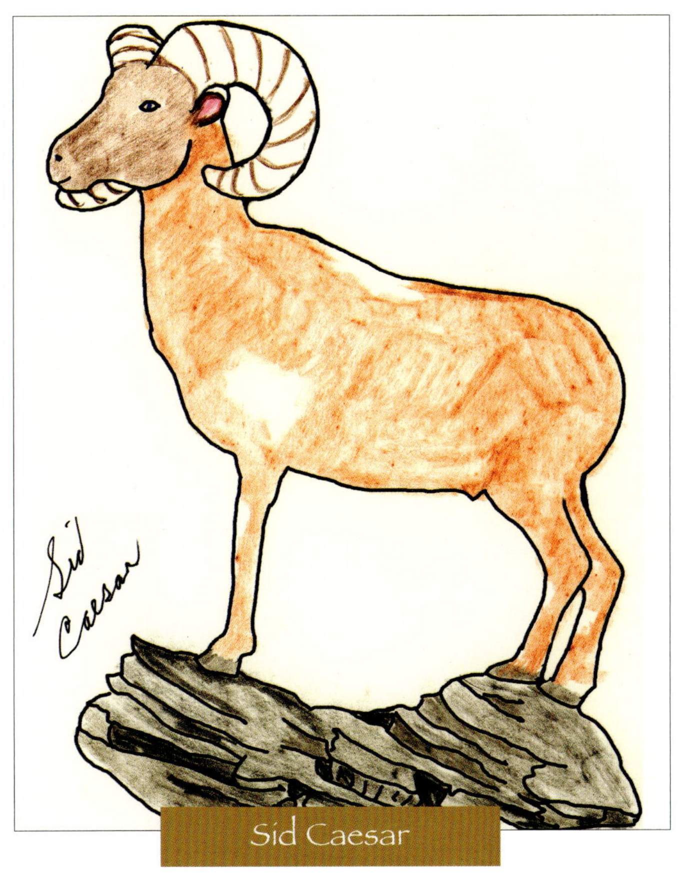

Sid Caesar

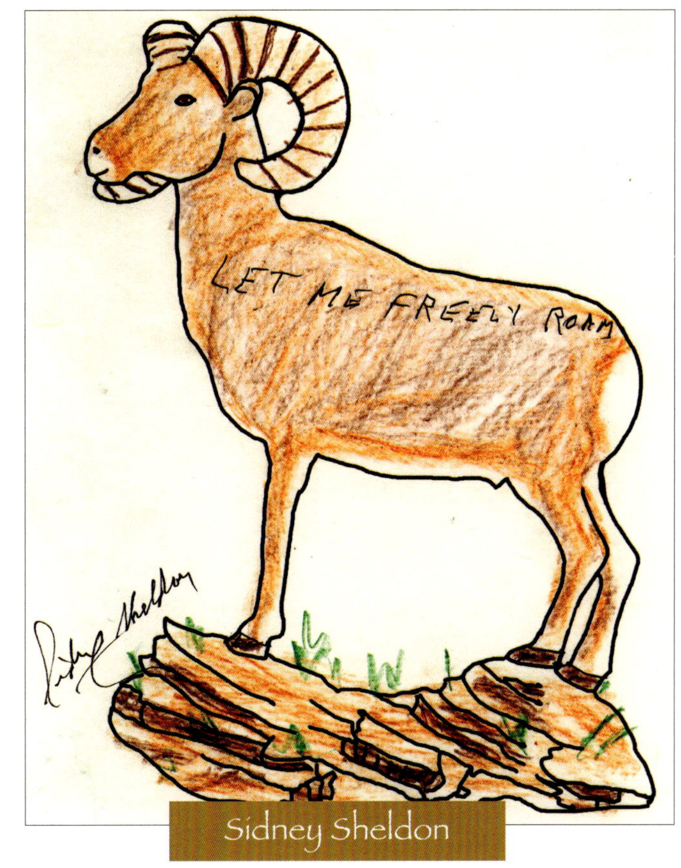

Sidney Sheldon

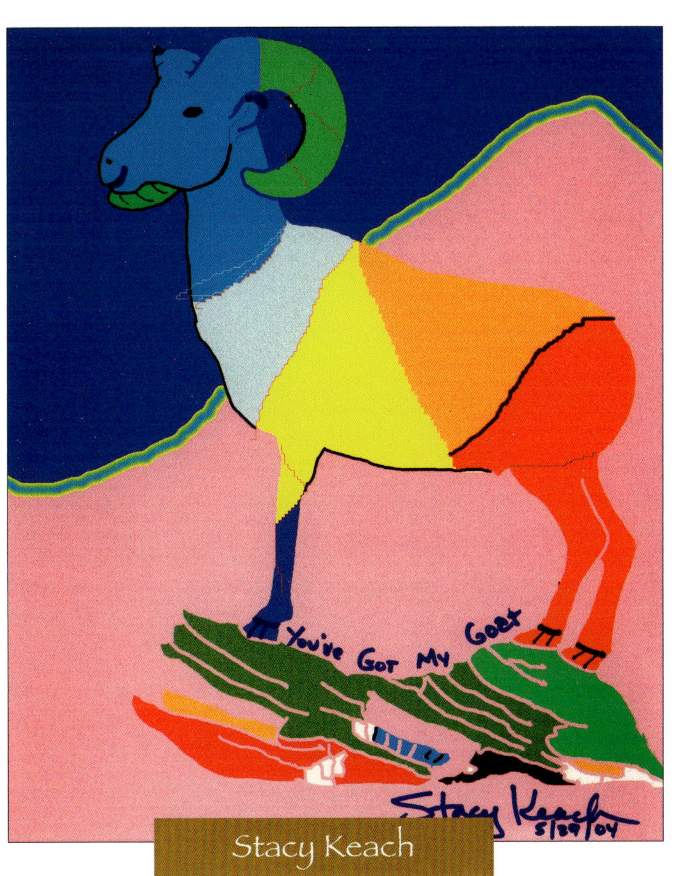

Stacy Keach

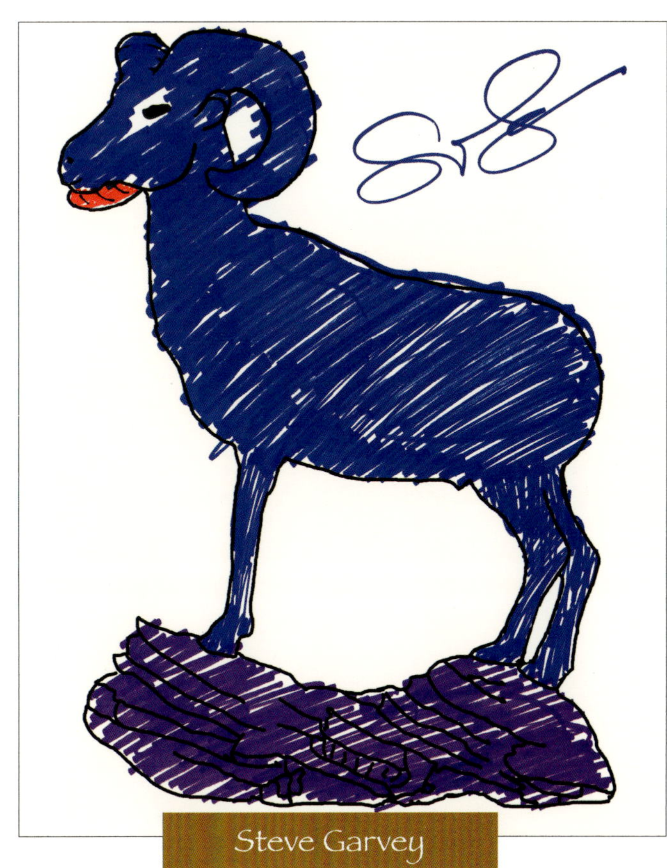

Steve Garvey

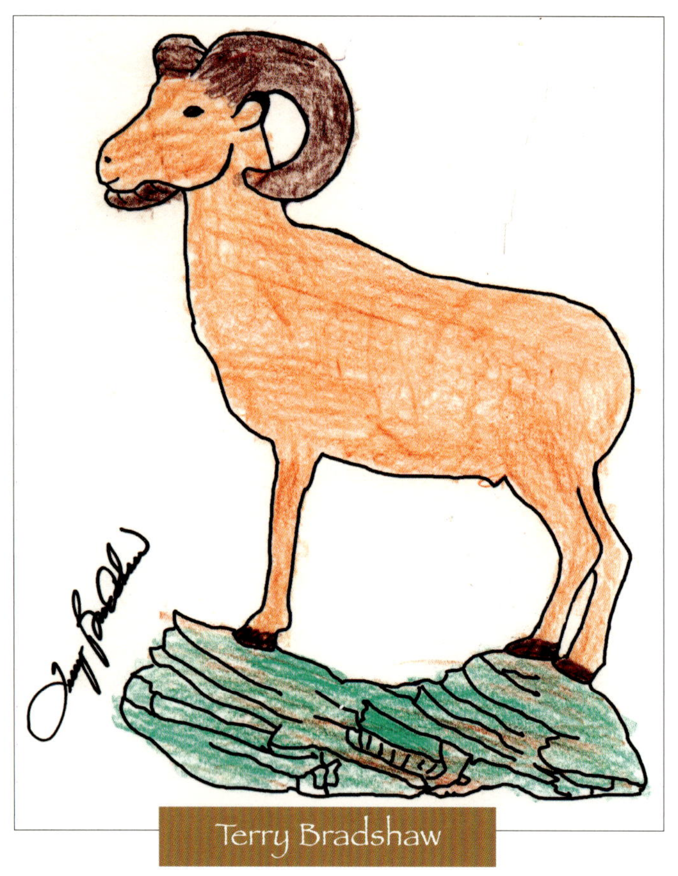

Terry Bradshaw

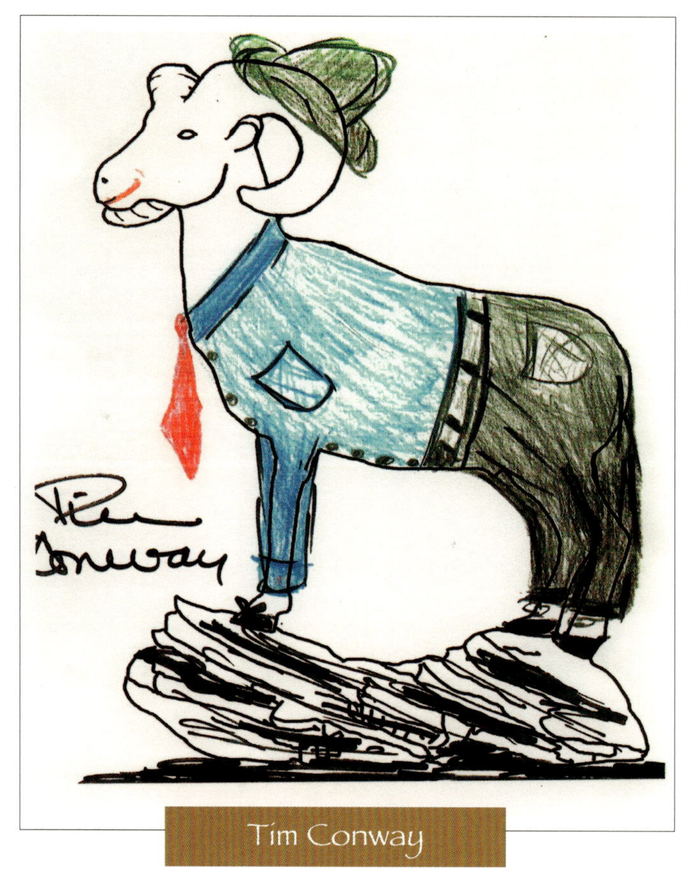

Tim Conway

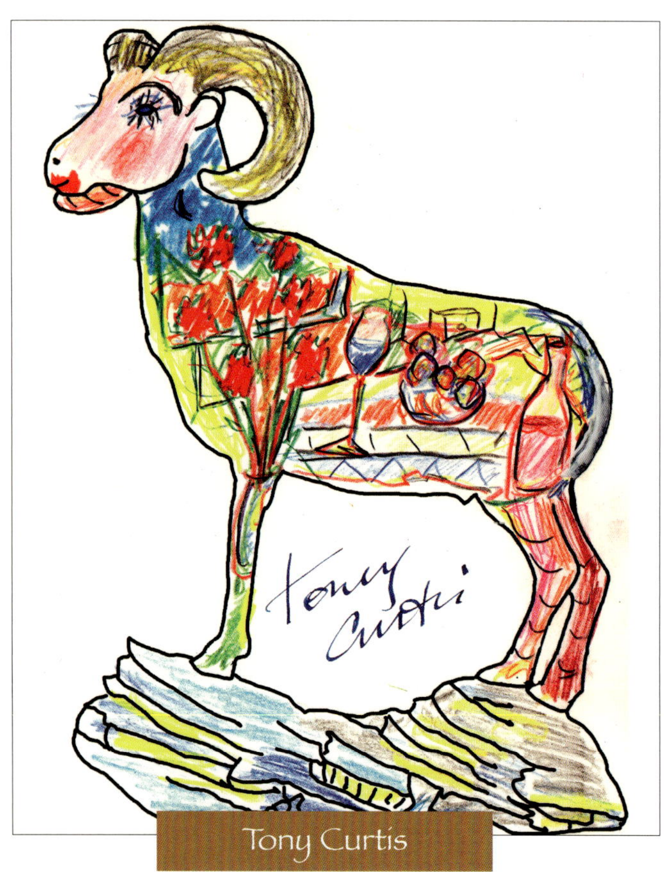

Tony Curtis

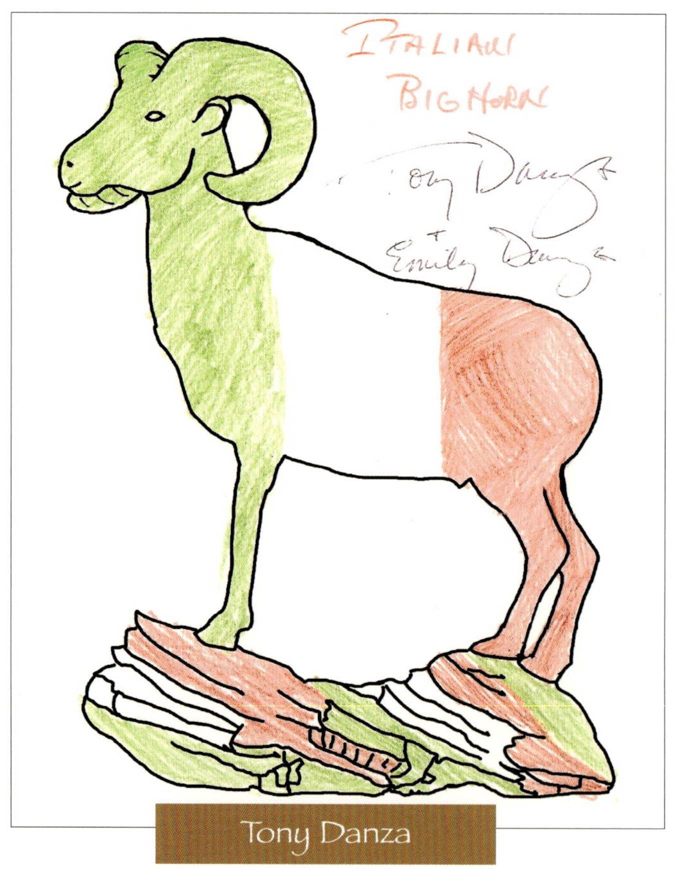

Tony Danza

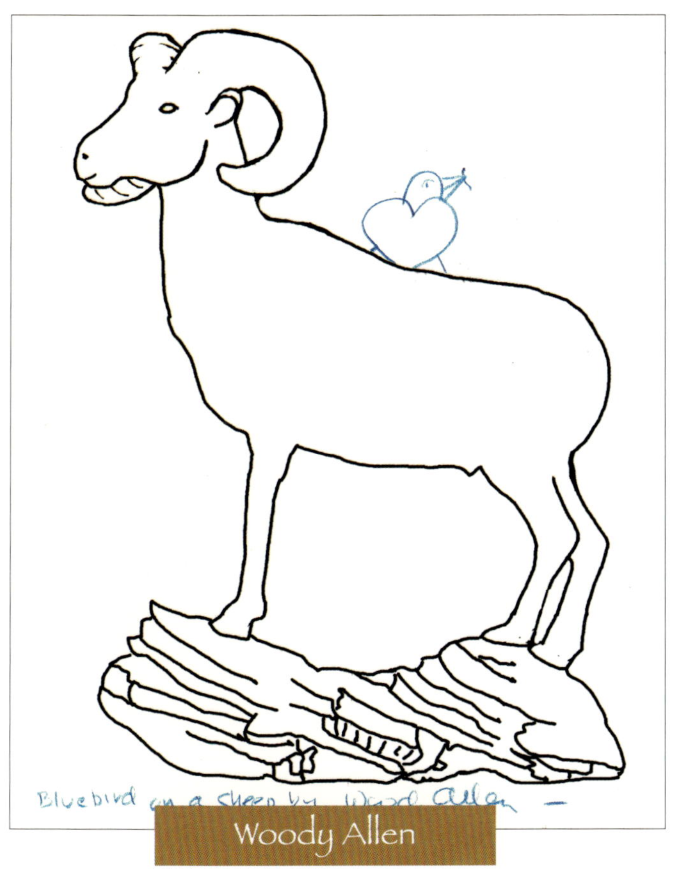

Woody Allen

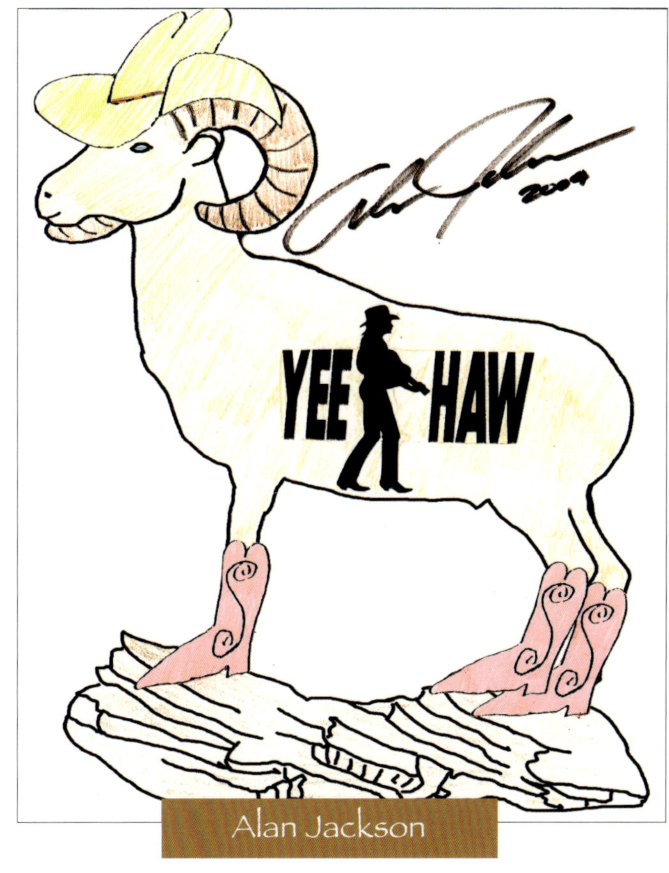

Alan Jackson

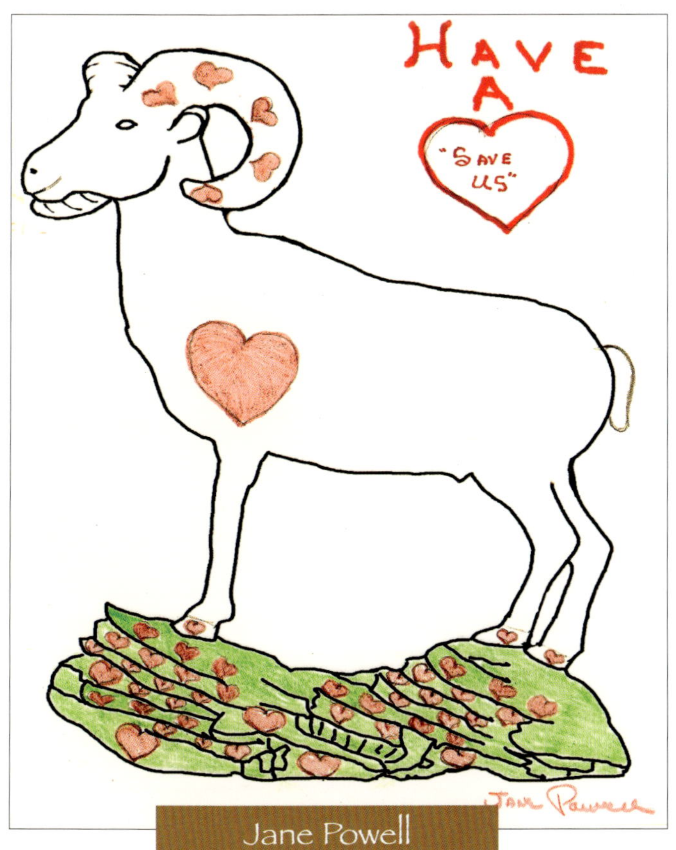

Jane Powell

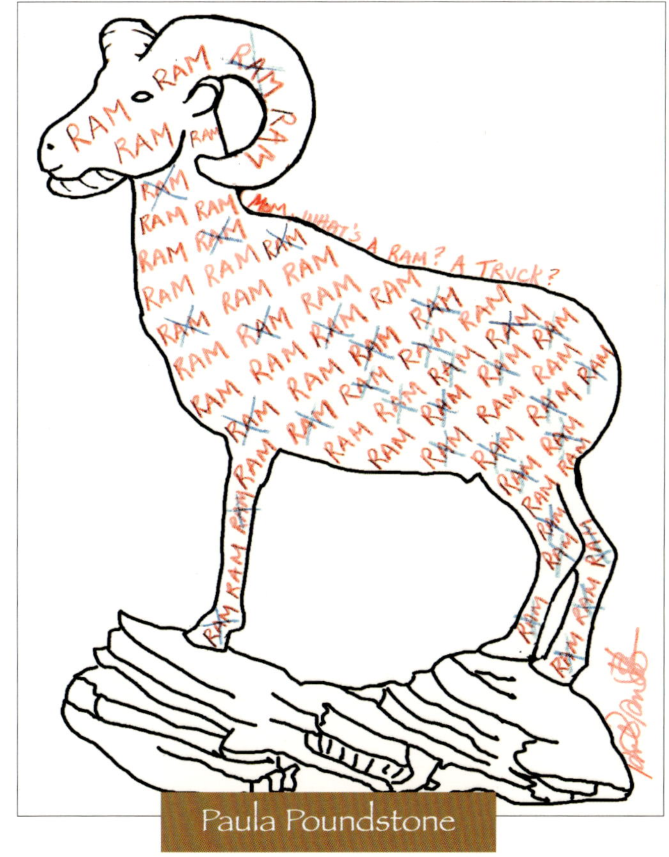

Paula Poundstone

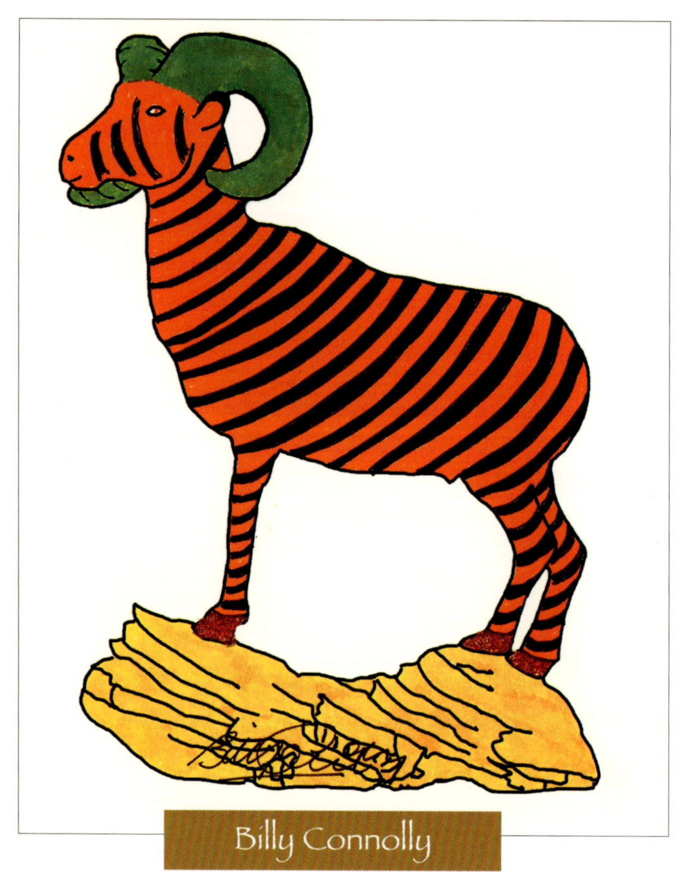

Billy Connolly

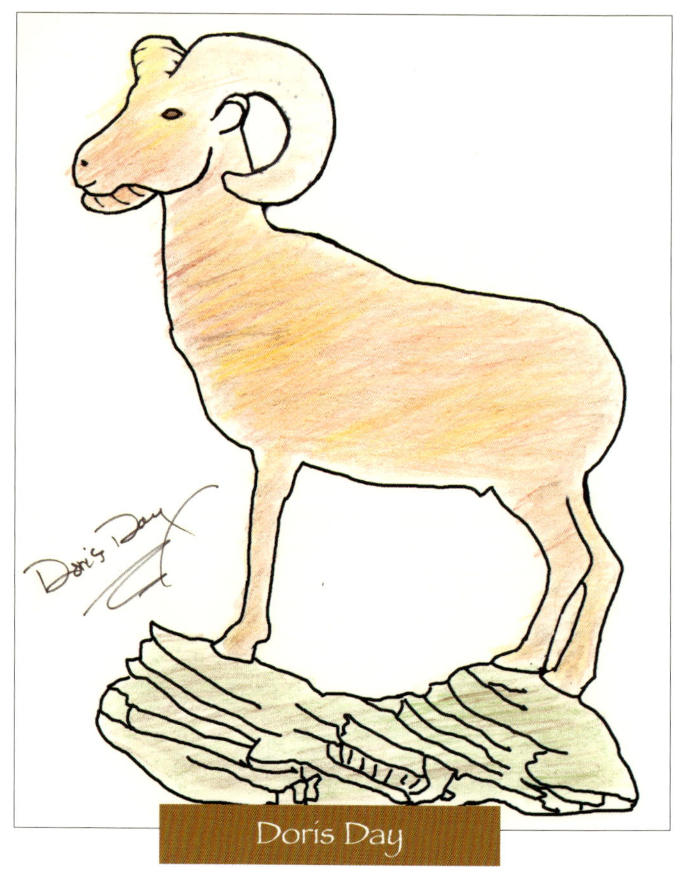

Doris Day

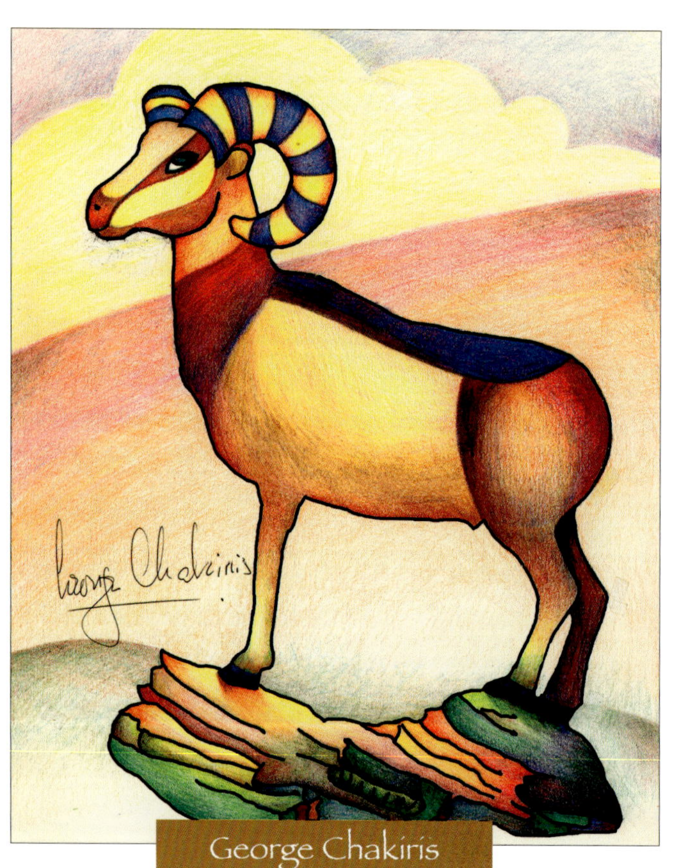

George Chakiris

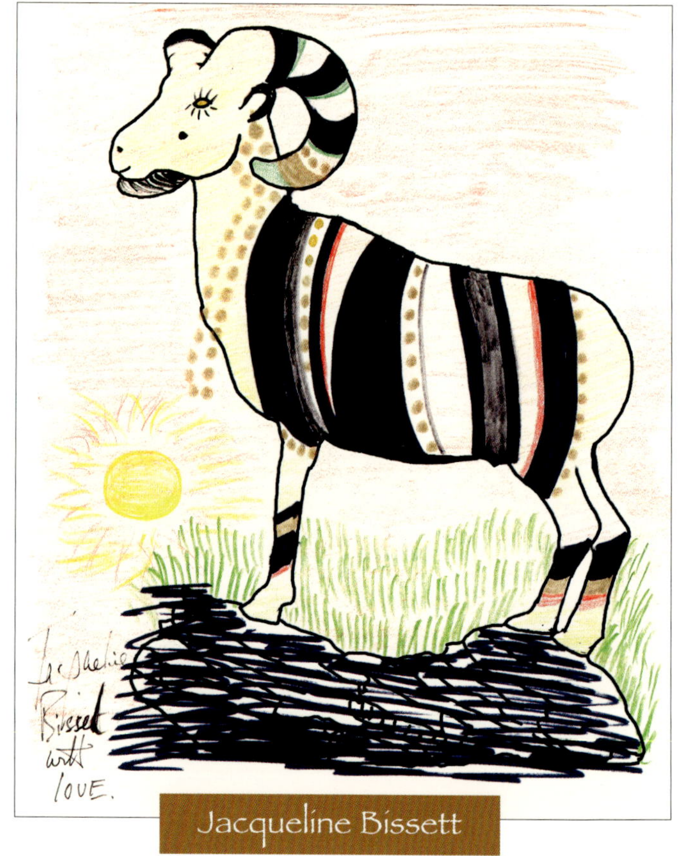

Jacqueline Bissett

Appendix

Narrative: *The Guardian*, p. 83

The boy in the center of the circle was captured and enslaved by a neighboring tribe. His captors cared little for him and allowed him only scraps of food; he became known to his captors as "Scavenger." On the side of a steep cliff, Scavenger's captors came upon an eagles' nest occupied by two eaglets. They wanted the young eagles but could not think of a way to get them. From a ledge above the nest, they decided to lower Scavenger in a willow basket, commanding him to throw the eaglets to them. Although they promised to pull Scavenger back up, they intended to leave him to his fate. The Wind had been listening to these plans and told "Talking God" and his companion that his Grandson was in trouble. In his sleep, Scavenger heard his Grandfather's voice telling him that his captors would try to kill him the next day. "They will let you down to the eagles' nest in a willow basket. Do not refuse to do this. Submit, but, when you reach the nest, do not throw the eaglets to them. If you do, your captors will leave you there to die. Let them pull up the basket empty, but do not be afraid. We will save you." The following day, Scavenger's captors took him to the top of the rock and lowered him as planned. All day long, his captors coaxed him to throw down the two eaglets (as depicted by the black shadow warriors with hands reaching toward the nest), but he refused. The parent birds were grateful and rewarded him by covering him with their wings at night for warmth. They brought him cooked corn suspended in packets from their bodies and water in hollow reeds tied to their tails. They also brought a yellow dish. They placed game animals and sacred animals around the nest to nurture and to protect him. This painting depicts Scavenger in the eagles' nest. The large blue circle is the house in the sky. The black line around it represents darkness, the white is the dawn or morning light, and the red is protection from danger. The boy's face is distinguished by eagle marks. The two birds in the circle (nest) with Scavenger are the young eagles. The parent birds hover outside the nest. The figures of rabbit, elk, mountain sheep, and lizard indicate nurturing and protection. Big fly in the circle (nest) warned Scavenger not to go with butterfly (shown in the lower right of the circle). The black tailed swallow is painted red because it bodes evil for Scavenger. The yellow circle is the food dish, and the basket is that used to lower Scavenger to the nest. The handle is lined with red to indicate rain or water.

Index

Sponsors